WITHDRAWN

The Spiritual Conversion of the Americas

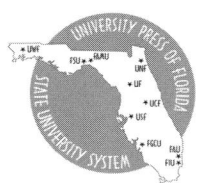

Florida A&M University, Tallahassee
Florida Atlantic University, Boca Raton
Florida Gulf Coast University, Ft. Myers
Florida International University, Miami
Florida State University, Tallahassee
University of Central Florida, Orlando
University of Florida, Gainesville
University of North Florida, Jacksonville
University of South Florida, Tampa
University of West Florida, Pensacola

Also by James Muldoon, from the University Press of Florida

Varieties of Religious Conversion in the Middle Ages (1997)

*Identity on the Medieval Irish Frontier: Degenerate Englishmen,
Wild Irishmen, Middle Nations* (2003)

The Spiritual Conversion of the Americas

Edited by James Muldoon

University Press of Florida
Gainesville/Tallahassee/Tampa/Boca Raton
Pensacola/Orlando/Miami/Jacksonville/Ft. Myers

Copyright 2004 by James Muldoon
Printed in the United States of America on recycled, acid-free paper
All rights reserved

09 08 07 06 05 04   6 5 4 3 2 1

Library of Congress Cataloging-in-Publication Data
The spiritual conversion of the Americas / edited by James Muldoon.
p. cm.
Includes bibliographical references and index.
ISBN 0-8130-2771-3 (cloth: alk. paper)
1. Catholic Church—Missions—America—History. 2. America—Church history.
I. Muldoon, James, 1935–
BV2755.S65 2004
266'.0230407—dc22   2004053708

The University Press of Florida is the scholarly publishing agency for the State University System of Florida, comprising Florida A&M University, Florida Atlantic University, Florida Gulf Coast University, Florida International University, Florida State University, University of Central Florida, University of Florida, University of North Florida, University of South Florida, and University of West Florida.

University Press of Florida
15 Northwest 15th Street
Gainesville, FL 32611-2079
http://www.upf.com

Contents

Preface   vii

Introduction: Seeking Spiritual Gold in the Americas   1
James Muldoon

1. Making the Land Holy: The Mission Frontier
   in Early Medieval Europe and Colonial Mexico   17
   Daniel T. Reff

2. Conversion Practices on the New Mexico Frontier   36
   Barbara De Marco

3. Two Kinds of Conversion ("Medieval" and "Modern")
   among the Hurons of New France   57
   Peter Goddard

4. Conversion in Theory and Practice: John Eliot's Mission
   to the Indians   78
   Annie Parker

5. Lutherans Meet the Indians: A Seventeenth-Century
   Conversion Debate   99
   Dennis C. Landis

6. Dutch Calvinism and Native Americans: A Comparative Study
   of the Motivations for Protestant Conversion among the Tupís
   in Northeastern Brazil (1630–1654) and the Mohawks
   in Central New York (1690–1710)   118
   Mark Meuwese

7. "None of These Wandering Nations Has Ever Been Reduced
   to the Faith": Missions and Mobility on the Spanish-American
   Frontier   142
   Amy Turner Bushnell

8. Confessing the Indians: Guilt Discourse and Acculturation in Early Spanish America   169
   Jaime Valenzuela Márquez

9. Conversion in Portuguese America   192
   Isabel dos Guimarães Sá

10. Making Papists of Puritans: Accounting for New English Conversions in New France   215
    Evan Haefeli

11. Gold for Glasse: The Trope of Trade in English Missionary Writings   231
    Laura M. Stevens

List of Contributors   253
Index   255

Preface

This volume of articles dealing with the religious conversion of the peoples of the Americas continues a line of research that began with the publication of *Varieties of Religious Conversion in the Middle Ages* (1997). The original proposal was for a volume that would deal with missionary efforts in the Old World and in the New, stressing the ways in which Catholic missionaries in the Americas initially attempted to apply the experience of medieval missionaries in the New World, only to learn that the New World was not just like the Old World after all.

The experience of missionaries in the Americas suggested that perhaps the medieval missionary experience was not relevant to the Americas and that new approaches would have to be developed if the inhabitants of the Americas were to become Christians. At the same time, the Protestant Reformers were criticizing the Catholic approach to conversion for producing shallow Christians who adhered to a corrupt version of Christianity. They applied this critique not only to the missionaries at work in the Americas but also to the initial conversion of the peoples of Europe in the early Middle Ages, arguing that not only did the people of the Americas require conversion to true Christianity, so also did the Catholics of Europe. All these pressures forced a reconsideration of what truly constituted religious conversion and what it meant to be a Christian. Indeed, they demanded a reexamination of the entire history of Christianity and reconsideration of the obligation of Christians to preach Christ's message to all mankind.

The initial proposal for a book was too long, however, and as a result the published volume dealt only with conversion in the medieval world. The hope at the time was that if there was sufficient interest in the history of conversion, then a second volume, one dealing with the Americas, would be developed. That hope is now fulfilled.

In bringing this project to fruition, I have incurred debts to a number of people. First, I want to thank the staff of the University Press of Florida who have worked on this project, especially Susan Fernandez, former acquisitions editor, and her successor, Amy Gorelick, both of whom must often have wondered if it would ever see the light of day.

Second, I wish to thank a number of people who contributed to the development of this volume. Foremost, I must thank Norman Fiering, the director of the John Carter Brown Library, who invited me to return to the library upon my retirement from teaching. Not only is the library a wonderful place to write and to do research, it also facilitates meeting people who have interesting things to say about topics such as conversion. Some of these have written articles, and others have taken time from their own research to read and critique parts of the project as it progressed: these include Fernando Gil, Kenneth Mills, Travis Glasson, Ed Osowski, and Amy Remensynder. I also want to thank Michael Hamerly for his assistance with the translation.

Finally, I must thank the two reviewers who read the original manuscript for the press. Their criticisms have made the book a better one than the one that I had initially proposed.

Introduction

Seeking Spiritual Gold in the Americas

James Muldoon

Sixteenth-century Europeans saw the newly revealed Americas in a variety of ways. For seekers after gold, it was El Dorado, a place of undreamed wealth. For Hernán Cortés, it gave Charles V an empire as great as the one he ruled in Europe.[1] For Christians, the Americas held even greater treasures. Some Catholics saw the Americas as a part of God's plan for restoring to the church the number of souls lost to the Protestant Reformation. Others, both Catholics and Protestants, saw the New World in apocalyptic terms, as the final stage in the implementation of Christ's injunction to preach His message to all mankind. The end of the world being near, Christians must complete their assigned task before Christ's return to earth.

The New World could also be placed within the context of the Reformation and Counter-Reformation. Efforts to convert the peoples of the New World would provide a test of the validity of different approaches to conversion. Protestants argued that Europe itself had not been truly converted to Christianity in the Middle Ages and that the barbarian peoples who had entered the declining Roman world had acquired only a corrupt version of the true faith that the bishops of Rome had created. Protestants would not repeat that mistake in the Americas. In contrast, Catholics often attempted to utilize in the Americas the same conversion methods employed during the early Middle Ages, thus implicitly validating the conversion of medieval Europe. The success or the failure of the various missionaries in the New World would presumably therefore determine whether or not Europeans had been converted to the true faith in the first place, thereby determining whose interpretation of the history of Christianity was the correct one.

A fundamental difference between Catholic and Protestant approaches to conversion in the Americas revolved around the sociocultural level of the potential converts. The early Christians (who provided the model of the conversion experience that Protestant missionaries followed) shared a common Mediterranean urban culture.[2] They were civilized in the classical use of the term, the inhabitants of agriculturally based city-states, which Aristotle defined as the highest form of human existence, the natural social environment for mankind. They were quite distinct from the *rustici* or *pagani,* the inhabitants of the rural areas surrounding the cities, people presumably capable of becoming civilized although they had not yet done so. The countrymen resisted Christianization, as use of the term *pagan* to label nonbelievers indicates.[3] From the very beginning, being Christian was associated with being civilized.

By the fourth century, as Christian missionaries began to reach out to the barbarian societies of early medieval Europe, the meaning of *conversion* gradually changed. Initially the term had referred to a change in an individual's way of life, a turning away from a sinful path and a turning to the Christian way or to stages in the Christian life as the individual moved from one level of Christian life to a higher one,[4] a process that Augustine of Hippo (d. 430) had described in his well-known *Confessions.* This meaning remained, but gradually conversion also came to refer to the mass baptism of an entire people. Such conversions usually accompanied some dramatic incident, such as winning a military victory and attributing it to the Christian God, as the Frankish king Clovis had done at the end of the fifth century.[5] Even this kind of conversion experience, however, usually required some previous exposure to Christianity, often by way of the Christian wife of the pagan leader who convinced her husband of the power of the Christian God.[6]

From the sixth century through the rest of the Middle Ages, the conversion of entire societies under the leadership of the rulers was the usual goal of missionaries.[7] This meant that conversion in the sense of a personal religious experience of the sort that Augustine described in his *Confessions* would be likely to occur only after several generations of instruction.[8] In recent years, some medieval historians have suggested distinguishing between conversion (a personal, interior spiritual transformation) and Christianization (the adoption of the external rules of Christian life). In his view, individuals are converted, whereas entire societies are Christianized.[9]

In practice, Christianization meant becoming civilized, moving from a seminomadic, pastoral, tribally organized way of life to a settled, agriculturally based, urban way of life, the life of the ancient Mediterranean city-state. The medieval Christian church was organized along the lines of the city-state regime of the ancient Mediterranean. The basic administrative unit, the diocese, was territorial in nature and followed Roman jurisdictional lines. The leaders of the early church tended to share the ancient view that those who lived outside of the city-state world were barbarians whose mode of existence was unsuitable for the fullest development of human life.

In addition to adopting the elements of civilized existence, the neophytes were also expected to adopt the behavioral standards required of Christians. Monogamy, for example, a requirement of church law, would be expected of the converts in place of the polygamous marriages that were the practice in the converts' society; or divorce would be banned where it was previously allowed. As a result, religious conversion and acculturation to the European Christian way of life required significant changes in a traditional way of life, changes that would require several generations to become the normal order of a society.

The chapters in this volume deal with a variety of aspects of the Christian encounter with the peoples of the New World. The discussions range over three continents and several centuries and deal with various approaches to the conversion and Christianization of the peoples encountered in the Americas, but the chapters do not stand in isolation. The authors converse, as it were, with one another. That is, they raise similar points and ask similar questions, forming a network of intersecting webs that suggest that Catholic and Protestant missionaries had more in common than is often recognized, faced many of the same problems in making converts, and developed similar techniques for dealing with these problems. Also apparent is the absence of a monolithic character within either Catholic or Protestant missionary efforts. That is, although Catholic missionaries worked within a common intellectual and cultural framework, the different religious orders involved based their missionary practice on principles derived from their own historical experience and theological insights. The same was true of Protestant missionaries as well, because they came from different theological traditions and had different understandings of the nature of conversion.

One of the fundamental themes in these articles is the applicability of the medieval missionary experience to the peoples of the Americas. Daniel Reff's opening chapter sets the scene for discussing this issue, emphasizing that Spanish missionary practices were deeply rooted in the medieval

Spanish experience. Reff points out that one important aspect of medieval Catholic missionary activity was the appropriation of pagan religious sites wherever possible and their transformation into Christian ones. The practice had received official papal encouragement in the late sixth century when Pope Gregory I encouraged Augustine of Canterbury (d. 604) to cleanse pagan places of worship and use them for Christian services. The goal was to make the transition from paganism to Christianity easier by softening the cultural shock that could occur when the new religion with its numerous ritual and social obligations was imposed.[10]

Reff has studied the theme of spiritually transforming space in Spain, describing in some detail how Spanish towns and villages created Christian spaces. Every community had not only a parish church but several small chapels, perhaps a monastery, and a variety of lesser shrines as well. The entire space within the municipal boundaries was dotted with a network of religious sites that demonstrated the victory of Christianity over paganism. By "baptizing" pagan sites and converting them to Christian use, missionaries could also be said to have brought the pagan spirits that inhabited these spaces into the fold. Reff argues that shrines honoring the Virgin Mary throughout the countryside made her "an ideal successor to the pre-Christian mother goddesses in the countryside." In this way, not only did the physical sites of paganism become Christian, but even the spirits who inhabited the spaces were converted.

Subsequently, according to Reff, the Jesuits brought this kind of "sacred geography" to the Americas. Perceiving the inhabitants of New Spain as being like the peasants of Old Spain (that is, small farmers living in villages and towns that were in turn "organized into larger sociopolitical systems"), the missionaries found it easy, even quite natural, to assume that the conversion of these people would follow the pattern of European conversion as the Jesuits understood it. The result would be a replication of the Spanish Christian way of life in the New World: organized communities characterized by churches, chapels, shrines, and other elements of the constant struggle between God and the Devil.

The Jesuit approach to conversion was not, however, the only one that Catholics employed. As Barbara De Marco points out in chapter 2, the Franciscans, an order whose members had been engaging in missionary work since the early thirteenth century, developed what she terms "theater of conversion." During the early fifteenth century, before going to the Americas, the Franciscans had engaged in missionary efforts in other regions only recently opened up to European settlement, such as the Canary

Islands.[11] De Marco stresses that the Franciscans utilized various kinds of visual and oral presentations of Christian doctrine and practices to teach the Indians by means of music, dance, and pictures. The Franciscan tradition also had another dramatic element derived from their long history: the missionary as martyr. Franciscan reports about the progress of their efforts in the New World stressed the sacrificial character of the missionaries, whose deaths at the hands of the Indians would pave the way for later missionaries to bring the Indians to the baptismal font. The stories of these deaths were an element of the theater of conversion directed not at potential converts but at other friars, to encourage them to replace their martyred brethren in the mission fields.

The significance of the Franciscan use of theater emerged in the aftermath of the Pueblo Revolt of 1680, a revolt that drove the Spanish out of New Mexico for a dozen years. The rebels had engaged in a kind of theater of unconversion, that is, destroying Christian symbols, rejecting Christian standards of behavior, and, in a dramatic gesture, washing Christian baptism off in the river. After the Spanish returned and reconquered Taos, the Franciscans held a public meeting in which the apostates were reconciled to the church in a series of actions that represented the punishment of the backsliders and the return of the people to the true faith.

Differing Franciscan and Jesuit approaches to the work of converting the peoples of the Americas were not restricted to the Spanish Americas. In chapter 3, Peter Goddard argues that missionaries in French Canada reflected those two missionary traditions as well. The Franciscans who had been involved in missionary activity since the early thirteenth century took one approach, while the recently founded Jesuits took another, based not on long historical experience but on a theory of education developed during the Renaissance.

Building on the work of John Leddy Phelan dealing with Franciscan missionaries in the Spanish world, Goddard demonstrates that the Franciscan missionaries approached the Indians of Canada from the perspective of an apocalyptic tradition that saw the end of the world as imminent, so that the conversion of the Indians had to proceed rapidly before the end came.[12] The apocalyptic tradition, however, was not part of the Jesuit spiritual outlook.

Goddard suggests that the conversion efforts of the Jesuits in Canada were linked to their educational program, which eventually led to a "sudden and total" conversion experience after a long period of instruction. The Franciscans, by contrast, appear to have been cautious about conversion, seeing it as a continual process during which the individual was in constant danger of backsliding. In Franciscan theology, the convert must always remain alert to spiritual dangers that threaten to deflect him from the true path.

Like the Jesuits, sixteenth- and seventeenth-century Protestant missionaries had no long medieval experience of missionary work to guide and inspire them or, as some might see it, to hinder them. Indeed, the Protestant view was that the medieval missionary experience was worthless. From the Protestant perspective, the use of pagan sites and customs as Gregory I suggested implied syncretism, the creation of a new religion that blended Christian and pagan beliefs and practices into a corrupt form of Christianity. Protestant missionaries denounced "all precontact activity as devil worship" and therefore to be shunned.[13] Protestant missionaries such as John Eliot, who created the Praying Towns in Massachusetts, insisted that potential converts make a complete break with their past, as Annie Parker points out in chapter 4, lest corruption creep into their practice of Christianity. The kinds of accommodations that Catholic missionaries might make to local practices were in Protestant eyes the same kind of accommodations that had corrupted Christianity in the early Middle Ages.

It is important to recognize at this point that although the Protestant Reformation began at about the same point in time as the New World was opening up to Europeans, Protestants did not immediately engage in missionary efforts outside of Europe. Their first goal was the reform of Christianity within Europe.

Furthermore, as Dennis Landis observes in chapter 5, among German Protestants there was a debate about whether or not Christians were obliged to preach the Gospel to the inhabitants of the New World at all. Because Martin Luther had focused on the reform of the church in Europe in his own day, his writings made no mention of missionary efforts, even though his critique of the Catholic Church was contemporary with the beginnings of Catholic missionary efforts in the New World. Subsequently, some Protestant theologians argued that the Gospel had been preached throughout the world by Christ's Apostles long ago, so that any society that has not accepted Christ's teachings was responsible for its spiritual fate and that it was not the responsibility of Europeans to preach it to them again.

In taking the position that the Gospel had once been preached universally, these German theologians employed evidence derived from reading Spanish Catholic sources dealing with religion among the Indians of the

New World. Some Catholic observers had suggested the possibility that one of the Apostles, Saint Thomas, had reached the Americas and made converts. The evidence for this was the existence of practices in the Americas that appeared to be either corruptions or inversions of Christian teachings.[14] From the Catholic perspective, the fact that the inhabitants of the Americas had lost any knowledge of Christianity and retained only some external practices did not excuse Europeans from any responsibility for seeking their salvation.

After the end of the bloody German wars of religion in 1648 and in response to the missionary efforts of both Catholics and Protestants in the New World, some German thinkers began to reconsider the theology of mission. With an ever-increasing amount of information about the peoples of the Americas becoming available, these German thinkers began to realize that indeed Christianity had not been preached everywhere. By the early eighteenth century, German missionaries were beginning to preach in the Americas, and the theory that missionary activity was no longer required of Christians generally faded along with the story of Saint Thomas.

Millennial and apocalyptic expectations motivated Catholics and Protestants alike. Mark Meuwese in chapter 6 stresses that even among the Dutch, not a group noted for extensive missionary work, there were "strong millenarian overtones" in the missionary efforts that they did undertake. In Massachusetts, the site of the most extensive Protestant effort to convert and to civilize the native population in British North America, some identified the Indians as descendants of the ten lost tribes of Israel, whose conversion to Christianity was one of the final stages of mankind's history before the millennium. As Parker suggests, John Eliot might not have believed this, but some of those who wrote about his work certainly did.

Regardless of the motives that inspired them, Catholic and Protestant missionaries alike faced similar problems in preaching to the peoples of the Americas. The Jesuits and the Franciscans that Reff and De Marco studied dealt with sedentary populations that fitted (or seemed to fit) the European conception of organized societies. That being the case, the missionaries could impose the European model of a territorial parish organization on the existing social structure. What of the peoples who did not live in organized, settled communities?

As Amy Turner Bushnell points out in chapter 7, Catholic missionaries found it difficult to convert many of the peoples of the New World because they were nomadic or seminomadic and therefore could not be easily fitted into the ecclesiastical structure based on the settled societies of the ancient Mediterranean that the missionaries took for granted. She emphasizes that the structure of the church assumed a hierarchically constructed society, in which peasants lived in villages and followed a daily routine that was punctuated by the sound of church bells announcing the time for prayer. Against this background the parish priest taught the truths of the new faith to the people, and it was in this context that Christianization took place.

Bushnell emphasizes the fact that missionaries going to the Americas took with them a theory of human development. That is, they assumed not only that Christianity was a universal faith but also that there was a universal course of human social development from hunter-gatherer to pastoralist to sedentary agriculturist. That being the case, when encountering societies that had not reached the highest stage of development, it was the responsibility of the missionaries to assist the people in rising to that level. Seen in the long term, the Catholic, and later the Protestant, insistence on linking conversion with sedentary, agricultural societies meant that the conversion of most of the peoples of the Americas, dwelling as they did in tribal, seminomadic societies, would be very difficult because two complex cultural transformations were involved, not just one, a fact not always fully appreciated by the missionaries.[15]

Bushnell concludes that experience with the migratory peoples of the Americas demonstrated that the "wild people" could be baptized, but they could not be successfully Christianized. To some extent, this conclusion reflected the earlier experience of Christian missionaries in medieval Ireland. The Irish whom Patrick and his successors had converted lived in a pastoral and tribally organized society. When the English entered Ireland in the late twelfth century, they had a papal bull authorizing them to reform the Irish Church. Over the next several centuries, English efforts to reform the Irish Church were only marginally successful, no more successful than their attempts to transform the Irish into farmers. At the end of the sixteenth century, Edmund Spenser asserted that the Irish were probably not even Christians, that having been badly taught by Patrick and his successors they were such poor Christians "ye woulde rather thinke them *Atheists* or infideles."[16]

The problem of dealing with nonsedentary societies was not restricted to Catholic missionaries. As Parker points out, John Eliot, the most important Protestant missionary to the Indians in seventeenth-century New

England, faced the same problem in Massachusetts. The Praying Towns he established were designed to provide potential converts not only with Christian instruction but with training in agriculture and town life as well. Only after the Indians had become town-dwelling agriculturists could they become members of the church.

Parker points out that historians "have sharply debated" the question of why Eliot did this. Seen from the perspective of the twentieth or twenty-first century, forcing potential converts into agricultural communities suggests placing them in what some historians have described as "proto-reservations." Seen against the millennium or more of experience of Christian missionaries with nonsedentary peoples, however, Eliot's Praying Towns have much in common with the famous Jesuit reductions in Paraguay. Both Eliot and the Jesuits were operating on the basis of the traditional belief that only civilized peoples could become true Christians. In effect, although he would no doubt have denied it, Eliot was engaged in Christianizing the Indians in order that they might become converted at some point, a position quite similar to the Catholic practice.

Missionaries, Catholic and Protestant, insisted on bringing the Christian neophytes into settled communities because Christianity required continuous instruction and regular ritual practice. Protestant missionaries engaged in a lengthy educational process before baptizing their converts. For Catholics, in addition to the ritual aspects of the faith, there were instructional elements as well.

As Jaime Valenzuela Márquez points out in chapter 8, both problems affected one of the most important elements in developing the Catholic life: the practice of regular confession of one's sins. The Fourth Lateran Council (1215) had mandated annual confession and reception of Communion as the minimum level of Christian practice. Parish priests had manuals that instructed them as to how the penitent was to be received. The priest was not simply to hear the record of sins and to grant absolution, he was also to instruct the sinner about how to avoid sinning in the future. Valenzuela also points out that in 1551 the Council of Trent reemphasized the importance of confession and the other sacraments in response to Protestant attacks on the entire sacramental system. This emphasis in turn placed even more pressure on the missionaries to establish the converts in settled communities.

Having brought potential converts into settled communities, the missionaries faced a series of complex problems. The first issue was linguistic, a problem for both Catholics and Protestants. What language would the missionaries employ in instructing the neophytes? They were entering a world in which scores, if not hundreds, of languages and dialects were spoken. Furthermore, even if the missionaries learned the local languages, instruction in Christian doctrine was complicated by the lack of terms for many Christian concepts in the indigenous languages. One solution was to develop a cadre of priests who were fluent in the language spoken by the peoples with whom they were dealing.[17] The second problem was how to explain Christian concepts in languages that lacked the concepts central to Christianity. One approach often used by Catholic missionaries was to identify Catholic practices and concepts with similar (or apparently similar) practices in the local culture. In this way, the conceptual gulf between pagan and Christian practice might be bridged. The other approach, more often employed by Protestants, was to reject any existing cultural practices as intrinsically evil and to require complete cultural transformation as a part of the process of conversion.

The Spanish made the most extensive efforts at converting the peoples of the Americas to Christianity, but they were not the only Catholic missionaries. The Portuguese and the French also engaged in missionary efforts, although on a smaller scale in keeping with the more limited geographical extent of their possessions in the Americas. Unlike the Spanish, neither the French nor the Portuguese encountered sophisticated societies such as those of the Aztecs and the Incas. They encountered various peoples who lived at an earlier stage of development. Furthermore, neither the Portuguese nor the French government provided the quantity of financial and other assistance that the Spanish government provided for missionaries.

Isabel dos Guimarães Sá points out in chapter 9 that the unwillingness of the Portuguese government to provide the funds necessary for extensive missionary work among the people of Brazil meant that the Jesuits, the order most actively involved in that region, owned and operated large estates employing African slaves to finance their missionary activities. This practice suggests one of the least examined aspects of the missionary efforts in the New World, the problem of financing the missionaries.

In Portuguese Brazil, as in the Spanish Empire, the Jesuits encouraged the settlement of the Indians in agricultural villages as the foundation of the work of conversion. In addition to the specific cultural issues attending the conversion efforts among Indians, African slaves, and mulattos, the clergy had to deal with a European population not inclined to live according to the highest standards of Christian morality.[18] One solution to this problem was to encourage the formation of separate communities for Indian converts, thereby protecting the converts from the bad example of the supposedly Christian Europeans.

Missionary efforts in the New World were not restricted to converting the non-Christian native peoples of the Americas. Catholics and Protestants were also anxious to convert each other, continuing in the New World the religious competition characteristic of Reformation and Counter-Reformation Europe. This occurred most often along the frontier that separated the Puritans of New England from the Catholics of New France. In chapter 10, Evan Haefeli points out that these two groups represented the radical extremes of the Reformation and Counter-Reformation and in a small corner of North America carried on the wars of religion with a fervor that Europe itself was starting to forget.

The conversion of Puritans to Catholicism took place against the background of the colonial wars in North America during the late seventeenth and the early eighteenth century. The converts were usually women and children captured in the course of the wars, taken to Canada, and incorporated into Indian tribes. In other cases, especially where adult men were involved, Jesuits and other priests entered into debate with the prisoners to convince them of the error of their ways.

Jesuits were not the only source of difficulties for Protestants. Another problem that hindered Dutch Protestant missionaries was disagreement between the leading officials of the Dutch Reformed Church and the missionaries in the field on how best to preach to the peoples of the Americas. The missionaries' translation of basic religious texts into local languages drew the wrath of the leadership of the Dutch church, as did the supposedly poor theological training of some of the missionaries. Meuwese in chapter 6 suggests that the declining interest in missionary work on the part of the Dutch church at home may have provided a freer hand for Calvinist ministers in New York, with the paradoxical result that with less interference from Europe, the missionaries were able to deal more effectively with potential converts.

Meuwese also points to another interesting paradox in the Dutch missionary efforts. Dutch missionaries in Brazil were successful at one point because they could build on the efforts of the Jesuits who had already worked among the Indians. Thus the missionaries in Brazil saw their task not as converting infidels who had no knowledge of Christianity but as transmitting the true form of Christianity to those who had been improperly converted. In that sense, the conversion efforts in Brazil could be understood in the same terms as the efforts to bring the correct form of Christianity to Europe, that is, bringing the merely Christianized to the point of true conversion.

By the beginning of the eighteenth century, Catholic and Protestant missionaries in the Americas had experienced a wide variety of responses to their preaching. There had been converts and there had been rejection of Christianity; there had been peaceful conversion and there had been conversion that employed force; there had been accommodation of Christian practice to local cultures and there had been the complete rejection of indigenous culture as a prelude to baptism.

What there had not been was what either Catholics or Protestants had expected. The Americas had not been completely converted as Catholics believed Europe had been in the early Middle Ages, but Protestants could not demonstrate that their missionary efforts produced more and better Christians than did Catholic methods. Furthermore, belief in the imminent return of Christ and the millennium cooled, as it always did, reducing the pressure to preach. Finally, two centuries of experience with the peoples of the Americas had weakened belief in the Aristotelian notion that all mankind was naturally inclined to life in settled communities and the related belief that the truth of Christianity would be readily apparent to the peoples of the New World. Neither Catholics nor Protestants found their initial ideas about conversion fully confirmed by their experience in the Americas.

The eighteenth century saw a great deal of discussion, criticism, and analysis of missionary efforts in the Americas and elsewhere. Among Catholics, a great battle was occurring between the representatives of the older missionary orders, Dominicans and Franciscans in particular, and the Jesuits about the degree of accommodation to local cultural practices that could be tolerated. The papal condemnation of Jesuit practices in China and India in 1742 was a sign that the papacy feared that the Jesuit approach to conversion, at least in Asia, would lead to syncretism rather than conversion. It also served as a warning to missionaries everywhere that there should be no accommodation to local cultural practices when engaging in missionary activities. The gulf between what Europe-based theologians considered suitable missionary techniques and conversion experience and what missionaries in the Americas found acceptable was also apparent among Protestants. Dutch missionaries in the New World faced criticism from their superiors in Europe for their seeming laxity in such matters. The clear definitions of doctrines and ritual practices drawn in the course of the Reformation and Counter-Reformation in Europe were difficult to apply in the Americas as Protestant and Catholic missionaries wrestled with the task of translating sophisticated theological concepts developed over centuries into languages that lacked the vocabulary for doing so.

Part of the Catholic response to the problems that missionary efforts around the world posed was to create the Congregation for the Propagation of the Faith in 1622. One of the important responsibilities of the Propaganda, as it was known, was to oversee the work of missionaries to ensure adherence to orthodox standards. The Propaganda settled the conflict between Jesuits and the other orders about the degree of accommodation that could be allowed in favor of the Franciscans and Dominicans. In so doing, it also condemned accommodation elsewhere.

As for Protestants, although they showed comparatively little interest in the actual work of conversion, this did not mean that they did not discuss such work. Laura Stevens in chapter 11 demonstrates that among Anglicans the conversion of the New World was a matter of great intellectual interest. She points out that one of the themes that characterized early modern European contact with the New World had been the relation between trade and missionary work. One of the most famous scenes in the encounter was that of Europeans trading worthless bits of glass and beads in return for gold. This scene, repeated in any number of travel and exploration narratives, had a moral significance: the Europeans were greedy and the Indians naive. Seen in this light, the story provided a basis for criticizing the explorers and conquerors. It was possible, however, to refigure this scene so that the exchange between Europe and America could be understood in positive terms, that the conversion of the Indians and their being brought to salvation by Christian missionaries provided them with a reward vastly disproportionate to the gold and other items that the Europeans took from them.

Ultimately, even the German theologians reconsidered their stance on the responsibility of Christians for preaching to all mankind. Whereas in the sixteenth and early seventeenth centuries they had argued that as the original Apostles had preached throughout the world, there was no need for contemporaries to repeat that mission, by the mid-seventeenth century, they were calling for missions. As a result, Landis points out, the first German Lutheran mission began in 1632.

As these chapters demonstrate, the process of converting the peoples of the New World to Christianity did not proceed as smoothly and as completely as the missionaries anticipated it would. That is, there was no Pentecost, no descent of the Holy Spirit enabling the missionaries to preach to every man in his own language; there were no miraculous victories over enemies that could be attributed to the Christian God's intervention and followed by the baptism of an entire society. There was even backsliding as converts rebelled against the new religion and the new political order that accompanied it. Much of the disillusionment that came in the wake of the failure to achieve the success of the conversion of Europe in the Americas stemmed from a misunderstanding of the history of the conversion of early medieval Europe itself. In fact, the conversion of European societies was slower and initially less successful than sixteenth-century Catholics seem to have recognized. In the sixteenth and seventeenth centuries, Catholic clergy often compared the state of Christianity in rural Europe to the state of Christianity in the Americas. European peasants were about as Christianized after a millennium of Christianization as were the Indians of the Americas after two or three generations.[19]

The work of converting the peoples of the Americas to Christianity was to be a test of conclusions about religion drawn from fifteen hundred years of Christian history. Protestants and Catholics read that history and acted in the Americas based on their understanding of that history. As things turned out, the religious situation in the Americas repeated neither the experience of the early medieval world as Catholics anticipated nor the experience of the primitive Christian church as the Protestants expected. The assumptions that each shared about the nature of society and about the expansion of Christianity, assumptions that stressed the universality of human nature and the Aristotelian conception of civilized society as well as the universality of the Christian Gospel, became suspect. Was it the sins of the Christians that prevented the peoples of the Americas from becoming civilized Christians or was it the nature of the people themselves? We know that after the initial enthusiasm wore off and the realities of the missionary experience (that is, indigenous resistance and backsliding) struck home, missionaries, both Catholic and Protestant, became discouraged.[20]

The history of missionary efforts in the colonial Americas as reflected in these chapters places the story of the conversion of the New World within the larger context of the European encounter with the New World that began in 1492. Above all, these discussions raise one of the most important issues in recent scholarship: precisely when did Europeans become fully aware that the New World was indeed a new world and not simply a world just like Europe but at an earlier stage of development?

Initially, Europeans placed the Americas and its peoples within existing intellectual frameworks, making the unfamiliar familiar in order to comprehend what they saw and to explain it to those who remained at home. As John Eliot and Anthony Grafton have demonstrated, a significant time lag ensued before Europeans came to realize that the Americas were different and that in fundamental ways the New World was indeed new.[21] The missionaries who saw the Americas in terms of the European experience and then attempted to repeat in the New World what they believed to be the conversion experience of the Old World eventually came to understand this.

Notes

1. Hernán Cortés, *Letters from Mexico,* trans. and ed. A. R. Pagden (New York: Grossman, 1971), 48.

2. Wayne A. Meeks, *The First Urban Christians* (New Haven: Yale University Press, 1983).

3. *Oxford English Dictionary,* 12 vols. (Oxford, U.K.: Clarendon Press, 1933), 7:372; see also R. A. Markus, *Christianity in the Roman World* (New York: Scribner's, 1974), 78–80; Jean Daniélou and Henri Marrou, *The Christian Centuries,* vol. 1, *The First Six Hundred Years,* trans. Vincent Cronin (London: Darton, Longman and Todd, 1964), 295–97.

4. Leonard P. Hindsley, O.P., "Monastic Conversion: The Case of Margaret Ebner," in *Varieties of Religious Conversion in the Middle Ages,* ed. James Muldoon (Gainesville: University Press of Florida, 1997), 32–46.

5. Concerning the conversion of Clovis, see Gregory of Tours, *History of the Franks,* trans. Ernest Brehaut (New York: Columbia University Press, 1916; reprint ed., New York: Octagon Books, 1965), 36–41. The best study of the medieval approach to corporate conversion is to be found in Bede, *A History of the English Church and People,* trans. Leo Sherley-Price (Harmondsworth: Penguin, 1955).

6. Cordula Nolte, "Gender and Conversion in the Merovingian Era," in Muldoon, *Varieties,* 81–99.

7. Christopher Dawson, *The Movement of World Revolution* (New York: Sheed and Ward, 1959), 79–80.

8. Augustine's *Confessions* provides the model for all subsequent discussions of personal conversion experience: see Frederick H. Russell, "Augustine: Conversion by the Book," in Muldoon, *Varieties,* 14–30.

9. This approach is developed in Guyda Armstrong and Ian Wood, eds., *Christianizing Peoples and Converting Individuals* (Turnhout, Belgium: Brepols, 2000); see also Birgit and Peter Sawyer, *Medieval Scandinavia: From Conversion to Reformation, circa 800–1500* (Minneapolis: University of Minnesota Press, 1993), 100–105.

10. John M. Howe, "The Conversion of the Physical World: The Creation of a Christian Landscape," in Muldoon, *Varieties*, 63–78.

11. Anthony M. Stevens-Arroyo, "The Inter-Atlantic Paradigm: The Failure of Spanish Medieval Colonization of the Canary and Caribbean Islands," *Comparative Studies in Society and History* 35 (1993): 515–43.

12. E. Randolph Daniel, *The Franciscan Concept of Mission in the High Middle Ages* (Lexington: University Press of Kentucky, 1975).

13. Henry Warner Bowden, *American Indians and Christian Missions: Studies in Cultural Conflict* (Chicago: University of Chicago Press, 1981), 122.

14. On the story of Saint Thomas, see D. A. Brading, *The First America* (Cambridge, U.K.: Cambridge University Press, 1991), 172–74, 273–74. Contemporary fundamentalists sometimes make a similar claim: see R. B. Thieme Jr., *Heathenism* (Houston, Tex.: Berachah Tapes and Publications, 1979), 9–13.

15. Peter A. Goddard, "Converting the *Sauvage:* Jesuit and Montagnais in Seventeenth-Century New France," *Catholic Historical Review* 84 (1998): 219–39 at 222–23.

16. Edmund Spenser, *Present State of Ireland*, vol. 10 of *Works*, ed. E. A. Greenlaw et al., 10 vols. (Baltimore: Johns Hopkins University Press, 1932–57), 136.

17. On the language issue in medieval Europe, see Richard Fletcher, *The Barbarian Conversion: From Paganism to Christianity* (New York: Henry Holt, 1997), esp. 7, 462–64. For the problem in the Americas, see Robert Ricard, *The Spiritual Conquest of Mexico: An Essay on the Apostolate and the Evangelizing Methods of the Mendicant Orders in New Spain, 1523–1572*, trans. Leslie Byrd Simpson (Berkeley: University of California Press, 1966, reprinted 1982), 39–60. Explorers and merchants also developed techniques for developing translators: see Ivana Elbl, "Cross-Cultural Trade and Diplomacy: Portuguese Relations with West Africa, 1441–1521," *Journal of World History* 3 (1992): 165–204 at 170–72.

18. This was not a new problem. Missionaries in Livonia, modern Estonia, and part of Latvia had feared the bad example of Christian settlers: see James Muldoon, *The Expansion of Europe: The First Phase* (Philadelphia: University of Pennsylvania Press, 1977), 107.

19. Goddard, "Converting the *Sauvage*," 222–23. As Richard Fletcher observed, efforts to convert the rural population of Europe "would continue to tax the energies of bishops for centuries to come." Fletcher, *Barbarian Conversion*, 64.

20. Ricard, *Spiritual Conquest*, 288.

21. J. H. Eliot, *The Old World and the New, 1492–1650* (Cambridge, U.K.: Cambridge University Press, 1970); and Anthony Grafton, *New Worlds, Ancient Texts: The Power of Tradition and the Shock of Discovery* (Cambridge, Mass.: Harvard University Press, 1992).

1

Making the Land Holy

The Mission Frontier in Early Medieval Europe and Colonial Mexico

Daniel T. Reff

Introduction

The Iberian conquest of the Americas appropriately has been understood in terms of a variety of processes (e.g., demographic, ecological, economic, political, literary). A neglected dimension of the invasion and conquest of the New World is that it entailed a significant reimagining and reconfiguring of the American landscape. I am not referring here to the fact that Europeans destroyed or transformed flora and fauna into commodities. Mercantilism and nascent capitalism certainly exercised a profound influence on how Europeans perceived and related to the physical environment. However, if Iberians and Europeans more generally felt it necessary to dominate and possess America, their motivation was more than economic. Significantly, one of the first and most enduring Iberian practices upon reaching the New World was to rename Indian settlements, islands, ports, rivers, and so forth, yielding Corpus Christi, Veracruz, Santa Maria, and San Salvador.[1] This naming practice was the beginning of a much more extensive process of inscribing the American landscape with Christian symbols and meaning, rendering it both intelligible and tractable.

In this chapter I focus on the Jesuit missionary experience in colonial Mexico and how Jesuit "orthographic practices" paralleled those of monks and bishops in medieval Europe. In both the Old World and the New,

Christian missionaries labored among gentiles who already had fashioned myths and other narratives of religious significance that were tied to the physical environment. Often these narratives focused on springs, caves, forests, mountains, or ordinary places that were understood as having experienced some in-breaking of the divine (e.g., an otherwise unpretentious battlefield where supernatural[s] ensured a military victory). These locales were perceived as points of access to supernaturals who were invoked during times of uncertainty or whose benevolence was maintained through rituals and sacrifice. Significantly, in both early medieval Europe (ca. 165–700 c.e.) and the New World (ca. 1492–1700 c.e.), profound dislocations coincident with epidemic disease, invasion, and the collapse of empire undermined the authority of native priests and shamans, the inscribers and maintainers of sacred space, thus setting the stage for Christian reinscription. Christian missionaries faced a fundamental dilemma of wanting to retain native belief in the in-breaking of the divine, even as they sought to discredit the pagan experience of divinity. It is never easy convincing people that they have been living a lie, that a devil has deceived them. This is the argument that was advanced by early medieval and Jesuit missionaries, with mixed success. Thus, in both medieval Europe and colonial Mexico, Catholicism entailed both universals (e.g., Holy Sacraments) and local contingencies of history and place.

Below I begin by examining how the advance of the mission frontier in medieval Europe gave rise to a particular sacred geography, which was still current in Iberia and elsewhere in 1492. I then explore how pioneer Jesuit missionaries sought to fashion an idealized Christian sacred geography in Indian Mexico, particularly along the northern frontier of Nueva España. I focus particularly on the period from roughly 1591 to 1640 in what is today northwestern Mexico, as it is revealed in the Jesuit *anuas* and Andrés Pérez de Ribas' history of the Jesuit missions, first published in 1645.[2]

The Medieval Origins of European Sacred Geography

By the time of Constantine (313 c.e.), Christian communities could be found in many cities of the Mediterranean. Christianity also had spread up the Rhine to Cologne, throughout the Rhône Valley, in eastern Gaul, in most of Auvergne, in south Aquitaine, along the Seine River, and to Britain.[3] Although such expansion bespeaks impressive growth, still only about 10 percent of the Roman world was Christian at the outset of the fourth century.[4] During this century various emperors and bishops encouraged the spread of Christianity to hinterland areas beyond major cities, as exemplified by the life of Martin of Tours. This expansion was facilitated by the monastic movement, which produced evangelistic monks who undertook missions both independent of and in cooperation with ecclesiastical organization.[5] Conversions continued during the fifth century among peoples who increasingly were more Germanic than Celtic, owing to a population collapse among the latter that began in the late second century, followed by the westward migration of Goths, Franks, Burgundians, and a host of other peoples from eastern Europe and western Asia. During the sixth century, fear of and contempt for these "barbarians" was replaced by a genuine desire to incorporate them into the Church.[6] By the end of the sixth century, the Franks, Burgundians, and Goths largely were brought into the Roman Catholic fold, and much of Europe could be said to be Christian.[7]

Although clearly by the seventh century people throughout western Europe had embraced Christianity (at least in part), surprisingly little scholarship has focused on the dynamics of the conversion process, particularly prior to 700 C.E.[8] Who were the pagan converts, and what precipitated and sustained their interest in Christianity? How representative was Martin of Tours, and what strategies did he and other bishops and monks employ that endeared pagans to Christianity? None of these questions has been answered satisfactorily, owing in part to a paucity of historical and archaeological data and a traditional scholarly emphasis on theological issues and controversies (e.g., Arianism, Pelagianism, Priscillianism).[9]

Regarding the pagans, we must rely on the Romans for narrative descriptions much as we must rely on the Spaniards for insight into Amerindian cultures. Europe during the late Iron Age was a world of mostly small farming communities in which individual rights and responsibilities were largely dictated by one's place in the local system of lineages and clans (e.g., with elders, particularly males, exercising the most authority). On occasion, particularly during times of war, these different kin groups would coalesce to form larger sociopolitical units, which were led by a "king" or paramount chief. During the last two centuries B.C.E., many paramount chiefs came under the influence of the imperial Roman state.

At first, Roman influence was extended through trade and diplomatic ties. In places such as Gaul and Iberia, Gallic nobles and chiefs imported large amounts of wine and pottery and, in turn, provided Roman cities with minerals, wool, and grain. This commerce apparently was a key factor in the rapid increase in the population, coincident with the appearance of towns and states and a privileged local "aristocracy" that adopted Greek and Latin writing.[10] Trade between Rome and Gaul boomed in the last century B.C.E. and continued during the first century C.E. During this period, Roman-style villas built by Gallic nobles came to dot the countryside in what is today southern France and Spain.[11]

Quite unlike their European descendants in America, the Romans were relatively tolerant—indeed, in some cases, respectful—of pagan religions. This was true even after Roman legions subdued or otherwise conquered pagan armies and much of western Europe ostensibly was incorporated into the empire.[12] The Celts saw the physical environment in which they lived out their lives as suffused with supernaturals. "Paganism," in general, has been characterized as truly a religion of place.[13] Mountains and most notably springs, trees, and groves were of particular religious significance and were viewed as "home" to primarily local and to some extent extraregional deities (e.g., Lugh, an apparent sun god) that were depicted in various ways, including shape shifters who assumed animal guises.[14] Often shrines to these deities were built nearby, as were more formal enclosures or templelike structures where the Celts petitioned their gods for good harvests, fortune, relief from disease, and the redress of wrongs. The Celts, and pagans more generally, are thought to have had various orders of holy men (e.g., priests, diviners) who fulfilled various functions, principally maintaining the calendar and fixing dates for festivals, sowing, and so forth, and acting as go-betweens with Celtic gods, the dead, and various spirits of rivers, springs, forests, and other natural "sites."[15]

Primarily as a result of Roman influence, pagan peoples began during the Late Iron Age to envision their deities in human shape and to build temples replete with altars and inscriptions. Later Germanic immigrants, who supplanted or assimilated what was a declining Celtic population in late antiquity (ca. 165–500 C.E.), also erected sacred buildings that housed figures of gods and cult objects. Although these temples occasionally were surrounded by a wall, Davidson notes that these sacred places must be understood as something not set apart from the ordinary secular world, but rather as providing a vital center for the needs of the community and for the maintenance of a kingdom.[16] Such a sacred space offered a means of communication with the Other World and was regarded as a source of power, inspiration, healing, and hidden knowledge.

As noted above, we know surprisingly little about how and why pagan peoples embraced Christianity and the particular methods and strategies employed by bishops and monks during the early Middle Ages. One thing that is apparent is that the conversions took place during a time of profound dislocations.

During the second century C.E., the population of the Roman Empire, which encompassed much of western Europe, witnessed a decided downturn in their fortunes owing to the appearance of new forms of infectious diseases, which were soon followed by Germanic invaders. There is a consensus that the population of Europe experienced a collapse beginning around the third century and continuing well into the Middle Ages.[17] Russell has estimated that the population of the Roman Empire declined by half between the time of Augustus and 543.[18] Biraben and Le Goff suggest that the great plagues of the sixth century, combined with smallpox, caused further catastrophic losses.[19] Boak notes that by the early fifth century the area of untilled land had reached astonishing proportions, and many of the cities of the Roman Empire had become ghost towns.[20]

Where town or urban life continued it was much attenuated.[21] Archaeological evidence indicates widespread abandonment of villas and other profound settlement system changes in Gaul beginning around the time of the Antonine Plague.[22] During the late third century—following the measles pandemic of 251–270 C.E.—Roman defenses against barbarian incursions became tenuous, and many towns drastically reduced the area contained within newly fortified walls.[23] It is perhaps a testament to the consequences of "crowd infections" that many of these newly fortified towns, after a brief revival, subsequently became impoverished and perished.[24]

In this context of demographic collapse and profound sociocultural upheaval, Christianity spread rapidly. Missionaries who ventured forth in the wake of epidemics to convert the pagans were well armed with a new perspective on human misery as well as rituals and sacrifices to combat uncertainty. This "new" perspective, which emerged during the third century, equated human suffering with Satan and his legion of fallen angels. Misfortune was represented as a consequence of a collective failure to fulfill some promise or covenant with supernaturals.[25] People who were possessed, ill, or otherwise harmed by the Devil were able to overcome Satan and correct prior imbalances through the sacraments and by enlisting one's guardian angel and the help of Christian martyrs and saints. Through prayer and sacrifice, the individual (and by extension, the community of which he or she was inextricably a part) would be rid of the Devil and his influence.

The biography of Gregory of Nyssa, whose thirty-year mission (243–

272 C.E.) to Pontus and Cappadocia coincided with the great measles epidemic of 252–266 C.E., recounts how he broke the hold of traditional priestly families by directly challenging their oracles and cures and replacing their festivals for pagan idols with celebrations for Christian martyrs.[26] In Sulpicius Severus' life of Saint Martin of Tours[27] (and indeed in many sacred biographies), missionary saints unabashedly toppled pagan shrines or destroyed pagan temples.[28] While such aggressive behavior often met with resignation, it apparently as often aroused the anger of pagans. For example, sixty Christians were killed at the turn of the fourth century after toppling a pagan statue of Hercules in Sufes, Byzacena.[29] As Flint suggests, the missionary who brazenly destroyed pagan idols or shrines took a tremendous gamble, because the missionaries' goal was to destroy the idols without dispelling the emotions and belief in the supernatural that had sustained them.[30] Similarly, destroying pagan sacred places or things did not necessarily induce respect for their Christian replacements, because religious shrines invariably embody traditions and sanctions that hold a society together, including sanctions that can recoil upon the missionary and his message. Indeed, the missionary who brashly toppled an idol (and in the process challenged the religious caretakers of the idol) established a precedent by which the missionary and his own "idols" were subsequently judged and replaced.

Thus, in addition to the aggressive approach to conversion, hagiographic sources reveal another approach that not only tolerated the older and competing magical practices, but also essentially resurrected them in the guise of the cult of the saints and their relics.[31] By the sixth century, a network of shrines with tombs or fragments of dead bodies covered the Mediterranean.[32] Through the introduction of relics, particularly the complete skeletons of widely known saints, Christian missionaries were able to provide pagan communities with what were touted as new supernatural advocates and protectors.[33] Relics were perceived as a permanent benevolent influence actively protecting the town and the church in which they were preserved and honored.[34] By translating the relics to a local church or shrine, which invariably was built over a pagan shrine, the missionaries effectively recouped prior passions and feelings for what, by tradition, was sacred space.[35] This transference of emotion presumably was facilitated by the Celts' prior personification of supernaturals and the construction of altars and formal shrines under the administration of the Romans, paralleling Christian belief and architecture.

Iberian Sacred Geography

Scholars concur that extension of the cult of the saints and their relics was instrumental in the rise of Christianity in western Europe.[36] Indeed, Brown has suggested that the central importance of the cults in western Europe is the key factor explaining the different histories of the Church in the west and Byzantium.[37] The cult of the saints and their relics remained central to religious life in Iberia at the time of the Spanish invasion and conquest of Mexico.[38] At the time, over 80 percent of Spain's population resided in small, close-knit agricultural communities, ranging in size from several dozen to upwards of several thousand people. Not only priests but Iberians in general saw the physical environment in which they lived out their lives as populated by a multiplicity of supernaturals who opposed the forces of evil. Arrayed against the Devil were the crucified Christ, his mother, and an army of saints. As noted, the power and voice of these supernaturals often was conveyed through relics and images that were housed in churches, chapels, monasteries, and shrines within and without many villages and towns. Through public vows and processions, Iberians were constantly in conversation with the supernaturals, negotiating continued protection against drought, plague, locusts, and a host of other misfortunes.

With renewed use of images beginning in the eleventh century, a further Christianization of the landscape occurred, such that by the sixteenth century, chapels and shrines dotted the landscape in and around many towns and villages. The *Relaciones Topográficas* (circa 1580) indicate that almost every community had at least two chapels with images of saints or Mary. Communities with populations of 2,500 or more often had five or six chapels dedicated to different saints. These chapels generally were a kilometer or more from the center of town and were likely to contain curing images, as opposed to relics.

The third and often most important center of religious devotion was the shrine, often constructed on the margins of a village adjoining the hinterland. Most shrines were dedicated to Mary and were near springs, near important trees, or on cliffs or peaks. There Mary was said to have appeared or requested devotion. Often such requests were conveyed indirectly, as in the case of a dog who incessantly scratched at the ground or some other such mysterious behavior. Because no relics for Mary existed, as a result of the assumption she became an ideal successor to the pre-Christian mother goddesses in the countryside.

Besides the parish church, nearby monasteries, and various chapels and shrines, each community also had its cemetery and sometimes oratories, which were at the outskirts of a village and oriented in accordance with the four cardinal directions.

The supernaturals who "resided" within and without each Iberian settlement were retained through processions and masses, which followed the Roman liturgy and calendar. Most Marian feasts, Holy Week, Corpus Christi, and the feasts of individual saints were all celebrated with processions to one or more nodes within the sacred geography of a village or town. During the spring, between April 25 and May 9, a particular flurry of processions to various chapels and shrines occurred, for the purpose of imploring Mary and the saints to protect crops. People, of course, also went to the shrines on their own. Additionally, during times of impending disaster a *rogativa* or petitionary procession to a local chapel or shrine was conducted to secure the intercessory help of saints who previously had been recognized as protectors of the community. The procedure invariably was to go to chapels on the outskirts of the town and then to a more distant shrine to Our Lady. Petitionary processions of this kind were predicated on a sense of collective responsibility for natural disasters.

The Jesuit Experience in Northern Nueva España

The Iberian sacred geography outlined above is what Jesuit missionaries knew best; not surprisingly, they sought to replicate it in Nueva España. Of course, when the Jesuits reached the mission frontier they found that the physical environment already had inscribed meanings. The natives of northern Mexico were largely sedentary agriculturists who also relied on hunted and gathered resources. The native population was distributed among innumerable *rancherias,* villages, and towns, ranging in size from one or two families up to a thousand or more. Permanent settlements were chiefly along the many rivers that originate in the Sierra Madre Occidental and flow eastward across the central plateau, or descend in the west through the foothills and then across the Sonoran Desert and subtropical coastal plain of Sinaloa.[39] Native settlements were governed by elites with differential access to and control of productive and organizational strategies and who wielded substantial political and military influence. Each community had what the Jesuits called *principales*—lineage- or kin-based elders. In many areas native peoples were organized into larger sociopolitical systems, perhaps best characterized as chiefdoms, which were led by a *principal cacique*.

Like the Celts of Iron Age Europe, the Indians in northwestern Mexico embraced a pan-American belief that spirits were present in or could manifest themselves through all natural phenomena, be it animals such as deer or rabbits, or inanimate forces such as the wind or lightning. Sedentary groups viewed the woods or desert scrubland (*monte*) beyond the village as the particular "haunt" of supernaturals.[40] Individuals or groups (e.g., hunters, traders) who ventured into what the Yaqui called the Huya Aniya did so only after petitioning for success and safe passage and always were mindful of the possibility of unsolicited contact with supernaturals.[41] During vision quests, individuals explicitly ventured into the Huya Aniya to numinous locations (e.g., mountaintops) to contact spirits and to secure guidance and rituals for controlling one's destiny or that of others. Those who were successful often returned with reports of encountering spirits in the form of animals or inanimate objects that spoke.

One Jesuit report, for example, relates an instance in which a Tepehuan Indian acquired an idol of stone while sitting at the base of a hill.[42] Reportedly, a stone rolled down the hill to where he was sitting, and it began speaking, soliciting his care and protection and promising, in return, strength in battle, the power to give or cure sickness, and advice on how to deal with other challenges.

The spirits of the Huya Aniya that were encountered or solicited by individuals often were described by the Jesuits in rather abstract terms, as if the spirits themselves lacked definite form.[43] At other times the Jesuits spoke of native worship of anthropomorphic deities. The sun and moon seem to have been universally worshiped, often as mates.[44]

Groups such as the Guasave, Mayo, Yaqui, and Acaxee also worshiped a variety of "lesser" or seemingly specialized deities who had dominion over arenas such as warfare, agriculture, hunting, carnal delights, and the discovery of lost or stolen items.[45] Many of these deities as well as the creator god were represented by idols of stone and wood, which, again, were associated with caves, thickets, or other physiographically distinctive areas away from Indian villages. Among the various deities worshiped by the Ahome and Guasave was one who provided good harvests, health, and success in war and was represented by an idol of stone approximately a meter in height, "in the form of a pyramid with certain characters carved in it that were unintelligible."[46] Similar Mesoamericanlike idols were found among the Tepehuan, including one that was described as a meter in height, of stone, with a realistic depiction of a man's head and a column for a body. The idol was kept at a shrine of sorts at the summit of a hill, along with a smaller idol in the shape of a caracole,[47] which is highly suggestive of the Mesoamerican deity Quetzalcoatl. Certain trees figured prominently in Acaxee religious beliefs and ceremonies. Hernando de Santarén, who had worked for five years among the Acaxee, noted in a letter in the *anua* of 1604 that to ensure victory in war the Acaxee placed offerings of arrows or enemy bones at the foot of a *zapote* tree, which grew in the plaza of their ceremonial houses.

Although in theory all members of native society apparently were privy to the spirit world, the Jesuits implied that certain individuals, often referred to as "wizards" (*hechiceros*), acted as intermediaries of the supernatural for other members of the community. Some of these *hechiceros* were solicited to deal with a variety of personal misfortunes, for which they received payments of food or other material items. The calamity most often mentioned by the Jesuits was sickness, which some wizards treated using sleight of hand, curing by blowing and sucking, and other forms of sympathetic magic.

Many native groups also had what amounted to a quasi-priesthood who cared for various idols or deities and secured appropriate offerings from fellow villagers to placate or enlist the support of the gods. In some instances, as among the Xixime, these "priests" were described as "petty kings" and fulfilled both political and religious offices.[48] Still others were reported to have inherited their idols and positions and appear to have formed a priestly hierarchy, as among the Zuni.

At least some of these "priests" were as important in death as they were in life. For example, shortly after Fathers Martin Azpilcueta and Lorenzo de Cardenas began working among the Ayvinos and Batucos (two branches of the Eudeve Opata), the priests learned that the natives had shrines where they worshiped the remains of what was described in one instance as an *hechicero* and in another an *indio principal*. The body of the so-called *principal* was kept inside a cave in a seated position and was apparently covered by an arbor of branches. Near the body the Ayvinos erected a ramada where shells, mantas, bird plumes, and other offerings were placed. Although Pérez de Ribas states that the Ayvinos made offerings to the *principal* to secure protection from lightning, the *principal* probably was a religious specialist who had earned the respect of the people for his ability to perform various public rites associated with the worship of Tlaloc, the god of thunder, rain, and lightning.[49]

This inference is supported by Father Lorenzo de Cardenas' account of another shrine, discovered by Father Azpilcueta apparently among the Batucos. The shrine was in a wooded area and consisted of a "sepulcher in the form of an altar" that contained the bones of a deceased *hechicero*. Reportedly the natives made offerings to the *hechicero* believing that "it was through him that they received beneficial rain."[50]

When the Jesuits came to the northern frontier of Nueva España in 1591–92, the indigenous population already had inscribed the world around them with narratives of religious significance. Not unlike pagan peoples in late antique Europe, the Indians of northern Nueva España saw springs, caves, and other unusual topographic features as foci where supernaturals could be accessed through ritual and sacrifice. Perhaps not surprisingly, the Jesuits had great difficulty making sense of indigenous categories and experience. In keeping with their Thomistic philosophy and a belief in the abundance of God's grace, the Jesuits saw both the Indians and the New World itself as blessed by God. Thus Pérez de Ribas noted that the Indians did not steal from each other and that women could live without fear of being raped. The land was so wholesome that one could perceive in birds' nests and trees Christian principles such as the Trinity.

Although both the Indians and the land reflected God's handiwork and grace, neither had ever been blessed by the word of God. In the absence of revealed truths, particularly the Gospels, Satan necessarily dominated the New World. Accordingly, the very same Jesuits who lauded the Indians for their honesty and modesty, and who saw the land itself as bespeaking profound truths, also noted the Indian proclivity for cannibalism, warfare, and intoxication—all vices that were introduced by the Devil. They flourished, as it were, because there was nobody enlightened by the Gospels and church teachings who could oppose them. During Satan's long reign he had effectively ensnared the people in lies that were visible in the physical environment—in shrines or caves to deceased sorcerers, in tree worship, in the very mountains themselves. Thus Pérez de Ribas quoted a Yaqui "sorceress":

> This nation was so entombed in darkness that a woman who had been enlightened by the teaching of the Gospel declared and so stated to one of the priests who preached the Gospel: "Father, look across the

river; do you see all those hills, mountains, peaks, and heights there? Well, we revered all of them and there we practiced and celebrated our superstitions." The old women certified that the devil appeared to them in the form of dogs, toads, coyotes, and snakes—forms that correspond to what he is. Indian principales and fiscales declared as a fact widely accepted among them that at night the sorceresses used to attend certain dances and gatherings with demons and that they returned through the air.[51]

Because the Jesuits perceived Indian symbols and sacred geography as the handiwork of Satan, one of their first priorities was to locate and destroy idols and then replace them with Christian symbols and images. The Jesuits essentially employed the favored strategy of medieval monks and bishops, substituting Christian for pagan rituals and practices. For instance, in Book 2 of his history of the Jesuit missions of Nueva España, Pérez de Ribas recounted how Father Gonzalo de Tapia destroyed a tree that was being worshiped by the Acaxee and replaced it with a cross:

> Before he [Father Tapia] departed, they reported to him that on a nearby mountain underneath an immense tree the Indians used to have an idol to whom they offered maize at planting time and weapons in time of war. The Spaniards had already taken it down and smashed it. The priest gathered together all the people he could and had a handsome cross fitted out. Then they went to the site of the tree singing the Christian doctrine. There, he had the tree destroyed, and in its place he planted the very beautiful cross. He blessed that place and in so doing erased the memory of that tree and those other superstitions.[52]

Note that Sulpicius Severus' *Life of Saint Martin* (circa 397 C.E.) recounted an incident of pagan tree worship that Saint Martin dealt with in the same way as Father Tapia.[53] Elsewhere, in Book XI of his *Historia*, Pérez de Ribas recounted how one of the first priests to work among the Laguneros of Parras learned of a cave where the Indians purportedly made offerings to the Devil. According to Pérez de Ribas, the priest

> organized a procession of the new Christians, and carrying a cross they proceeded to the devil's cavern. There they performed the exorcisms and blessings of the Church, and an altar was erected and the priest said mass. A holy cross was then placed in the cave, which from then on they called Santiago, because this was the feast day of the

great Patron Saint of the Spaniards [July 25], under whose protection they have planted the Faith and the Catholic Empire in the Indies.[54]

It is worth emphasizing that in northern Mexico—as in early medieval Europe—the advance of the mission frontier was coincident with profound demographic and sociocultural changes wrought by new forms of infectious disease.[55] Everywhere the Jesuits went, smallpox, measles, malaria, and other maladies accompanied or preceded the "black robes," as these missionaries were known. Old World diseases not only devastated populations but also undermined the structure and functioning of native societies, including the power and influence of Indian priests and shamans, who had no knowledge of, or experience with, epidemic diseases comparable to smallpox.[56]

Coincident with the replacement of Indian "shrines" with crosses, the Jesuits established a hierarchical network of sacred places, modeled after what was found in Iberia. The highest-order place in this network was the head mission or *cabecera*, which invariably was in the chief Indian pueblo of a region. Here the Jesuits supervised the construction of what was essentially the parish church. Unlike parish churches in Iberia, which were understood to house the prized relics of local saints, the mission churches established by the Jesuits were represented as privileged and powerful by virtue of the fact that they were permanent home to the Holy Sacrament (although in time the fact that many missionaries died, particularly as martyrs, meant that the landscape did take on Jesuit bodies and body parts).

In nearby, smaller Indian settlements—or what were called *visitas*—the Jesuits established what essentially were chapels. Most *visitas* were dedicated to Mary, to her mother, and to Jesuit saints and martyrs. On the appropriate feast day, mass was said under elaborate ramadas or simple churches in the *visita*, but otherwise the consecrated host resided in the *cabecera* church. During Holy Week and Corpus Christi the *cabecera* church was the point of origin for what were often elaborate processions that encompassed outlying *visitas* and topographical features that were rendered sacred through the installation of crosses. This process is exemplified in Pérez de Ribas' account of the first Holy Week celebration among the Guasave Indians: "To make the stations of the cross, they erected crosses in the most appropriate sites, for there were not many churches or shrines to visit. On the designated day, they conducted processions to each station, singing hymns and doing penance by scourging themselves and drawing blood."[57]

Within years of the establishment of a mission with its *cabecera* and *visitas*, the Jesuits often encouraged the Indians of a particular mission to establish shrines to saints and to Mary. These shrines characteristically were built in places that already were understood as "sacred" or having evidenced some in-breaking of the divine:

> The Zuaque women were so spirited in the construction of their principal church that they decided to also build a small shrine to the Most Holy Virgin. It was erected next to their pueblo at the top of a pretty little pinnacle of rock, the base of which was bathed by their river. This pinnacle was mentioned earlier when it was told how it broke open due to the unusual trembling through which God had threatened to punish this nation for their rebelliousness. Therefore, this shrine and church were a sign that this nation's hearts had softened and that they had dedicated themselves to God.[58]

As was the case in Iberia, some of these shrines took on a regional importance, attracting processions from many settlements that came seeking relief from disease or drought:

> On one occasion during a great drought, the fields belonging to the pueblo of Torim began to dry up. This prompted the children to hold a scourging procession to a shrine of Our Lady that they had erected on a little hill near their pueblo. Because of these little innocents' prayers, and in honor of His Most Blessed Mother, Our Lord let abundant rain fall on the fields of the pueblo; no rain fell on the fields of other nearby pueblos. The Indians were amazed and the neighboring pueblos became fond of imitating the people of Torim in their devotion to the Most Holy Virgin.[59]

As noted earlier, the sacred geography of Iberia was not simply a collection of religious points in space. The supernaturals who resided in or frequented the parish church, chapels, shrines, and other locales required regular sacrifices. These sacrifices, which were realized through processions and the sacrament of the Eucharist, were regularized by the Roman liturgy and calendar. The Jesuit missions largely followed the church's ritual of feasts. The regulations drawn up for the missions in 1662, however, indicate that processions to the cemetery for the dead were to be held each Monday.[60] The high frequency of these processions and the corresponding importance of the cemetery reflect the fact that the mission frontier was a disease environment. With missionaries came diseases that wreaked havoc on Indian populations during the sixteenth and seventeenth centuries.

Conclusion

As Zamora has noted, "Although space takes shape through the traveler's experience of the journey, the spatiotemporal paradigm is always present at the beginning of the journey, to set the traveler in motion."[61] The Jesuit's spatiotemporal paradigm was a land to be freed from Satan and remade in the image of idealized Christian Iberia.

In colonial Mexico, as in early medieval Europe, the Jesuits worked with native societies that had experienced profound dislocations coincident with invasions, migrations, epidemics, and conquest. Like medieval missionaries, the Jesuits imagined themselves at war with the Devil and his heathen familiar, the dreaded shaman. The Jesuits directly challenged these religious leaders and just as often deployed accommodated pagan belief, chiefly through the cult of the saints and their relics.

Like medieval missionaries, the Jesuits retained the sacred spaces of the Indians, inscribing new figures or narratives onto them and in the process extending existing narratives. Thus, most place names in northern Mexico have a saint's name and an Indian name (e.g., San Pedro y San Pablo de Tubutama). Along these lines, it has been suggested that the mission system supplanted most traces and memories of aboriginal culture among groups such as the Yaqui.[62]

The reality is that many Christian beliefs and rituals that were accepted by native peoples appear to be modifications or extensions of preexisting native beliefs and rituals. Pérez de Ribas and other Jesuits would no doubt wince at the suggestion that Christian theology was polytheistic. Yet the Santoria introduced by the Jesuits (including the crucified Christ, Christ the Child, the various portrayals of Mary, and the patron saints of the church and town) all accorded well with the natives' prior belief in a multiplicity of spirits and deities of both sexes who oversaw matters of war, weather, health, and the heart. Christian theology may be universal in scope, but the history of Christianity has been characterized by the adaptation of this theology to local settings; Christianity is not everywhere the same beliefs and rituals, however much the Vatican and church hierarchy may endeavor to legislate norms.

Notes

1. Patricia Seed, *Ceremonies of Possession in Europe's Conquest of the New World, 1492–1640* (Cambridge, U.K.: Cambridge University Press, 1995), 190.

2. D. Reff, M. Ahern, and D. Danford, eds. and trans., *History of the Triumphs of Our Holy Faith amongst the Most Barbarous and Fierce Peoples of the New World*, by Andrés Pérez de Ribas (Tucson: University of Arizona Press, 1999).

3. Yitzhak Hen, *Culture and Religion in Merovingian Gaul A.D. 481–751* (New York: Brill, 1995), 8.

4. K. S. Latourette, *A History of the Expansion of Christianity*, 7 vols. (London: Eyre and Spottiswood, 1938–45), 1:163.

5. W.H.C. Frend, *Religion Popular and Unpopular in the Early Christian Centuries* (London: Variorum Reprints, 1976), 9–10; E. Glenn Hinson, *The Evangelization of the Roman Empire* (Macon, Ga.: Mercer University Press, 1981), 38, 57.

6. Frend, *Religion Popular and Unpopular*, 17.

7. Darrel W. Amundsen, "The Medieval Catholic Tradition," in *Caring and Curing: Health and Medicine in the Western Religious Tradition*, ed. R. Numbers and D. Amundsen (London: Macmillan, 1986), 66; Peter Brown, *Religion and Society in the Age of Saint Augustine* (New York: Harper and Row, 1972), 140–41.

8. James Muldoon, "The Conversion of Europe," in *Varieties of Religious Conversion in the Middle Ages*, ed. James Muldoon (Gainesville: University Press of Florida, 1997), 1–10; Richard Sullivan, "What Was Carolingian Monasticism?" in *After Rome's Fall, Narrators and Sources of Early Medieval History, Essays Presented to Walter Goffart*, ed. A. Callander Murray (Toronto: University of Toronto Press, 1998), 251–89.

9. Roger Collins, *Early Medieval Europe, 300–1000* (New York: St. Martin's Press, 1999); Richard Sullivan, *Christian Missionary Activity in the Early Middle Ages* (Brookfield, Vt.: Variorum, 1994).

10. The population of Gaul has been estimated at perhaps 8 million at the time of the Roman conquest (ca. B.C.E. 61) and is said to have grown to 12 million by the third century, when it declined significantly; see Simon James, *Exploring the World of the Celts* (London: Thames and Hudson, 1993), 147, 151.

11. Ibid., 118–21, 137–47.

12. Béatrice Caseau, "Sacred Landscapes," in *Late Antiquity: A Guide to the Postclassical World*, ed. G. W. Bowerstock, P. Brown, and O. Grabar (Cambridge, Mass.: Belknap Press, 1999), 21–60.

13. Pierre Chuvin, *A Chronicle of the Last Pagans*, trans. B. A. Archer (Cambridge, Mass.: Harvard University Press, 1990), 8–9.

14. Ibid.

15. Ton Derks, *Gods, Temples, and Ritual Practices: The Transformation of Religious Ideas and Values in Roman Gaul* (Amsterdam: Amsterdam University Press, 1998); James, *Exploring*, 52–53, 95.

16. H. R. Ellis Davidson, *Gods and Myths of Northern Europe* (Baltimore: Penguin, 1964), 34–35.

17. A. E. Boak, *Manpower Shortage and the Fall of the Roman Empire in the West* (Ann Arbor: University of Michigan Press, 1955); William McNeill, *Plagues and Peoples* (New York: Anchor Books, 1976), 116; N. J. Pounds, *An Historical Geography of Europe* (Cambridge, U.K.: Cambridge University Press, 1990), 77.

18. J. C. Russell, "Late Ancient and Medieval Population," *Transactions of the American Philosophical Society,* New Series, vol. 48, pt. 3 (Philadelphia: American Philosophical Society, 1958).

19. J. N. Biraben and Jacques Le Goff, "The Plague in the Early Middle Ages," in *Biology of Man in History,* ed. E. Forster and O. Ranum (Baltimore: Johns Hopkins University Press, 1975), 62.

20. Boak, *Manpower Shortage,* 127.

21. Pounds, *Historical Geography,* 70.

22. William E. Klingshirn, *Caesarius of Arles: The Making of a Christian Community in Late Antique Gaul* (Cambridge, U.K.: Cambridge University Press, 1994), 203–6; C. R. Whittaker, *Frontiers of the Roman Empire: A Social and Economic Study* (Baltimore: Johns Hopkins University Press, 1994), 232.

23. Christopher Pickles, *Texts and Monuments: A Study of Ten Anglo-Saxon Churches of the Pre-Viking Period* (Oxford, U.K.: Archaeopress, 1999), 102; Whittaker, *Frontiers,* 207–8.

24. J. F. Drinkwater, *Roman Gaul: The Three Provinces, 58 B.C.–A.D. 260* (London: Croom Helm, 1983), 157–58; Colin Haselgrove, "Roman Impact on Rural Settlement and Society in Southern Picardy," in *From the Sword to the Plough: Three Studies on the Earliest Romanisation of Northern Gaul,* ed. N. Roymans (Amsterdam: Amsterdam University Press, 1996), 166–68; Whittaker, *Frontiers,* 211.

25. Brown, *Religion and Society,* 135.

26. Frend, *Religion Popular and Unpopular,* 8.

27. F. R. Hoare, trans. and ed., *The Western Fathers, Being the Lives of SS. Martin of Tours, Ambrose, Augustine of Hippo, Honoratus of Arles, and Germanus of Auxerre* (New York: Sheed and Ward, 1954), 26–29.

28. Clare Stancliffe, "From Town to Country: The Christianization of the Touraine, 370–600," in *The Church in Town and Countryside,* ed. Derek Baker (Oxford, U.K.: Basil Blackwell, 1979), 43–59.

29. Hinson, *Evangelization,* 64–65.

30. Valerie I. J. Flint, *The Rise of Magic in Early Medieval Europe* (Princeton: Princeton University Press, 1991), 94.

31. Flint, *Rise of Magic,* 76; Hinson, *Evangelization,* 64–65; Klingshirn, *Caesarius of Arles,* 212.

32. Peter Brown, *Society and the Holy in Late Antiquity* (Berkeley: University of California Press, 1982), 6.

33. Ronald C. Finucane, *Miracles and Pilgrims: Popular Beliefs in Medieval England* (Totowa, N.J.: Rowman and Littlefield, 1977).

34. Joaquín Martínez Pizarro, *A Rhetoric of the Scene: Dramatic Narrative in the Early Middle Ages* (Toronto: University of Toronto Press, 1989), 201.

35. John Howe, "The Conversion of the Physical World," in *Varieties of Religious Conversion in the Middle Ages*, ed. James Muldoon (Gainesville: University Press of Florida), 66.

36. Amundsen, "Medieval Catholic Tradition," 71; Finucane, *Miracles and Pilgrims*, 20; Flint, *Rise of Magic*, 79.

37. Peter Brown, *Society and the Holy*, 139–40.

38. William A. Christian, *Local Religion in Sixteenth-Century Spain* (Princeton: Princeton University Press, 1981).

39. Peter Gerhard, *The Northern Frontier of New Spain* (Princeton: Princeton University Press, 1982); Daniel T. Reff, *Disease, Depopulation, and Culture Change in Northwestern New Spain, 1518–1764* (Salt Lake City: University of Utah Press, 1991); Carroll L. Riley, *The Frontier People* (Albuquerque: University of New Mexico Press, 1987); Carl O. Sauer, "The Distribution of Aboriginal Tribes and Languages in Northwest Mexico," *Ibero-Americana* 5 (1935).

40. Ralph Beals, "The Aboriginal Culture of the Cahita Indians," *Ibero-Americana* 19 (1943): 18; Edward Spicer, *The Yaquis: A Cultural History* (Tucson: University of Arizona Press, 1980), 65–67.

41. Although Spicer suggested that the Yaqui conception of the Huya Aniya was a postcontact phenomenon (*The Yaquis*, 63–65), Jesuit materials suggest otherwise (Reff, *Disease, Depopulation*, 267).

42. *Documentos para la historia de Mexico, 1853–57*, Serie IV, "Anua del año de 1596" (Mexico City, 1857), 24.

43. Ralph Beals, "The Acaxee, a Mountain Tribe of Durango and Sinaloa," *Ibero-Americana* 6 (1933): 22ff.

44. Archivo General de la Nacion, Mexico City, Historia 15, "Anua del año de mil quininetos noventa y seis."

45. Reff et al., *History*, by Pérez de Ribas, 96–98.

46. Archivo General de la Nacion, "Anua del año de mil quininetos noventa y seis."

47. Reff et al., *History*, by Pérez de Ribas, 586.

48. Ibid., 546.

49. Ibid., 404.

50. Andrés Pérez de Ribas, *Corónica y historia religiosa de la Provincia de la Compañía de Jesús de México*, 2 vols. (Mexico City: Sagrado Corazon, 1896 [1653]), 2:502.

51. Reff et al., *History*, by Pérez de Ribas, 368.

52. Ibid., 119.

53. Hoare, *Western Fathers*.

54. Reff et al., *History,* by Pérez de Ribas, 668.

55. A. Ferreiro, "Early Medieval Missionary Tactics: The Example of Martin and Caesarius," *Studia Historica* (1988): 225–38; Frend, *Religion Popular and Unpopular,* 18. Note that during the Hun invasion of 451 C.E., the invaders beheaded the bishop of Reims because he apparently failed to halt an epidemic; see Donald R. Hopkins, *Princes and Peasants: Smallpox in History* (Chicago: University of Chicago Press, 1983), 23.

56. Reff, *Disease, Depopulation;* Gerhard, *Northern Frontier.*

57. Reff et al., *History,* by Pérez de Ribas, 146.

58. Ibid., 225.

59. Ibid., 367.

60. Charles W. Polzer, S.J., *Rules and Precepts of the Jesuit Missions of Northwestern New Spain, 1600–1767* (Tucson: University of Arizona Press, 1976), 79.

61. Margarita Zamora, *Reading Columbus* (Berkeley: University of California Press), 100.

62. Evelyn Hu-DeHart, *Missionaries, Miners, and Indians* (Tucson: University of Arizona Press, 1981), 23–25.

2

Conversion Practices on the New Mexico Frontier

Barbara De Marco

Not long after his arrival in Mexico City in 1523, Pedro de Gante, one of the first Franciscans to embark upon the mission of evangelization in the New World, realized the value of song and dance and visual representation as fundamental aids to the process of conversion. In a letter to King Philip II, he recounts how, faced with the native peoples' resistance to doctrine and sermons,

> by the grace of God, I began to know them and to realize . . . that their adoration for their gods consisted in singing and dancing before them . . . and when I saw this, and that all their songs were dedicated to their gods, I composed solemn verses concerning the Law of God and the faith, and how God became man to save the human race, and how he was born of the Virgin Mary.
>
> . . . and this was about two months before Christmas, and I also gave them designs (*libreas*) to paint on their capes so they could dance in them, because that is what they used to do—depending on the dances and songs they were performing, they would dress for rejoicing or for mourning or for victory; then, as Christmas was drawing near, I summoned everyone within twenty leagues' distance of Mexico City to attend the celebration of the birth of Christ our Redeemer. So many came that they could not all fit in the *patio* [the open atrium in front of the church] . . . and on the night of the Nativity they heard the angels sing "today is born the Redeemer of the world." In this way . . . they came to the obedience of the Holy Church and Your Majesty.[1]

In a similar fashion, the Franciscan Bernardino de Sahagún, one of the *primeros doce* who arrived in Mexico in 1524, fashioned the *Psalmodia*

Christiana, a composition of hymns and canticles in Nahuatl, designed "for song-dance adaptations to be performed in the churches, or for composing sermons, or for catechizing the natives and, in any case, for making them praise God and His saints rather than their old gods—the demons and devils who until lately had been masters of New Spain."[2]

It is not my purpose here to discuss the degree to which these performance pieces represent a fusion of European and native traditions, but rather to underscore the Franciscans' deliberate employment of performance techniques as a method to attract converts to the faith, whether in the urban center of México-Tenochtitlán or in the frontier wilderness of the province of New Mexico.[3] One example of performance techniques in the latter region is evident from a 1629 expedition to the Zuni pueblos in which the governor and military escort promoted the work of the Franciscans "with standard theater rather than force of arms," kneeling before the friars and kissing their feet to demonstrate the veneration due to the Franciscans.[4]

The performance at Zuni is typical of the episodes that fall under the rubric "theater of conversion," a term which I deliberately extend to signify any visual and verbal enticements—song, dance, ritual, ceremonial, art, and artifact—employed by the Franciscans for the purpose of conversion. Understood in this sense, the celebration of the Mass is no less performance for the purpose of catechesis than is Gante's elaborately staged Christmas play.

Writing of the early missions in Mexico, Robert Ricard makes a similar point:

> Processions were the natural and necessary complement of the religious services . . . held on almost all Sundays and feast days, accompanied, it goes without saying, by singing and playing, and also, if I may be forgiven the expression, by a complete theatrical setting. The way was covered with flowers and boughs, and decorated with arches. . . . [Processions] were much more frequent during certain religious seasons, but they were held throughout the year and brought together all classes and all ages. Like the pagan festivals, they were a part of life, and with them and by them Christianity penetrated that life a little more deeply.[5]

Original documents concerning early conversion practices in Mexico are to be found in the many chronicles, letters, histories, and *memoriales* written by those first Franciscans. In addition to the letter from Pedro de

Gante to King Philip II, already mentioned, is the *Tratado de las antigüedades mexicanas* (1533–1539) by Andrés de Olmos. His work has been lost and is now known to modern scholars only through several subsequent texts, among them the *Historia Eclesiástica Indiana* by Jerónimo de Mendieta (1525–1604) and the *Monarquía Indiana* (1609–13) by Juan de Torquemada. From the hands of the *primeros doce* came such works as Toribio de Benavente de Motolinía's *Memoriales* and *Historia de los Indios de la Nueva España*, and the *Historia general de las cosas de la Nueva España*, compiled under the direction of Bernardino de Sahagún.[6]

The New Mexican frontier also had its Franciscan chroniclers; this chapter offers a representative selection from some of those narratives, derived from critical periods in the early history (sixteenth and seventeenth centuries) of the Franciscan attempts to convert New Mexico. Obviously, what follows is not meant to be an exhaustive but rather a selective illustration of the creation of a theater of conversion.[7]

Fray Marcos de Niza's *Relación* of 1539 picks up the thread of the remarkable tale spun by the shipwrecked Cabeza de Vaca, thereby ushering in the first major exploration of New Mexico. That story is continued by Fray Antonio Tello (writing in 1653), who, borrowing in large part from earlier chroniclers, tells of the Franciscans who accompanied Coronado on his 1540 expedition into New Mexico. In 1598, New Mexico saw the establishment of the first Spanish settlements, under the direction of Juan de Oñate in 1598, himself an able practitioner of theater. Fray Alonso de Benavides' *memorial* of 1640, written at the height of missionary endeavor in the territory, tells a remarkable tale of conversion at a distance. This early period was brought to a close by the 1680 Pueblo Revolt in northern New Mexico, carrying with it the martyrdom of twenty-one Franciscans and a nearly successful eradication of the Spanish presence; eyewitness testimony to the revolt and its aftermath comes in the form of a retrospective *memorial* to the viceroy, written by Fray Francisco de Ayeta in 1693.

Fray Marcos de Niza's *Relación* of 1539

Fray Marcos de Niza and the provocative tale of the Seven Cities of Cíbola contained in his *Relación* of 1539 usher in the first serious expedition to what is now the American Southwest. His narrative contains many instances of public ceremonies, notably the welcome he received on the way north: "I took to the road until I arrived at the Pueblo of Petatlán, receiving along the way many welcoming greetings and gifts of food, rose garlands, and other things of this nature, and they made me dwellings of palm fronds and branches" (3r, 16–19).[8]

One of the many purposes of this journey, as explicitly stated in the *Relación* (fols. 1r–2r), was to discover whether there was an Indian settlement large enough to justify the establishment of a mission. Information on conversion techniques employed during Fray Marcos' journey is interspersed with his attempts to elicit information on the fabled cities of Cíbola, as well as with various pieces of ethnographic detail:[9] "I met other Indians who wondered upon seeing me, because they had never seen Christians.... They indicated their welcome and gave me a great quantity of food, and they tried to touch my clothes and they called me *sayota* which means in their language 'man of the heavens.' As best I could I tried to give them ... knowledge of our Lord in heaven and of his Majesty on earth and in any way I could I tried to gain information about populated lands" (3v, 4–15).

The mood of the Indians turned sour, apparently because of a misappropriation of ceremonial usage on the part of Fray Marcos' assigned guide, Esteban de Dorantes. Esteban had formed an advance party with some three hundred Indian companions, one of whom returned to Fray Marcos with the following report. Arriving at one day's journey from Cíbola, Esteban sent messengers ahead, carrying his ceremonial gourd, as was his custom, to advise the people of his coming. The gourd was decorated with bells and feathers. However, when the chief received the gourd and saw the bells, he threw it on the ground and told the messengers to get out, that he knew who they were (because the bells were not the same as the ones his people used), and that he would not allow them to enter his city, but rather he would kill them. When messengers reported all this to Esteban, he waved away the angry threat and proceeded to the city, where he was taken prisoner and, along with many of his companions, killed.

As a result of Esteban's miscalculation of his audience, Fray Marcos was left pretty much to his own resources, the once-friendly Indians having turned hostile at the loss of their relatives to Esteban's reckless adventure. His account of Cíbola, though later dismissed as so much nonsense by Coronado, is largely credited for reawakening interest in government-sponsored expeditions northward.[10]

Fray Antonio Tello's *Crónica miscelánea*

Upon the heels of Fray Marcos' report, in 1540 Francisco Vásquez de Coronado set out on a full-scale expedition in search of the fabled cities to the north. After two years of fruitless endeavor and increasing antagonism from the native peoples, Coronado decided to return to Mexico City; however, three Franciscan missionaries in his company were determined to remain. Over a century later, in his *Crónica miscelánea y conquista espiritual y temporal,* Fray Antonio Tello takes up the tale of Fray Juan de Padilla and his companions, thereby presenting an important variation on the conversion theme: the narrative of martyrdom.[11]

Repeated scenes of "glorious martyrdom" on the frontier were intended to sway other Franciscans to take up the task of conversion in the hostile environment of the New World. Inasmuch as the narratives often reveal important details of conversion practices, the story of the first martyr in New Mexico merits close examination. Fray Tello begins:

> No land or province of New Spain has been discovered where one does not find the first preachers and teachers of the faith, the religious of our father St. Francis, and the shedding of their blood and the glorious martyrdom that they undergo for love of our Lord God, the foundation stone of the edifice of the church. With holy zeal they go out to unknown lands, distant and remote, to serve him in the conversion of infidels. One worthy of eternal fame and perpetual memory was the illustrious martyr Fray Juan de Padilla, son of the holy province of Andalucia. He went out to New Spain with the intention of preaching and converting to our faith the many infidels. . . . He was guardian in the province of Tzapotlán when, unable to quiet his spirit in its most burning desire to save souls, he sought the permission and blessing of his prelate to go to the discovery of Cíbola. (487–88)

After Coronado departed in 1542, Fray Padilla remained behind in the province of Tiguex to continue with his program of conversion. In the company of Andrés de Campo and two Indians from Michoacán, Fray Padilla went out in search of potential converts. Seeing hostile Indians approach, Padilla instructed the others to flee, whereupon "the blessed Fray Juan, kneeling in prayer, commended his soul to the Lord for whose love and faith he had placed himself in danger." The Indians, having shot Padilla with arrows, dismounted to steal his vestments and supplies and threw his body into a ditch. Fray Tello finishes the story with a postscript appropriate to a holy martyr. Fray Padilla's death was marked with many portents: the sun grew dark, comets coursed the heavens, and the earth was struck with balls of fire (489–91).

As to the companions left behind at the pueblo, Fray Juan de la Cruz and Fray Luis de Ubeda, Tello continues with their stories of martyrdom, each couched in suitably hagiographic terms: Fray Juan de la Cruz was a man of "great patience, humility, abstinence, and mildness, and imbued with such charity that . . . when he entered the pueblos, the Indians carried him in their arms" (491). Even the Spanish soldiers revered him, so much so that Coronado ordered that "whenever his name was mentioned, [the soldiers] were to bow or uncover their heads in a sign of the veneration and honor that was due to the virtue and sanctity of so excellent a servant of God" (491). Of Fray Luis de Ubeda, Tello admits, little was known, but it was commonly accepted that he was a martyr "and a perfect religious . . . of upright life, and esteemed and respected by all, so that Coronado ordered his soldiers to treat him with esteem and reverence" (492).

Fray Angélico Chávez, in his twentieth-century work *Coronado's Friars*, has carefully pieced together the same stories as told by various Franciscan chroniclers. Fray Angélico writes: "The chroniclers and others relate that Fray Juan de Padilla was easily aroused to anger when the soldiery did or said anything wrong, and we can suppose that with this short temper went a stubbornness when he had set his mind on something" (21). Fray Angélico also suggests that Fray Padilla's motivating force for remaining behind was not so much the desire to convert souls, but rather the desire to find the Seven Cities of Cíbola (50n.3). What is significant about these narratives is not the strict veracity of the details but the overall effect of the staging: stories of martyrdom in particular are to be understood as *exempla*.[12]

Fray Juan de Padilla himself is thought to have written the following account of a significant combination of Christian and native rituals:

> In the places where we erected crosses, we taught the natives to venerate them, and they offered them their powders [sacred corn meal] and feathers, some even the blankets they were wearing. They did it with such eagerness that some climbed on the backs of others in order to reach the arms of the crosses to put plumes and roses [feather rosettes] on them. Others brought ladders, and while some held them others climbed up to tie strings in order to fasten the roses and feathers.[13]

Juan de Oñate Takes Possession of New Mexico

After the Coronado expedition, forty years passed before the resumption of authorized and significant explorations of New Mexico. In 1581, a lay brother, Fray Agustín Rodríguez, set out with two other Franciscans and Captain Francisco Sánchez Chamuscado; together with a small party of soldiers and Indians they explored the territory of the Pueblo Indians. In 1582, Antonio de Espejo went beyond that country into the buffalo plains and present-day Arizona.

Out of such tentative forays into the New Mexico frontier grew the first real settlement of the province of New Mexico in 1598, under the leadership of Juan de Oñate. It seems from all reports that Oñate also appreciated the value of staging public ceremonies, and he did so to mark his formal taking possession of the territory of New Mexico. In addition to the performance of an open-air drama specially composed for the occasion, Oñate conducted a series of public gestures that, in the manner of Fray Marcos before him, served the dual focus of "knowledge of our Lord in heaven and of his Majesty on earth." After nailing a crucifix to a tree near the riverbank to invoke safe crossing, Oñate then knelt to pray before this same crucifix, that it might "open the doors of Heaven to these heathens, establish the church and altars where the body and blood of the son of God may be offered, open to us the way to security and peace for their preservation and ours, and give to our king, and to me in his royal name, peaceful possession of these kingdoms and provinces for His blessed glory." Oñate then walked into an open field and raised the royal standard, accompanied by a salvo of weapons.[14]

Supply Wagons to New Mexico

By 1609, the Crown had assumed responsibility for the government of the province of New Mexico, as well as for the support of the missions. With this development, a regular supply caravan began to wend its way between Mexico City and the northern province. It is of some interest to read, in the contractual agreement of 1631, that the list of supplies to be distributed every three years to each friar-priest serving in the *Conversión del Nuevo México* included not just what was needed for survival—blankets, scissors, yarn, needles, horseshoes, grindstones, paper, bridles, spurs, medicines, and the like—but also what was required for the conduct of the Catholic rituals and devotional practices. Among the items listed were forty-five gallons of sacramental wine, eighty-five and a half pounds of prepared candle wax, twenty-six gallons of oil for illuminating the Holy Sacrament, six common rosaries, two tin-plate lanterns for saying Mass, one rug for the base of the altar, tables and benches with which to construct an altar, six staffs with iron mountings for the awning to cover the altar, and two cruets made of tin-plate.[15]

The items listed in the contract are cited here in some detail inasmuch as they implicitly provide an inventory of the various means, visual and verbal, by which conversion to the faith was effected: church architecture and manipulation of space for processions and other ritual performances; the decoration of that space with statues and pictures, bells and crosses; the constant invocation of the persons of God, the Virgin Mary, and particular saints; the sequences of music and prayers learned by heart and recited out loud; and the elaborate ceremonials required in the celebration of the Mass, including the vestments for the celebrant and the various articles for the altar. Robert Ricard makes this point in his fundamental work on Mexico, and clearly the Franciscans were aiming for the same effects on the northern frontier: "The same motives that led the religious to construct vast and beautiful churches and decorate them luxuriously led them also to surround the Mass and the services with the most solemn pomp. This had a double advantage. It maintained the enthusiasm of the Indians, who were very sensitive to external spectacles, and it enhanced their devotion and their respect for the ceremony at the altar."[16]

The sudden appearance on the New Mexico frontier of silver chalices and gilded crucifixes, of chasubles made of damask, and perfectly rounded hosts can hardly provide a more severe contrast to the feathers, herbs, powders, and masks that were part of the native repertory. The 1631 inventory assumed a new significance in the context of the 1680 Pueblo Revolt, when it was transformed from a straightforward listing of necessities to a bitter reckoning of the natives' repudiation of the Franciscan program of conversion.

In addition to hardware and foodstuffs, the "Statement of Ornaments and other things for Divine Worship to be given each Friar-Priest the first time that he goes to those Conversions" stipulated the provision of a chasuble, stole, and other clothing that constitute the wardrobe of the priest when saying Mass; for the holy services, the list included altar cloths, missals, a silver chalice, a gilded paten and cup, one small *Sanctus* bell, one two-hundred-pound bell and framework, one pair of gilded wooden processional candlesticks, one pair of brass candlesticks, cupboards and vessels to hold the host, holy oils and holy water, cruets for water and wine, a crucifix with a gilded brass handle, and two and a half pounds of incense. To be shared among every five priests were two choir robes, two carved images of Christ, a ciborium, the utensils for making hosts, a set of clarions and bassoons, a set of trumpets, and three books of chants.

Fray Alonso de Benavides' 1634 *Memorial*

Returning to Franciscan narratives of conversion, perhaps one of the best known is the *memorial* written by Alonso de Benavides, director of the Franciscan missions in New Mexico. The *memorial* has enjoyed a recent resurgence in fame, largely due to the story of the Spanish nun María de Agreda, whose remarkable manipulation of time and space enabled her to preach to the Jumano Indians of New Mexico while never actually leaving the comfort of her native Soria.

Whatever one is to make of the legend of the Lady in Blue, Fray Alonso's *memorial* yields further testimony of conversion practices in New Mexico:

> We soon noticed that the great care and solicitude with which the Xumana Indians came to us every summer to plead for friars to go and baptize them must have been through inspiration from heaven. . . . We called them to the convent and asked them their motive in coming every year to ask for baptism with such insistency. Gazing at a portrait of Mother Luisa in the convent, they said: "A woman in similar garb wanders among us over there, always preaching". . . . Immediately we decided to send [Fathers Juan de Salas and Diego López]. . . . After traveling more than one hundred leagues, crossing the country of the Apache Vaqueros toward the east, they reached the Xumana nation, who came out to receive them in procession, carrying a large cross and garlands of flowers. They learned from the Indians that the same nun had instructed them as to how they should come out in procession to receive them, and she had helped them to decorate the cross. A very large number of people stopped in that place and asked for baptism with loud cries. The Indian women with suckling babes seized their little arms and lifted them on high, shouting also for baptism for them since they were incapable of asking for it themselves. . . . The chief captain said: "Father, we are as yet of no value before God, because we are not baptized; we are like the beasts in the fields. You are a priest of God and can do much with that holy

cross; heal our many sick before you depart." They brought people with all kinds of infirmities, and when these two friars made the sign of the cross over them and recited the gospel of Saint Luke, *Loquente Jesu,* and the prayer of our Lady, *Concédenos,* and the one of our father, Saint Francis, they immediately arose, well and healed. More than two hundred of the latter were counted. In this manner the Indians were strongly confirmed in our holy Catholic faith.[17]

Fray Francisco de Ayeta and the 1680 Pueblo Revolt

After several unsuccessful attempts at armed rebellion, a general insurrection of pueblos in northern New Mexico was staged on 10 August 1680, under the direction of leaders from Taos Pueblo. The Spanish soldiers and settlers from the Taos–Santa Fe region were driven as far south as present-day El Paso, Texas. Meanwhile, the Franciscan *procurador general* Francisco de Ayeta was heading northward from Mexico City with the regular supply wagons. Pausing at El Paso, on 25 August 1680, he received news that the governor of New Mexico, Antonio de Otermín, was in retreat from Santa Fe in the company of those who had managed to survive the revolt. Ayeta thus became a central figure in the subsequent efforts to maintain a Spanish presence in New Mexico. His name figures prominently in the several hundred folios' worth of official documentation that records the details of the revolt and its aftermath, including the martyrdom of twenty-one Franciscans.[18]

Drawing on this copious documentation, in 1693 Fray Ayeta wrote a *memorial* to the viceroy, offering a retrospective on the events of the revolt and its aftermath. The immediate cause for his writing was news of don Diego de Vargas' reconquest of the province of New Mexico in 1692.[19] Among the information included in the *memorial* are specific details of conversion practices. Ayeta describes several public ceremonies designed to reclaim the apostate souls. He also gives full weight to the evidence of Indian resistance (as expressed, for example, in the desecration of the missions) and in particular to the testimony of an Indian captive whose testimony on the causes of the 1680 Pueblo Revolt offers the counterpoint to the Franciscans' attempts at conversion.

One of the most striking and elaborate of staged rituals is played out in the course of Governor Otermín's attempt to regain the lost Spanish territory in New Mexico. He began the *entrada* in November 1681, some fifteen months after the 1680 Pueblo Revolt. Moving slowly northward from

El Paso, by 6 December 1681 he arrived at the Pueblo de Isleta. After a dawn raid in which Otermín and seventy of his men encircled the pueblo, quickly overpowering the surprised inhabitants, Governor Otermín summoned Fray Francisco de Ayeta to Isleta.

Arriving in Isleta, Ayeta was met by the governor, his escort, and all the Indians. Dismounting, he was embraced by all. The *Ave Maria* was played on the bugle, and the Indians recited the Angelic salutation out loud three times.[20]

The next day, the governor ordered everyone in Isleta and in the nearby pueblos to gather in the plaza. Fray Ayeta set up a portable altar in the middle of the plaza, where he dressed in his alb and stole. He then preached a sermon to the apostates (by means of an interpreter, because the Indians present spoke many different languages), giving them to understand the serious faults they had committed, admonishing them to return to the holy faith, making clear to them what was pleasing to God and what was offensive to Him, and explaining the holy commandments. He absolved all the apostates and baptized many children, giving to the first child the name of Carlos, in honor of His Majesty, with the governor standing as godfather to the child. He then ordered all the married Indian males to come forth with their "legitimate" wives and united them with their children.

The governor, for his part, ordered them to take from their houses the idols, feathers, herbs, powders, masks, and everything that had to do with superstition and idolatry. They did so, and they gathered together everything else in the pueblo that was to be burned. These and other scenes of purification and reconsecration were performed, Ayeta writes, on the eve of the feast of the Immaculate Conception of Our Lady, the most Holy Virgin Mary Mother of God.

On the actual feast day, 8 December, the Indians of the pueblo were again gathered together in the plaza, and in another carefully staged ritual, Fray Ayeta blessed a huge cross made of pine wood. He and the governor then placed the cross on their shoulders and carried it to exactly the place where previously a cross had stood, a cross that had been desecrated and destroyed in the Pueblo Revolt. He then celebrated Mass in the plaza and again preached to the Indians, reiterating the substance of the previous day's sermon.

The backdrop to this elaborate and public ritual of reconsecration is to be found in Governor Otermín's report of his attempted *entrada*. On 17

December 1681, Otermín, with twenty soldiers and a squadron of Indian allies (*yndios amigos*), arrived at the pueblo of Sandia. The report of what they found there is repeated numerous times in the course of the *entrada*. The scouting party detailed the extent of the havoc wreaked in the revolt: the church and convent had been burned and demolished, bells had been broken into pieces, items used in the service of the Mass or to decorate the churches had been destroyed or desecrated. A particular outrage was recorded at Sandia: a *retablo* image of the Immaculate Conception of the Virgin was found in one of the houses: her eyes and mouth showed signs of disfigurement, and the rest of her body had been stoned, whereas the figure at her feet—the depiction of the Devil as a dragon—was left whole.[21]

Following this discovery at Sandia, the governor took down the testimony of Pedro Naranjo, a known *hechicero*—that is, from the Spanish point of view, a practitioner of witchcraft. Naranjo, along with three or four other Indians, had been captured at Sandia. Asked to give testimony regarding the revolt, Naranjo described the long-standing resentment against the Spanish presence and traced the 1680 rebellion to the direction of an Indian named Popé from Taos Pueblo. Naranjo reported that Popé had ordered everyone in all the pueblos to burn and destroy the images of Christ, the Virgin, and the other saints, as well as the crosses and anything having to do with Christianity. They were to burn down the churches and destroy the bells. They were also instructed to leave their wives (that is, those given in the sacrament of matrimony) and to take whomever they pleased. Furthermore, they were never and nowhere to pronounce the name of Jesus or Mary, nor were they any longer to use the Christian names given them at baptism. They were to remove the traces of baptism by immersing themselves in the river, washing themselves and even their clothes with yucca root. All this was done so that they might return to their former way of life. Popé told them that the Spanish God was worthless, whereas their own was very strong; the Christian God was only made of wood, and even though they had obeyed his commandments, all his promises had proven false. Popé's orders were obeyed by all the Indians except a few who, moved by Catholic zeal, refused, and these Popé immediately had put to death.

Thereupon, Ayeta continues, they rebuilt their houses of idolatry, making masks in honor of the Devil, so as to dance the *kachina* dance (Naranjo stated that it was for this purpose that he had gone to the pueblo of

Sandia). Naranjo added that Popé had ordered that no one should feel in his heart any affection for the priests, the governor, or the Spanish, at the risk of cruel punishment.

Details from Naranjo's lengthy testimony are echoed in declarations of other Indians taken into custody during Otermín's attempted *entrada* in 1681. As regards the manipulation of ritual, however, Naranjo's testimony is by far the most detailed. It is also the most telling: What could be clearer proof of the acknowledged efficacy of the ritual of baptism than Popé's command to engage in a ritual of unbaptism? The Christian rites were turned upside down, as with the desecration of the image of the Virgin, which simultaneously exalted the image of the Devil. Matrimony was repudiated, and the sanctity of holy images and sacred objects violated.

Similar evidence is brought forth by Ricard, writing of the Mixton War, the 1541 rebellion of the Indians of Nueva Galicia:

> When the insurgents entered the village of Tlaltenango (Zacatecas), they burned the church and the cross. In Tepechitlán (Zacatecas), they gave themselves up to sacrilegious ceremonies and parodied the Mass by pretending to worship a *tortilla*. In Juchipila (Zacatecas) . . . they burned the monastery, defiled the cross, celebrated their sacrifices, and performed pagan dances. . . . When the Christian Indians abjured their faith, [the rebels] washed their heads to remove the mark of baptism and made them to penance for the time they had been Christians.[22]

The mirror image of these desecrations is to be found in the actions of the Spaniards, of course. During the *entrada*, Governor Otermín regularly gave the order to burn down the *kivas* and to gather up and destroy the ritual objects. Nonetheless, that Popé must command the people to drive the Spanish not just out of the land but out of their hearts also suggests how complex were the relations between the two peoples. Indeed, other Indian testimony taken down at the same time as that of Pedro Naranjo makes clear that there often was dissension in the assembly, some Indians going so far as to suggest that, nearly a century after their first settlements in New Mexico, the Spanish were also "children of the land who had grown up with the natives."[23]

The Program of Conversion

In the preface to his edition of Sahagún's *Psalmodia Christiana,* Arthur Anderson writes that "religious transformation [of Mexico] was a part of a whole social program of conversion and replacement." He recommends further study of "such literary means of acculturation as sermons and devotional works" that might yield valuable evidence of that transformation (xii).

The Franciscan letters and chronicles excerpted here surely belong within that program of study. Though written for different purposes and different audiences, they are all, in some fashion, narratives of conversion. They also provide evidence of the creation of a Franciscan architecture and the proliferation of religious artifacts, material items that weighed heavily in the transformation of the physical and spiritual focus of the New Mexican frontier. At different times in the history of the Franciscan theater of conversion, the most eloquent testimony to the perceived effectiveness of these transforming symbols may be found, paradoxically, in the litanies of repudiation, that is, in the reports of the desecration of the missions and in testimonies of the Indians' purposeful attempts to exterminate Christian devotional practices.

Notes

1. Unless otherwise noted, the English translations in this article are my own. The letter from Pedro de Gante to King Philip II, dated 23 June 1558, is quoted by Othón Arróniz, *Teatro de evangelización en Nueva España* (México: UNAM, 1979), 31–32, who reproduces it from Joaquín García Icazbalceta's *Nueva colección de documentos para la historia de México* (1886). Fernando Horcasitas, "Experiencia educativa de los Franciscanos en México," in *Ocho escritores mexicanos hablan de 750 años de presencia franciscana* (México: Centro de Estudios Bernardino de Sahagún, 1977), 45–56, focuses on the person of Pedro de Gante as both an innovator in methods of education and a creator of popular theater. Horcasitas, referring to the Christmas performance in 1526, calls it "without a doubt the first and most spectacular psychological stroke of genius (*golpe*) on the part of the missionaries; Gante himself seems to have been surprised at the results, since he attributes a mass conversion to the performance" (50).

Of Miguel León-Portilla's extensive publications on precolonial customs and rituals in Mexico, see *Los antiguos mexicanos a través de sus crónicas y cantares,* 3d ed. (México: Fondo de Cultura Económica, 1983); and *Aztec Thought and Culture,* trans. Jack Emory Davis (Norman: University of Oklahoma Press, 1963).

2. Cited in Arthur J. O. Anderson's edition and translation of Bernardino de Sahagún's *Psalmodia Christiana* (Salt Lake City: University of Utah Press, 1993), xxxii. Christian Duverger, in *La Conversión de los indios de la Nueva España con el texto de "los Coloquios de los Doce" de Bernardino de Sahagún (1564)* (Quito, Ecuador: Ediciones ABYA-YALA, 1990), discusses the Franciscans' desire to understand in detail the native psychology, so as to better serve the purposes of their conversion. As to "the demons and devils who until lately had been masters of New Spain," that this was a real belief can be seen from Fray Antonio Tello's lengthy description of the Devil's assumption of power of the peoples of Mexico in the *Crónica miscelánea y conquista espiritual y temporal de la Santa Provincia de Xalisco en el Nuevo Reino de la Galicia y Nueva Vizcaya y descubrimiento del Nuevo Mexico,* chap. 2, pp. 13–23 (Guadalajara: Tip. de La República Literaria, 1890), written in 1653: "No one knows who were the first people after the flood to inhabit the provinces of Aztatlán, but they are presumed to belong to the families of the ten tribes [referring to the lost tribes of Israel].... There appeared to them a demon, the first time to two Indian chiefs, one named Tecpatzin and the other Huitziton, and he ordered them to leave that sterile land ... and they obeyed, going in search of new lands in the year 1113 ... and in their travels he made them adore him, they having adored previous to this only the sun and the moon ... and everything that Holy Scripture teaches of God he abrogated to himself ... and he persuaded them that he was a god" (14–16).

3. On the question of cultural fusion, see Arróniz, *Teatro de evangelización:* "As specimens of cultural history, the works of the theater of evangelization in America are full of unsettling questions: Are they survivals of medieval Spanish theater ... or are they the product of the religious syncretism of those first years [of Franciscan evangelization], or are they, finally, the original creation of the Franciscans, a weapon of battle in the spiritual conquest of New Spain?" (15). The discussion is taken up by Armando Partida (*Teatro Mexicano, historia y dramaturgia,* vol. 2, *Teatro de evangelización en náhuatl* [México: Consejo Nacional para la Cultura y las Artes, 1992], 40–46), who is clearly a partisan of Arróniz's claim for the originality of the theater.

On the *auto sacramental,* see Luis Weckmann, *La herencia medieval de México,* 2d rev. ed. (México: Colegio de México and Fondo de Cultura Económica, 1994), 510–23, esp. 510–15. An English translation of Weckmann, *The Medieval Heritage of Mexico,* trans. Frances M. López Morillas (New York: Fordham University Press, 1992) is based on the first edition, which appeared in 1984. See also Robert Ricard, *Conquête spirituelle du Mexique* (Paris: University of Paris, 1933), 194–206 (chap. 12, "The Edifying Play"). All citations of Ricard are from the English translation by Lesley Bird Simpson, *The Spiritual Conquest of Mexico: An Essay on the Apostolate and the Evangelizing Methods of the Mendicant Orders in New Spain, 1523–1572* (Berkeley: University of California, 1966), which contains, as Appendix I, Ricard's preface to the 1947 Spanish edition by Angel María Garibay K.

The idea that Nahuatl theater was a continuation of European *autos sacra-*

mentales has been explored by several scholars of Spanish theater, among them Alfonso Reyes, "Los Autos Sacramentales en España e América," in *Capítulos de literatura española* (México: Colegio de México, 1945), 115–28; Hermenegildo Corbató, "Misterios y Autos del teatro misionero en Méjico durante el siglo xvi y sus relaciones con los de Valencia," in *Anales del Centro de cultura Valenciana*, anejo 1 (Valencia: CSIC, 1949); and Joseph E. Gillet, "Valencian 'misterios' and Mexican Missionary Plays in the Early Sixteenth Century," *Hispanic Review* 19 (1951): 59–61. The most recent discussion of the question is to be found in Charlotte Stern's detailed review of Louise Burkhart's *Holy Wednesday: A Nahua Drama from Early Colonial Mexico* (Philadelphia: University of Pennsylvania Press, 1996), in *Romance Philology* 55 (fall 2001): 173–81.

4. David J. Weber, *The Spanish Frontier in North America* (New Haven: Yale University Press, 1992), 97.

5. Ricard, *The Spiritual Conquest*, 179–81. The connection between theater and religious ceremonies is reiterated by Lino Gómez Canedo, "Aspectos característicos de la acción franciscana en América," in *Franciscanos en América*, ed. Francisco Morales, 103–17: "We know that the Mexicans loved [the theatrical], for their religious ceremonies abounded in song and dance. The missionaries, who also brought their own tradition in this respect . . . made abundant use of song and processions. . . . For the Franciscans, these were the two pillars of their evangelization" (116–17).

6. A listing of Franciscan works written between 1524 and 1572 is given in Ricard, *The Spiritual Conquest*, 407–12. See also the exhaustive bibliography in Weckmann, *La herencia medieval de México*, 587–658. Compilations of early documents were undertaken by Joaquín García Icazbalceta in *Colección de documentos para la historia de México*, 2 vols. (1858) and *Nueva Colección de documentos para la historia de México*, 5 vols. (1886–92); and by Mariano Cuevas, *Documentos inéditos del siglo XVI para la historia de México* (México: Museo Nacional de Arqueología, Historia y Etnología, 1914). On these and other sources, see Ricard's essay, Appendix II in *The Spiritual Conquest*, 310–22.

As to modern editions of specific authors, Pedro de Gante's correspondence is included in Fray Fidel Chauvet's *Cartas de Fray Pedro de Gante, primer educador de América* (México: Talleres Junípero Serra, n.d.). Christian Duverger, ranking Andrés de Olmos with Motolinía and Sahagún as the three "pioneros de la aventura mexicana" (*La Conversión de los indios*, 188–90), refers to Georges Baudot's attempt to reconstruct Olmos' work (189n.6). A text entitled *Historia de los mexicanos por sus pinturas*, attributed to Fray Andrés de Olmos, is included in Angel María Garibay K.'s *Teogonía e historia de los mexicanos—Tres opúsculos del siglo XVI* (México: Porrúa, 1973). Mendieta's *Historia* was also lost until Icazbalceta's publication, in 1870, of a copy of the work that came into his hands in 1860; this is recounted in Fray Angélico Chávez, *Coronado's Friars* (Washington, D.C.: Academy of American Franciscan History, 1968), viiin.2.

For Motolinía, we are fortunate to have several editions, among them: a recent edition of the *Memoriales* by Nancy Joe Dyer (México: Colegio de México, 1996), with a complete bibliography of manuscripts and editions on pp. 563–66; the facsimile edition of the *Códice Fiorentino* containing Sahagún's *Historia general de las cosas de Nueva España* (México: Secretario de Gobernación, 1979); Georges Baudot's 1985 edition of the *Historia de los indios de la Nueva España* (Madrid: Clásicos Castalia); and the four-volume edition by Angel María Garibay K. (México: Porrúa, 1977).

7. A quick outline of the Franciscan presence in New Mexico may be found in Kieran McCarty, "Franciscanos en Nuevo México y California," in *Franciscanos en America: Quinientos años de presencia evangelizadora,* ed. Francisco Morales (México: Conferencia Franciscana de Santa María de Guadalupe, 1993), 273–75. Also useful as an overview and guide to primary documentation is the "Historical Introduction" to J. Manuel Espinosa, *The Pueblo Indian Revolt of 1696 and the Franciscan Missions in New Mexico: Letters of the Missionaries and Related Documents* (Norman: University of Oklahoma Press, 1988), 3–58.

8. An interesting and intelligent portrait of Fray Marcos is given by Fray Angélico Chávez in *Coronado's Friars,* esp. 1–8, 10–13, and 40–49. The English citations of the *Relación* given here are based on the 1999 edition published by Jerry R. Craddock in *Romance Philology* 53 (fall 1999): 69–118.

9. On Cíbola, Quivira, and the search for other marvelous sites and kingdoms in the New World, see Weckmann, *La herencia medieval de México,* 48–58.

10. On the Coronado expedition, see the edition and translation by George P. Hammond and Agapito Rey, *Narratives of the Coronado Expedition, 1540–1542* (Albuquerque: University of New Mexico Press, 1940), and Herbert E. Bolton, *Coronado on the Turquoise Trail* (Albuquerque: University of New Mexico Press, 1949), "the descriptive and interpretative account of the expedition based on the foregoing critical edition" (Fray Angélico Chávez [*Coronado's Friars,* p. x] adds, "These two works are the last word on the Coronado Expedition, unless a major contemporary document . . . should turn up"). To this critical bibliography we would add Bolton's *Coronado on the Turquoise Trail: Knight of Pueblos and Plains* (1949; Albuquerque: University of New Mexico Press, 1990) and the edition and translation by George Parker Winship, *The Coronado Expedition, 1540–1542* (Washington, D.C.: Government Printing Office, 1896).

Fray Angélico Chávez describes Coronado's disappointment in Fray Marcos' account in *Coronado's Friars,* pp. 43–44. Summary accounts of the expedition are contained in John Kessell, *Kiva, Cross, and Crown: The Pecos Indians and New Mexico, 1540–1840* (1979; Albuquerque: University of New Mexico, 1987), 1–27; and Weber, *The Spanish Frontier,* 45–49.

11. The episodes reported here are taken from chapters 146–48 of Tello's *Crónica,* pp. 484–97 of the 1890 edition (my translation). On the genesis of Tello's *Crónica* and the sources upon whom Tello relied, see Chávez, *Coronado's Friars,* p. ix and n. 4; on Tello's confusion of certain details, see pp. 6–7, 58–63, 84. Fray Juan de Padilla is the subject of chaps. 3, 10, and 11, and pp. 44–47, 50–57, 85–86; Fray Luis de Ubeda, of chap. 4 and pp. 28–29, 62–63, 73–74; Fray Juan de la Cruz, of chap. 6, pp. 32–36.

12. On the deliberate construction of narratives of martyrdom as both a justification of the New World enterprise and a hagiographic gloss on the first religious to lose their lives in that enterprise, see Maureen Ahern's article on the Jesuit Andrés Pérez de Ribas' *Historia de los Triumphos de Nuestra Santa Fee* (1645), "*Dichosas muertes:* Jesuit Martyrdom on the Northern Frontier of La Florida," in *Romance Philology* 53 (fall 1999): 1–21. See also Weckmann, *La herencia medieval de México,* chap. 33, "La historiografía, la cronología y la imprenta...," esp. 485–87.

Kessell (*Kiva, Cross, and Crown,* 5n.5) refers to Fray Angélico Chávez' "lively characterization" of Fray Juan de Padilla in *Coronado's Friars,* a study, Kessell says, that "cuts through 'the pious imaginings' of the later chroniclers to get at what can be known of the sixteenth-century Franciscans brought together by the Coronado expedition." This remark is somewhat misleading. Fray Angélico's purpose was to determine the number and identity of the friars who accompanied Coronado (see his introduction, esp. p. viii), and to do so, he examined in great detail the testimony in the "later chroniclers." His characterization of Fray Juan de Padilla as short-tempered and stubborn, for example, begins, "The chroniclers and others relate" (21), a phrasing later reiterated: "As all our chroniclers relate" (27). In regard to specific episodes, he does distinguish between what was likely to have happened and how the chroniclers chose to present the episode: "Later Franciscan writers made much of this cross in their pious imaginings" (57); "The Franciscan chroniclers have their own simple pious versions" (60). He also refers to "pious chroniclers" (73), though never with the disdain suggested in the note by Kessell. The chroniclers had their own purposes in constructing their narratives, as I have no doubt Fray Angélico well understood, for he himself occasionally indulged in "pious imaginings" for the sake of constructing a narrative; see Barbara De Marco, "*Cantaron la victoria:* Spanish Literary Tradition and the 1680 Pueblo Revolt," in *Recovering the U.S. Hispanic Literary Heritage,* vol. 3, ed. María Herrera-Sobek and Virginia Sánchez Korrol (Houston: Arte Público Press, 1999), 163–72.

13. Chávez, *Coronado's Friars,* 51–52; on p. 50, n. 2, Chávez elaborates on why Padilla is believed to be the author of this account.

14. These ceremonies are reported by Felix D. Almaráz, Jr., "Transplanting 'Deep, Living Roots': Franciscan Missionaries and the Colonization of New Mexico—the Fledgling Years, 1598–1616," in *Seeds of Struggle, Harvest of Faith: The Papers of the Archdiocese of Santa Fe,* ed. Thomas J. Steele, S.J., et al. (Albuquerque: LPD, 1998), 9–11. Almaráz's sources are Gaspar Pérez de Villagrà's epic poem of the period, *Historia de la nueva México,* ed. Miguel Encinias et al. (Albuquerque: University of New Mexico Press, 1992), and George Hammond and Agapito Rey's edition and translation of *Don Juan de Oñate: Colonizer of New Mexico, 1595–1628,* 2 vols. (Albuquerque: University of New Mexico Press, 1953). Almaráz describes a succession of rituals performed in the course of Oñate's expedition, including the Act of Obedience and Vassalage required from the Pueblo Indians.

15. The source for the background information and inventory of supplies presented in this section is France V. Scholes, "The Supply Service of the New Mexican

Missions in the Seventeenth Century," *New Mexico Historical Review* 5 (1930): 93–115. See also his "Documents for the History of the New Mexican Missions in the Seventeenth Century," *New Mexico Historical Review* 4 (1929): 45–58, 195–201, as well as his series, coauthored with Lansing B. Bloom, "Friar Personnel and Mission Chronology, 1598–1629," *New Mexico Historical Review* 19 (1944): 319–36, and 20 (1945): 58–82.

16. Ricard, *The Spiritual Conquest,* 176. On Franciscan architecture in Mexico, see Ernest de la Torre Villar, "Florecillas de San Francisco en Nueva España" and Justino Fernández, "Las construcciones franciscanas del siglo xvi en la Nueva España," both published in *Ocho escritores mexicanos,* pp. 57–74 and 121–33 respectively; see also Raffaele Davanzo, "Il territorio sacro. Gli insediamenti dei Francescani nel Nuovo Mondo: spazi e tipologie," in *Diffusione del Francescanesimo nelle Americhe, Atti del X Convegno Internazionale, Assisi, 14–16 ottobre 1982* (Assisi: Università di Perugia, Centro di Studi Francescani, 1984), 197–215, and Jesús Palomera Páramo, "Franciscanos, arte sacro y evangelización," in *Franciscanos en America,* ed. Morales, 177–86.

On the use and decoration of space both inside and outside the church structure, see the discussion in Partida, *Teatro Mexicano,* pp. 30–33, based largely on Ricard, *The Spiritual Conquest,* and Fernando Horcasitas, *El Teatro náhuatl: épocas novohispana y moderna* (México: UNAM, Instituto de Investigaciones Históricas, 1974).

17. Quoted in Clark Colahan, *The Visions of Sor María de Agreda: Writing, Knowledge, and Power* (Tucson: University of Arizona Press, 1994), 103. On the controversy surrounding María de Agreda, see his introduction, pp. 1–15. On her story as reported by Benavides, see Colahan, *Visions,* 93–127, as well as Kessell, *Kiva, Cross, and Crown,* 140–42, and Weckmann, *La herencia medieval de México,* 244–45. A facsimile edition of Benavides' *Memorial of 1630* (Madrid) was privately printed and translated by Mrs. Edward E. Ayer (1916), with notes by Frederick Webb Hodge and Charles Fletcher Lummis. A translation of Fray Alonso de Benavides' *Revised Memorial of 1634* was published by Frederick Webb Hodge, George P. Hammond, and Agapito Rey (Albuquerque: University of New Mexico Press, 1945).

Benavides' *memorial* also contains, according to J. Manuel Espinosa, "the best description of the daily life led by the friars and their Pueblo Indian converts at the missions in New Mexico," including details of the manner of church decoration and inventories of religious articles; see Espinosa, *The Pueblo Indian Revolt of 1696,* pp. 20–24 and the notes therein.

18. English translations of a selection of these documents are to be found in the two-volume collection, *Revolt of the Pueblo Indians of New Mexico and Otermín's Attempted Reconquest, 1680–1682,* ed. Charles Wilson Hackett and trans. Charmion C. Shelby (Albuquerque: University of New Mexico Press, 1942). Most of the subsequent literature on the revolt is based on these two volumes. Volume 3 of the Bandelier papers, *Historical Documents Relating to New Mexico, Nueva Vizcaya and Approaches thereto, to 1773,* collected by Adolph F.A. Bandelier and Fanny R. Bandelier, ed. Charles Wilson Hackett (Washington: The Carnegie Institution of

Washington, 1923–37), also contains English translations of "Miscellaneous general documents relating to Indian uprisings in New Mexico, 1680–1698," pp. 327–48. Spanish editions of these documents are being prepared as part of a comprehensive project to make available reliable Spanish editions of original documents relating to the early exploration and settlement of New Mexico. The project is described in the introduction to Barbara De Marco, "Voices from the Archives, I: Testimony of the Pueblo Indians in the 1680 Pueblo Revolt," *Romance Philology* 53 (spring 2000): 375–448.

19. The first edition of the full Spanish text of the *memorial* was published in Barbara De Marco, "Voices from the Archives, II: Ayeta's 1693 Letter to the Viceroy," *Romance Philology* 53 (spring 2000): 449–508.

The Vargas documents have been published in several volumes by the University of New Mexico Press; see John Kessell et al., eds., *Remote beyond Compare: Letters of don Diego de Vargas to His Family from New Spain and New Mexico, 1675–1706* (1989); *By Force of Arms: The Journals of Don Diego de Vargas, New Mexico, 1691–93* (1992); *To the Royal Crown Restored: The Journals of Don Diego de Vargas, New Mexico, 1692–94* (1995); *Blood on the Boulders: The Journals of Don Diego de Vargas, New Mexico, 1694–97* (1998).

20. The version presented here is an English paraphrase of Ayeta's report, based on my transcription of his 1693 *memorial;* English translations of documents on which Ayeta's *memorial* was based are published in Hackett and Shelby, *Revolt of the Pueblo Indians*.

21. This episode takes on particular significance in light of the widespread devotion to the Virgin Mary. On the development of cults to the Virgin in Nueva España, see Joaquín Antonio Peñalosa, *La práctica religiosa en México, siglo xvi* (México: Editorial Jus, 1969), 206–13, and the sections on Mexico in Rubén Vargas Ugarte, S.J., *Historia del culto de María en Iberoamérica y de sus imágenes y santuarios más celebrados*, 3d ed. (Madrid: Talleres Gráficos Jura, 1956). On devotional practices, specifically miraculous images of the Virgin, see Weckmann, *La herencia medieval de México*, 168–72, 274–83.

In addition to the episode at Sandia, the *cabildo* of the Villa of Santa Fe described other outrages, in more graphic terms, in a report to Governor Otermín dated 16 October 1680. An edition of the report, based on the original (Archivo General de la Nación, Provincias Internas, vol. 37, fols. 377r–379v), was published by Jerry R. Craddock and Barbara De Marco in "La profanación de lo sagrado: modalidades medieval y novomexicana" *Anuario de Letras* 35 (1997): 193–213.

22. Ricard, *The Spiritual Conquest*, 264–66. Fray Silvestre Vélez de Escalante, in his 1778 report on the revolt, adds another telling episode (reported in Espinosa, *The Pueblo Indian Revolt of 1696*, 36–37): "At Santa Ana a large feast was prepared with food from the kitchens of the missionaries and the Spanish governor and served on a long table in the manner of the Spaniards. Popé sat at the head, and Catiti at the other end, and the other leaders were seated around. Popé and Catiti were brought holy chalices, and they both used them to toast curses to the Spaniards and to the

Christian religion. Popé, raising his chalice, and as though addressing the father custodian, addressed Catiti, saying, 'To your health, reverend father.' Catiti replied, 'The same to you, your excellency, the Governor.'"

23. This testimony is given on 18 December 1681 by Juan, a Tewa from Tesuque. The Spanish text of Juan's testimony appears on pp. 389–402 of De Marco, "Voices from the Archives, I."

3

Two Kinds of Conversion ("Medieval" and "Modern") among the Hurons of New France

Peter Goddard

Introduction

In his important study of missionaries, J. Leddy Phelan observed the effect of medieval millenarianism on the Franciscan outlook in sixteenth-century New Spain. Gerónimo de Mendieta, a "missionary visionary," asserted that the conversion of the Mexicans would herald the renewal of Christianity and inexorable progress to the Last Days. In contrast, the Jesuits who arrived in New Spain in 1579 were "missionary realists": their conversion strategy embraced the modern colonial project and dispensed with thoughts of a chiliast utopia. Franciscans, this interpretation suggested, were committed to an idealistic concept of conversion, in which poverty and simplicity within intact traditional communities would signify purity of belief—a state of grace inaccessible to most Spanish themselves. Further, conversion of the Indians was a project dependent on the millennial framework, as Franciscan pastoralism would shepherd this flock through time toward a better end.[1] Phelan's argument suggests two points of division: "medieval" and "modern," corresponding to his "visionary" and "realist."

This chapter tests this assertion of difference through comparison of Jesuit and Franciscan ideas of conversion in missions to the Hurons of New France in the first half of the seventeenth century and finds that Phelan's distinction can be further sharpened and even taken in new directions.

Although both missionary orders necessarily upheld Saint Jerome's dictum that "Christians are made, not born," early modern French Jesuits, deeply invested in the formation of self through education, leaned toward what Karl F. Morrison describes (for an earlier period) as the "peripety paradigm" of rapid transformation, creating a new person, atomized and autonomous in the faith.[2] Conversion was dependent on effective pedagogy and discipline but produced a total break with past culture and a "new" person. Conversion could be verified through quantifiable means, and recidivism warranted strong censure.

In contrast, French Franciscans, belonging to the Capuchin and Recollect branches of the order, were typically less optimistic: they viewed conversion as a gradual and even indeterminate process, as true religion was adopted and the individual transformed, constantly subject to backsliding. They also identified worldly interests as barriers to conversions. Reflecting the institutional bias of the itinerant friars, this approach was more admitting of "natural" behaviors and of the vulnerability that persisted even after conversion; indeed, "nature" could be a force working both for and against conversion. Recollects did not speak of converts as "supermen" and "superwomen" in the way Jesuit accounts sometimes do; instead, their accounts stress the vulnerability and the somewhat infantile nature of the new Christians. Franciscan preaching emphasized the constant need for vigilance as well as the theme of forgiveness and drew attention to the shortcomings of European Christians.

These differences emerge through comparison of Franciscan and Jesuit approaches—particularly their preaching to converted and unconverted alike—to the Hurons, an Iroquoian people whose agriculture, social organization, and spiritual inclinations appeared to make them good candidates for relatively rapid Christianization. Recollects and Jesuits campaigned to convert the Hurons from their first contact with the French in 1615 to their destruction by Iroquois in 1649. Such competing visions produced a large corpus of writings that aimed to edify Christians by illuminating the progress of different kinds of conversion in the New World.

Recollects were first to enter this mission field: Father Joseph le Caron traveled to the Huron country in 1615, and lay brother Gabriel Sagard-Théodat overwintered in 1624–25. Sagard wrote two accounts of his travels—one, his *Histoire du Canada* (*History of Canada*, 1636), the first of its kind. Le Caron strategized the mission in an important memorandum of 1626.

Jesuits followed in the Franciscans' footsteps, taking up residence in (and then taking over) the Recollect house at Québec in 1632. The Jesuits subsequently developed their most important mission in New France, the mission of Saint Joseph to the Hurons, whose promise was eclipsed by famine, disease, and war; it was finally destroyed in 1649. Their monopoly on missions continued to 1670, when the Recollects were reestablished in New France.

Relations between the two groups were not warm: for Recollects, the Jesuits were as usual the cats who got the cream, while for the Jesuits, conscious of their growing difficulties with Gallicans and Jansenists in France, the Recollects were amateurs whose interference in the Canadian mission program could have dire pastoral but also political effects.[3] A prime example of the sharp confessional conflict that marked these relations in the later period is the Recollect Chrestien le Clercq's *First Establishment of the Faith in New France* (1691), which conveys a bleak assessment of mission (especially Jesuit) progress and emphasizes the intractability of native superstition and resistance to Christianity.[4]

Only recently has the question of religious conversion been problematized in the history of missions in the early modern world. The field has oscillated between "confessional" history, in which the missionaries are portrayed as "spiritual conquerors" (or, failing that, as holy martyrs), and a stridently secular historiography that sees missionaries as front-men for the fur trade or other forms of colonialism and as indiscriminate wielders of the *pastorale de la peur* (or "pastoral of fear"), a brutal regime of instruction and extirpation.[5] But recent research inquires into the mental equipment of the missionaries themselves: What were their systems of reference; How did they understand their project? Theological, social, and political contexts mattered: missionaries to the New World were generally mature products of Jesuit or Franciscan systems of education and training, deeply embedded in their original social and institutional culture.[6] Long before reaching the mission field, their values were formed and their loyalties solidified, their *modo de procedar* (way of proceeding) clear. Understanding the dynamic of mission and the concept of conversion that lies at the heart of it involves understanding missionary mentalities and the institutional experience that shaped them.

From the founding of the *fratres minorum* in 1209, Franciscan culture, while antimonastic in that it sought engagement in the world, was explicitly antiworldly as well. "Pilgrims and strangers in this world," Franciscans followed the dictates of apostolic poverty, going barefoot and begging for sustenance. "Declared enemies of the world," asserted seventeenth-century Capuchin Yves de Paris, Franciscans denounced the powerful and the complacent, and idealized the poor as the favored receptacles of God's grace.[7] The Recollects, a reformed branch of the order founded in 1592, embodied a return to the primitive ideal and a heightened spirituality, with a commitment to missionary activism. They claimed to recruit from the better social elements; the order was not the "sweeper-upper of the world."[8] In turn they formed a new spiritual elite, "citizens of a new world," brimming with the certainty that Saint Francis's arduous path was the right one.[9]

In New France, these brown-robed friars wore wooden clogs, spurned property, and praised the apparent antimaterialism and the charity of Amerindian peoples. The Franciscan vocation was to preach. In an urban space, this took on the form of the chastisement of a sinful population and urgings to repentance. In the Canadian wilderness, their preaching tended to emphasize on one hand the vast gulf that separated the Indians from grace, but on the other the instrumentality and effectiveness of a long-term preaching commitment.

Here is a perhaps typical Franciscan view, in which Indian depravity calls forth the enlightened reign of the friars:

> These poor savages who maintain no other order except that which a corrupt nature has taught them, who have no other observance but that which the Devil has taught them, and who with the ferocity of beasts kill and eat one another, have however immortal souls purchased by the blood of Christ. They have angels as their guardians and sufficient grace to conduct them to their proper ends. Nevertheless, their ignorance and their lack of faith have made these universal aids useless. It is necessary, then, to go and pull these souls from the captivity of demons: to make actual Christians of those who were such only in potential, in order to conduct them to their proper ends.[10]

Such preaching emphasized the perdurable nature of sin and the necessity of a long-term pastoral guidance: conversion for Christian old and new alike was a life's work, and even the saintly were beset by temptations that might derail them. Conversion was in fact a retrospective boon: one was sure of it only at the point of meeting one's maker. The repetitive quality of Franciscan preaching resulted from the certainty that humanity sinned again and again and that there were only variations on the themes of sin and penance, whether among the burghers of the late medieval town or the rustic-looking *sauvages* of the early modern New World.

Franciscans also operated within the framework of an institutional history that included the key stages of the Spanish *conquista*. Franciscans had implemented a regime of punishment and repression among the Maya of the Yucatán, and the Franciscan bishop Diego de Landa was the leading exemplar of "spiritual conquest" in the Americas. The triumphal elements of the Franciscans' experience in New Spain conflicted with the contrary drive to establish a pure and simple Christianity of the Indians, buffered from the colonial power, as promoted by Mendieta and others. While Recollects in France announced their allegiance to the Crown and to a "civilizing mission," they too eschewed such triumphalism in favor of the urge to recover simplicity and humility in religious life in mission, "not to improve our minds and become wiser and better recognized among ourselves, but in helping our brothers (the Savages) of Canada to bring there the torch of the knowledge of God and to chase out the shadows of barbarism and infidelity."[11]

Early modern Jesuit mentality owed much to the example of the itinerant friars. The history of mission, most recently as part of the fabulous conquest of America, and the antimonastic stance were echoed in the formation of the new religious order in 1540. While setting aside the Franciscan stress on poverty, Jesuits added their distinctive regime of "spiritual exercise," which expedited Jesuit self-formation.

Institutionally, Jesuits went beyond Franciscans—whose pastoral mission embraced preaching, confession, and charity—in developing a specialization in formal liberal education. Jesuits in seventeenth-century France were first and foremost teachers in their order's college system: their *ratio studiorum* promised the spectacular transformation of untamed youth into Christian adulthood. From the *collège*, or seminary teaching, many Jesuits proceeded to missions either within or beyond France, or to service in various elite capacities. To a striking extent, though, French Jesuits operated within a pedagogical paradigm and proceeded in important ways as if the world were a classroom. They foregrounded rationality and emphasized the teacherly nature of their apostolic mission. This stance was of particular importance in New France, where missions operated not as an adjunct of conquest but rather as part of an evolving relationship between the tiny French settlement in the Saint Lawrence valley and the extensive Iroquoian and Algonquian alliances of the Great Lakes interior, over which neither church nor state could exercise coercive power.

Jesuits interpreted the situation as one in which enlightened rhetoric alone would win converts:

> We have not here, nor can we have, either the power of constraint or the chains of benefits, to the extent that would be necessary to render these people entirely ours. All our power lies at the end of our tongues, in the exhibition and production of our books and Writings, the effects of which they never cease to wonder at. This is the only thing that avails us with these people, in lieu of all other ground for credibility."[12]

Yet Jesuits also expressed great optimism that this reasonable project would produce a mighty boon to the missionary church. Conversion of the Amerindians was a matter of making clear Christianity's rationality and introducing the pedagogical mechanism to transform understanding and outlook.

From this basic difference in culture—the Franciscan sense of the universality and the enduring character of sin, and of the possibility of mass conversion through grace, with the attendant yearning for a Christian utopia, contrasting with the Jesuit sense of the teachability of the lay population and its capacity for transformation—flowed two modes of conversion: the "medieval" (Franciscan) and the "modern" (Jesuit). What follows is a discussion of the further characteristics of each mode and consideration of the implication of these for the study of missions and French-Indian contact in seventeenth-century New France.

"Medieval" Conversion: Conversion as Life's Work or Millennial Event

In 1626, the Recollect Joseph le Caron suggested, in dire terms, the challenge of converting the Amerindians: "Their licentious and slothful life, their crude intellect which can hardly understand, the poverty of their language when it comes to explaining divine mystery, for never have they had any true religion."[13] This was not so different from the Capuchin Charles de Genève's summation of the remote Savoyard villagers, subject to Franciscan missionizing at approximately the same time, as "this rough, rustic people of a deeply corrupt language."[14] The Hurons offered the most promise of all the *sauvage* peoples of New France, however. Sagard suggested in 1630, "These people are not so mired in primitiveness (*"la rudesse"*) and rusticity as one imagines."[15] It would take time to reform such people, in the case of the Savoyards, or to introduce Christianity among them, in the case of the Hurons.

Recollect prescriptions for the larger project of Christianization were conventional: they observed a basic difference between "ordered peoples" ("*gens policés*") and the *sauvage*. This latter, the Amerindians, would have to be civilized before they could be converted. To defeat idolatry and to "tame the barbaric customs of pagans" ("*polir les moeurs barbares des Gentils*") were the ostensible goals.[16] Conversion had a social dimension— the adoption of a new set of specifically French manners and customs—as well as a spiritual one. Recollects viewed this "civil conversion" as a daunting problem in its own right and demanded that the constituents of colonial enterprise—traders and settlers—serve as exemplars for the new Christians.[17] Colonial development was in their view central to effective Christianization: "In settling and cultivating the land, we find a means of cultivating souls."[18]

Beyond this stereotypical approach, which called for the effacement of the un-Christianized culture, an intention readily ascribable to most missionaries operating on most European colonial frontiers, lay a way of proceeding rather at odds with this goal. Specifically, the combination of castigatory preaching and implicit recognition of the human failings of a backwards people led to elevated rhetoric about their spiritual condition but at the same time equated conversion with a long-term and possibly interminable process. Such a paradox suggests that the Recollects adopted a posture toward the Hurons that posited the inextricability of conversion and a slow process of development. Conversion was a matter of history— yet the history of all humanity.

Sagard's "farewell" to the Hurons, which concludes his 1632 *Grand Voyage*, emphasizes the great regret and sadness he feels upon leaving, "since I see you still frozen in the thick shadows of infidelity, so little illuminated by heaven, so little enlightened by reason, and so deadened in the habits of your wicked customs." It is not enough to believe; baptism is required and, in turn, an ongoing rejection of "everything which is depraved in you." The fate of Hurons will be shared by "many Christians who live worse than you and yet are better instructed than you, who have not yet encountered we friars."[19]

Sagard's *Histoire du Canada* is a sweeping sermon on the frailty of human nature without God. "You will see like an in-depth picture and a rich engraving," Sagard advises the reader, "of the misery of human nature ... deprived of the knowledge of the faith, destitute of good morality, and prey to the most deplorable barbarisms which the distance from heavenly light could grotesquely conceive." He describes the processes that would free the Amerindians from diabolical slavery, "embellish their reason with salutary discourse and civilize their rough barbarism into the courtesy of good morality, so that, having learned that they are men, they can become Christians."[20] However, as Gilbert Chinard and Jacques Warwick have pointed out, Sagard convinces the reader that these "savages" possessed unquestionable humanity and abundant "natural" virtues. Such admirable traits allowed for the long-term cultivation of the faith among them.[21]

Recollects respected the Amerindians in their "natural" state but distinguished between natural virtue and *civilité*. By lauding the virtues of uncivilized pagans, they were able to criticize European excess and hypocrisy, against which the Franciscan "stranger and pilgrim in this world" stood sentry. To become Christian, though, the Hurons had to take up "a decent and civil life."[22]

The Recollects' tendency to idealize the Hurons, and indeed to locate the site of a possible Christian utopia in their midst, derived from an understanding that their agrarian way of life had already featured many favorable aspects in what the modern anthropologist might call their "culture." The Huron way of life produced not quite "polite and civil mores, as in people who are civilized by religion and piety, or by magistrates and philosophers"—but certainly a promising foundation.[23] Conventionally, Sagard and others portrayed Indian physical attractiveness, despite their climate- and custom-induced skin color, as a sign of virtue.[24] Sagard also noted the various social failings, well short of French ideas of *civilité*. Hurons, claimed Sagard, cleaned themselves with dog's hair, washed only when extremely filthy, and belched during meals.[25] Yet this lack of manners did not deter appreciation of social organization: Recollects especially approved of the charity and reciprocity present in Huron communities. This mutual support reflected liberality toward neighbors—by Sagard's account increasingly rare in France. He suggested that the Hurons were repelled by the cruel culture of poverty and begging in France: "Our savages have no need to establish hospitals for the sick, or to ban begging by vagabonds, because each one care for his sick, and no-one is so vagabond that he must live at another's expense." Nor did charity involve public righteousness: the Hurons never accumulated so much food that it had to be conspicuously redistributed to the poor, for, as they maintained no superfluous supplies, there were no really poor among them.[26] Instead, they regulated material appetites and organized work around the principle of mutual aid rather than the pursuit of individual interests.

As a consequence, Hurons enjoyed a radically different disposition of labor and also human relations than did the French. Lacking acquisitiveness, they had repose in abundance, for "they have not a single passion for wealth and the riches of the earth, which they enjoy without possessing."[27] They were mercifully free of "trials, quarrels or debates" and knew nothing of judges, taxes, or prisons.[28] Even Huron women, despite working much more than the men, had time to spare. In their case, it was spent on dancing.[29] This sense of the "naturally happy" Indian resurfaces in later Recollect writing: the Micmac peoples of the Gaspé peninsula Chrestien le Clercq estimated as "incomparably happier than us."[30]

It was indeed an idyllic picture, but the Recollects feared that such precivilized innocence would not last. In language that evokes Mendieta's condemnation in his *Historia eclesiástica* of the corrupting effects of European contact, Sagard expressed doubt for the Huron future: "[P]lease be to God that they be converted, but at the same time they become Christian, I fear that they will lose their simplicity and their repose, not that God's law demands it, but corruption creeps up on the converted Barbarians, who taste alongside the doctrine of the Saints, the bad influence of wicked Europeans who trade among them." Yet as long as it remained isolated from this commerce of the world, Huron life was especially enviable and instructive because it was not extreme but instead feasible, and in ways lost to Europeans, it was pure: "The savages are men like us, of the same nature, and I myself have lived on their diet, without salt, bread or wine, for more than a year without experiencing any incommodity," affirmed Sagard.[31] These virtues flowed from nature and reflected isolation from the currents of a sometimes corrupt civilization.

Sagard also described the failings of Huron society. If virtue flourished in the absence of European vices, sins resulted from Satanic manipulation. The Devil was responsible for deviations from the norms of natural virtue. Contrary to expectations (voiced by Cicero and others) that there were no peoples on earth who lacked an intimation of superior nature, the *sauvages* of New France had no exercise that the Recollects could equate to religion. Indeed, the Canadians lived "beast-like, without adoration, without Religion, and without vain superstitions which grow up in the shadow of Religion either." They did not recognize holy days except those ordered for purely social ceremony. The moon held greater sway over the organization of time than did divine order. Without religion, "each one forged his own observations, ceremonies, and a God or Creator of his own design, to whom nevertheless he attributes less than absolute power over life, as we do to our true God." The Hurons believed in the immortality of spirits but attached no salutary power thereto. Indeed, their greatest god, Yoscaha, was thought to live in the same infirmity as other men, although eternal. Sagard ridiculed this "earth-bound God" ("Dieu terrestre"), suggesting that if he was like men he would die like men.[32] Huron spiritual life was governed not by hopes of futurity but by concerns of the present: illnesses, dreams, curses, and the all-important relations with nature, which influenced the outcome of corn planting, fishing, hunting, and trading. Ignorance rather than superstition characterized such concerns. Their mythology reflected such ignorance: "The savages, like many simple people, had never imagined that the world was round and suspended in space."[33]

Diabolical intervention was a thornier matter. The Devil could enliven an account, but did he actually play a role in the lives of these Amerindians? The Hurons believed that *diables* and *malins esprits* abounded; "they believed in an infinite number, and feared them strongly," blaming them for sickness, injury, bad luck, and nightmares. Indeed, the Hurons produced "dins and rackets to chase them away"—as if the demons were a flock of birds. The Devil amused the Hurons and enthralled them, like children, "in strange superstitions, lending them aid and favour as to people abandoned of God."[34]

Sagard's approach to traditional Huron belief depended upon mockery and derision. Even effective curses and auguries were ridiculed. He was amused by "the ceremonies and ridiculous ways" surrounding hunting and fishing, such as the practice of guarding bones from the fire. He chuckled with his readers when the Hurons interpreted his gestures of explanation as (superstitious) signs that guaranteed good fishing and begged him to do some more.

To a certain extent, Recollects countered with belief in rational explanation and in the obvious virtue of European institutions. Their arguments often appealed to reason—apparently deeply seductive to the Hurons. "They call on us from time to time to teach them things which surpass their understanding, and they admire these teachings—not hard to imagine given their ignorance." At the same time, the Recollects maintained a view of diabolical influence as animating the wrongheadedness of the Indians. Recollect skepticism about diabolical agency was attenuated, and the circulation of diabolic influence generally credited. In any case, the situation of a devil-ridden, ignorant population called for a program of proper pastoral supervision: "One cannot hope for very much reason among people born and raised in the gross ignorance of paganism if they are not first instructed in the school of Jesus Christ, and in the knowledge which comes with this, which is why we must have compassion, and understand that if we had been born with barbarian parents, we would be the same as them, and possibly even worse."[35]

Recollect actions sometimes belied these pious sentiments. It seems clear that in addition to quite faithfully representing reformed Catholicism, these missionaries engaged in a range of "shamanistic" practices that engaged traditional Indian spirituality on its own level. They organized collective prayers to influence the weather, for example, rivaling the invocations of the "sorcerers," and much of the tone of the refutation of magical powers in traditional native practice suggests an element of credulity.[36]

While Sagard as mission pioneer produced descriptions of Huron rituals and beliefs of enormous benefit to future missionaries and ethnographers, he was more concerned with edification—not only of the Indians, but also of the French reader. Thus he presented the conversion experience as a disavowal of misguided belief and custom and commensurate adoption of Catholic practice under the tutelage of the friars.

Some Hurons besought Sagard to pray for them, "confessing ingenuously that all their ceremonies, dances, songs, feasts and other clowning about, served for absolutely nothing." The French undertook to support a newly baptized Huron in the event of his recovery from a life-threatening illness, "for fear that necessity would constrain him to return to his former station, that is his barbarian life." Conversion represented the arduous switch from a barbarian to a civilized way of life. The faith could only be lived in the context of such a life, and even there only with difficulty given the temptations of the world. Huron maxims had lasted for centuries until the arrival of Christianity and would have lasted forever, given their limited conformity to natural reason. But now "it was necessary for them to change their life, laws, and maxims, which for the most part were as much savage as brutal and impertinent."[37] Conversion was a lifelong path to a redeemed end, buttressed at every point by pastoral care and the guidance of a Christian civilization.

What did the Hurons understand of the new faith that the "gray robes" conveyed across the linguistic and the cultural gap? According to Sagard, those to whom the Recollects had preached possessed a complete understanding of at least a censorious and hectoring missionary Christianity, especially its emphasis on reward and punishment:

Among the things that the Hurons had most admired, as we instructed them, was that there was a Paradise, where were found all of the blessed dead together with God, and a subterranean Hell, where the souls of the wicked, together with the souls of their deceased parents and friends, alongside their enemies, were tormented by Devils in an abyss of fire: all for having neither known nor adored God our creator, and for having led a life so wicked and having lived with so much dissolution and vice.[38]

The disproportionate attention to Hell was typical of the seventeenth-century missionary movement; like others, the Recollects employed the *pastorale de la peur* as part of their approach to conversion. Mention that the relatives of sinners would also endure this unimaginably awful punishment is a reminder of the problem that bedeviled agents of Catholic reform in rural Europe—converting individuals within kinship networks.[39] Sagard does not say whether these tactics were counterbalanced by gentleness in confession. His writing, however, like Franciscan preaching in missions to the French countryside or to the poorer quarters of French towns (evident in the preaching of François de Toulouse, for example), suggests that the order relied more heavily on castigation than tenderness in conveying the specifics of Christianity.

Recollect writing thus emphasized the qualities of charity, simplicity, and finally childishness of the Hurons and other Indian peoples, together with a fire-and-brimstone approach to their conversion. Sagard additionally depicted an alternative world in which the reforming energies of France might be deployed. The formidable task of changing maxims and educating Indians in Christianity, creating in effect a Christian community, might reform old France, especially the clergy: "All France overflows with monks and nuns, benefice-holders, and secular priests, but few work hard for the salvation of unbelievers. There are an infinity who live lazily here [i.e., France], eating the bread of the poor and chasing after benefices. If only they were to come to the Indies, not only would these infidel countries benefit, but so would they."[40]

Recollects idealized the Amerindians yet at the same time could not help but promote their transformation and hence the likely disappearance of their traditional harmonious communities and other manifestations of natural virtue. Yet through a sympathetic account of this pagan people, the Recollects established the case for Christianizing the Indians on the basis of ideal elements of their own community. Hurons and others would overcome the liabilities of their pagan past through engagement with the preaching and teaching of the friars; they would be brought as a group into the church. Nature, in this analysis, was no more a barrier to Christianization than was childhood; but, as with immaturity, it would take time for the Hurons to grow into the faith.

"Modern" Conversion

Peripeteia is the Greek term for sudden change of fortune in a drama or in a life. For Jesuits, conversion meant a clean break with the past, the fashioning of a new self through God's grace.

A relatively new order, and facing hostility from the Gallican faction in the French church, Jesuits were under pressure to produce an impressive tally of converts and to demonstrate the efficacy of their program regardless of the challenges. Their New France mission served the important purpose of publicizing both the courageous spirit of the Society and the rigor with which they approached the work of proselytization. This latter goal gained in importance as Jansenist criticism of Jesuit "laxism" grew over the course of the century. Despite their commitment to the education of youth—a long-term investment—Jesuits wanted to demonstrate rapid progress. Moreover, they believed that they possessed the means to achieve relatively fast acting conversions: means that would allow them to move beyond the Franciscan stance of idealization and castigation.

For the Jesuits, as for the Recollects, the Hurons, *terrestre* and *barbare*,[41] were the rustics of the New World—farming folk, spiritually ill-informed and apathetic yet peaceable and docile enough for instruction. Like peasants, they had limited understanding and needed instruction. In certain respects, Hurons were advantaged, for as one author noted, "they are even more intelligent than our country folk."[42] Native wit, as it were, would provide the springboard to conversion.

Beginning in Messina in 1548, Jesuits developed a system of Christianized humanism that came to be known as the *ratio studiorum*. The *ratio* emphasized the liberal arts and the classical languages, and it encouraged civility, self-control, and rhetorical polish.[43] The program was designed to subordinate "everything to the end of forming the devout Christian soldier."[44] Rules specified that "the principal goal for being in College is to acquire piety, to study, and to learn good manners."[45] More than any other agency in the early modern West, Jesuits were aware of the capacity of rigorous education to transform the individual in matters of faith as well as power of mind and ability to progress in the world.

In setting out the essentially pedagogical direction of the mission in his first *Relation* of 1633, Paul Le Jeune optimistically suggested that conversion of the Amerindians was a matter of making clear Christianity's rationality: "[W]hen one makes them see the conformity of God's law with reason, I do not believe that we will find great resistance in their understanding."[46] Jesuit missionaries consequently taught the orthodox account of Christianity as a set of rational principles, rather than invoking miraculous intervention or performing the role of shaman in competition with the Amerindian *sagamos* (witch-doctors). In his preaching to the Hurons, for example, Jean de Brébeuf insisted that Christian doctrine reflected only that which "nature itself teaches us"; Christianity was reasonable. Jesuits occasionally resorted to "supernatural" effects, such as moving needles about with an unseen magnet, which of course were subject to rational deconstruction as part of their "school of Truth."[47] Scientific demonstration countered the prospective converts' ignorance about the world and supported the missionaries' other claims to superior truth.[48]

Jesuit missionaries attempted to bridge from Indian experience to Christian truth, responding to the Ignatian injunction to find God in all things. In the teaching of Huron children and catechumens, this could result in such innovations as Jean Pierron's board game "Point to Point," in which players who might otherwise be gambling, a wildly popular activity, were instructed "without difficulty, in what they must know in order to be saved."[49] The emphasis on correct belief never wavered, despite the reliance on cultural linkage and association. Always missionaries emphasized the alliance between Christian revelation and reasonableness: if the all-powerful nature of God was explained and the universal power of Christ spelled out as well, and even buttressed by scientific, geographical, and cultural proofs, who could refuse to consider instruction in the new faith?

Religious vocation demanded a sundering of bonds with the old (exemplified by the religious practice of assuming a new name upon joining the order, or the Jesuit case of relying on Latin and not vernacular languages for communication). Jesuits proposed a similar radical step for their prospective pupils in New France. The young Huron would first be decontextualized: removed from the home, that traditional seat of error, and placed within the quarantined space of the college, where the contagion of past practice could not penetrate and a pure new set of beliefs could be inculcated. At most this process could involve *dépaïsement* or removal to an entirely new life in France, as was proposed in 1636 for a group of girls under the charge of the Hospitalières; at very least, it involved *déracination* ("uprooting") of young Huron boys in the new seminary at Québec, many hundreds of leagues from their Georgian Bay homeland.[50]

Reflecting brutal contemporary standards of classroom education, Jesuit advocacy of strict schooling was rejected by Huron parents.

> The reason [seminaries are necessary] is, that the savages prevent their instruction; they will not tolerate the chastisement of their children, whatever they may do; they permit only a simple reprimand. Moreover, they think they are doing you some great favour in giving you their children to instruct, to feed and to dress. Besides, they will ask for a great many things in return, and will be very importunate in threatening to withdraw their children if you do not accede to their demands.[51]

In the short term, this policy threatened to produce the same effects that it had achieved on a large scale in Europe: a means of reproducing an exclusive elite and reinforcing social divisions between educated and uneducated. In New France, this meant a division between Christianized and "civilized"—that is, individuals introduced to idealized European civility—and the *sauvage* community, which remained untouched by formal education at Québec or the new Christianized Algonquin community of Sillery. Many prospective Hurons and other Indian pupils rebelled against the system, thus preserving their attachment to their traditional worldview. In Jesuit accounts, the drop-outs remained *sauvage*, depriving themselves of a means of exit from barbarian life. The new converts, in contrast, stood as exemplars of a individualized, godly piety—building blocks of a new society.

Limitations of the reasonable, pedagogical approach were evident, however, even beyond the desultory results of the seminary program in distant Québec: "[T]he evil is, they are so attached to their old customs, that, knowing the beauty of the truth, they content themselves to approve of it without embracing it."[52] This opened the door not to further discourse of reason but rather to the dismal *pastorale de la peur*. More generally, the pedagogical approach involving patient but insistent catechizing of new converts undermined other potent pastoral approaches derived from the older tradition of mission as espoused by the Recollects—especially the invocation of an enchanted world or a millennial augury, or the assertion of a common ascetic, otherworldy spirituality or way of life.

By emphasizing the discourse of reason over "white magic" and by emphasizing the exclusive power of God, Jesuits deviated from the overall thrust of baroque catholicism with its appeal to the senses and its claim to supernatural efficacy and departed in most cases at least from the strategy of identification and idealization adopted by their Franciscan colleagues.[53] Jesuit missionaries may have relied upon symbolic display and collective ritual to a considerable extent, but unlike the Recollects, the Jesuits' concern for conveying an essentially learned version of Christianity limited their capacity to recognize native spirituality, let alone to assimilate it. In combination with the missionary tendency to castigate native error or superstition, deeming it wrong because of its ignorance if not its suggestion of diabolical influence, this emphasis on conveying truth through formal instruction (and expecting it to produce an immediate response on the part of the hearer) tended to undermine other means of demonstrating Christianity. Of course, Jesuits would be constrained to play the role of shaman in the context of epidemic disease or starvation in the Huron country in the later 1630s and 1640s; the subsequent theme of martyrdom, as a number of missionaries were killed by Iroquois invaders, dominated representations of the Huron mission.

With the poor results from a decade of mission before him, the local superior Jérôme Lalemant expressed doubts about a strategy of intensive pedagogy leading to the production of individual converts opposed to their traditional way of life. The gulf between Christian civilization and Huron society was simply too large to be bridged in a single generation or even several generations: "They have no usage of letters, no historical monuments, and no idea of a Divinity who created the world and who has care of its government."[54]

Yet interaction with Hurons had taken place on the level of reasonable dialogue rather than magic and countermagic or displays of cultural closeness or affinity with the poor and the pure. Products of a post-Reformation world, with its emphasis on the individual believer, the power of education to transform, and the disciplined community, Jesuits in the Huron country may have forgone some of the most tried and tested—most recently by Franciscans—techniques of mission.

Conclusion

Testy relations between Jesuits and Recollects as well as the constant backdrop of confessional sparring mark their respective mission accounts. This situation made Sagard, le Clercq, and other Recollect writers inclined to emphasize difference and to trumpet the Franciscan case.[55] Another way to compare the more idealizing and possibly quixotic Franciscan view with the systematic but eventually disillusioned view of the Jesuits is in terms of the size, strength, and level of support of the two missions both in France and among the colonial interests in New France. Recollects were "also-rans" here, while the French Province of Jesuits made the Huron mission their largest effort and most publicized undertaking of the century. Their mission to the Hurons benefited from superior resources and a stronger political base both in France and on the New France frontier, as the Hurons rose to prominence as key commercial and military allies of the French.

This chapter has, however, concentrated on the different Franciscan and Jesuit "ways of proceeding" and ways of understanding conversion in the Huron mission. Unquestionably much was shared: conviction of the inherent superiority of French civilization together with varying degrees of faith in ideas of rationality and order typical of reformed Catholic elites; reliance on fear-raising preaching; and a tendency to be, over time, less optimistic about the progress of conversion. Differences highlighted here have included a Franciscan tendency to idealize but also to infantilize the Indian population, together with a more credulous view of the workings of supernatural power in their midst. Jesuits in contrast tended to see conversion as a product of correct instruction and education, producing a more definite break with the old culture and, implicitly, a greater responsibility on the part of converts for their own continence and self-control. Jesuits appear to have operated in a distinctly desacralized world, in that for most Jesuits New France seems to have been neither an enchanted place nor particularly diabolized; Jesuit work was quite straightforwardly the conversion of the Indian population and the extension of Christian civilization. Both Franciscans and Jesuits were interested in linguistic and cultural exploration: Sagard's *Dictionary of the Huron Language* (*Dictionnaire de la langue huronne*), a product of his 1624–25 sojourn, would form the basis for subsequent linguistic investigation undertaken by Jesuits.[56] Both missions tried to understand the Hurons in order to convert them.

The brevity of the Recollect mission, however, invites speculation on how a Franciscan approach may have evolved had exogenous factors such as French religious politics or Iroquoian wars permitted. Would a Franciscan idealization of poverty and the organic simplicity of traditional Indian cultures have worked against the "civilizing mission" as articulated in early French colonial policy? Would the tendency to favor the conversion of the whole community, rather than individuals within it, have produced a situation different from the atomized society of converts living scattered throughout the Huron country in the later 1630s and 1640s? Would a syncretic approach toward Christianity among the Indians have produced a greater movement toward conversion, and if so, how resilient would such a Christianity be in the face of the massive Iroquoian assault in the 1640s? Our understanding of conversion among the Hurons is dominated by Jesuit accounts, and we have a sense too of how Jesuits were changed by their eventual defeat in the Huron country. For the Hurons, the disintegration of their way of life in 1649 after a sustained Jesuit mission meant that their experience of conversion was overwhelmingly the modern one, under Jesuit direction, rather the medieval one, under the tutelage of friars.

Notes

1. J. Leddy Phelan, *The Millennial Kingdom of the Franciscans in the New World*, 2d ed. (Berkeley: University of California Press, 1970), 109.

2. Karl F. Morrison, *Understanding Conversion* (Charlottesville: University Press of Virginia, 1992), xii, 3–4.

3. See Peter A. Goddard, "Canada in Early Modern Jesuit Thought: Backwater or Opportunity?" in *Decentring the Renaissance*, ed. Germaine Warkentin (Toronto: University of Toronto Press, 2002), 186–99.

4. Chrestien le Clercq, *Premier Etablissement de la foi dans la Nouvelle France* (Paris: Amable Auroy, 1691).

5. A classic statement of the former view is found in Lionel Groulx, *Le Canada français missionnaire* (Montreal: Fides, 1962), 40, 49, 59. For the latter, typically unflattering views of missionaries in New France, see the essays in *Rhétorique et conquête missionnaire: le jésuite Paul Lejeune*, ed. R. Ouellet (Sillery: Septentrion, 1993); Marie-Christine Pioffet, *La tentation de l'épopée dans les Relations des jésuites* (Sillery: Septentrion, 1997); and Yvon Le Bras, *L'Amérindien dans les Relations du père Paul Lejeune (1632–1641)* (Sainte-Foy: Editions de la Huit, 1994). See also Réal Ouellet, "Monde sauvage et monde chrétien dans les Relations des jésuites," in *La Notion de "Monde" au XVIIe siècle. Littératures classiques* 22 (1995): 59–72.

6. Studies of the culture of Jesuits include A. Lynn Martin, *The Jesuit Mind: The Mentality of an Elite in Early Modern France* (Ithaca: Cornell University Press,

1988) and John O'Malley, *The First Jesuits* (Cambridge, Mass.: Harvard University Press, 1993). Studies of early modern Franciscanism are less available; useful studies include J. Moorman, *A History of the Franciscan Order* (Oxford, U.K.: Oxford University Press, 1968) and M. D. Lambert, *Franciscan Poverty* (London: S.P.C.K., 1961).

7. "Ennemis declarez du monde." Yves de Paris, *Les heureux succès de la piété* (Paris: Vve N. Buon, 1634), 657.

8. François d'Angoumois cited in Bernard Dompnier, *Enquête au pays des frères des anges* (St. Etienne: Publications de l'Université de Saint-Etienne, 1993), 68.

9. Nicolas de Dijon, *L'esprit du religieux formé sur celui de Jésus Christ* (Lyon: J.-B. De Ville, 1688), 18.

10. François de Toulouse, *Jésus-Christ ou le parfait missionnaire* (Paris: Vve D. Thierry, 1662), 53–54.

11. Gabriel Sagard, *Histoire du Canada* (1636; Paris: Librarie Tross, 1866), 5–6.

12. *Relation de ce qui s'est passé en Nouvelle-France*, 1639 (Paris: Cramoisy, 1640), part II, 116–17. Authoritative modern editions include *Jesuit Relations and Allied Documents*, ed. Reuben Gold Thwaites et al., 73 vols. (Cleveland: Burroughs Brothers, 1896–1901; reprint, New York: Pageant, 1959), and a critical French and Latin edition, *Monumenta Novae Francia*, ed. Lucien Campeau, 9 vols. (Montreal and Rome: Monumenta Hist. Soc. Iesu, 1967–), which contains a large set of ancillary documentation from the Jesuit Archives in Rome.

13. Campeau, ed., *Monumenta Novae Francia*, vol. 2, 52. See Luca Codignola, "The Holy See and the Conversion of the Indians in French and British North America, 1486–1760," in *America in European Consciousness*, ed. Karen Ordahl Kupperman (Chapel Hill: University of North Carolina Press, 1995), 204–5, for missionary ideas of North American primitiveness.

14. Charles de Genève, *Les trophées sacrées*, ed. Félix Tisserand (Lausanne: Société d'Histoire de la Suisse Romande, 1976), 41.

15. Sagard, *Histoire du Canada*, 60, 83–85.

16. Gabriel Sagard, *Grand voyage du pays des Hurons* (Paris, 1632), p. 1; reprint, Paris, 1885, translated by H. H. Langton as *The Long Journey into the Country of the Hurons* (Toronto: Champlain Society, 1939).

17. "Au Roy" (1621) in Sagard, *Histoire du Canada*, 79.

18. Denis Jamet, *Coppie de la lettre escripte par le R.P. Denys Iamet, Commissaire des Recollects au Canada, à monsieur de Rancé, grand vicaire de Pontoyse*, 15 August 1620, 3 (Bibliothèque Nationale, Paris, FRBNF 30644111).

19. Sagard, *Grand Voyage*, 356.

20. Sagard, *Histoire du Canada*, 6, 8.

21. Gilbert Chinard, *L'Amérique et le rêve exotique dans la littérature française au 17e et au 18e siècle* (Paris: Droz 1934), 117; J. Warwick, "Humanisme chrétien et bons sauvages (Gabriel Sagard, 1623–36)," *XVIIe siècle* 97 (1972): 25–49.

22. Sagard, *Histoire du Canada*, 398.

23. Sagard, *Grand Voyage*, 81.

24. Sagard, *Histoire du Canada*, 28.

25. Sagard, *Grand Voyage*, 186–87.
26. Sagard, *Histoire du Canada*, 112, 255, 291.
27. Sagard, *Histoire du Canada*, 255.
28. Sagard, *Histoire du Canada*, 255–57.
29. Sagard, *Histoire du Canada*, 273.
30. Chrestien le Clercq, *Nouvelle relation de la Gaspésie* (Paris: Amable Auroy, 1691), 85–86.
31. Sagard, *Histoire du Canada*, 255–56, 280.
32. Sagard, *Histoire du Canada*, 485–88, 492.
33. Sagard, *Grand Voyage*, 251; cf. Elisabeth Tooker, *An Ethnography of the Huron Indians, 1615–1649* (Midland, Ont.: Huronia Historical Development Council and Ontario Department of Education through the cooperation of the Smithsonian Institution, 1967), 72–123, 140–48.
34. Sagard, *Histoire du Canada*, 486, 496.
35. Sagard, *Histoire du Canada*, 495, 498.
36. Sagard, *Grand Voyage*, 189.
37. Sagard, *Histoire du Canada*, 278, 94, 419–20.
38. Sagard, *Grand Voyage*, 234.
39. J. Bossy, "The Counter-Reformation and the People of Catholic Europe," *Past and Present* 47 (1970): 55–57.
40. Sagard, *Histoire du Canada*, 25.
41. *Relation de ce qui s'est passé en La Nouvelle France, en l'année 1639* (Paris: Cramoisy, 1640), part II, p. 9.
42. J. M. Chaumonot to Vitelleschi, Sainte-Marie, 26 May 1640, in *Jesuit Relations and Allied Documents*, vol. 18, 18–20.
43. Early modern Jesuit education is analyzed in François de Dainville, *L'éducation des jésuites*, ed. Madelaine Compère (Paris: Editions de Minuit, 1978), 157–533; Aldo Scaglione, *The Liberal Arts and the Jesuit College System* (Amsterdam and Philadelphia: J. Benjamins Pub. Co., 1986); and O'Malley, *The First Jesuits*, 200–42.
44. Scaglione, *The Liberal Arts and the Jesuit College System*, 124.
45. Scaglione, *The Liberal Arts and the Jesuit College System*, 179 ("Rules and Established Customs for the Royal College of Savoy in Torino," trans. A. Scaglione).
46. *Relation de ce qui s'est passé en La Nouvelle France, en l'année 1633* (Paris: Cramoisy, 1634), 119; *Relation de ce qui s'est passé en La Nouvelle France, en l'année 1637* (Paris: Cramoisy, 1638), 115, 118–19.
47. *Jesuit Relations and Allied Documents*, vol. 12, 36.
48. For a discussion of the role of rationalism in Jesuit mission practice, see Peter A. Goddard, "Science and Scepticism in the Early Mission to New France," *Journal of the Canadian Historical Association* 6 (1995): 43–58.
49. *Jesuit Relations and Allied Documents*, vol. 53, 113–15.
50. *Relation de ce qui s'est passé en La Nouvelle France, en l'année 1636* (Paris: Cramoisy, 1637), part I, 123.

51. *Relation de ce qui s'est passé en La Nouvelle France, en l'année 1633* (Paris: Cramoisy, 1634), 120, 197.

52. *Relation de ce qui s'est passé en La Nouvelle France, en l'année 1636*, part II, 10.

53. The concept of Catholic "white magic" is advanced by R.J.W. Evans, *The Making of the Habsburg Monarchy, 1550–1700* (Oxford, U.K.: Oxford University Press, 1979), 386–91.

54. *Relation de ce qui s'est passé en La Nouvelle France, en les années 1644 et 1645* (Paris: Cramoisy, 1646), part II, 143.

55. For a helpful and still unsurpassed account of the politics of Jesuit-Franciscan relations, see J. M. Lenhart, "Who Kept the Récollets Out of Canada?" *Franciscan Studies* 5 (1945): 277–300.

56. Gabriel Sagard, *Dictionnaire de la langue huronne: necessaire a ceux qui n'ont l'intelligence d'icelle, & ont a traiter avec les sauvages du pays* (Paris: Chez Denys Moreau, 1632).

4

Conversion in Theory and Practice

John Eliot's Mission to the Indians

Annie Parker

Although the story of John Eliot's mission to the Indians in early New England has been written and rewritten many times, both by its contemporary observers and by modern historians, interpretations vary widely. None doubt the mission's significance, yet broader implications of the experience are still in dispute.

Eliot (1604–1690) was the first Puritan minister to implement a formal mission to the Indians in New England. He began to study a local Algonquian dialect in 1643, began preaching to the Indians in 1646, and translated many religious works into the native language, continuing preaching to the Indians until he was over eighty years old. Historians agree that Eliot reached a significant number of Indians, estimating that approximately 2,500 to 4,000 Indians inhabited the Christian Praying Towns that he established. King Philip's War (1675–76) marked the mission's decline: the scale of opposition between the Indians and the English settlers, and the extent of violence during the conflict, hardened racial lines for both groups and hindered cultural interaction.[1]

Although the visible results of Eliot's mission were not permanent, the images of conversion that Puritan authors recorded remain firmly etched in historical memory. One of the earliest interpreters of Eliot's story invoked a textual metaphor to denote the mission's larger significance. He wrote, "[I]f thou wilt (Reader) thou mayest eye *this work of God* as a full *text:* affording, matter both for *Theoretick* and *practick* conclusions."[2] This author's suggestion to interpret the events of Eliot's mission as one might examine a written text illustrates an important aspect of the Puritan system of understanding. Those who believed in absolute divine providence applied a type of hermeneutics to everyday events in their lives, as they did in studying scriptures. For the authors of the Eliot Tracts, Eliot's mission was a text, requiring the attempt to read larger meanings from the symbolic figures of human acts and decisions, as well as events.[3] Therefore, the Eliot Tracts include a rich depiction of how some Puritans tried to understand their world through their religion, particularly through their beliefs and the practice of conversion.

Historians extend the textual metaphor by continuing to interpret and debate the significance of Eliot's story, demonstrating the implications of historical theory and practice. At the center of these different approaches are separate theoretical bases of historical-critical research, which significantly shape the conclusions that historians draw from Eliot's experience.[4]

The year after Eliot's death, Cotton Mather published a memoir entitled *The Triumphs of Reformed Religion in America: The Life of the Renowned John Eliot.*[5] In the late nineteenth century, some writers in the reformed tradition continued to link Eliot's image with the providential origins of both America and reformed religion.[6]

Since 1975, historians have been more critical of Eliot's enterprise, linking it to the political and cultural conquest of Native Americans.[7] Ethnohistorical studies argue that the New England missions, in general, were more coercive and less successful than the Jesuit missions farther north. As Charles Cohen has noted, the Puritans killed many more Indians than they converted.[8] In addition, historians often compare Eliot's mission unfavorably to Thomas Mayhew's Indian mission on the islands of Nantucket and Martha's Vineyard. Eliot, unlike Mayhew, removed the converted Indians from their place of habitation to towns under English jurisdiction.

Historians who have opposed the ethnohistorical and critical trend have created a controversy in the literature over the respective motivations of Puritans and Indians, as well as the mission's relative costs and benefits in economic, political, and affective terms. The current historical assessment of Eliot's mission reflects the larger challenges of writing about Puritan and Indian cultural interaction. One cannot come away from the current literature without a heightened sense of the cultural divide between Native Americans and Europeans in America and the divide that historians still encounter and contest as they attempt to retell Eliot's story.

However, the ethnohistorical model obscures the motives and reasoning of the Puritan authors who wrote about Eliot's mission. The model projects a power motive onto the missionaries that is theoretical rather than historical in origin. While economic and political power explain the end result of interaction between Indians and Europeans in the New World, "power" has little to do with understanding how those involved made sense of the events, their motivations, and systems of meaning at the time.

The aim of this chapter is to generate new insights into this cultural interaction by exploring more fully the Puritan theory and practice of conversion when confronted by "praying Indians." Eliot's decision to preach to the Indians and his methods for their instruction were informed by Puritan beliefs about conversion and human nature. Puritan ideas about sin and salvation shaped how Eliot implemented the mission and how he and other Puritan authors defined the mission's significance. Puritan authors presented Eliot's mission as a communal struggle against sin, as embodied in images of Indian "depravity." Furthermore, the mission was an opportunity for Massachusetts Bay Puritans to demonstrate and validate the efficacy of their doctrine in transforming Indians into Puritans. However, Eliot could not control, or even predict, how the Indians responded to and adapted his message. Thus, the Eliot Tracts portray a tension between the authors' ideas about salvation and the practice of Indian conversion.

In this chapter I first contextualize Eliot's conversion initiative and methods by examining the contemporary issues in conversion theory in the 1630s and 1640s in the Massachusetts Bay area. I have selected documents pertaining to the Antinomian Controversy and Thomas Shepard's lecture sermons and conversion narratives to demonstrate certain aspects of preparationist theology that are relevant to Eliot's conversion methods. Themes of hypocrisy, original sin, and human depravity illuminate the content and form of Eliot's mission. I also examine various writings by Eliot, drawn primarily from the Eliot Tracts, to determine his message and methods of conversion and to read the Indian responses through these reports, specifically, by assessing how the response of the Praying Indians contradicted or shaped the contours of Puritan interpretation.

To examine connections between Puritan ideas about salvation and Eliot's conversion methods requires a basic understanding of Puritan soteriology, that is, the theology of salvation. English Puritans as early as 1560 assumed they could be reasonably certain of salvation, and they had a prescribed form for recognizing it.[9] The conversion experience is an important defining feature of Puritanism for scholars, especially in how it reflects covenant theology.[10] According to this theory, the first man, Adam, was under a covenant of works with God, which required Adam's obedience to God's commands. When Adam disobeyed, he broke the covenant with God, and his progeny were born into original sin, a type of hereditary moral disability.[11] The punishment for disobedience (sin) was death. However, Puritans taught that God in his mercy offered humanity a covenant of grace. This covenant depended upon God's mercy in dispensing grace to those he chose for salvation, rather than upon human will or action. Grace provided the elect not only with justification (redemption from eternal damnation), but also with sanctification (exemplary moral behavior).

The affective, in addition to the theological, aspect of Puritan conversion is essential to understanding its powerful place in Puritan religious experience. Puritan conversions tended to follow a particular progression of experiences: first a period of preparation and active searching for truth; then an intense awareness of one's sinfulness; next an emotional release of love and joy in realizing God's mercy; and finally the desire to do good works. In *God's Caress* (1986), Cohen argues that the psychological and social system of Puritanism emerged as a way of restoring order in a chaotic world. The theme of helplessness dominated the messages of Puritan ministers. The Puritan religious system dealt with feelings of inadequacy by organizing conceptual (theological) locations for these feelings: guilt for sin, fear of God's wrath, and an unrelenting sense of moral inadequacy due to original sin.[12] Cohen argues that the affective cycle of Puritan conversion not only occurred initially when one was "saved," but also continued to occur throughout the believer's religious experience, to renew assurance of one's calling. Anxiety over one's salvation occurred not only through guilt over actual (performed) sins, but also over hypocrisy (unregeneration masked by outward compliance). These fears could threaten a person's faith in the authenticity of his or her conversion experience. Thus, maintaining assurance of salvation depended not only on having undergone the conversion experience, but also by reconverting—repeating the affective cycle—many times throughout one's life.[13]

During the Antinomian Controversy (1636–38), certain persons, called "Antinomians" by their detractors, redefined hypocrisy and the significance of anxiety in the believer's experience. As outlined above, most Puritan ministers taught that the struggle against sin, balanced by moments of assurance, was necessary throughout the believer's experience. Not only did the Antinomians claim that the anxiety this tension produced was unnecessary, they claimed that it was legalism (and thus hypocrisy) to struggle over one's sins, signaling an erroneous understanding of unconditional saving grace. The Antinomian articulation invalidated the orthodox

Puritan understanding of conversion by redefining hypocrites as those who struggle and through that redefinition eliminating the role of anxiety and preparation in the process of salvation.

Historian David Hall argues that the Antinomian Controversy occurred in New England as a result of the exponential growth of new churches in the context of freedom that brought Puritans to New England during the Great Migration.[14] When a revival during the years 1633–36 waned, in its place developed a "mood of acute religious anxiety" among clergy and church members.[15] In response, John Cotton, an influential Puritan clergyman at the First Church in Boston, began to emphasize the dangers of relying upon outward signs of grace for assurance, teaching that hypocrites might easily pass for Christians outwardly.[16] Anne Hutchinson, a woman who held private religious meetings in her home, adapted Cotton's message to say that assurance of salvation was immediate with conversion and lasted throughout the believer's experience, regardless of any behavioral failings. Among the heresies that, in John Winthrop's words, Hutchinson "hatched and dandled"[17] were two that struck at the heart of the Puritan reconversion experience: that "the law, and the preaching of it is of no use at all, to drive a man to Christ"; and that the "graces of Saints and Hypocrits differ not."[18] She also accused other ministers of preaching a covenant of works rather than faith.[19] Antinomians defined the act of struggling against sin as hypocrisy rather than as a demonstration of sincerity. The church synod and civil court proceedings duly disciplined the Antinomians. Anne Hutchinson was excommunicated from the church and banished from the colony, and many others faced banishment and warnings as well. Although the Antinomians had provided an alternative formulation for assurance, it was one that most of the colonists chose to reject.[20]

Thomas Shepard, minister of the Cambridge Church, articulated the primary theological response to the Antinomian challenge in a series of sermons he began to preach in the summer of 1636.[21] He defined the differences between Massachusetts Bay saints and heretics by an experience of continual struggle, driven by anxiety over the authenticity of one's salvation. According to Shepard, sanctification could be a sign of justification, and anxiety over the authenticity of one's belief could bring assurance.[22] His response, which still adamantly stressed the danger of hypocrisy, affirmed the previous understanding of hypocrisy as an outward appearance of compliance masking inward unregeneration.[23] Shepard defined a hypocrite as one who tastes briefly of "means" but only insofar as it is pleasant and easy.[24] He charged true believers that they might recognize their status by their constant struggle of recognizing and seeking to overcome sin.[25] The definition of true and false (heretical) believers was critical to defining an orthodoxy that was persuasive in identifying and explaining authentic religious experience.

In the preparationist view of salvation, recognizing and struggling with sin was continual throughout the believer's life.[26] According to Shepard, sin was omnipresent in human life: "There is something that doth oppose God in every lawful thing, in whole or in part, (for flesh is in it,) or else you are blinded if you see it not."[27] If a person was unable to see the presence of sin in his or her life, even in good deeds, that itself signaled a sinful heart. Shepard's language reflected his awe at the pervasiveness of sin in human endeavors: "O, therefore, feel the breadth of evil in it."[28] Yet the Christian's goal was total annihilation of sin, that even "every thought may be brought into subjection and obedience to Christ."[29] If sin was everywhere, even in good and lawful actions, how could it be conquered? Shepard wrote that sin could not be entirely overcome but must always be a struggle: "The eternal efficacy of the word may be preserved in a power of conflict against the power of sin; for therein the Lord's power of the word does principally appear in this life, though not in a power of victory; I mean a complete victory."[30] A partial and temporary victory was the best a believer could hope for in this life, for the power of God's word was evident only in the struggle.

What constitutes human existence if removed from the "power of the word"? Obviously, from Shepard's words, we might expect a lack of resistance to sin. However, Shepard has an even more powerful visual image to impress upon his listeners. He charged them to "think within yourselves, What if the Lord had left me without the word? I will tell you what ye would have been. Look upon these poor Indians."[31] To the colonial Puritans, Indians were an accessible symbol of human life without grace or the word, a life of total depravity. Therefore, Shepard used the image of Indians to personify sin to his congregation and to illustrate lives removed from the struggle with sin in a godly community. This understanding of the nature of Indian experience shaped the way Eliot taught the Indians and how Puritans interpreted their subsequent conversions.

As minister of the Cambridge Church, Shepard transcribed confessions, or conversion narratives, of his members during the years 1638–45.[32] These confessions illustrate Shepard's articulation of the central importance of anxiety regarding false faith (also discussed variously as an over-reliance on "means," "form," and "works") in obtaining assurance.[33] As much as the confessions represented the standard form of conversion, they also mirrored the intense fears of Puritans regarding hypocrisy. Repeatedly, the voices in Shepard's collection reported that a critical moment in their preparation came in realizing their hypocrisy,[34] indicating that fears of hypocrisy were a common route to salvation for persons in this New England parish.[35] These confessions demonstrated in experience Shepard's articulation of the central importance of anxiety, particularly over false faith, in obtaining assurance.[36]

In addition to searching one's own life for sin, mourning for the sins of others could be an important sign of genuine faith, as well.[37] One of Shepard's confessors, William Hamlet, said that he obtained a measure of assurance after hearing the words of a minister who told him that "one difference between hypocrits and saints was mourning for the sins of others to whom we have no relation."[38] Hamlet reported that he could not bear sin or unbelief without "annoying" the sinner and laboring against unbelief. His response to his minister's injunction to mourn the sin of others is an isolated report. However, the logic in Hamlet's understanding of assurance has important implications for how Massachusetts Bay Puritans viewed their relations with the Indians in the 1640s. If mourning the sins of others was a sign of assurance, then Eliot's mission provided a unique opportunity for communal assurance.[39] The central role that conversion played in Puritan understanding provides an ideological framework for understanding Eliot's mission that historians have not yet examined.

One of the questions that historians struggle to answer is why no one began a mission to the Indians in Massachusetts Bay before 1646. One line of historical explanation argues that Eliot began the mission when he did for various reasons of personal and political gain. Richard Cogley has revised this line of historical interpretation by exploring a combination of factors that preceded the mission's origin in 1646, such as Indian desire to assume Puritan life and competition with other "heretical" factions for favor with England in a territory dispute.[40] In addition, Cogley reviews Eliot's writings about the early stages of the mission, such as Eliot's efforts to learn the Massachuset dialect of Algonquian. Although we cannot assert with certainty Eliot's motives in initiating the mission, we can be sure that he (and other Puritan clergy) viewed its origin as providential and read theoretical and practical implications from its events.

Three themes in the Eliot Tracts indicate how its authors defined the importance of Eliot's mission. These rhetorical themes highlight tensions and inconsistencies in the tracts as the authors struggled to articulate the significance of Eliot's mission to English Puritans. The first theme is a rhetorical emphasis on the depravity of Indians and their status as separate from the American Puritan community. Eliot's methods of conversion involved imposing certain expectations and categories of meaning (especially regarding sin) upon the Indians. Another (conflicting) theme is an emphasis on correct doctrine among the Massachuset Indian converts. In the confusion over the correct method of obtaining assurance following the Antinomian Controversy, Eliot's mission provided an opportunity to observe the authenticity of the means of grace in transforming persons outside the covenant into Puritans.[41] A third theme is a recurring emphasis on the importance of struggling against, and mourning for, sin. The authors of the Eliot Tracts employed a rhetorical strategy of portraying the mission as a metaphorical and communal struggle against sin. In this way, the struggle to convert Indians (who seemingly personified sin) resembled a sign of grace.

Eliot's emphasis on "Indian" depravity is evident in his conversion methods. In 1646, when he first preached to a group of Massachuset Indians in Nonatum in their own language, he introduced the concept of God's law and punishment to them. Yet Eliot did not just teach about sin as an abstract concept. He taught that "Indians" were sinful. Eliot began by explaining the Ten Commandments, then

> shewing the curse and dreadfull wrath of God against all those who brake them . . .
> and so applied it unto the condition of the *Indians* present . . . and then preached
> Jesus Christ to them the onely meanes of recovery from sinne and wrath and eternall
> death . . . and of the blessed estate of all those that by faith beleeve in Christ, and
> know him feelingly.[42]

After the sermon, which Eliot estimated as lasting about an hour and fifteen minutes, Eliot and the three English men with him began to teach the Massachuset Indians who were gathered there in a catechetical question-and-answer format, with the assistance of a native interpreter.

In addition to teaching the Praying Indians about sin, the language in which Eliot and the other authors of the tracts described "Indians" is steeped in the imagery of human depravity. Their language denotes the

Indians as "Sonnes of Adam,"[43] the "very servants of sin and Satan,"[44] and the "verriest ruins of mankind."[45] When several of these Indians later related their conversion narratives, they used similar terms to refer to themselves. Eliot must have used these terms in instruction as well as description. Many Puritan authors assumed that Indian life and culture represented humanity as reduced to its barest frame, thus equating Indians with the doctrine of human depravity.

Eliot's rhetorical emphasis on sin in instructing the Praying Indians is also evident in their responses to his message. He listed the questions that the Praying Indians asked him on several occasions, and their queries indicate their reactions to as well as their understanding of the new religion.[46] Their questions did not mirror the catechetical questions that Eliot taught. Rather, questions such as "Why did God make Hell?" and "Why must we be like Salt?"[47] represent the reactions of a people completely new to the culture of Christianity. Moreover, many of the Indians' questions indicated that the Indians perceived subtle ethical complexities in Puritan views about sin. Some saw far-reaching implications of the Puritan concept of sin and were concerned.[48] The Indians' questions and ethical discussion represent the extent to which Eliot impressed the Indians with the importance of sin in Puritan religious experience.[49]

After beginning to teach the Praying Indians the essential elements of Christianity, Eliot decided that they needed towns to live in. Eliot set about organizing the Praying Towns just one month after he began the mission in 1646, although the towns were not fully established until 1651.[50] This move is indicative of Eliot's emphasis on demonstrating the authenticity of the Indians' conversion to others, to transform them into "believers." Eliot concluded after his initial sermons to the local Indians that "such as are so extremely degenerate, must bee brought to some civility before religion can prosper, or the word take place."[51] Eliot set out to change the Indians, as he described them, "from these wild and wandring course of life, until a settling unto particular Townes and Cities."[52]

Moving the Indians into towns to teach them "civility" is an aspect of Eliot's mission that historians have sharply debated, for Eliot's first order of business in these towns was to establish laws in them, both civil and religious.[53] On one side of the controversy are the historians who call Eliot's towns "proto-reservations" and cite the legal imposition of English civility and religion as a significant difference from the Mayhews' voluntaristic methods. Francis Jennings and other historians have interpreted the legal forms that Eliot's "instruction" took as coercive conversion.[54]

However, as Cogley points out, Eliot's move to incorporate Indians into English towns also provided them with property rights under English law, which Eliot defended throughout his life.[55] In addition, religious laws were rarely enforced in the Praying Towns, in contrast to English Puritan towns.[56]

A 1648 tract written by Thomas Shepard suggests that Puritans may have considered the new towns to be as significant for themselves and the larger world of English Puritanism as for the Praying Indians. So eager was Shepard to demonstrate the sincerity of the Indians in joining a covenant and setting up a town that he sent the original copy of the Indians' covenant with the letters to England. As Shepard proudly introduced it: "I have sent you their owne copy and their owne hands to it."[57] Puritans placed a great deal of emphasis on written covenants. The particular importance that Puritans placed on Indian conversion is indicated by the fact that the covenant was held by English Puritans in London rather than by its authors. Shepard was at least as interested in presenting Indian missions to other English Puritans as in the actual conduct of missions in New England.

After the changes began in the Indians' civil and religious life, four tracts were published with a changed emphasis from the previous tracts.[58] These authors presented warnings to English believers in light of the perceived altered spiritual status of the Indians. Instead of emphasizing the degeneracy of the Indians, they stressed the failings of the English. This new rhetorical emphasis in the mission reports was similar to the Puritan literary and sermonic form of the jeremiad, lamenting the corruption of the English and calling for reform to primitive zeal. Puritans viewed the history of God's chosen people as conforming to a cyclical pattern of reform, corruption, repentance, and reform again. This framework excluded any progressive view of society. Instead, for Puritans, improvement meant returning to primitive Christianity, making the cycle complete.[59] This primitivist drive explains why the Eliot Tracts assumed a new tone once the Indian towns were established. The religious "progress" of the Indians served a rhetorical purpose as a warning to English believers. Although the jeremiad was a part of the larger intellectual context in New England at this time, in the case of Puritan and Indian relations it illustrates how the rhetoric of struggling with sin in the Eliot Tracts precluded the possibility that the two communities might progress together.

The epistle dedicatory to a 1648 tract warned its English audience: "We have as many sad symptoms of a declining, as these poor outcasts have glad presages of a Rising Sun among them."[60] The successes of Eliot's mission provided a new way of viewing the comparative sins of the Indians and the English. The authors of the Eliot Tracts warned their readers of the prospect of a reversal of spiritual fortunes. As another author wrote: "God is preparing them a table in the Wilderness; where our satieties, will be their sufficiencies; our complaints, their contents; our burdens, their comforts; if He cannot have an England here, He will have an England there."[61] The dichotomy that this author sets up places the spiritual interests of the two groups in opposition. The theoretical and practical implications that this author extrapolated were based on the assumption that the mission existed to teach spiritual lessons to the English.

When Eliot first began his mission efforts, one way in which many English contemporaries understood Indian acceptance of Christianity was in eschatological terms. Some of the English conjectured that the Indians in North America were the descendants of the ten lost tribes of Israel.[62] Some thought that the conversion of the Indians (if they were part of Israel) fulfilled a scriptural promise: "Israel has experienced a hardening in part until the full number of the Gentiles has come in. And so all Israel shall be saved" (Romans 11:25–26). Many conjectured that the ten lost tribes had come to America and that their conversion now was a sign of the "fullness of times," indicating an imminent end to the world. Initially, the English authors who wrote about Eliot's mission frequently suggested that the Indians were descendants, or "lost tribes," of Israel to persuade their readers of the importance of the mission endeavor.[63] However, as the Indians began to embrace Christianity and live in Praying Towns, Richard Mather reversed the analogy.[64] He designated the Indians as gentiles who received the gospel only to make Israel (the English) realize her sins, make her jealous, and make her return to God. He warned his readers: "And oh, let the English take heed, both in our dear Native Country, and here, lest for our unthankfulness, and many other sins, the Lord should take the Gospel from us, and bestow our mercy therein upon them as upon a Nation that would yield the fruits thereof in better sort than many of us have done."[65] The spiritual progress of the Praying Indians, then, was not necessarily positive news.

However, as far as the Indians exhibited correct doctrine, Eliot could interpret the mission positively. In a 1650 letter, Eliot related a story to illustrate the status of "the work of the Lord among the Indians."[66] Two Praying Indians had "travelled to Providence and Warwick where Gorton liveth," and because the men stayed in the town over a Sunday, they attended a church there.⁶⁷ The members of the church were very curious about the Indian believers and talked with them for some time after the service, questioning them about their religious beliefs. The persons in Providence had attempted to challenge the Praying Indians' doctrine: "They perceiving that they had some knowledge in religion, and were of my hearers; they endeavor[ed] to possess their minds with their opinions."⁶⁸ After their return, the two Indians expressed their surprise that the English could believe such different things when they all professed to believe the same Bible. The two Indians had debated and defended their beliefs regarding heaven and hell, infant baptism, and the authority of ministers and magistrates. Eliot asked the Indians how they had responded on each point, and he affirmed their responses as correct. For example, the persons in Providence told the Indians that magistrates were unnecessary: since they could not grant life, they should not have the power to take it away. The Indians responded that they would do as God commanded, for "if God commands us to magistrate, and commands them to punish sinners, then we must obey."⁶⁹ Eliot affirmed this response, linking correct doctrine with legitimate authority and heresy with heterodoxy.

Eliot was very encouraged by the Indians' rejoinders to the heretics in Providence. He interpreted the story as reflecting not only the orthodox beliefs of his converts, but also his own spiritual success. This unexpected confrontation of the Indians with heretics was Eliot's one moment of unabashed rejoicing over his work with the Indians. For Eliot, the encounter affirmed orthodoxy, displayed the legitimate conversion of Indians, and was the reward for his labors.⁷⁰

The last tract that Eliot wrote about the Praying Indians (1673) illustrates some of the tensions that he faced in reproducing English Puritanism among the local Indians. He wrote the tract in response to a number of questions that had been sent to him from England. Several questions pertained to matters of form, such as the requirements for gathering churches among the Praying Indians. Eliot assured his readers that the practice of church building among Indians was the "same (as near as we can) that is practiced in gathering churches among the English."⁷¹ However, his admission "as near as we can" indicates that Puritan ecclesiology, at least, did not replicate itself exactly in Praying Indian practice. Two of the questions also dealt with the problem of heresy. In response to a question regarding Anabaptist doctrine, Eliot admitted that two had been swayed, "but the rest are stedfast."⁷² An additional question asked whether the Praying Indians tolerated heterodoxy, allowing multiple interpretations of doctrine or religious experience. Eliot's response was unequivocal: "Not any; they have a deep sense of their own darkness and ignorance, and a reverent esteem of the light and goodness of the English, and that such English as wasp [sic] into errors doe also decline from goodness, by which means satan hath yet found no door of interest into them."[73] Eliot stressed the significance of the Praying Indians' sinfulness and corresponding humility and their correct doctrine, affirming both orthodox doctrines and his efforts among the Indians.

Historians have proposed many reasons to explain why the Indians converted. Whether as a strategy of political and economic survival, as a desire for community with the English, or as a way of understanding their experience, there is consensus that conversion was a significant experience for the Praying Indians.[74] Indians readily and accurately accepted Christian understandings of sin, guilt, and eternal punishment. As discussed previously, Eliot taught the Praying Indians that they were children of Adam, inheritors of original sin, corrupt, and outside the covenant. It seems evident that the Indians identified with the state of sinfulness to a great degree, although this identification may also have represented Eliot's emphasis on this theme.[75] Among those Indians who chose to listen to Eliot's message, many expressed deep emotional responses.[76]

In 1653, Eliot reported on the Indians' desire to partake of ordinances, to become full members of the church. To do so they would have to recount their conversion experience, their confessions, to a panel of ministers who would then judge whether they were fit for church membership. Therefore, Eliot began to examine the Indians, recording their confessions. The Indian confessions are similar to Shepard's Cambridge confessions in doctrine, length, and form, yet differ in how they articulate their guilt and the means of obtaining assurance.[77] In Shepard's confessions, as previously discussed, the theme of hypocrisy was a prevalent means of coming to salvation. Shepard's converts who cited hypocrisy in their confessions feared that although they were outwardly moral, they still lacked inward regeneration. In contrast, although repentance was central to the Indian confessions, they emphasized actual sins rather than false religion. The Praying Indians negotiated Eliot's message of their greater depravity to their own spiritual advantage. The Indians' spiritual poverty afforded them a claim to profound humility and thus assured themselves of divine mercy without fearing for the authenticity of their conversion.

For Shepard's confessors, original sin was an impersonal explanation of human selfishness and the need for salvation. These confessions referred to human depravity in distant, highly abstracted terms, far removed from any personal ties to themselves. They only reference their natural spiritual state variously as "my condition, fallen in Adam," "my estate by Adam's fall," or "my original corruption." Adding to this balanced, distant tone regarding their fallen state is its ready correction in the conversion narrative: "And herein the Lord made me look up to the Lord to be reconciled and change my nature."[78]

While Shepard's confessors exhibited anxiety regarding false religion in their conversion narratives, the Praying Indians stressed their identification with original sin in their confessions. A Praying Indian named Totherswamp explained his spiritual status through the story of the fall and his claim to Adam as a father: *"The first man God made was named Adam & God made a Covenant with him, do and live, thou and thy Children; if thou do not thou must die, thou and thy children:* And we are Children of Adam poor sinners."[79] When he said "we are Children of Adam" he undoubtedly meant himself and his Indian relatives. Eliot also used this exact phrase to denote the Indians' status as persons born outside of the covenant of grace. As Eliot explained in a question session with the Praying Indians in 1647, "when God chooses a man or a woman to be his servant, he chooses all their children to be so also."[80]

Another difference between the two sets of confessions is in the affective aspect of the experience. One Indian noted, "I heard that my heart must break and melt with sin."[81] Another declared, "My heart is broken for [my sins] . . . and melteth in me."[82] Moreover, one Indian man wept through the entire period of his examination and the recitation of his confession.[83] However, in the Shepard confessions, the two persons who used the word *melt* to describe their affective experience in conversion used it to denote the warmth that drew them to God. This contrasts with the Indians' stronger usage and meaning of the term to describe being heartbroken over one's sins.[84]

The differences between Shepard's English confessions and Eliot's Indian confessions must derive partly from the Indians' adaptation of Christianity to their own values and ways of expressing meaning. However, the differences also reflect the ways in which Eliot's message to the Indians presented them with a different soteriology than the English, by stressing their status as persons outside the covenant, who had further to journey in their path to conversion. Whereas Shepard's confessors expressed anxiety regarding hypocrisy, the Indian confessions professed anxiety over original sin. Moreover, whereas Shepard's converts related moments of peace and assurance of salvation, the Indians' confessions dwelt on sorrow and repentance.[85]

The board of Puritan ministers who examined the Indians' confessions in 1653 did not accept them into church membership immediately. Richard Mather defended the actions of the ministers by explaining that the "delay in churching of Indians, [was] evidence of the sincerity of missions."[86] It was unremarkable for even English Puritans to be delayed in establishing churches.[87] In fact, these same Indian confessors were later accepted into church membership. However, denying the Indians full membership was an action consistent with the Puritan rhetoric of struggling with sin evident in the Eliot Tracts. Some historians have concluded that Eliot's mission was a failure because it did not achieve religious and civil integration between the two communities.[88] Perhaps the authors of the Eliot Tracts looked for meaning in the mission's efforts rather than its results, just as struggling against—not eradicating—sin was a sign of grace for Puritans.

Whether as confirmed "visible saints" or not, the Praying Indians continued to practice Puritan religion with some modifications when it came to discussing hypocrisy and anxiety over sin. In a 1658 report to the corporation, Eliot transcribed some of the exhortations of the male Indian leaders in the town of Natick. They had gathered for a public fast "in preparation for gathering a church, and because of much rain, and sicknesse and other tryalls."[89] I have selected two of the exhortations to shed light on how the Indians' reconversion experience may have altered over time, as both of these men were Indians whose conversion narratives Eliot had recorded six years earlier.

The first exhortation is from a man named Waban. He began by citing Matthew 9:12–13: "But when Jesus heard that, he said unto them, they that be whole need not a Physittan, but they that are sick. But goe ye and learne what that meaneth; I will have mercy and not sacrifice; for I came not to call the righteous, but sinners to repentance."[90] Waban's message was that they were sick in their souls as well as their bodies and that sin made their souls sick. If they repented, their souls could be made well. He instanced such actual sins among them as idleness, Sabbath-breaking, and passion. Waban was careful to explain this scriptural verse in terms of hypocrisy:

> what is the lesson, which Christ would have us learne, that he *came not to call the righteous, but sinners to repentance.* What! Doth not God love them that be

> righteous? . . . The righteous here are not meant those that are
> truly righteous,
> but those that are Hypocrits; that seem righteous, and are not; that think
> themselves righteous, but are not so indeed; such God calleth not, neither doth he
> care for them: but such as see their sins, and are sick of sin, them Christ calleth to
> repentance, and to believe in Christ, therefore let us see our need of Christ, to heal
> all our diseases of soul and body.[91]

Here, Waban clearly distinguished between hypocrites and sinners and identified his community with the latter. The sins that he listed were actual sins and do not reflect a fear of false religion, or hypocrisy. Waban's lack of identification with hypocrisy indicates that he experienced reconversion somewhat differently than did English Puritans in New England.

This exhortation indicates an adaptation of meaning in the Puritan belief and practice of religion. Waban manipulated his identification with original sin, whether imposed on him or appropriated by him, to the Praying Indians' spiritual advantage. Spiritual poverty afforded the Praying Indians a claim to profound humility and thus a greater assurance of divine mercy. Their reconversion experience appeared to capitalize on actual sins rather than hypocrisy, thus avoiding English Puritan anxieties over false faith and works.

Historians typically conclude the story of Eliot's mission with King Philip's War. For those sympathetic to Eliot's aims, the war was an unfortunate interruption to his work, with tragic consequences. For ethnohistorians, the war was the logical end of European attempts at physical and cultural domination of Native Americans.

However, understanding Puritan beliefs about conversion illuminates how Eliot and other colonists viewed their relationship with the Praying Indians without oversimplifying their world of understanding to the historical conventions of the benevolent (if misinformed) missionary, or the missionary as a political, economic, and cultural conqueror. In addition, study of the Puritan theories and practices of conversion sheds new light on how the Praying Indians adapted the message they received to their advantage. Eliot's mission efforts are clearer when situated within contemporary theological beliefs about conversion and struggling against sin. The cosmic struggle between good and evil was as much a part of the Puritan understanding of their experience as were their actual interactions with the local Massachuset Indians. In the Eliot Tracts, Puritan theories of "Indian" degeneracy vied with the need to present examples of correct doctrine and the success of the mission. Both of these ideas were implicated in Puritan ideas about conversion that were central to how Puritans in New England conceived of themselves and their place in the world. Thus, the story of Eliot's mission highlights tensions in Puritan theories and practices of conversion when confronted with Praying Indians.

Notes

1. For Eliot's biographical information, see Francis Bremer, *The Puritan Experiment: New England Society from Bradford to Edwards*, rev. ed. (Hanover, N.H.: University Press of New England, 1995), 169, 205; and Roy Harvey Pearce, *Savagism and Civilization: A Study of the Indian and the American Mind* (Los Angeles: University of California Press, 1988), 29–30.

2. J.D., appendix to "The Glorious Progress of the Gospel amongst the Indians in New England," ed. Edward Winslow (London, 1649), in *Massachusetts Historical Society Collections* (hereafter cited as MHSC) 3:4 (Boston: Massachusetts Historical Society Collections, 1834), 93.

3. The Eliot Tracts are a series of reports about Eliot's mission, written by Eliot and other Puritan ministers during the years 1648–55 and published in MHSC 3:4 (Boston, 1834).

4. In a book review, Edward G. Gray referred to the opposing lines of historiography as "institutional" and "ethnohistorical." In the first category are works such as William Kellaway, *The New England Company, 1649–1776* (New York: Barnes and Noble, 1963); Alden T. Vaughan, *New England Frontier: Puritans and Indians, 1620–1675* (Norman: University of Oklahoma Press, 1965); and Richard W. Cogley, *John Eliot's Mission to the Indians before King Philip's War* (Cambridge: Harvard University Press, 1999). Gray cites the following as examples of the ethnohistorical approach: Neal Salisbury, "Red Puritans: The 'Praying Indians' of Massachusetts Bay and John Eliot," *William and Mary Quarterly*, 3d Ser., 31 (1975): 27–54; Francis Jennings, *The Invasion of America: Indians, Colonialism, and the Cant of Conquest* (Chapel Hill: University of North Carolina Press, 1975); James Axtell, *The Invasion Within: The Contest of Cultures in Colonial North America* (New York: Oxford University Press, 1985). Edward G. Gray, review of *John Eliot's Mission to the Indians before King Philip's War* by Richard W. Cogley, *American Historical Review* 105:3 (June 2000): 917–18.

5. Cotton Mather, *The Triumphs of Reformed Religion in America: The Life of the Renowned John Eliot* (Boston: Harris and Allen, 1691).

6. Chalmers Martin, "Apostolic and Modern Missions, II: The Problem," *Presby-*

terian and Reformed Review 8 (April 1897): 246; "Apostolic and Modern Missions, IV: Results," *Presbyterian and Reformed Review* 8 (October 1897): 726.

7. James Axtell, "Invading America: Puritans and Jesuits," *Journal of Interdisciplinary History* 14:3 (winter 1984): 635–46; Axtell, *The Invasion Within;* Francis Jennings, "Apostles to the Indians," chap. 14 in *Invasion of America*, 228–53; Kenneth M. Morrison, "'That Art of Coyning Christians': John Eliot and the Praying Indians of Massachusetts," *Ethnohistory* 21:1 (1974): 77–92; James P. Ronda, "'We Are Well as We Are': An Indian Critique of Seventeenth-Century Christian Missions," *William and Mary Quarterly*, 3d Ser., 34 (1977): 66–82; Salisbury, "Red Puritans."

8. Charles L. Cohen, "Conversion among Puritans and Amerindians: A Theological and Cultural Perspective," in *Puritanism: Transatlantic Perspectives on a Seventeenth-Century Anglo-American Faith*, ed. Francis J. Bremer (Boston: Massachusetts Historical Society, 1993), 234.

9. David Hall, ed., *The Antinomian Controversy, 1636–1638: A Documentary History*, 2d ed. (Durham, N.C.: Duke University Press, 1990), 12.

10. Regarding conversion as a defining element of Puritanism, see Theodore Dwight Bozeman, *To Live Ancient Lives: The Primitivist Dimension in Puritanism* (Chapel Hill: University of North Carolina Press, 1988), 9; Charles Cohen, *God's Caress: The Psychology of Puritan Religious Experience* (New York: Oxford University Press, 1986), 4; Perry Miller, *The New England Mind: The Seventeenth Century* (ca. 1954; reprint, Cambridge, Mass.: Harvard University Press, 1982), 287; Alan Simpson, *Puritanism in Old and New England* (Chicago: University of Chicago Press, 1961), 2.

11. Cohen, "Conversion among Puritans and Amerindians," 238.

12. Cohen, *God's Caress*, 271–72.

13. Ibid., 12–13, 22.

14. Hall, *The Antinomian Controversy*, 14–17.

15. Ibid., 15.

16. Regarding this shift in John Cotton's sermons, see Hall, *The Antinomian Controversy*, 16; see also William Stoever, *A Faire and Easie Way to Heaven: Covenant Theology and Antinomianism in Early Massachusetts* (Middletown, Conn.: Wesleyan University Press, ca. 1978), 48–57.

17. John Winthrop, "A Short Story," in *The Antinomian Controversy*, ed. David Hall, 202.

18. Ibid.

19. Stoever, *A Faire and Easie Way to Heaven*, 10.

20. Hall, *The Antinomian Controversy*, 18.

21. Ibid., 19. On Shepard's considerable influence on preparationist theology in America and the implications for Puritan communities in America, see Norman Pettit, *The Heart Prepared: Grace and Conversion in Puritan Spiritual Life* (New Haven: Yale University Press, 1966), 86–87, 104–5.

22. Hall, *The Antinomian Controversy,* 18–19.

23. On the centrality of hypocrisy to Shepard's test for assurance, see Michael McGiffert, *God's Plot* (Amherst: University of Massachusetts Press, 1972), 17–18; William Stoever has defined hypocrisy in the context of the Antinomian Controversy as the question of determining which people "merely appear regenerate in outward behavior" in *A Faire and Easie Way to Heaven,* 49.

24. Thomas Shepard, *The Works of Thomas Shepard,* vol. 2 (Boston: Doctrinal Book and Tract Society, 1853; reprint, New York: AMS Press, 1967), 250–51.

25. Ibid., 252.

26. On the role of repentance in Puritan reconversion, see Patricia Caldwell, *The Puritan Conversion Narrative: The Beginnings of American Expression* (New York: Cambridge University Press, 1983).

27. Thomas Shepard, "Means to Submit to Christ," *The Works of Thomas Shepard,* vol. 3 (Boston: Doctrinal Book and Tract Society, 1853; reprint, New York: AMS Press, 1967), 360.

28. Ibid.

29. Ibid.

30. Ibid., 378.

31. Ibid., 382.

32. George Selement and Bruce Woolley, eds., *Thomas Shepard's Confessions* (Boston: Colonial Society of Massachusetts, 1981), 2.

33. See, as examples, *Thomas Shepard's Confessions,* ed. Selement and Woolley, 32, 45–46, 64, 71, 74, 83, 102, 104–5, 108, 112, 120, 122, 158, 162, 185.

34. See, as examples, ibid., 48, 51, 59, 80, 88, 94, 109, 113, 124, 126–27, 154.

35. Cohen has noted that fears about false belief were a typical phase in the Puritan conversion experience, in "Conversion among Puritans and Amerindians," 238; McGiffert has noted the centrality of anxiety regarding false faith in Shepard's writings, in *God's Plot,* 20–21.

36. Shepard, *Works,* vol. 2, 250–51.

37. Regarding "mourning" one's sins, see, as examples, *Thomas Shepard's Confessions,* ed. Selement and Woolley, 36–37, 40, 43, 52, 61, 120, 123–24, 127, 134–35, 143, 149, 153, 166, 180–81, 186, 188.

38. Ibid., 127.

39. For discussions of the communal implications of Puritan conversion, see Cohen, *God's Caress,* and McGiffert, introduction to *God's Plot.*

40. Cogley, *John Eliot's Mission,* 48–51.

41. Perry Miller has noted a general pattern among Puritan ministers of looking for evidence or models of God's will in nature in *The New England Mind,* 166–67, 288.

42. Eliot, "Day-Breaking" (1647), MHSC 3:4 (1834): 4.

43. Multiple authors, epistle dedicatory to "Strength Out of Weaknesse" (1652), MHSC 3:4 (1834): 152.

44. Thomas Mayhew, "Tears of Repentance" (1653), MHSC 3:4 (1834): 207.
45. Eliot, "Tears of Repentance" (1653), MHSC 3:4 (1834): 215.
46. Eliot, MHSC 3:4 (1834), 45–48, 84–86, 128–30, 132–33.
47. Eliot, "Glorious Progress" (1649), MHSC 3:4 (1834): 85; Eliot, "Light Appearing" (1651), MHSC 3:4 (1834): 129.
48. See, as examples, Eliot, "Clear Sun-shine" (1649), MHSC 3:4 (1834): 47, 55; Eliot, "Glorious Progress," MHSC 3:4 (1834): 85.
49. Cohen has noted the orthodoxy of the Indians' articulation of sin in their conversion narratives, although he finds these expressions "formulaic," in "Conversion among Puritans and Amerindians," 246. Robert Naeher notes the centrality of emphasis on sin in Eliot's teaching the Indians' questions, in "Dialogue in the Wilderness: John Eliot and the Indian Exploration of Puritanism," *New England Quarterly* 62 (1989): 351.
50. Eliot, "Day-Breaking" (1647), MHSC 3:4 (1834): 15.
51. Eliot, "Clear Sun-shine" (1648), MHSC 3:4 (1834): 42.
52. Ibid., 49.
53. On the Puritan association of "civility" with "religion," see Cogley, *John Eliot's Mission*, 6–8.
54. Axtell, *The Invasion Within*, 137; James Axtell, *The European and the Indian: Essays in the Ethnohistory of Colonial North America* (New York: Oxford University Press, 1981), 61; Jennings, *Invasion of America*, 239–42, 253; Salisbury, "Red Puritans," 28–29.
55. Cogley, *John Eliot's Mission*, 237–45.
56. Ibid., 42–43.
57. Shepard, "Clear Sun-shine" (1648), MHSC 3:4 (1834): 39.
58. "Clear Sun-shine" (1648), MHSC 3:4 (1834): 25–67; "Light Appearing" (1651), MHSC 3:4 (1834): 101–47; epistle dedicatory, "Strength Out of Weaknesse" (1652), MHSC 3:4 (1834): 158; "Tears of Repentance" (1653), MHSC 3:4 (1834): 197–260.
59. Miller, *New England Mind* (1982), 465, 468.
60. Multiple authors, epistle dedicatory, "Clear Sun-shine" (1648), MHSC 3:4 (1834): 39.
61. Eliot, "Clear Sun-shine" (1648), MHSC 3:4 (1834): 39.
62. Shepard, "Clear Sun-shine" (1648), MHSC 3:4 (1834): 64; J.D., "Glorious Progress" (1649), MHSC 3:4 (1834): 93.
63. On the "lost tribes" theory, see Cogley, *John Eliot's Mission*, 83–85.
64. Richard Mather was an orthodox member of the clergy in Massachusetts Bay colony and a participant in the Antinomian Controversy.
65. Richard Mather, "Tears of Repentance" (1653), MHSC 3:4 (1834): 224.
66. Eliot, "Light Appearing" (1651), MHSC 3:4 (1834): 135.
67. Ibid.
68. Ibid., 136.
69. Ibid., 135.

70. Ibid., 137.

71. Eliot, "An Account of the Indian Churches in New-England" (1673), MHSC 1:10 (1809): 124.

72. Ibid., 127.

73. Ibid., 128.

74. Salisbury, "Red Puritans," 28–54; Naeher, "Dialogue in the Wilderness," 346–68; Morrison, "'That Art of Coyning Christians,'" 77–92; Axtell, "Were Indian Conversions *Bona Fide?*" in *After Columbus: Essays in the Ethnohistory of Colonial North America* (New York: Oxford University Press, 1988), 100–121; Cohen, "Conversion among Puritans and Amerindians," 246.

75. Cohen, "Conversion among Puritans and Amerindians," 246.

76. See, for example, Eliot, "Day-Breaking" (1647), MHSC 3:4 (1809): 9, 13, 16–17, 18; various authors, "Clear Sun-shine" (1649), MHSC 3:4 (1809): 31, 53, 56. In contrast to Shepard's confessors, who—while they may have expressed more anxiety than their counterparts in England (as Patricia Caldwell argues)—only twice reference weeping, and then only as a response to God's mercy, not judgment, see, for example, *Thomas Shepard's Confessions*, ed. Selement and Woolley, 63, 143.

77. Cohen, "Conversion among Puritans and Amerindians," 247–49.

78. *Thomas Shepard's Confessions*, ed. Selement and Woolley, 95, 115, 131; see also 126, 157, 210, 119.

79. Eliot, "Tears of Repentance" (1653), MHSC 3:4 (1809): 230; emphasis in the published edition.

80. Eliot, "Clear Sun-shine" (1649), MHSC 3:4 (1809): 55–56.

81. Ibid., 272.

82. Ibid., 230.

83. Ibid., 232.

84. *Thomas Shepard's Confessions*, ed. Selement and Woolley, 48, 143.

85. As Cohen has noted in "Conversion among Puritans and Amerindians," 252.

86. Mather, "Tears of Repentance" (1653), MHSC 3:4 (1809): 221.

87. Bremer, *The Puritan Experiment*, 107.

88. Morrison, "'That Art of Coyning Christians,'" 88–89; Salisbury, "Red Puritans," 54.

89. Eliot, "Here Followeth a Brief Epitomy" (1658), in "A Further Accompt of the Progresse of the Gospel amongst the Indians in New-England" (London, 1659), 8 (microfilm copy in Early English Books, 1641–1700, reel 491).

90. Ibid., 9.

91. Ibid.

5

Lutherans Meet the Indians

A Seventeenth-Century Conversion Debate

Dennis C. Landis

German Protestant missionaries were in the eighteenth century newcomers to a colonial world where other national groups were well established and Spanish Catholics had been proselytizing for centuries. Spain's New World colonization rights were from 1493 tied to the dissemination of the Christian message, and the technology of printing was harnessed for this objective from the time the first press was established in Mexico City in 1539. The English, the Dutch, and the French all established American missions during the seventeenth century.

Englishmen, plagued to some extent by uncertainties over the suitability of native Americans for conversion, would nevertheless produce great landmarks of missionary literature. Roger Williams's Narraganset vocabularies (1643) and John Eliot's Massachuset Bible (1661) provide fundamental records of those languages.[1] Moreover, English-speaking theologians would, in the course of the seventeenth century, strive to incorporate native American races and the American continent itself into their understanding of Divine plans for the human race. Often their writings were couched in an apocalyptic context, viewing earthly life as near its end. A sense of the cosmic importance of America reached even into metaphysical poetry, prompting George Herbert to warn in *The Temple* that the gospel was poised to depart from England "for the American strand."[2]

In this same period of missionary experimentation by multiple nations—even by Swedes—most Germans remained at home. German missions were scarcely thinkable in the seventeenth century; there were not yet any successful German colonies abroad, and German society was internally disrupted by the Thirty Years' War. It would also seem that the theological underpinnings existed to free German Protestants from any missionary quest. The very idea of mounting world missions is absent from the copious writings of Martin Luther.[3] Luther and his early successors in the canon of Protestant orthodoxy accepted the principle that the biblical injunction to spread the gospel throughout the world had in fact been achieved and the Apostolic Age was past. Setting the tone for the next two centuries, Luther regarded the Apostle Paul as the one responsible for the dissemination of the divine message to the heathen. Christians were taken to be present in the four corners of the world, although the conversion of individual heathens remained as a task to be undertaken modestly at the parish level.[4]

In time, the great orthodox theologians would carefully examine Catholic sources on New World peoples drafted a few decades before, in the sixteenth century. These writings provided a kind of geographical enlightenment and also contained numerous bits of evidence encountered by Spanish explorers and priests, suggesting that folkloric and practical residue of missions long ago persisted in numerous parts of the New World. If the gospel had been carried throughout the Americas but was rejected or forgotten by the indigenous peoples there, then it was argued that European Christians bore no responsibility to propagate the message any further.

Whatever the merits of this comfortable assertion, its validity for German theologians began dissipating soon after the Thirty Years' War ended in 1648. The record of printed books and pamphlets in the mid-seventeenth century establishes that the question of American missions was being taken up afresh. Again under the stimulus of Catholic publications, and those by English and Dutch Protestants, German religious writers were examining the idea that missions should be carried to the American natives. Had not every people been reached?[5] The growing perception that collective terms such as "Indians" and "Americans" masked a host of linguistically distinct populations led to a suspicion that there must surely be vast pockets of territory where the Christian Word had not penetrated. Accepting and incorporating this new information into the long-established canon of theological teachings and understanding its implications for Christian practice was, however, a long and torturous process that would stretch throughout the seventeenth century and a bit beyond.

The Chaos of Dogma

To Catholic writers in the seventeenth century, Protestant theologians inhabited a chaotic environment of independent, undirected thought. Indeed, the absence of a central, controlling authority such as the Vatican meant that Protestant thought would continue unabated for decades on such topics as missions, matters that could have been handily resolved in a short stretch of time through authoritative councils or hierarchical decision making. Protestants indeed held numerous councils that were effective in controlling the spread of a range of movements deemed heretical, but alternative thinking on heathen conversion remained lively. The idea that the gospel might not have reached all the way to the Indies found its way into discussion as early as the 1620s but was not actively treated before 1648.

The discussion of missions occurred within a great framework of the question of the very authority over Christendom itself. Protestants were aware of the vast undertaking mounted by Spanish Catholics in the New World but long remained indifferent to it and regarded this missionary work as but another aspect of failed church leadership. The Catholic Church in Europe was corrupted by worldliness, they thought, and had led its flock into idolatry and habit and away from the personal religious experience that would make the true difference in eternity. Moreover, the Catholic achievement had been marred by a record of human rights abuses that overshadowed whatever superficial advances had been made among the heathen. More positive exemplars of religious truth in the American environment, in the view of continental Protestants, were a handful of English Calvinists whose work in New England had come to their attention: John Eliot, John Cotton, and Thomas Mayhew.[6] Dutch and German writers viewed these spiritual workers as a hopeful sign of mission work that Christians might properly carry out.

To the Catholic perspective, however, the very absence of a missionary program or endeavor was itself essential proof that the Protestants lacked the validity of a universal church. Polemics were directed at the Lutheran Church for its lack of missions, inspiring Lutheran responses throughout the seventeenth century. Cardinal Robert Bellarmine, writing before even the English had made furtive steps toward conversion, ridiculed Protestant assertions of a religious leadership role in the face of Spain's army of priests and its multitudes of converted souls in Mexico, Peru, and other colonies. Because of the cardinal's leadership role in denouncing Protestant presumptuousness, he came to be regarded as the principal exponent of Catholic orthodoxy, and every Protestant theologian who chose to address the need for competitive missions was also compelled to treat the assertions of Cardinal Bellarmine.

Thomas Brightman typified the most extreme English and German responses to Bellarmine's arguments by casting the pope in an apocalyptic context as the reigning Antichrist for the preceding five hundred years, with minions preaching as far abroad as America and the East Indies.[7] Lutherans by and large produced a more measured response to Bellarmine, seizing the opportunity to address individual issues. The first of the many to comment on the Jesuit's charges was Heinrich Eckard, professor at Giessen. His *Pandectis controversiarum religionis inter A.C. Theologos et inter Pontificios* (1611) offered that it was no special monument for the church to have an outpost in every country.[8] Johann Brutscher, a Jesuit in Augsburg, renewed Bellarmine's query through a 1628 letter about the absence of Lutheran missions. Elias Ehinger (1573–1653) responded to it in his 1631 *Velitatio epistolaris* with the prevailing view that no one today had the responsibility that had been entrusted to the apostles. Johannes Müller (1598–1672), pastor of the main church of Saint Peter in Hamburg, laid down the essential story in his *Gründliche Antwort und Widerlegung* (1631): every teacher of the Lutheran Church has his own flock to tend, and it is beyond his calling to go among the heathen. Such missions would be conceivable only for those lacking their own flock. Any mission would have to be duly called into being by the authorities and could proceed only with the spoken word and sacraments, abjuring force. Müller offered that the size of a religious body was not in itself an important issue but that Lutheran countries did in fact cover a substantial territory; moreover, the work by the kings of Denmark and Sweden to Christianize Iceland and Greenland demonstrated that Lutherans had indeed mounted missions.[9] Finally, Müller offered the interesting view that the Lutheran conversion of Catholics also represented a kind of heathen conversion, that church having descended in his assessment into heathen idolatry and misdeeds.

How Far the Gospel?

Martin Chemnitz (1522–1586), who served as mediator between the adherents of Luther and Melancthon, may be viewed as representative of the position that universal preaching had been achieved in ancient times. His *Loci Theologici* (1604), addressing the spread of the gospel, noted that "this doctrine was being proclaimed not so much to the Jews as to all the peoples in the entire world."[10] Chemnitz was writing in advance of José de Acosta's seminal work that—once disseminated in German lands—established the fundamental awareness of distinct American peoples as opposed to a hazy image of heathens living at the borders of civilization. It was in the sixteenth century not yet customary for Protestants to address the question of New World peoples, and it was entirely normal that Chemnitz should omit any mention of America. Not until the 1620s did this issue come even slightly under discussion.

For nearly two hundred years, the view prevailed that the Apostolic Age was over, with no duty existing to disseminate the gospel further.[11] This perception held sway among theological writers from Ägidius Hunnius (1591), *Tractatus de s.s. majestate* (1591), to Ludwig Dunte (Erfurt, 1648) and Christian Eichsfeld in Döbeln (Leipzig, 1655): though not passed on to posterity, the rest of the world had in fact received the message. Konrad Porta, pastor in Eisleben, explained (1591) that preaching to the heathen was a task peculiar to the apostles, essentially delegated to every bishop or churchman (*Pfarrherr*). In elucidating his view that the apostles had borne the gospel throughout the world, Friedrich Balduin cited the testimony of Eusebius and Saint Jerome that no people had been left untouched. Importantly, he noted that lay people may have accomplished this preaching, having been authorized to do so by Luther.[12]

A somewhat different insight came from Philipp Nicolai in his *Historia regni Christi* (Frankfurt, 1624), explaining in chapter 1 of Book 1 that the Word was carried to the four corners of the globe and continues to be carried on, expanded, and developed (*"fortgetrieben, erweitert und ausgebreitet"*). That is, even with mission offices widely established, work remained to be done. The resident authorities were recognized as responsible for religious indoctrination. In the course of time, Lutherans would plow through methodological territory already cultivated by the Spanish fathers in the previous century, such as the crucial question of how the intended subjects would be moved to conversion. Felix Bidembach (1608), Leonhart Hutter (1610), and Georg Dedekennus (1671), writing unspecifically of heathens or with reference to the Turks (in the case of Dedekennus), advocated the use of force to carry out conversion, though Bidembach held back from punishing with execution those who refused to accept conversion. To the contrary, Melchior Sylvester Eckhard (1658) held that it was not reasonable to spread religion with the sword, and similar views were expressed by Johann Conrad Dannhauer (1707).

The first true recognition of a Lutheran duty to conduct formal missions appeared in the lectures of Balthasar Meisner (1587–1626) in Wittenberg, though these remained unpublished until 1679, long past his death. Meisner regarded the absence of missions to heathens, Turks, and Jews as a churchly fault. At this same time, to exercise some control over the chaotic missionary enterprise in the Catholic world, Pope Gregory XV was calling the Congregatio de Propaganda Fidei formally into being (bull of 2 June 1622). Urban VIII followed up by founding the Seminarium in 1627 to provide training to European and native missionaries. However, Georg Calixt stood practically alone among Lutheran churchmen when he acknowledged the necessity of missions in a 1629 speech. Calixt's pathbreaking address, "De populis a nobis in religione dissidentibus," seems to have had little immediate impact and was not published until 1659 (in his son's posthumous edition of selected orations).[13] Calixt propounded the then-remarkable view that it is a duty to convert the heathen to true belief, if one found the opportunity to do it, especially those next door to heathens, and princes with jurisdiction over them had responsibility to do everything in their power. Special emphasis was understandably laid on Muslims and Jews, the non-Christians best known in the German lands. In time others would accept this same view, and it would be well represented among German theologians by the century's end.

Georg Calixt's *Discurs von der wahren Christlichen Religion und Kirchen* (Helmstedt, 1687)—actually written fifty years before and not previously published—sought to undermine the assertion of the universality of the Catholic Church, noting the independence of the Greek, Eastern Orthodox, Armenian, and Abyssinian churches, and suggested that the conversion of Islamic remnants in Spain had been purely superficial. Other nations, he thought, would also break away if freed from the yoke of the Inquisition. Calixt accepted the notion disseminated by Pierre Belon that the Greek and Eastern churches held sway over a far greater territory than did the Roman church.

However, it was in the writing of the foremost articulator of Protestant orthodoxy, Johann Gerhard, that the essential view of American populations would be formed; Gerhard's *Loci theologici* was printed for the first time in 1610–22, remaining in print as late as 1762 and appearing again in the nineteenth century. The widely read Gerhard, building on the work of Nicolai, took a broad range of publications by Catholic writers into his understanding and received from them some appreciation of Amerindian cultures. Reading Acosta, Bartolomé de las Casas, Francisco de Vitoria, Luis de Granada (as well as Antoine Arnauld), and others, he regarded what had been done in Spanish missions as wrong in the extreme: "The method of conversion of the Indians usurped by the Jesuits is plainly frivolous, preposterous, inept, alien, fanciful, ludicrous, tenuous, truculent, violent, ridiculous, childish and finally Simoniacal."[14] This corrupt method of conversion, in Gerhard's view, could not have been approved by the apostles who carried the message into the world; on the contrary, the avarice borne into those distant islands had rendered them alien to the Christian religion.[15]

Gerhard thought the Catholic effort had been a grand blending of good and bad: the modes and doctrines delivered were a mixture both precious and vile, Christian and anti-Christian, apostolic and pseudo-apostolic. What was precious, Christian, and apostolic were the uncorrupted Holy Scripture, the mystery of the Trinity, the Mediation of Christ, baptism, eternal life, and other traditional precepts, whereas the vile, anti-Christian, and pseudo-apostolical—echoing the Protestant perception in Europe—were the papal dogmatism of human tradition, the invocation of saints, the value of works, Purgatory, the primacy of the pope, and so on.

However, Gerhard's judgment on this manner of conversion was also informed by the perception that the Christian message had been heard in America once before. Drawing on a reading of Johannes Goropius (1518–1572) and other authorities, he accepted the view long before disseminated in other parts of Europe that America was that part of the world known to the ancients as Atlantis.[16] The statement in Paul's letter to the Colossians 1:23 and Romans 10:18 that the gospel had been distributed throughout the world was to be taken literally. As reported in Justinian's dialogues, there was no people on earth to whom the name of Christ was not known. In support of this view, Gerhard cited Peter Martyr on Spanish discovery of the use of rites of baptism and circumcision in Mexico; Lery's report that Brazilians knew of the immortality of the spirit and other vestigial remnants of an earlier Christian belief; and Benzoni's remarks concerning knowledge among the Peruvians of immortality, the Flood, and the resurrection of the dead. With the knowledge that Europeans had penetrated distant continents and indeed circumnavigated the entire world, Gerhard accepted the century-old notion propagated by early Portuguese explorers that Saint Thomas had in fact borne the Good News throughout the world.

Finally, Gerhard was compelled to take up the discussion of Cardinal

Bellarmine's attitude toward Lutherans, Cajetanus on the just war, and the cruelties meted out by the Spaniards in the New World; he concluded above all to abjure the use of force to propagate Christianity.

If the salient distinguishing feature of Protestantism in the Reformation era is the direct and individual interpretation of the Bible, then it is entirely fitting that the essential discussion of this subject—whether American natives had been preached to—should find its first serious discussion in a work of biblical exegesis. Johann Quistorp's *Annotationes in omnes libros Biblicos* (1648) takes up this essential question in the section on the letter to the Colossians, chapter 1, focusing on the phrase "Omni creaturae."[17] Publishing in the year of the peace agreement ending the Thirty Years' War, Quistorp asserted that the world to which the letter referred was of course the world known to the ancients; to suggest to the contrary that this had extended to the New World of recent discovery was hyperbolic.[18] Quistorp approached the matter once again in his commentary on the Epistle of Paul to the Ephesians, chapter 4.[19] In his consideration of the relationship between the India known to the ancients and those of the new Indies, he cites the rather modest treatment of this subject in the writings of Philipp Camerarius (*Operae horarum succisivarum*, Centuria 1, cap. 15; Centuria 2, cap. 32–33).[20] Finally, in the passage on Matthew 24, on the phrase "In toto mundo," he reiterates that this is an exaggerated locution like that in Romans 1:8, Colossians 1:6, 1 Timothy 3:16, and elsewhere. The Christian message was not literally carried to the entire globe, merely to the lands known at the time. He cites Strabo and Polybius as further demonstration of the limits of ancient geography.

The view that Americans had already been exposed to the gospel would continue to find expression in standard theologies well after the contrary idea had been introduced. In Wittenberg in 1655, Abraham Calov's *Systema locorum theologicorum . . . Tomus primus [-secundus]* would continue to find in the writings of Acosta and Peter Martyr adequate demonstration that the apostles had introduced the message to America (vol. 1, p. 156), invoking also the confirmation of this in the orthodox example of Philipp Nicolai's *Tractatus de regno Christi*.

But it would be necessary for Protestants to reap the historical lessons of the first century of Spanish missions. The accounts of that hundred years reveal not only the possibility that the residue of Christian teaching still existed in folklore and practice, but also the legacy of native depopulation and enormous suffering. The latter story, reported by Las Casas and others, was perceived as of surpassing importance. Some theologians felt that it was this very suffering that made American natives ideal subjects for conversion.

The question of how far the gospel had been disseminated was widely enough under discussion to require more direct academic focus in the 1660 edition of a dissertation by Georg Moebius.[21] There, on pages 113 to 136 of what was otherwise a treatise already published in 1657 without any mention of America, Moebius undertook to settle this vital question. Moebius drew upon travel accounts such as those of Johann Albrecht von Mandelslo and the compendium of Johann Ludwig Gottfried, by which many of the great travel narratives were disseminated to a German public.[22] The disputation occurred in 1660 in Martisburg. Moebius took up his own reading of Acosta, Peter Martyr, and Hernán Cortés. He lined up in turn each of the major Protestant interpreters of this question, beginning with part 2 of Wendelin's *Exercitationes theologicae*, which assumed that the apostles had penetrated into every land occupied by men, including the distant islands.[23] He pursued the writings of Calvin, Bellarmine, and Valentin Weigel and then came to the important turning point of Johann Quistorp's *Annotationes*, asserting that it was only the then-inhabited world that had received the message. Then he turned to the work of Johann Heinrich Ursinus, which theorized that America at the time of the apostles was scarcely cultivated or inhabited by human beings.[24] Moebius parsed out the assumptions inherent in Ursinus's assertions and noted that the orthodox to a man (Gerhard, Philipp Nicolai, D. Franz, D. Huelsemann, Carpzovius) comprehended universal ancient propagation of the gospel.[25]

However, Moebius took a mental leap not available to theologians by employing the writings of secular authorities in equal measure. Ortelius, for example, wrote that the ocean to the west of Europe was a dangerous realm not navigable by the ancients. Moebius suggested then that there was a gap in truth between these authorities ("*Ergo veritati non est congruum*").[26] He cited Philippus Mornaeus, *De veritate religionis Christianae* (Leyden, 1605, cap. 26, p. 589), on the impossibility of crossing the ocean without the use of the modern invention of the magnetic compass. Taking a sober view of modern geographical knowledge in the mid-seventeenth century, Moebius then asked whether it was believable that the apostles should have been able to cross the ocean and penetrate what appeared to be a vast American continent, notwithstanding Mandelslo's demonstration that it was possible to travel far into Asia on foot.[27] Much the same attitude was represented in the academic dissertation of Valentin Heinrich Voegler (overseen by Friedrich Ulrich Calixt in 1686 in Helmstedt), *De religione Judaica et Judaeurum conversione dissertatio,* which listed the New World and America among those to whom Christ was unknown (p. 44).

Conservative voices continued to counterbalance the impact of these liberal and moderate theorists. Writing in 1677, Johann Adam Osiander was able to draw on still further studies than Moebius—though to different ends—such as Joannes Hoornbeek's *De conversione Indorum & Gentilium* (Amsterdam, 1669, pp. 196–97).[28] Osiander cited John Davenant (Salisbury) on this subject, as well as Pareus in his *Ad Romanos S. Pauli apostoli epistolam Commentarius,* cap. 10, Dubio. 13, also viewing America as little cultivated or inhabited. Osiander cited Spanish authorities on vestiges of Christian belief and relied on Alexander Ross and Georg Horn, who believed that Saint Thomas had gone to Brazil and distributed the Christian message there.

In much the same vein, Johann Andreas Quenstedt, writing in 1715, considered the writings of Marcus Friedrich Wendelin, Daniel Chamier, and Bellarmine, the dissertation of Moebius, and Dannhauer; Quenstedt thought particularly important the assessment of Georg Horn in the reader's preface to his *De origine Americanarum.*[29] Quenstedt remarked that Saint Jerome said about Matthew 24 that there is now no people that does not know the name of Christ (*"Non puto aliquam remansisse gentem, quae Christi nomen ignoret"*). Quenstedt felt that America was known to the ancients and that the gospel had been proclaimed there, citing among others Huelsemann (*Tra. de auxil. grat.,* l. c., p. 145), quoting Horn on the announcement of Christian doctrine in the West. The utter absence of any direct American reference in the *Dissertatio historico-theologica de statu ecclesiae evangelicae* of Samuel Schelguigius (Wittenberg, 1699), a disputation supervised by Quenstedt, demonstrates the persistence of the orthodox Lutheran outlook, there being only a slight reference to Jesuit conversion with Pelagian overtones and atrocities, and America itself being of little importance.

What, then, were the first halting steps toward missions? The earliest undertaking of a German Lutheran mission began in 1632, when the Lübeck jurist Peter Heyling set out from Paris for Abyssinia; however, Abyssinia was acknowledged at this time to be a Christian country.

By contrast, Protestants from Holland and England were mounting very real missionary endeavors. The conception was laid down by Justus van Heurn in *De legatione Evangelica ad Indos capessenda admonitio* (Leyden, 1618). Along with a logical framework justifying missions,

Heurn admonished the secular authorities to take up this cause, and he urged soldiers and sailors not to abuse and alienate the natives. Heurn's plan also called for the translation of materials into the indigenous languages. The missionary training seminar in Leyden (1622–32) mounted by Anton van Wale trained twelve missionaries who were dispatched to the East Indies. As professor in Leyden, Hoornbeek promoted a new missionary effort modeled on the Roman church example, outlined in his *De conversione Indorum & Gentilium*, published just after his death in 1666. However, in methodology he mostly relied on what van Wale had taught.

The Dutch achievements, such as they were, were delivered to a German audience in Willem Tentzel's *Monatliche Unterredungen* from 1694. Tentzel wrote with particular approval of what the English (Eliot, Cotton, Treat) were doing in America.[30]

The English resolve to mount missions had taken earnest form with Parliament's decision in 1647 to start a missionary college; this was undertaken in 1648 with the formation of the Society for the Propagation of the Gospel in New England. The Englishman John Dury tried to arouse interest for missions in Germany in the mid-seventeenth century but did not find support for his plan to utilize merchants to missionize. For the first half of the century, most German thinking rejected the idea of missions; the second half of the century may be characterized as an earnest struggle between opponents and supporters of missions. A council at Wittenberg in 1651 decreed that the command to spread the gospel was a "personal privilege" of the apostles and not passed on to others; the apostolic mission was inextricably of the past.[31] Wolfgang Grössel's thorough study of this subject identified three groups of theologians in the seventeenth century: those who denied any mission duty; those who accepted the duty but felt the time was not yet ripe and who therefore awaited a divine sign; and those who thought missions were absolutely necessary.[32] Dannhauer sided with those who wanted missions to go forward, while others urged patience.

Beyond the theoretical basis, the real controversy may be said to have begun in 1666 by Justinianus von Welz, who challenged German seminarians to undertake a role in missionary work. His first formal invitation to take on missions appeared in *Ein kurtzer Bericht, wie eine newe Gesellschaft auffzurichten wäre unter den rechtgläubigen Christen der Augspurgischen Confession* (ca. 1664). However, the formal call to action came in his *Eine Christliche und treuhertzige Vermahnung an alle rechtgläubige Christen/ der Augspurgischen Confession, betreffend eine sonder-*

bahre Gesellschaft . . . (1664).[33] Welz called upon the German princes to finance this undertaking, but in the climate of understanding that existed, it is understandable that they were unmoved to accept the challenge. Welz proceeded to direct a letter to major theologians, calling for mission agents to be stationed in Paris, London, Amsterdam, Abyssinia, the East Indies, and America.

Mostly positive responses were received, but major resistance came from Superintendent Johann Heinrich Ursinus, who regarded Welz's plan as unworkable. The sense of urgency Welz held regarding the mission endeavor is betrayed by his publication in response, the *Widerholte treuhertzige und ernsthaffte Erinnerung und Vermahnung die Bekehrung . . . vorzunehmen* (Amsterdam, 1664). The tone of this work, a complaint that Welz's entreaties had been ignored, served only to alienate the German theological community further, and Welz left Regensburg. Landing in additional trouble in Germany, including brief imprisonment, the nobleman departed his homeland for good. In Holland, where Reformed missions had a generation-long history, Welz expected to find the merited support. However, the Dutch were also unprepared to undertake his ambitious plan.[34]

Welz's understanding of the need for missions was formed within a millenarian context, sensing a fast-approaching Judgment Day threatening thousands of souls in distant lands. In the absence of help from religious authorities in any country, he felt impelled to assume direct responsibility for missionary work himself. Therefore he arranged to set forth for the Dutch colonies of Surinam and Essequibo in Guiana.[35] However, he was ill-prepared for colonial life, and by the beginning of 1668 he was dead on the river Serena. The letters he directed from Essequibo have been lost since 1748.[36]

Ursinus regarded Welz's planning as inadequate, but Welz for his part thought it dangerous to reveal the details in print lest the Catholic authorities be enabled to subvert the undertaking. From the time Welz left Germany, his cause was taken up by his friend Friedrich Breckling (1629–1711). Breckling was similarly convinced of the need to follow the apostolic example, mindful of the coming end of time and impending thousand-year reign, and began a series of bitter publications in 1664, regretting the lost momentum and seeking to refute the objections of Ursinus. However, his efforts seemed only to harden the orthodox Lutheran resolve that the brief to convert the heathen was long past.

Johann Gerhard (d. 1637) had taken the lead in attacking the assumptions crucial to Welz's thinking (*Loci theologici*, p. 220) by exposing the errors he thought present in the writings of the mission proponents Raymund Caron and Adrian Saravia. Johann Joachim Zentgraf (1643–1707) took it upon himself to refute in 1699 (*De obligatione Evangelicorum*) all the positive claims for missions by Catholic and Reformed theologians; his was one of the few seventeenth-century works exclusively concerned with missions to the heathens.[37] Zentgraf tried to put the matter to rest permanently through this all-encompassing treatise and by establishing that the Apostolic Age was over. Through application of the writings of Grotius, Zentgraf also sought to demonstrate that war on heathens and Christianizing through force were unjustified.[38]

In Ursinus's subsequent *Wiederholte Erinnerung*, he attacked Welz as a hopeless visionary; it was impossible, in the view of Ursinus, to do the customary work of the church and undertake missions at the same time. Attempting to do so would instead be the work of Satan. The journal *Unschuldige Nachrichten* (1702) discusses Ursinus and his assessment of Breckling as a chiliast. Breckling's "Widerlegung der Schrift Joh. Heinrich Ursini" was published in 1666 in his *Synagoga Satanae*. In it Breckling attempted to refute also Ursinus's *Richtiges Zeigerhändlein* (1654), which was an earlier attack on the chiliasm of German enthusiasts, reframing their interpretation of the Book of Revelation in an orthodox manner.

Ursinus did not reject the idea of missions out of hand. In his *Historisch- und theologischer Bericht* (Nuremberg, 1666, first issued in 1663), he reported on the failed mission to America (i.e., the Catholic one). Stepping back for a long view of Christendom, Ursinus laid out a vast historic and mythic panorama in which the preaching of the divine word had overspread the world, maintaining itself in part up to present times. At the same time this mission went forward, however, Satan spread his powerful grip over the "children of unbelief," so that by Ursinus's time he held sway over most of Europe, Asia, Africa, and America, as well as the earth's extreme borders.[39] Ursinus's claim in 1666 of Satanic hegemony over the farthest reaches of the world echoed the view of Thomas Shepard (*The Sincere Convert*, London, 1640) that huge chunks of the world were "covered with a deluge of prophaneness and superstition."

Ursinus viewed this development as a complicated matter. Perhaps the heathen peoples had not accepted the Christian God in the very beginning because of their wild, barbaric state and their "blindness," or they may have pushed it aside, partly because Christians did not concern themselves with the salvation of such peoples, or because the Christians angered them in the highest degree with their internal divisions and unconsidered ways of living among them—which, of course, every reader understood as referring to the Spaniards in America. The Regensburg pastor and superintendent reasonably asked: "Why in justice should the heathens be punished with such horrifying darkness and be set before the thankless Christians as an example of the awful judgment of God?"[40]

Grössel has documented enthusiastic support for Welz's project and a Lutheran missionary effort from several quarters. Among others, Philipp Spener reminded his congregation in a 1677 sermon of the duty to conduct missions.[41] Christian Gerber seems almost a disciple of Welz, his *Unerkannte Sünden der Welt* containing a chapter on "negligence and lethargy" in the promotion of Christianity.[42] And if conservative theologians fell back rather easily on the assertion that foreign missions would exert unreasonable costs for the home church, this issue was finally addressed by Elias Veiel in 1678 (in *Hundert-Jährige Bedencken*), supporting the mission question. Far better, Veiel thought, for the money to be directed to missions abroad than to have been extracted from millions of German subjects for the purposes of war in the decades past. Pointing to the imperative set forth in Isaiah 49, Veiel offered that the putative Christian Lutherans would find damnation at the final court of judgment for their failure to promote the work that they could and should have supported.[43]

A pivotal position was occupied by Johann Amos Comenius (1592–1670), who had begun his missionary thinking in 1644–47, writing *Methodus linguarum novissima*. Comenius had become aware of the Spanish fathers and probably of Acosta's support for the acquisition of native languages in *De procuranda Indorum salute* (lib. iv., cap. vi).[44] Comenius believed in the persuasive power of the Holy Scripture if it could just be provided to the heathens, accessible linguistically. In his "Vorrede an die Europäer," Comenius wrote that the last days were nigh and the Word must be disseminated throughout mankind. Living in Amsterdam, he was aware of Hoornbeek's work and of Saravia and Welz, as well as of the Puritans in New England and the message of Las Casas. His "Panorthosia" delineated how missions were to be sent out everywhere. The fulfillment of Comenius's broad missionary plan would be effected by August Hermann Francke and taken by him into Lutheran missionary thought as a whole.

Pietism has been regarded as the last vital development in religious thinking on the road to a missionary ethos. Francke, the foremost exponent of Protestant missionary thinking, was closely in touch with the New

England Puritans, who had real contact with some of the target populations and were therefore regarded as having some expertise. At the same time, he was a master of the most developed German theory of missions as set forth by Comenius, who in turn had incorporated thinking all the way from the radical theoretical forefront by Welz to the latest practical developments in the field, as discussed in Amsterdam. Inspired by Gottfried Wilhelm Leibniz, Francke drew on all the mission thinking that had been developed to date and set the plans in motion for the work to come.

Regardless of how clearly the path from Luther to the pietists, as laid out by Grössel, is borne out and further delineated by examination of other early theological texts, there was a revisionist effort from the 1930s through the 1950s to establish that Lutherans had, after all, been oriented to missions from the start and had been thwarted by circumstances.[45] Among other arguments, a postwar commentator held that the Lutherans had been caught up in a "two-front war" between papists on one side and enthusiasts on the other and thus had no remaining resources to turn to missions.[46] However, the debate acknowledged and charted in large part by Grössel remains an undeniable chapter in the intellectual history of central Europe and a standard for assessment of the range of theological thinking in this period.[47]

Conclusion

It was in the course of the seventeenth century that European intellectuals truly incorporated the experience of America—in large part colonial Latin America—into their consciousness and work. Isolated thinkers of the sixteenth century may be said to have done this, but of them there were relatively few. Writers in the chiefly Catholic world of southern Europe played a key role in interpreting American history to northern Europe. The wide availability of printed books guaranteed that their witness to the events of the Spanish conquest would be read throughout European civilization among those trained in Latin. Pietro Martire d'Anghiera, Acosta, Las Casas, Garcilasso de la Vega, and Vitoria were among the primary sources for the leading thinkers of the seventeenth and early eighteenth centuries. Their writings were integrated with the existing knowledge of biblical and classical writers to produce a new vision of what had happened in America under the Spaniards, a tragic vision that was meant to serve as a lesson to other Europeans on how civilization should conduct itself.

The practical result of this new thinking by Comenius and others, once the ravaged German lands had been rebuilt and their population in part replenished, was the beginning of Protestant missions by German speakers to India (1706), later to Greenland and the West Indies, and finally to the mainland of South and North America. Thus seventeenth-century German theologians were, despite their remove from the Americas, much like the English. The Germans were also seeking—albeit through a disputatious process—to incorporate the existence of American populations into a system of religious thought and ultimately into a missionary objective. They thus enlivened theological judgements that had seemed fixed and immutable a few decades before.

Some added perspective on this difficult subject may be gained by departing from the works of theologians and considering the assessment of a jurist and historian. Samuel Pufendorf's posthumous *Politische Betrachtung der geistlichen Monarchie des Stuhls zu Rom* (1714) noted how Protestant missionary zeal and industriousness (*"Eifer, Mühe und Industrie"*) near the end of the seventeenth century rivaled the Catholic,[48] but in it Pufendorf regretted the implacable jealousy that afflicted the Protestant nations, preventing unity. Protestant missions differed, he thought, in their effort to expunge Pharisee-like and "jesuitical" notions from all teaching. That Pufendorf should make these observations demonstrates how much the intellectual framework had changed. His other posthumous work, *Heiliges Religions-Recht* (1696), discussed the different times at which the gospel had been delivered and accepted by different peoples.[49] Pufendorf rejected Pierre Jurieu's notion that divine grace had not been granted to the Tartars and Chinese, and he proposed that it was knowable only by God himself when each group would finally accept the gospel, accounting for the great variance in time and circumstance in its acceptance.

Notes

For access to many of the works most useful to this chapter, I am indebted to a fellowship granted by the Herzog August Bibliothek, Wolfenbüttel, Germany. Additional sources were located during fellowships from the William Andrews Clark Library, Los Angeles, and the Huntington Library, San Marino.

1. Roger Williams, *A Key into the Language of America* (London: G. Dexter, 1643); Bible. N.T. Massachuset. Eliot, 1661, *The New Testament . . . Translated into the Indian Language* (Cambridge, Mass.: S. Green and M. Johnson, 1661).

2. George Herbert, "The Church Militant," in *The Temple: Sacred Poems* (Cambridge, Eng., 1633).

3. Martin Luther, *Works,* ed. Jaroslav Pelikan, 55 vols. (St. Louis: Concordia Publishing House, 1955–86).

4. Luther, *Works,* II:184f, XIV:9f, XIV:334n, XIII:342.

5. Complicating this subject further were the competing seventeenth-century Protestant theories that American populations were descended from known peoples in Europe and Asia, who may or may not have received the gospel. Principal theoreticians were Johan de Laet, Hugo Grotius, and Georg Horn.

6. See Johann Berkendal, *Neue Schwarmgeister-Brut. Oder Historische Erzählung . . . V. Die Bekehrung der Indianer in Neu-England* ([Hamburg?], 1661), 220–23.

7. Thomas Brightman, *The Revelation of St. John, illustrated with analysis* (Amsterdam, 1644), 195–240.

8. Heinrich Eckard, *Pandectis controversiarum religionis inter A.C. Theologos et inter Pontificios* (Leipzig, 1611), cap. 8, quaest. 10, 441ff.

9. Johannes Müller, *Gründliche Antwort und Widerlegung* (1631), 17–18.

10. Martin Chemnitz, *Loci Theologici* (1604), vol. 2, 549–91. "Porrò quia doctrina illa praedicanda erat, non tantùm Judaeis, sed omnibus gentibus in universo terrarum orbe" (554).

11. The essential study of this subject remains that of Wolfgang Grössel, first published as a dissertation, *Die Stellung der lutherischen Kirche Deutschlands zur Mission im 17. Jahrhundert* (Leipzig, 1895), and then as a monograph, *Die Mission der evangelischen Kirche im 17. Jahrhundert* (Gotha, 1897).

12. Cf. Martin Luther, *Das eynn Christliche versamlu[n]g oder gemeyne: recht un[d] macht habe: alle lere zu urteylen; unnd lerer zu beruffen: eyn unnd abtzusetzen* (Wittenberg, 1523).

13. Georg Calixt, *Orationes selectae* (1659; reprint, Helmstedt: H. Müller, 1660).

14. Johann Gerhard, *Locorum theologicorum tomus undecimus* (Tübingen: J. G. Cotta, 1772), 282. "Modus convertendi Indos a Jesuitis usurpatus est plane frivolus, praeposterus, ineptus, alienus, umbratilis, ludicrus, tenuis, truculentis, violentis, ridiculus, puerilis ac denique simoniacus."

15. Johann Gerhard, *Locorum theologicorum. . . . Tomus primus [-nonus]* (Geneva: P. Gamonet, 1639), lib. v, 354.

16. Ibid., 355.

17. Johann Quistorp, *Annotationes in omnes libros Biblicos* (Frankfurt and Rostock, 1648), pt. 2, 348.

18. Ibid. "Verum quum ex indiciis non obscuris colligatur, nunquam Evangelium in novo ut apellatur orbe, ante nuperam hujus partis terrae detectionem praedicatum fuisse. Videntur tum Apostoli, tum Patrum in toto orbe praedicatum esse Evangelium, asserentia dicta accipienda esse vel de orbe tum cognito, vel hyperbolice. Quemadmodum de Romanis Apostolus scribit, eorum fidem annunciari in toto mundo, Rom. I, 8. obedientiam corundē–omnibus innotuisee, Rom. 16, 19."

19. Ibid., 337, v. 28.

20. The views of Camerarius were well distributed, from the first edition at

Nuremberg in 1591 through five Frankfurt editions up to 1658. For listings, see John Alden, *European Americana: A Chronological Guide*, 6 vols. (New York and New Canaan: Readex, 1980–97), v. 1–3.

21. Georg Moebius, *Tractatus philologico-theologicus de oraculorum ethnicorum origine.... Dissertationes duae philologico-theologicae.... Altera tractat quaestionum illam An Evangelium ab Apostolis etiam Americanis fuerit annunciatum?* (Leipzig: J. Wittigau, 1660).

22. Johann Ludwig Gottfried, *Newe Welt und Americanische Historien* (Frankfurt a.M.: M. Merian, 1631).

23. Marcus Friedrich Wendelin, *Exercitationes theologicae vindices* (Cassel: S. Schadewitz, 1652).

24. "Americam iis temporibus, quibus Apostoli mundo annunciarunt Evangelium, ab hominibus minime fuisse cultam, aut habitam" (Johann Heinrich Ursinus as cited in Moebius, *Tractatus philologico-theologicus de oraculorum ethnicorum origine*, 118–19).

25. Ibid., 121–22.

26. Ibid., 129.

27. Moebius was referring to Johann Albrecht von Mandelslo's *Morgenländische Reisebeschreibung* (Hamburg, 1658), which appeared in various editions.

28. Johann Adam Osiander, *Dissertatio de jubilaeo Ebraeorum, Christianorum, Academicorum* (Tüebingen: J. G. Cotta, 1677).

29. Johann Andreas Quenstedt, *Theologica didactico-polemica, sive Systema theologicum, in duas sectiones* (Leipzig: T. Fritsch, 1715).

30. Willem Tentzel, ed., *Monatliche Unterredungen einiger guten Freunde ... 1694* (Leipzig: J. T. Fritsch, 1694), 713–21.

31. *Consilia theologica Vitembergensia, d.i. Wittenbergische geistl. Ratschläge Lutheri* (Frankfurt a.M., 1664).

32. Grössel, 94–95.

33. Justinianus von Welz, *Eine Christliche und treuhertzige Vermahnung an alle rechtgläubige Christen/ der Augspurgischen Confession, betreffend eine sonderbahre Gesellschaft....* (n.p., 1664). A second edition appeared at Halberstadt in 1666, but the work is best known from a Leipzig 1890 reprint.

34. In *Monatliche Unterredungen ... 1694* (p. 719), Tentzel notes the atmosphere of opprobrium met by mission enthusiasts in Reformed circles, despite notable Dutch achievements in the field. Another correspondent cited by Tentzel wondered, "daß man unter uns Lutheranern nicht auch Leute ausschickt, die Heyden, Türcken und Jüden zu bekehren, da wir eine solche Menge *Studiosos Theologiae* auf allen Universitäten haben."

35. The degree of millennial angst experienced by Welz is unique to him among Lutherans, though present to a lesser extent of personal commitment among his close supporters. A similar level of enthusiasm had occurred earlier in the century, however, with a Calvinist Fleming named Jan van Avontroot. A merchant based on the Canary Islands who came in contact with native Americans in South America,

Avontroot was impelled to have printed in 2,000 copies a "letter to the Peruvians" which he attempted to distribute, along with the Heidelberg Catechism. Spanish colonial authorities took possession of them upon arrival, and Avontroot was ultimately burned at the stake. A Dutch version of the letter survives as *Sendt-brief aen die van Peru* (Amsterdam: P.A. van Ravesteyn, 1630). Quite different circumstances prevailed for those enabled to undertake a supported mission among the Indians, as exemplified by Vincent Soler's *Cort ende sonderlingh Verhael van eenen brief van Monsieur Soler, bedienaer des H. Evangelij inde Ghereformeerde Kercke van Brasilien* (Amsterdam: B. de Preys, 1639). A Calvinist missionary in Dutch Brazil, Soler declared in the letter that he had never felt better in his life and was hard at work on the salvation of the Brazilian Indians, whom he thought promising, guilty only of the sins of drunkenness and dancing.

36. Essential details on Welz's short career are conveyed by Wolfgang Grössel's mission history cited previously, and in particular by his monograph, *Justinianus von Welz: der Vorkämpfer der lutherischen Mission* (Leipzig: Faber, 1891).

37. Johann Joachim Zentgraf, *De obligatione evangelicorum ministrorum praedicandi evangelium per terras infidelium* (Strasbourg: Spoor, 1699).

38. Johann Joachim Zentgraf, praeses, *De Europaeorum ad Indorum regiones jure . . . respondebit Joh. Paulus Silberrad* (Strasbourg, 1689).

39. Johann Heinrich Ursinus, *Historisch- und theologischer Bericht vom Unterschied der Religionen heutiges Tags auf Erden* (Nuremberg, 1663), p. 6 §6.

40. My translation from ibid., p. 6 §7: "Worum denn die Heiden mit solcher greulichen Finsternis von Rechts wegen gstraft und den undankbaren Christen zum Exempel des erschröcklichen Gerichts Gottes vor Augen gestellet werden."

41. See Grössel, 96.

42. Christian Gerber, "Von der Nachlässigkeit und Schlafsucht in Ausbreitung und Förderung des Reiches Christi und seiner Ehre," *Unerkannte Sünden der Welt* (Dresden, 1699), chap. 105.

43. Elias Veiel, *Hundert-Jährige Bedencken* (Ulm, 1678), 100ff. and 137.

44. Heinrich Geissler, "Johann Amos Comenius als Wegbereiter evangelischen Missionsdenkens," *Evangelische Missions-Zeitschrift* 14 (1957): 74–82.

45. See Walter Holsten, *Das Evangelium und die Völker: Beiträge zur Geschichte und Theorie der Mission* (Berlin-Friedenau, 1939); Wilhelm Maurer, "Die lutherische Kirche und ihre Mission," *Lutherisches Missionsjahrbuch* (1953–54): 22–50.

46. Maurer, "Die lutherische Kirche und ihre Mission."

47. Hans-Werner Gensichen, *Missionsgeschichte der neueren Zeit. Dritte, verbesserte, und ergänzte Auflage* (Göttingen: Vandenhoek and Ruprecht, 1976), 12.

48. Samuel Pufendorf, *Politische Betrachtung der geistlichen Monarchie des Stuhls zu Rom* (Halle: Renger, 1714), 356.

49. Samuel Pufendorf, *Heiliges Religions-Recht* (Frankfurt a.d.O.: J. Völcker, 1696), 398ff.

6

Dutch Calvinism and Native Americans

A Comparative Study of the Motivations for Protestant Conversion among the Tupís in Northeastern Brazil (1630–1654) and the Mohawks in Central New York (1690–1710)

Mark Meuwese

In an official report written for the directors of the Dutch West India Company (WIC) in January 1638, the governor-general of Dutch-controlled northeastern Brazil Johan Maurits and his councilors observed that the local Tupí-speaking Indian peoples had recently requested Protestant ministers to instruct their people in Calvinist principles and educate their children in reading and writing. Maurits and his officials were especially delighted that the Indians had driven the Portuguese Jesuit missionaries from their villages. The WIC officials enthusiastically noted that the Tupís "have expelled the papists from their communities themselves"; further, "They ask us frequently for our preachers, and wish for nothing better than one or two ministers to be sent among them who would communicate with them and instruct them and baptize their children and marry their young folk."[1]

Similarly, in 1690, the Dutch Reformed Church council in Albany, New York, wrote to the Amsterdam Classis, or church organization, in the United Provinces that "much to the astonishment of everybody," the local minister Godfried Dellius had made dramatic success in converting the nearby Mohawk Indians to Protestant Christianity. Dellius' progress was "astonishing" because successive Dutch Calvinist ministers had been unsuccessful in bringing the gospel to the Mohawks. Ever since the WIC had established a colonial government in New Netherland in the early 1620s, some well qualified and some less qualified Protestant missionaries had attempted to bring Protestant Christianity to the Mohawks who lived west of Albany. Despite several decades of close Dutch-Mohawk interactions based upon cross-cultural trade, the Calvinist church of the Dutch communities in the upper Hudson valley had failed to make any documented progress among the Mohawks by the time of the English conquest of New Netherland in 1664. However, in the late 1680s many Mohawks suddenly became interested in the Dutch Reformed religion. From 1691 to 1710, Calvinist ministers baptized no less than 170 Mohawk men, women, and children at the Dutch Reformed church in Albany.[2]

Scholars of Dutch-Indian relations in northeastern Brazil and North America have treated the Dutch Protestant evangelization programs among the Tupís in northeastern Brazil (1630–54) and the Mohawks in central New York (1690–1710) as separate historical events. This is unfortunate because a comparative study of Tupí and Mohawk responses to Dutch Calvinist missionaries reveals that there were significant similarities as well as differences. In pursuing a comparative approach I show that the missionary program of the Dutch Reformed Church was much more extensive in colonial Brazil than in colonial New York. At the same time, by analyzing the natives' attraction to Dutch Calvinism I argue that both the Tupís and the Mohawks converted to Protestant Christianity to strengthen political and economic alliances with the Dutch. Furthermore, Dutch Calvinism appealed to Tupí and Mohawk converts because it emphasized the written word in evangelization. By adopting literacy, the Tupís and Mohawks were consequently better equipped to deal with the challenges created by European colonialism. Finally, despite their conversion to Protestant Christianity, many Tupís and Mohawks continued practicing not only their traditional religious beliefs, but also aspects of Catholicism that they had adopted earlier from Jesuit missionaries.[3]

For practical purposes, in this chapter I have defined the ambiguous term *conversion* as the process in which one individual or group adopts a new set of religious beliefs without necessarily giving up previously established religious practices or worldviews. By allowing for the persistence of earlier developed spiritual beliefs and traditions among American Indians, I argue that conversion was not a sudden break with the past but rather an integral part of the creative responses by which indigenous peoples accommodated European expansion.[4]

Contrary to traditional scholarly interpretations of the Dutch Reformed Church as not interested in overseas evangelization, the orthodox Protestant church in the United Provinces during the first half of the seventeenth century was sincerely concerned with bringing the gospel to non-European peoples. After the Dutch Reformed Church had established itself as the most powerful and privileged religious denomination in the Dutch Republic by the early 1600s, an influential faction of hard-line Calvinists began to call for the implementation of orthodox Protestant morals in the United Provinces.[5]

Although this radical faction within the Calvinist church was primarily interested in purifying Dutch society, it was also concerned with spreading the gospel among non-Christian peoples. In their quest to evangelize non-European peoples and societies, the militant Dutch Calvinists were strongly motivated by a belief in the universal character of the Protestant church. According to this ideology, Calvinism was the only true religion and to honor God it was the duty of every Calvinist to evangelize all the peoples on earth. It is important to realize that the Dutch Reformed Church wanted to evangelize not only among Catholics, Lutherans, and Jews, but also among Muslims, Buddhists, Hindus, and the practitioners of any other religion that was not based on the principles of Calvinism. According to Dutch Calvinists, all these "blind heathens" had to be brought into the "light of the true Christian religion." This aggressive missionary ideology also had strong millenarian overtones because the militant Calvinists believed that the conversion of non-Christians across the world would directly lead to the return of Christ to earth.[6]

The interest of the Dutch Reformed Church in the evangelization of the Brazilian and North American Indians was clear from the early years of the WIC's existence. The States General, the assembly of representatives of the seven United Provinces that made up the Dutch Republic, chartered the WIC in 1621 as a hybrid between a trade company and a military organization. One of the main tasks of the WIC was to extend the Dutch war against Spain to Spain's overseas possessions in the Atlantic world. In a number of Calvinist sermons the company was called upon to use its recently gained profits for spreading Protestantism among the indigenous peoples of the Americas. After the WIC had captured Salvador de Bahia, the capital of Portuguese Brazil, in 1624, the prominent minister Willem Teellinck published a sermon that called upon the newly chartered company to set up an extensive missionary program among the native peoples of Brazil. In Dutch North America the missionary zeal was less pronounced but still important. In 1625, company officials instructed Willem Verhulst, the first director of New Netherland, to be mindful "that the Indians be instructed in the Christian religion out of God's Holy Word."[7]

One important similarity between the Protestant evangelization program in Brazil and that in New Netherland is the emphasis on education and literacy. The Calvinist church in the United Provinces looked down upon Catholic missionary strategies such as group baptisms and instead concentrated on evangelization programs that would enable potential converts to better understand and learn the word of God as it was written down in the Bible. For instance, the Dutch Reformed Church was instrumental in supporting an extensive school system in the United Provinces, making it one of the most literate societies of early modern Europe.[8]

This emphasis on fostering literacy was also extended to indigenous peoples. Like other European Protestants at the time, Dutch Calvinists believed that all human beings were capable of receiving the word of God. But because the word of God could be properly understood only by reading the Bible, Dutch Calvinists consequently saw reading and writing as primary tools for the evangelization of the native societies. Moreover, as instruction in the Dutch language posed formidable barriers for non-European peoples, Dutch Calvinists supported educational materials that were written in the Indians' own languages or in regional trade languages that were widely spoken by native peoples.[9]

As a result, in both northeastern Brazil and colonial New York, Calvinist missionaries developed educational tracts that were partly or completely written in the native languages. In Brazil, several Calvinist missionaries developed a catechism that was written in Tupí-Guaraní, a widely used native language. The catechism was also written in Portuguese, a language that many of the coastal natives understood because of their extensive contacts with Jesuit missionaries. For their part, Dutch Calvinist preachers working among the Mohawks during the late seventeenth and early eighteenth centuries constructed missionary pamphlets that were written in the Iroquoian Mohawk language. Finally, in both Brazil and New York, Protestant preachers and schoolteachers organized schools in which Indian children were instructed in reading and writing.[10]

Despite the active interest of the Dutch Reformed Church in the conversion of indigenous peoples, the missionary program in Brazil and New York was plagued by several structural problems. First, religious personnel in the two colonies were often badly paid by their WIC employer. The company usually hired Calvinist ministers and other religious instructors for a period of several years. However, the WIC was notoriously slow in compensating its employees, and after 1645 the company was practically bankrupt because of the costly invasion of Brazil. Although the WIC attempted to shift the responsibilities for paying the salaries of the Calvinist ministers to local colonists, Dutch settlers were often unwilling or unable to provide salaries for their ministers, lay-preachers, and schoolteachers. When Calvinist preachers—many of whom traveled to Brazil and colonial New York with their families—realized that they were not well paid, a considerable number of them returned to the Dutch Republic once their contracts with the WIC expired.[11]

Another structural problem was the tendency of Calvinist church leaders in the republic to keep a tight ideological grip on missionary activities in the colonies. Whenever ministers or lay-preachers in Brazil or colonial New York deviated from the official line of Calvinist preaching, they were reprimanded or even recalled by their superiors in the republic. For instance, when several Calvinist missionaries in Brazil translated a catechism from Dutch into the Tupí language, their church superiors in Amsterdam prohibited the printing and distribution of this catechism because the missionary text did not follow Calvinist orthodoxy closely enough. Likewise, when the minister Bernardus Freeman developed a rudimentary form of written Mohawk to aid the missionary work among these Indians during the early eighteenth century, the Amsterdam church council remained unsupportive of Freeman simply because he was not a university-trained minister.[12]

Yet another similarity between the evangelization programs in the two colonies is that in both Brazil and New York, Dutch Reformed Church personnel had to fulfill multiple tasks beyond the evangelizing of native peoples. Contrary to the Catholic Church in Spanish, Portuguese, and French America, the relatively new Dutch Calvinist church did not have separate religious orders that concentrated on the conversion of indigenous peoples. Instead, Calvinist personnel in Brazil and New York were expected to both administer religious services to European Protestants and spread the gospel among followers of other religions. Because the populations of colonial Brazil and New York consisted of multiple non-Calvinist religious minorities such as Portuguese Catholics and Sephardic Jews in Brazil and Lutherans and Quakers in New York, evangelization of the indigenous peoples in the two colonies was only one of the many tasks for the Calvinist ministers and lay-preachers in both colonies. Furthermore, Calvinist ministers were also expected to evangelize the African slave population in both colonies.[13]

Along with these similarities, there are also differences between the orthodox Protestant church in Brazil and that in North America. The most important difference is that northeastern Brazil was a much more popular destination for Calvinist ministers and lay-preachers than North America. According to recent studies, no less than fifty-three fully ordained or candidate ministers were active in Brazil during the relatively short period between 1625 and 1654, whereas only twelve Calvinist ministers were employed in New Netherland between 1628 and 1674. In addition, a significant reflection of the importance of the evangelization program among the Tupís is that several ministers in colonial Brazil were employed as full-time missionaries among the Indians. This is in marked contrast to New Netherland and colonial New York, where Calvinist ministers could devote only a limited amount of time to the conversion of American Indians. Although the number of Calvinist ministers in colonial New York did increase after the English conquest of New Netherland, the number of church personnel sent out by the Dutch Reformed Church in the United Provinces remained small in comparison to Brazil. Significantly, during the peak of the Dutch Calvinist missionary program among the Mohawks from 1690 to 1715, only one or at the most two ministers at a time were employed in the Dutch communities of Albany and Schenectady in the upper Hudson valley.[14]

The discrepancy in the number of ministers in Brazil and New York can best be explained by the role of anti-Catholicism among the Dutch Reformed clergy during the first half of the seventeenth century. Because the Catholic Church was the archenemy of the Calvinists, Dutch Protestants sought to defeat the hated papists anywhere across the globe. Because the Catholic Church held a prominent position in the overseas Iberian empires, Dutch Calvinists hoped that the WIC's campaigns against Spain's overseas empire in the Atlantic would weaken the power of the Catholic Church. Because the Spanish Crown had incorporated Portugal and its overseas colonies into its empire in 1580, Dutch Calvinist hard-liners considered Portuguese Brazil a legitimate target. When the WIC invaded northeastern Brazil in the late 1620s, Dutch Calvinist ministers were therefore eager to replace the Catholic Church in Brazil.[15]

This anti-Catholicism was also extended to the coastal Tupí Indian peoples whom the Calvinist ministers encountered in Brazil. When the Dutch arrived in Brazil, they came in contact with the Tupí-speaking Indians who lived in mission villages that had been established there by the Jesuits in the second half of the sixteenth century. Because Dutch Calvinists strongly detested the Jesuits, converting the Catholic Tupí Indians to Protestantism was seen as an important and prestigious task for the Dutch

Reformed Church. Ironically, these same fiercely anti-Catholic Calvinist preachers found it convenient to use the infrastructure of the Catholic mission villages to convert the Tupí Indians more effectively. Like their Catholic counterparts, Dutch Protestant missionaries not only wished to convert the Indians to Christianity but also attempted to transform the "savage" Tupís into civilized and sedentary peoples. By placing the natives in fixed agricultural settlements, both Catholic and Protestant missionaries hoped to accomplish the spiritual and the cultural conversion of Native Americans.[16]

In contrast to the Calvinist anti-Catholicism in Brazil, the Dutch Reformed Church lacked any similar ideological incentives for the evangelization of Indians in North America. Instead, the mid-Atlantic region of North America was colonized by the fellow Protestant nation-states of England and, to a lesser extent, Sweden. Moreover, the various Algonquian- and Iroquoian-speaking native peoples there had not yet been exposed to Christian missionaries by the time of Dutch contact in the early 1600s. Surprisingly, the presence of Jesuit missionaries in nearby French Canada did not lead Dutch Calvinists to consider North America as equally important missionary terrain as northeastern Brazil. On the contrary, relations between the Dutch and the Jesuits in North America were generally peaceful. Dutch Calvinists probably considered the Jesuits in French North America less of a threat than the Jesuits in Brazil because the latter were closely associated with the Spanish Crown. Moreover, whereas the Jesuits had already established an extensive missionary program in colonial Brazil since the mid-sixteenth century, French Jesuits had only recently undertaken missionary activities in Canada.[17]

A second major difference between the Dutch Reformed Church in Brazil and that of colonial New York is that the Calvinist church was expelled from northeastern Brazil after the WIC surrendered its colony to the Portuguese in 1654, whereas the Reformed Church was able to continue its religious activities after the English conquest of New Netherland in 1664. After ten years of brutal and vicious warfare, the Portuguese colonists forced the Dutch from Brazil in January 1654. Following the official WIC surrender, the ambitious Calvinist evangelization program among the Tupí Indians abruptly ended. Although the Tupís continued to practice Protestant rituals for several decades, by the early eighteenth century the Portuguese Crown, the Catholic Church, and Portuguese colonists had aggressively suppressed any sign of Protestantism among the native peoples in northeastern Brazil.[18]

In contrast, the English Crown permitted the Dutch Reformed Church to hold public services and evangelization work in New York after 1664. To avoid resentment among the thousands of Dutch Protestant colonists who had remained in mid-Atlantic North America after the English conquest, New York colonial officials granted religious freedom to the Calvinist church. The Dutch Reformed Church therefore continued to be an influential cultural and religious force in New York throughout the colonial period.[19]

Before discussing the Indian motives for converting to Dutch Calvinism, I think it is important to outline the traditional beliefs of the Tupís and the Mohawks. Both were deeply spiritual peoples for whom religion was an integral part of their everyday lives. The Tupís and the Mohawks believed in prominent deities as well as spirits that inhabited the inanimate and animate world. These beliefs were expressed in ceremonies and ritual practices that permeated the daily lives of Tupís and Mohawks. Although both peoples lacked a specific group of ordained religious specialists, shamans were influential individuals in the daily lives of the Tupís and Mohawks. Shamans were held in great awe and respect because of their purported supernatural powers to heal sick and afflicted people. At the same time, the shamans were greatly feared for their ability to bewitch and even kill individuals.[20]

The traditional beliefs of the Tupís and Mohawks were greatly shaken by several crises brought on by European colonialism. Of these crises, newly introduced diseases had perhaps the most disastrous impact upon Indian peoples. Without prior exposure to Old World diseases such as smallpox and influenza, native populations throughout the Americas declined dramatically once these diseases were introduced among them. Native depopulation was especially high in coastal Brazil, where the Tupís suffered from several epidemics of smallpox that had been inadvertently introduced by Portuguese colonists and their African slaves during the sixteenth century. Upon arriving in Brazil in the early 1630s, WIC officials consequently encountered heavily depopulated Tupí communities. Similarly, the Mohawk communities west of the upper Hudson valley suffered tremendously from a series of epidemic diseases throughout the seventeenth century.[21]

Because traditional healing practices such as curing rites by shamans proved ineffective in preventing the spread of unknown contagious diseases, some Tupís and Mohawks became attracted to the ceremonies of Jesuit missionaries in the hope that the spiritual power of the Christian God would protect them from further afflictions. By adopting Catholic rituals such as baptisms and communion, Tupí and Mohawk individuals hoped to find solace and ward off more devastating epidemics. Although most Tupís and Mohawks continued to hold onto their traditional beliefs and to revere the spiritual powers of their shamans, they integrated many ritualistic aspects of Catholicism into their daily lives.[22]

In addition to diseases, colonial exploitation and warfare were also major factors in persuading the Tupís and Mohawks to adopt Catholicism. After private ventures had largely failed to develop a viable Portuguese colony on the Brazilian coast during the early sixteenth century, the Portuguese Crown dispatched royal officials and members of the newly founded Jesuit order to Brazil in the 1550s to strengthen the fledgling colony. Upon arriving in Brazil, the Jesuits quickly clashed with the colonists over the issue of Indian slavery. While the Jesuits wanted to abolish Indian slavery and integrate the coastal Tupís as Christian peasants into colonial society, Portuguese colonists increasingly relied on enslaved Tupís to fulfill the ever-growing demand for labor on the sugar plantations. Although the Jesuits never did fully succeed in abolishing Indian slavery, support from prominent royal officials enabled the Jesuits to establish an extensive system of *aldeias* or mission villages throughout coastal Brazil. Because these mission villages offered protection from slave raids and allowed the Indians to cultivate their primary food source (manioc) on a communal basis, a considerable number of Tupís subsequently converted to Catholicism and resettled in the *aldeias* during the second half of the sixteenth century.[23]

Like the Tupís, many Mohawks converted to Catholicism in the wake of European contact. Soon after the establishment of New France in the St. Lawrence valley and the founding of Dutch New Netherland along the Hudson valley during the early seventeenth century, the Mohawks became actively involved in a complicated and multisided contest for power in the region. On one side were the French and their Indian allies such as the Hurons and many Algonquian-speaking Indians. On the other side were the Mohawks and their Iroquoian neighbors the Senecas, Cayugas, Onondagas, and Oneidas. These five Indian peoples had formed the Iroquois League of peace and friendship, which predated the arrival of Europeans.

Because of their close proximity to the Dutch communities in the upper Hudson valley, the Mohawks were able to obtain large amounts of manufactured goods such as firearms from the Dutch in return for beaver pelts.

However, the Mohawks soon became involved in a deadly competition for beaver furs with the Hurons and other Indian peoples who were closely allied with the French. Moreover, because epidemic diseases had depopulated many Mohawk villages, the Mohawks sought to counter their losses by incorporating peoples from other native groups into their communities. Although the Mohawks and the other peoples of the Iroquois League were temporarily successful in dominating the fur trade and replenishing their numbers by forcibly adopting the defeated Hurons into their midst, by the 1650s the French and their Indian allies began to successfully counter Iroquois expansion. Especially devastating for the Mohawks were several French campaigns during the late 1660s that resulted in the destruction of several Mohawk villages and their agricultural fields. To avoid further destructive French attacks, some Mohawk leaders welcomed French Jesuits and converted to Catholicism. Ironically, recently adopted Huron captives who had been baptized by Jesuit missionaries before being forcibly incorporated into the Iroquois League were especially supportive of the activities of Jesuit missionaries in Mohawk villages.[24]

Although a considerable number of Mohawks converted to Catholicism for spiritual and diplomatic reasons, they were at first not attracted to the Protestant religion of their Dutch neighbors of the upper Hudson valley. The Mohawks remained indifferent to Dutch Calvinism because Mohawk-Dutch relations were primarily shaped by practical considerations. Although the Mohawks were in frequent contact with Dutch colonists to exchange animal hides for manufactured goods, the Mohawks were not interested in the Calvinist religion of their Dutch trade partners. As we have seen, the Dutch Reformed Church was unconcerned with the conversion of North American Indians. In addition, because New Netherland was not a popular destination for ministers compared to Brazil, the Dutch Reformed Church lacked enough personnel to convert the Indians in New Netherland. One Calvinist preacher who did try to convert the Mohawks during the early 1640s quickly encountered Mohawk indifference.[25]

Despite the early hesitance of many Tupís and Mohawks to convert to Protestantism, in contrast to Catholicism, a considerable segment of these native peoples did become attracted to Dutch Calvinism. Like earlier Indian converts to Catholicism, some Tupís and Mohawks were drawn to Protestantism to spiritually revitalize their individual lives. Living on the margins of their native communities, these persons embraced Protestant Christianity to obtain new spiritual power in a time of demographic, political, and economic crises. Moreover, some Tupís and Mohawks converted to Dutch Calvinism to strengthen political and economic ties with Dutch colonists. By adopting Protestant Christianity the Tupís and Mohawks sought to foster alliances with the Dutch in the face of increasing pressure by, respectively, the Portuguese and the French.[26]

Tupí and Mohawk leaders and headmen played a prominent role in persuading their kinsmen to adopt Protestant Christianity. The Tupí envoys who visited the Dutch Republic from 1625 to 1630 provide a good example of the important function of indigenous leaders in the process of Indian conversion to the Reformed religion. Although many Tupís in Brazil sided with the Portuguese against the Dutch invaders, a considerable number of Indian communities desired to establish an anti-Portuguese alliance with the WIC. While the Tupís in the sugar provinces of Bahia and Pernambuco remained generally loyal to the Portuguese, the Tupí inhabitants of the relatively underdeveloped frontier provinces of Paraíba and Rio Grande showed the most enthusiasm for a Dutch alliance. By the time of the Dutch invasion, Portuguese soldiers and colonists had only recently subjugated most of the Tupí-speaking Potiguars of Paraíba and Rio Grande in a series of brutal frontier wars. When a WIC fleet visited the coast of Paraíba in the spring of 1625, many members of the Tupí-speaking Potiguars welcomed the Dutch as allies in their ongoing war against the Portuguese colonizers.

To foster an alliance with the Dutch visitors, a group of Potiguar leaders accompanied the company fleet back to the United Provinces. During their five-year stay in the republic, the handful of Potiguar visitors learned the Dutch language and provided the WIC with a considerable amount of intelligence for a future invasion of Brazil. Moreover, to foster the alliance with their Dutch hosts, the Potiguar leaders were "instructed in the principles of the Christian religion" and adopted Dutch Calvinism. After the successful Dutch invasion of northeastern Brazil in the early 1630s, the Potiguar envoys returned to their native communities, where they became important mediators between the Dutch and the Tupís. The Potiguar leaders also continued to identify with Protestant Christianity as a sign of their close ties with the Dutch.[27]

Like the Tupís, some Mohawks also converted to Dutch Calvinism for political reasons. After the devastating raids by the French in the 1660s, some Mohawk leaders increasingly looked toward the colony of New York as an ally. Although the Mohawks had established a "Covenant Chain" or diplomatic alliance with New York colonial officials soon after the English conquest of New Netherland in 1664, this alliance was often ineffective in preventing the French and their Indian allies from attacking the Mohawks.

Moreover, the ongoing migration of pro-French Mohawks to Jesuit mission towns near Montreal steadily eroded the authority and influence of the anti-French Mohawk headmen. To foster a closer alliance with New York and to offset the continuing movement of Catholic Mohawks to Jesuit missions, several anti-French Mohawk leaders appealed to the English colonial authorities in New York in 1691 to evangelize their people. Since the colonial communities on the Upper Hudson Valley were still dominated by Dutch Protestant colonists, English colonial officials encouraged local Dutch Calvinist ministers to evangelize the nearby Mohawks.[28]

In converting to Dutch Calvinism, the Mohawk leaders not only expected to obtain more military support from colonial New York, but also hoped to divert those Mohawks with an interest in Christianity to the Dutch Reformed religion rather than to French Catholicism. As a result of this political strategy, Dutch Calvinist preachers baptized a considerable number of Mohawk men and women during the 1680s and 1690s. Some of the Reformed ministers who worked among the Mohawks were well aware of their strategic role as agents of the English colonial empire. Although the Reformed Church in the Dutch Republic had strictly prohibited the baptism of non-Christians before they had shown an adequate knowledge of the Christian catechism, local Calvinist preachers such as Godfridius Dellius neglected these stringent guidelines to ensure that potential Mohawk converts would not turn to the French Jesuit missions. As a result, by 1693, minister Dellius enthusiastically reported to his superiors in the republic that he had baptized no less than two hundred Mohawks.[29]

These mass baptisms in colonial New York stand in marked contrast to the Dutch Calvinist missionary program in Brazil in the first half of the seventeenth century. Reformed ministers in Dutch Brazil did not baptize large numbers of Tupís, because most missionaries during the early seventeenth century were ideological hard-liners. Whenever Calvinist preachers suspected that the Tupís did not yet fully understand the word of God, they refused to baptize the Indians. Moreover, because group baptisms had been an important strategic tool of the Jesuits in converting the Tupís, the fiercely anti-Catholic Calvinist ministers logically rejected the large-scale baptisms of natives in Brazil. To differentiate themselves from the Jesuits, the Dutch Calvinist ministers in Brazil therefore emphasized education and catechization rather than baptisms.[30]

Another motive for the Tupís and Mohawks to adopt Protestant Christianity was intertwined with the need to foster political alliances and concerned the growing necessity of both Indian peoples to gain better access to European trade goods. Throughout the era of European colonization in northeastern Brazil and the upper Hudson valley, the Tupís and Mohawks had increasingly become dependent upon a wide variety of material goods. To obtain a steady flow of European material goods to their communities, the Tupís and Mohawks subsequently established commercial ties with the Dutch. To cement this economic alliance with the Dutch more firmly, the Tupís and Mohawks converted to the religion of their trading partners. This process of conversion was not so much intended to maximize profits but was instead a reflection of traditional native values. Because the Tupís and Mohawks did not make sharp distinctions between the sacred and the secular world, both indigenous peoples considered adoption of the Dutch Reformed religion as a spiritual affirmation of the existing secular alliance with the Dutch.[31]

The relationship between conversion and the Indian demands for material goods became especially apparent when Dutch Reformed missionaries directly supplied trade goods to the natives. When Portuguese colonists rebelled against the Dutch in Brazil in the summer of 1645, many Tupís who had allied themselves with the Dutch were forced to seek shelter in WIC forts. While their husbands joined company soldiers in military campaigns against the Portuguese rebels, Tupí women and children soon became dependent upon the distribution of food and clothes by WIC officials. Protestant ministers called upon their superiors in the United Provinces to organize monetary collections in local Dutch Calvinist churches to aid their impoverished Tupí allies. From 1646 to 1648, the Dutch Reformed Church subsequently shipped large amounts of linen and cloth to Brazil to be distributed among destitute Tupí families. Unfortunately, it is unknown how many of these Tupís receiving material aid from the Dutch were actually Christian converts. However, it is unlikely that the Dutch Reformed Church distributed costly trade goods to native peoples who showed no interest in Protestant Christianity.[32]

Likewise, the Mohawks adopted Protestant Christianity to obtain essential trade goods from their Dutch neighbors at Albany. A considerable number of Mohawk men and women who are recorded as having been baptized in public ceremonies in the Calvinist church of the town of Albany in the upper Hudson valley all had prominent local Dutch traders as their godparents. In addition, the earlier mentioned minister Dellius relied extensively on gift giving while evangelizing to the Mohawk communities during the 1690s. Because generosity was an important social value among the Mohawks, the distribution of trade goods by Dellius considerably enhanced the status and prestige of Dutch Calvinism among potential Mohawk converts.[33]

Yet another important motivation for the Tupís and Mohawks to convert to Protestant Christianity was to become literate. Dutch evangelization strategies emphasized instruction in reading and writing so that indigenous peoples were able to read and understand the Bible in their own languages. By attending Calvinist educational programs, the Tupís and Mohawks were therefore able to master the skills of reading and writing. In actively adopting literacy, both native peoples could better adapt to the "new world" in which they were living. Reading and writing not only enabled the Tupís and Mohawks to understand God's word, but also enabled them to communicate better with their European neighbors. In this respect, acquiring literacy provided an important tool to contest European colonization. By turning their own native languages into written forms the Tupís and Mohawks were culturally empowered in a time of political crisis and social turmoil. Like the Cherokees, who developed their own written alphabet and language in the early nineteenth century, the seventeenth-century Tupís and early eighteenth-century Mohawks utilized literacy to revitalize their communities.[34]

Before adopting literacy through association with the Dutch Reformed Church, many Tupís had already learned reading and writing from Jesuit missionaries during the sixteenth century. The languages used in this Catholic mission program were Portuguese as well as a regional version of the Tupí-Guaraní language. By the early seventeenth century, several Jesuit missionaries had even printed a Tupí-Guaraní grammar that they used in the missionization of the Brazilian Indians. When Calvinist preachers initiated their own educational programs among the Tupís during the early 1630s, they quickly noticed a strong willingness on the part of these Indians to participate in reading, writing, and catechism classes. This educational program was so successful that the Dutch Reformed Church in Brazil soon appointed several Tupí men as schoolteachers. Although Calvinist ministers saw this as evidence that their evangelization work was succeeding, the emergence of native teachers at the same time revealed that the Tupís were increasingly controlling and shaping the Calvinist missionary program.[35]

The Mohawks of the upper Hudson valley also adopted the literacy programs of the Dutch Reformed Church to revitalize their communities. However, in contrast to the Calvinist schools among the Tupís in Brazil,

Reformed ministers were unable to establish mission schools among the Mohawks during the late seventeenth and early eighteenth centuries. Those Mohawks who showed an interest in converting to Calvinism traveled to the nearby Dutch communities of Albany and Schenectady to receive instruction in reading and writing from Reformed ministers.

The small group of interpreters between the Dutch and Iroquois played an important role in the fostering of literacy among the Mohawks. Because of the importance of intercultural trade in the upper Hudson valley, a considerable number of Dutchmen had learned the Mohawk language, whereas some individual Mohawks had become familiar with the Dutch language. In addition, some of the interpreters were persons born of the liaisons between Mohawk women and Dutch men. Hilletie van Olinda was an especially useful interpreter because she was not only of Mohawk-Dutch descent and therefore well versed in both languages, but also a convert to Protestant Christianity herself. Some Dutch Reformed ministers eventually learned the Mohawk language through the help of interpreters. With the aid of Dutch and Mohawk interpreters, the previously mentioned minister Freeman translated passages of the Bible into Mohawk; he also used psalms in Mohawk language versions. Freeman developed a sixteen-letter written alphabet into the Mohawk language during his tenure as minister among the Dutch communities in the early eighteenth century. Because of these teachings, the Mohawks were able to shape and control their own version of Protestant Christianity. By the mid-eighteenth century, a considerable number of Mohawks had become catechist teachers (unlike the situation in northeastern Brazil, where the Tupís had been unable to sustain a similar cadre of native teachers following the expulsion of the Dutch from Brazil in 1654).[36]

Although the Tupís and Mohawks converted in large numbers to Dutch Calvinism to strengthen alliances and foster literacy, it is important to emphasize that both native peoples did not simply abandon earlier adopted religious traditions. Although some Tupí and Mohawk men and women were attracted to Calvinist notions of individual piety, for the majority of Tupís and Mohawks Protestant conceptions such as original sin and personal guilt were difficult to grasp because they were completely alien to the traditional cultural beliefs of both peoples. For the most part, the Tupís and Mohawks selectively adopted the aspects of Dutch Protestantism that they considered spiritually powerful. As with their prior adoption of Catholicism, many Tupís and Mohawks appropriated Protestant Christianity to obtain more supernatural protection in a volatile world of deadly epidemics and European colonialism.[37]

Tupí and Mohawk converts to Protestantism continued practicing their traditional religious ceremonies. The records of the Reformed Church in Brazil are filled with references to the continuation of non-Christian religious practices by the Tupís. For instance, in a church council held in Recife, the colonial capital of Dutch Brazil, in September 1644, the assembled Calvinist ministers were alarmed at the ongoing use of body painting and decorating by the Tupís living in the *aldeias*. For the Tupís, body adornments were closely linked with traditional beliefs in spirits. However, these practices were abhorrent to Dutch Protestant ministers, and they angrily proclaimed that from then on "no one will be allowed to paint his body or represent in another way the depiction of the devil." Similarly, Dutch Reformed preachers in colonial New York were irritated by the persistence of traditional Indian religious practices among Mohawk converts. To the consternation of Anglican missionaries who arrived in Albany during the early eighteenth century, the Protestant Mohawks continued to consult shamans and make offerings to personal guardian spirits even after being baptized.[38]

In addition to the continuing practice of non-Christian beliefs and customs by Protestant Tupís and Mohawks, both peoples also persevered in adhering to Catholic rituals that they had adopted earlier from Jesuit missionaries. For instance, in the previously mentioned church council meeting in Recife of September 1644, the Calvinist ministers issued an ordinance prohibiting any Indians from "going to the papists or any other heathenish servants, whoever they may be, in order to obtain letters, beads, or crucifixes of St. John from them for superstitious practices." Likewise, during the early eighteenth century, the Anglican missionary Thomas Barclay noted how one Protestant Mohawk woman, Marie Tsiaonentes, sat at services in the Dutch Reformed Church in Albany while reciting her rosary. Thus, even as many Tupís and Mohawks converted to Protestant Christianity, they simultaneously continued to practice previously adopted Catholic rituals.[39]

This comparative perspective shows that the Tupís of northeastern Brazil and the Mohawks of central New York adopted Dutch Calvinism for very similar reasons. At the same time, several differences reveal the distinctiveness of each situation.

The most important similarity is that both the Tupís and the Mohawks turned to the Christian Reformed religion to strengthen political and economic alliances with the Dutch. In the face of political and military threats by the Portuguese and French respectively, the Tupís and Mohawks converted to Dutch Calvinism to foster a stronger alliance with Dutch colonists. A growing dependency upon material goods supplied by the Dutch also led many Tupís and Mohawks to associate closely with the Reformed religion. Because their frequent interactions with Dutch officials and traders provided them with prestige and influence, Tupí and Mohawk leaders were especially interested in converting to the religion of their Dutch allies.

Yet another important similarity is that the Dutch Calvinist emphasis on education and literacy provided useful tools of cultural revitalization for both native peoples. By attending catechism classes taught by Dutch and, later, native instructors, Tupís and Mohawks gained the ability to read and write in their own language. The acquisition of literacy was culturally empowering in a time of devastating epidemics, colonial conflicts, and economic dependency. Moreover, in learning the language of the colonizers, the Tupís and Mohawks were also better equipped to deal with the challenges created by European colonialism.

A final important similarity is that the Protestant Tupís and Mohawks continued to practice their traditional religious beliefs as well as Catholic ceremonies. The perseverance of non-Christian religious practices and the ongoing adherence to Catholic rituals should not necessarily be seen as a failed conversion of the natives to Protestant Christianity. For the Tupís and Mohawks, converting to Protestant Christianity never meant abandoning their earlier religious beliefs.

Despite these significant similarities there are also considerable differences. Whereas the evangelization program of the Dutch Reformed Church in Brazil was extensive because it was an intrinsic part of the global Calvinist Dutch struggle against the Catholic Church and the Spanish Crown, Dutch attempts to convert the Indians of North America to Protestantism lacked any strong ideological fervor. Even when the Mohawks showed a strong willingness to adopt Protestant Christianity during the 1690s and 1700s, the Reformed Church in the Dutch Republic remained largely uninterested in the conversion of North American Indians. Ironically, the strong dislike of Jesuit missionary tactics among the Calvinist ministers in colonial Brazil prevented many Tupís from being baptized. At the same time, the relative indifference of the Dutch Reformed Church toward the conversion of indigenous peoples in North America allowed several Protestant ministers in colonial New York to act on their own and baptize a considerable number of Mohawks.

Another major difference between the Tupís and the Mohawks is that the Tupí were never able to establish their own Protestant religious tradition, whereas the Mohawks succeeded in incorporating Protestantism into their religious and cultural beliefs. After the Portuguese forced the Dutch out of Brazil in 1654, the Tupís were left without Dutch support and without Calvinist ministers. After 1654, any vestiges of Protestantism among the Tupís were brutally repressed by the Portuguese colonists and the Catholic Church. Like the Dutch colonial project in Brazil, the Dutch attempt at colonization in North America was also prematurely terminated by a European power. However, whereas the Catholic Portuguese forced the Dutch Reformed Church from Brazil, the Protestant English Crown allowed Dutch Calvinists to continue services in colonial New York after 1664. In fact, English colonial officials actively supported the evangelization attempts of Dutch Protestant ministers among the Mohawks because their missionary work fostered a closer alliance between the Mohawks and colonial New York. While the Tupí experiment with Dutch Calvinism therefore turned out to be a historical dead end, the Mohawks constructed a Protestant religious tradition that nurtured literacy and helped the Mohawks to survive in a world that was increasingly dominated by European colonial powers.

Notes

An earlier version of this essay was delivered at the 2000 Annual Meeting of the Organization of American Historians in Saint Louis, Missouri. For comments on that paper I would like to thank James Carrott, Sarah Fatherly, Joe Hall, Margaret Hogan, and Alice Nash. I also thank James Muldoon and Kristin Lovrien. All translations from the Dutch are mine, except where otherwise noted.

1. For this report, see Johan Maurits, Mathias van Ceulen, and Adriaen van der Dussen, "Sommier Discours ouer den Staet van de Vier Geconquesteerde Capitanias Parnambuco, Itamarica, Paraiba, ende Rio Grande inde Noorderdelen van Brasil (January 19, 1638)," *Bijdragen en Mededeelingen van het Historisch Genootschap (Gevestigd te Utrecht)* 2 (1879): 257–317. For the quotes, see 291–92. I have somewhat loosely used here the term *Tupís* to describe all the coastal Indian peoples that lived in northeastern Brazil. Although they were divided into different polities such as the Potiguars, I have used the more generic linguistic term *Tupís* because contemporary Dutch sources are usually obscure about the identity of the Indians. For a historical overview of the Tupís of coastal Brazil in the early colonial period, see John

M. Monteiro, "The Crises and Transformations of Invaded Societies: Coastal Brazil in the Sixteenth Century," in *South America,* ed. Frank Salomon and Stuart B. Schwartz, vol. 3, part 1 of *The Cambridge History of the Native Peoples of America* (New York: Cambridge University Press, 1999): 973–1023. See also Alfred Métraux, "The Tupínamba," in *The Tropical Forest Tribes,* ed. Julian H. Steward, vol. 3 of *Handbook of South American Indians,* Smithsonian Institution Bureau of American Ethnology Bulletin 143 (Washington, D.C.: Smithsonian Institution, 1946): 95–133.

2. Edward Tanjore Corwin and Hugh Hastings, eds., *Ecclesiastical Records of the State of New York,* 7 vols. (Albany: State of New York, 1901–16), vol. 2, 1000–1004. For the number of Mohawk baptisms, see Lois M. Feister, "Indian-Dutch Relations in the Upper Hudson Valley: A Study of Baptism Records in the Dutch Reformed Church, Albany, New York," *Man in the Northeast* 24 (1984): 89–113, especially the table on page 96.

3. For scholarship on the evangelization program among the Brazilian Indians, see Jose Antonio Gonsalves de Mello, *Tempo dos Flamengos: Influência da Ocupação Holandesa na Vida e na Cultura do Norte do Brasil* (1947; Recife: Fundação Joaquim Nabuco, 1987), chap. 4. See also Ernst van den Boogaart, "De Nederlandse Expansie in het Atlantische Gebied, 1590–1674," in *Overzee: Nederlandse Koloniale Geschiedenis, 1590–1975,* ed. Ernst van den Boogaart (Haarlem: Fibula-van Dishoeck, 1982), 124–25; and F. L. Schalkwijk, *The Reformed Church in Dutch Brazil (1630–1654)* (Zoetermeer: Boekencentrum, 1998), chaps. 8–11. For the scholarship on the evangelization of Indians in Dutch North America, it is important to make distinctions between the period of WIC rule (1624–64) and the post-WIC period, when Dutch Reformed ministers continued missionizing activities in the Dutch communities across New York and New Jersey. For scholarship dealing with the WIC period, see Jaap Jacobs, *Een zegenrijk gewest: Nieuw-Nederland in de zeventiende eeuw* (Amsterdam: Prometheus-Bert Bakker, 1999), 271–75; and Oliver A. Rink, "Private Interest and Godly Gain: The West India Company and the Dutch Reformed Church in New Netherland, 1624–1664," *New York History* 75 (July 1994): 245–64. Most scholars agree that the Dutch evangelization program in the WIC period was a failure. See Allen W. Trelease, *Indian Affairs in Colonial New York: The Seventeenth Century* (Ithaca, N.Y.: Cornell University Press, 1960), 38–40, 169–72; and Matthew Dennis, *Cultivating a Landscape of Peace: Iroquois-European Encounters in Seventeenth-Century America* (Ithaca, N.Y.: Cornell University Press, 1993), 142, 166. For scholarship on the post-1664 period, see Daniel K. Richter, "'Some of Them . . . Would Always Have a Minister with Them': Mohawk Protestantism, 1683–1719," *American Indian Quarterly* 16, no. 4 (1992): 471–84; Feister, "Indian-Dutch Relations in the Upper Hudson Valley"; and William Bryan Hart, "For the Good of Our Souls: Mohawk Authority, Accommodation, and Resistance to Protestant Evangelism, 1700–1780," Ph.D. diss., Brown University, 1998. For the uses of comparative history, see, for instance, George M. Fredrickson, *The Comparative Imagination: On the History of Racism, Nationalism, and Social Movements* (Berkeley: University

of California Press, 1997). For earlier examples of studies of Dutch-Native interactions from a comparative perspective, see Laurence M. Hauptman and Ronald G. Knapp, "Dutch-Aboriginal Interaction in New Netherland and Formosa: An Historical Geography of Empire," *Proceedings of the American Philosophical Society* 121 (1977): 166–82.

4. For the different meanings and definitions of conversion, see James Muldoon, "Introduction: The Conversion of Europe," in *Varieties of Religious Conversion in Medieval Europe*, ed. James Muldoon (Gainesville: University Press of Florida, 1997), 1–10.

5. For the militant Calvinists, see Jonathan I. Israel, *The Dutch Republic: Its Rise, Greatness, and Fall, 1477–1806* (New York: Oxford University Press, 1995), 474–77.

6. Leendert Jan Joosse, *"Scoone dingen sijn swaere dingen": Een onderzoek naar de motieven en activiteiten in de Nederlanden tot verbreiding van de Gereformeerde Religie gedurende de eerste helft van de zeventiende eeuw* (Leiden: J.J. Groen en Zoon, 1992): 97–137.

7. For the WIC and the Dutch Reformed Church, see Willem Frijhoff, "The West India Company and the Reformed Church: Neglect or Concern," *De Halve Maen: Magazine of the Dutch Colonial Period in America* 70 (1997): 59–68. For the pamphlet by Teellinck, see A. Th. Boone, "'Tot Verbreydinge van het Rijcke onses Heeren Jesu Christ': Een Inleiding tot de Zendingsgedachten binnen het Gereformeerd Pietisme in Nederland," *Documentatieblad Nadere Reformatie* 17 (1993): 1–18, esp. 2–4. For the instructions to Verhulst, see *Documents Relating to New Netherland, 1624–1626, in the Henry E. Huntington Library*, trans. and ed. A.J.F. van Laer (San Marino, Calif.: Henry E. Huntington Library and Art Gallery, 1924), 36.

8. Israel, *Dutch Republic*, 686–90.

9. The importance of education in the Calvinist evangelization in the overseas world is discussed extensively in G.M.J.M. Koolen, *Een seer Bequaem Middel: Onderwijs en Kerk onder de 17e-Eeuwse VOC* (Kampen: J. H. Kok, 1993), English summary on 248–52.

10. For schools in Brazil, see Schalkwijk, *Reformed Church in Dutch Brazil*, 142–45, 191–92, 196–97. For Calvinist educational programs in colonial New York, see Richter, "Mohawk Protestantism," and Hart, "For the Good of Our Souls."

11. For a discussion of this problem, see Jaap Jacobs, "The Dutch Protestant Church in North America during the Seventeenth and Eighteenth Centuries: Some Comments on Historiography and Sources," *Documentatieblad voor de Geschiedenis van de Nederlandse Zending en Overzeese Kerken* 1, no. 1 (1994): 62–79.

12. For the Tupí catechism, see Schalkwijk, *Reformed Church in Dutch Brazil*, chap. 11. For Freeman, see Hart, "For the Good of Our Souls," 124–29.

13. For Calvinist concerns with religious plurality in Brazil, see Schalkwijk, *Reformed Church in Dutch Brazil*, chap. 7. For New York, see Jacobs, *Een zegenrijk gewest*, chap. 5.

14. For the number of preachers in Brazil, see Schalkwijk, *Reformed Church in Dutch Brazil*, 305–6; see 176–84 for the individual careers of those ministers in-

volved in evangelizing the Tupís. For New Netherland, see the appendix in Jacobs, *Een zegenrijk gewest*, 486, table 10. For colonial New York, see Gerald F. De Jong, *The Dutch Reformed Church in the American Colonies* (Grand Rapids, Mich.: Eerdmans, 1978), 153–61.

15. For the Dutch Reformed Church and its relationship with the WIC in the 1620s and 1630s, see Willem Frijhoff, *Wegen van Evert Willemsz.: Een Hollands weeskind op zoek naar zichzelf, 1607–1647* (Nijmegen: Sun, 1995), 497–98. For the diplomatic context of the Dutch in Brazil, see Charles R. Boxer, *The Dutch in Brazil, 1624–1654* (Oxford, U.K.: Clarendon Press, 1957).

16. For the Jesuit missions among the Tupís, see John Hemming, *Red Gold: The Conquest of the Brazilian Indians, 1500–1760* (Cambridge, Mass.: Harvard University Press, 1978), chap. 5; and Dauril Alden, *The Making of an Enterprise: The Society of Jesus in Portugal, Its Empire, and Beyond, 1540–1750* (Stanford: Stanford University Press, 1996), 71–75. On the similarity between Catholic and Protestant missionary policies regarding the use of fixed settlements, see James Axtell, *The Invasion Within: The Contest of Cultures in Colonial North America* (New York: Oxford University Press, 1985), esp. chaps. 4 and 7.

17. For Catholic missions among the Mohawks, see Daniel K. Richter, "Iroquois versus Iroquois: Jesuit Missions and Christianity in Village Politics, 1642–1686," *Ethnohistory* 32, no. 1 (1985): 1–16. For the Jesuits in New France, see Axtell, *The Invasion Within*.

18. Schalkwijk, *Reformed Church in Dutch Brazil*, 215–17. For the Portuguese-Indian wars in the Northeast after 1654, see Beatriz G. Dantas et al., "Os povos indígenas no Nordeste brasileiro: um esboço histórico," in *História dos Índios no Brasil*, ed. Manuela Carneiro da Cunha (São Paulo: Companhia das Letras, Secretaria Municipal de Cultura, 1992), 431–56, esp. 442–44.

19. For the continuation of the Dutch Reformed Church in New York after 1664, see De Jong, *Dutch Reformed Church in the American Colonies*. See also Randall H. Balmer, *A Perfect Babel of Confusion: Dutch Religion and English Culture in the Middle Colonies* (New York: Oxford University Press, 1989).

20. For traditional Tupí religion, see Métraux, "The Tupínamba," 127–31; and Eduardo Viveiros de Castro, *From the Enemy's Point of View: Humanity and Divinity in an Amazonian Society*, trans. Catherine V. Howard (Chicago: University of Chicago Press, 1992). For traditional Mohawk religion, see Daniel K. Richter, *The Ordeal of the Longhouse: The Peoples of the Iroquois League in the Era of European Colonization* (Chapel Hill: University of North Carolina Press for the Institute of Early American History and Culture, 1992), 24–25; and Hart, "For the Good of Our Souls," 40–49.

21. For Indian depopulation in the wake of Old World diseases, see Noble David Cook, *Born to Die: Disease and New World Conquest, 1492–1650* (New York: Cambridge University Press, 1998). For Dutch reports about the depopulation of the Tupís, see, for instance, Dutch National Archives, The Hague, Netherlands (hereafter cited as DNA), Section 1, Archive of the First West India Company (hereafter cited as

AFWIC), Inv. 69: *Daily Minutes,* February 17, 1642. For the depopulation among the Mohawks, as well as other Iroquois peoples, see Richter, *Ordeal of the Longhouse,* 58–60.

22. The protection from diseases by the spiritual power of the Christian God was also a motivation for New England Indians to adopt Protestant Christianity. See Charles L. Cohen, "Conversion among Puritans and Amerindians: A Theological and Cultural Perspective," in *Puritanism: Transatlantic Perspectives on a Seventeenth-Century Anglo-American Faith,* ed. Francis J. Bremer (Boston: Massachusetts Historical Society Press, 1993), 233–56.

23. For the conflict between Jesuits and Portuguese colonists in coastal Brazil, see Alden, *Making of an Enterprise,* chap. 19.

24. For the "mourning wars," see Daniel K. Richter, "War and Culture: The Iroquois Experience," *William and Mary Quarterly,* 3d Ser., 40 (1983): 528–59; and José Antonio Brandão, *"Your Fire Shall Burn No More": Iroquois Policy toward New France and Its Native Allies to 1701* (Lincoln: University of Nebraska Press, 1997). For the Mohawks in this period, see Richter, *Ordeal of the Longhouse,* chap. 5, esp. 102–4 (French expeditions of the 1660s), 108 (Huron captives as converts), 114 (Mohawk leaders welcoming Jesuit missionaries). For the Iroquois League, see Richter, *Ordeal of the Longhouse.*

25. For the Dutch Calvinist mission program among the Indians of New Netherland before 1664, see Jacobs, *Een zegenrijk gewest,* 271–75; and Rink, "Private Interest and Godly Gain," 252–56.

26. For examples of the conversion of marginalized persons to Christianity, see Hart, "For the Good of Our Souls," 62–68, 75–83.

27. For the wars between the Potiguars and the Portuguese, see Hemming, *Red Gold,* chap. 8. About the visit of the Potiguars to the United Provinces, see *Beschrijvinge van de Custen van Brasil, en verder zuidelijk tot Rio de la Plata; toestand der forten, enz. Getrokken uit scheepsjournalen, officiële verklaringe enz. van 1624–1637,* anonymous manuscript (late 1630s?), John Carter Brown Library, Ms. Codex Du-1, 11–14. For the quotation, see Joannes de Laet, *L'Histoire du Nouveau Monde ou description des Indes Occidentales* (Leiden: Elzeviers, 1640), 539–40. I thank Peter Cook and Jennifer Cage for helping me read the French edition.

28. For the "Covenant Chain" alliance, see Francis Jennings, *The Ambiguous Iroquois Empire: The Covenant Chain Confederation of Indian Tribes with English Colonies from Its Beginnings to the Lancaster Treaty of 1744* (New York: Norton, 1984). For the attraction of Protestant Christianity to the anti-French and anti-Catholic Mohawk leaders, see Richter, *Ordeal of the Longhouse,* 164–65; and Richter, "Mohawk Protestantism," 474–75. See also Hart, "For the Good of Our Souls," 68–75. For the importance of the Dutch in Albany, see Donna Merwick, *Possessing Albany, 1630–1710: The Dutch and English Experiences* (New York: Cambridge University Press, 1990).

29. For Dellius and his Mohawk baptisms, see Feister, "Indian-Dutch Relations in the Upper Hudson Valley," 93.

30. For the small number of Tupí baptisms performed by the Dutch Reformed ministers, see Schalkwijk, *Reformed Church in Dutch Brazil*, 188–89.

31. For the economic exchange between the Tupís and the Dutch, see Van den Boogaart, "Nederlandse Expansie in het Atlantische Gebied," 124–25. For the commercial relationship between the Dutch and the Mohawks, see Richter, *Ordeal of the Longhouse*, chap. 4; and Dennis, *Cultivating a Landscape of Peace*, chap. 5.

32. For a good discussion of this aid, see Schalkwijk, *Reformed Church in Dutch Brazil*, 208–10.

33. For Dellius and gift giving among the Mohawks, see Hart, "For the Good of Our Souls," 73–75. For the importance of gift giving among the Mohawks in the eighteenth century, see Timothy J. Shannon, "Dressing for Success on the Mohawk Frontier: Hendrick, William Johnson, and the Indian Fashion," *William and Mary Quarterly*, 3d Ser., 52 (January 1996): 13–42.

34. On the idea that Indians found themselves in a "new world" just like Europeans, see James H. Merrell, *The Indians' New World: The Catawbas and Their Neighbors from European Contact through the Era of Removal* (Chapel Hill: University of North Carolina Press, 1989). For literacy as revitalization among the Cherokees, see William B. McLoughlin, *The Renascence of the Cherokee Republic* (Princeton: Princeton University Press, 1986).

35. For the Jesuit missionary program among the Tupís and the role of literacy in this process, see Maria Cândida D. M. Barros, "The Office of *Lingua* (Interpreter): A Portrait of the Religious Interpreter in Brazil in the Sixteenth Century," *Itinerario* 25, no. 2 (2001): 110–40. For the Calvinist school program among the Tupís, see "Classicale Acta van Brazilië," *Archief voor de Geschiedenis der Oude Hollandsche Zending* 2, ed. J.A. Grothe (Utrecht: Van Bentum, 1885): Brazilian Classis meetings of January 5, 1638, session 1 (233–36); April 20, 1640, sessions 4 (273–74) and 7 (277–78); November 21, 1640, session 2 (282–85); July 1644, sessions 2 (311–12) and 9 (315–17). For native schoolteachers, see DNA, AFWIC, Inv. No. 69: *Daily Minutes*, July 12, 1642; AFWIC, Inv. No. 75: *Daily Minutes*, August 31, 1651. See also Schalkwijk, *Reformed Church in Dutch Brazil*, chaps. 9 and 10.

36. Hart, "For the Good of Our Souls," 74–78 (Hilletie van Olinda), 124–29 (Freeman). See also Nancy Lee Hagedorn, "Brokers of Understanding: Interpreters as Agents of Cultural Exchange in Colonial New York," *New York History* 76 (1995): 379–408. For later adaptations of literacy by the Mohawks, see William B. Hart, "Mohawk Schoolmasters and Catechists in Mid-Eighteenth-Century Iroquoia: An Experiment in Fostering Literacy and Religious Change," in *The Language Encounter in the Americas, 1492–1800: A Collection of Essays*, ed. Edward G. Gray and Norman Fiering, European Expansion and Global Interaction 1 (New York: Berghahn Books, 2000), 230–57.

37. The argument that most Indians did interpret central tenets of Protestant Christianity differently is discussed in Cohen, "Conversion among Puritans and Amerindians."

38. For the ordinance against decorating the body, see the church council meeting in Recife in September 1644, DNA, AFWIC, Inv. No. 70: *Daily Minutes,* September 20, 1644, point 1. On the significance of tattooing and body painting for the Tupís, see Castro, *From the Enemy's Point of View,* 40, 70. For similar complaints by Protestant ministers about the persistence of traditional religious practices, see also Schalkwijk, *Reformed Church in Dutch Brazil,* 171, 199. For the persistence of religious practices among the Mohawks, see Richter, "Mohawk Protestantism," 479–80; and Hart, "For the Good of Our Souls," 34.

39. For the church council meeting in September 1644, see DNA, AFWIC, Inv. No. 70: *Daily Minutes,* September 20, 1644, section 1. See also Schalkwijk, *Reformed Church in Dutch Brazil,* 171. For the Mohawk woman in the Calvinist church in the 1690s, see Hart, "For the Good of Our Souls," 32.

7

"None of These Wandering Nations Has Ever Been Reduced to the Faith"

Missions and Mobility on the Spanish-American Frontier

Amy Turner Bushnell

Shortly before the first centennial of Spanish settlement in America, the Jesuit José de Acosta published two tracts: *De procuranda Indorum salute* (1588), on missionary rationale and tactics, and *Historia natural y moral de las Indias* (1590), on the natural history and customs of native Americans. Like the Dominican Bartolomé de Las Casas, his predecessor in ethnography, Acosta followed the classical authors Aristotle and Cicero on the common nature of man and the ascent of mankind from antisocial nomadism to orderly community and the pastoral and agricultural arts of peace. His contribution was to classify, in terms of cultural evolution, the non-Christians with whom the Society dealt.

First were the Chinese, the Japanese, and some East Indians. Possessing cities, laws, and written scripts, they lacked nothing of civilization except Christianity, which, he predicted, reason and the wonders of Western technology would lead them to accept. Next were the native American peoples of villages and settlements. These ranged from the imperial Mexica and Inca, who lived in cities under the rule of law and worshiped idols, to the loosely organized tribes of Chile and New Granada, who had smaller settlements and simpler hierarchies and worshiped animals. The Christianizing of these barbarians could be accomplished by means of preaching and substituting Christian for pagan symbols. Although the settled peoples owed gratitude and submission to the representatives of Church and Crown, their republics and customs were to be respected, for Christianity did not demand that they be Spanish in all things.

Lowest on Acosta's scale of civilization were America's savages, who, he understood, shunned human society, material goods, and permanent settlements and wandered about naked, eating unclean things and worshiping stones, streams, and mountains. In this category he placed the first human occupants of the Americas, most of the natives of Brazil and Florida, the Chiriguanás, and the Chichimecos. Living like beasts in the jungles, deserts, and mountains, the "wild men" lacked the capacity to understand the gospel. Before they could be Christianized, they must be driven into settlements to acquire the social, linguistic, and laboring skills of rational men. In Acosta's view, Christianity demanded a higher level of civilization than the wandering peoples possessed.[1]

Spain had come to America with an arsenal of weapons for spiritual conquest drawn from the three militant, monotheistic faiths that had long shared Iberia: Judaism, with a pastoral past and an urban present; Roman Catholicism, a religion of cities, distrusting the countryside; and Islam, brought from North Africa by nomads and flourishing in cities such as Córdoba and Toledo under caliphs who valued their Christian tributaries, invited Jewish scholars to grace their courts, and understood horticulture. In their seven centuries of *convivencia* alternating with conquest, Spain's Christians, Jews, and Moslems had ample time to develop the workable system for dealing with subject peoples, complete with unequal treaties, tribute, and self-governing republics, that Spaniards carried to the New World.

Ironically, 1492 was also the year when the *"reyes católicos"* Ferdinand and Isabel, determined to end confessional pluralism in their realms, seized the Moslem stronghold of Granada after an eight-year war and pronounced a sentence of exile on unconverted Jews. A Spain prepared to sacrifice religious tolerance for national unity broke into the Americas with issues of conquest and forced conversion unresolved.

In the first Spanish-American century, the people of settlements bore the brunt of adjustment to the new order: first the islanders of the Greater Antilles, then the imperial peoples of the Mesoamerican and Andean highlands. How small companies of Spaniards striking into unknown territory could defeat armies of seasoned warriors and subjugate powerful empires has always excited wonder, but the success of the "high conquest" is usually accounted for by the superiority of European military technology, the tactical support of tributary nations in revolt, the disastrous effects of Old World pathogens, and the fact that an expedition was a venture enterprise in which fighting men risked their capital as well as their lives and divided the spoils on share.

Hard on the heels of the conquerors came the missionaries. Emperor Charles V sent twelve Franciscan apostles to central Mexico to instruct and baptize his millions of new subjects. Aspiring to reconstruct the primitive church in America, the friars were openhanded with the sacrament, asking only that the Indians renounce paganism and polygamy and be able to recite a few prayers, bless themselves, and have some sense of Catholic obligations, like European peasants. In this charismatic, millenarian phase, evangelists entered a region, preached, founded churches, and moved on. A similar system was followed thirty years later in Peru. In both viceroyalties, bands of itinerant preachers gave way to domiciled friars, who sallied from their convents on "flying missions" to visit their converts. The institutional phase began when the "holy vagabonds" were set to tending Indian parishes.[2]

The mandate to Christianize America had come at a bad time. For a faith that preached "one fold and one shepherd," Roman Catholicism was becoming singularly suspicious of converts. In the control centers of the Catholic Reformation, Augustinian thought revived, with its darker view of human nature. The Christianizing of Peru coincided with the final sessions of the Council of Trent (1545–63), a council marked by preoccupation with hierarchy, order, dogma, and the minimum rites for sacramental validity. The Tridentine answer to the state-sponsored heresies of the "Lutherans" was to retrench and purify the core and not, in trying times, to expand the peripheries.[3] In Spain, grotesque claims to "purity of blood," signifying a lineage without *conversos* or other religious suspects for four generations, split the faithful into New and Old Christians.

By 1555, Mexican churchmen had persuaded themselves that Indians too made inferior Christians, unfit to be ordained or to touch the sacred vessels. Unaccountable by virtue of mental incapacity, like minors and European rustics, they were subject to incremental conversion, surveillance, and paternal correction.[4] "Regardless of how many generations of baptized forebears the Indians might eventually accumulate," writes historian Nancy Farriss, "they were always considered neophytes in the Christian faith," adding to "the ordinary lapses caused by human frailty . . . their own peculiarly perverse—that is, non-Spanish—ways."[5]

The conquest of the imperial peoples had been consolidated through *congregación*, the process of collecting the inhabitants of remote or depopulated places into larger, more accessible settlements for their better administration and indoctrination. Fray Toribio de Benavente (Motolinía) advised his emperor to gather the Indians of New Spain into villages like the peasants of Spain so they could be civilized and evangelized. Las Casas experimented with *congregación* in Cumaná, Venezuela, and Vera Paz, Guatemala. In Michoacán, Bishop Vasco de Quiroga gathered the survivors of epidemics into pueblo-hospitals called "republics of Indians." In Peru, Viceroy Francisco de Toledo initiated a massive resettlement program, consolidating hamlets into towns of four hundred tributaries—the optimal size for exacting tribute and labor and imposing religious control.[6] *Población*, by contrast, was the sponsored migration of *pobladores*, usually Indian families of farmers or weavers, to regions short on sedentary inhabitants. *Reducción*, the process of reducing mobile people to fixed settlements and the constraints of municipal government, was the form of directed settlement associated with the Christianization of nonsedentary peoples. Reduction—the sacrifice of mobility—was the starting point for evangelism on the frontiers.

Like the Incas and Aztecs before them, Spaniards were unable to subdue the mobile peoples. The days when Christians held the military advantage were over, warned Acosta: the natives of Chile had lost all fear of horses and harquebuses, and the naked Chichimecos grew bolder daily. Wandering peoples avoided battle, preferring to raid; they had no property to destroy or treasure to seize; and their decentralized organization made it necessary to defeat them band by band. Unlike the subjects of native empires, they had never borne the yoke of tribute, labor conscription, or agricultural taxation. Nor were they easily stamped by a new religion of state. The religion of the conquerors was a demanding one, with a castelike priesthood, immutable doctrines, unvarying rituals, and fixed temples to house the sacred. In spirit the church may have been universal, but in the flesh it was seigneurial, campanilist, and Mediterranean, subscribing to a social order fast disappearing in Europe itself, in which persons from the lower orders were farmers who obeyed their natural superiors and lived "beneath the bell" in villages centuries old. When a missionary's hearers dissolved into bands to move from place to place, they were rejecting more than the preaching of the gospel. People unwilling to be peasants were unfit to be Christians.

The peoples that Acosta and others labeled "wild" were not true nomads, but they were indeed poor candidates for evangelization. Some of these groups simply continued their seasonal rounds, avoiding contact with Spaniards. Others adopted horse pastoralism and expanded their territory at the expense of their neighbors. Still others, unable to maintain the old ways nor yet to feel at home with the new, sought a middle way, sometimes advancing, sometimes reversing the course of Christianization. In their time, they were charged with inconstancy, rebellion, and "gypsy" habits if they reverted to the old ways; in ours, they are accused of collusion, compromise, and a failure of solidarity if they coped with change.[7]

Elsewhere I have examined the corollaries of early modern conversion, arguing that the Spanish had a "sacramental imperative" to impose a pattern of nucleated settlement with residence year-round.[8] The purpose of the present chapter is to advance a broader Christianization model, neither Eurocentric nor indigenocentric, that takes mobility into account.

In terms of mobility, anthropologists conventionally classify groups as wandering (free, restricted, or central-based) or sedentary (semipermanent or permanent). Free wandering, which is high in subsistence risk, occurs mainly in the course of mass migration. In restricted wandering, hunter-gatherers systematically move from site to site, harvesting resources in a seasonal round. In central-based wandering, the group keeps its foodstores in a central place and small bands visit satellite sites to hunt, fish, and gather. A group becomes sedentary when its mobility is reduced to the point of having at least part of its population in residence year-round. A sedentary group that changes settlement sites every few years is semipermanent. Only a group that remains in place, farming intensively and building houses to last, is considered permanent. On the mobility continuum, on which reduced wandering equals increased sedentism, the difference between "semisedentary" and "seminomadic" is usually a matter of the balance between food gathering and food production, with the caveat that a forest can be managed and a garden left to fend for itself.

When subsistence economies are arranged in order of mobility, the most nomadic is that of predators and foragers. The difference between these and hunters and gatherers is technological: a hunter is a predator with projectile weapons; a gatherer is a forager with carrying devices. In the "extensive mixed" economy, hunter-gatherers add food production to their subsistence repertoire but continue to emphasize wild food sources. Food production gains the ascendancy in the "extensive agricultural" economy, which combines forest clearing, hoe cultivation, and long periods of fallow in a system variously known as slash-and-burn farming, swidden farming, shifting cultivation, and forest colonizing. This economy is semipermanently sedentary in that it requires the periodic relocation of village sites. The "intensive agricultural" economy is permanently sedentary, thanks to the rapid recovery of soil fertility by seasonal floods or the manure of domestic animals, which also provide the draft power to plow the permanent fields. To Europeans accustomed to fields that were fenced, manured, and furrowed, the Indians' fenceless fields, with their irregular plantings and blackened stumps, looked ill tended, but hoe-farmers knew that a burned clearing was good for only two or three years, that most garden raiders could be trapped and eaten, and that grazing animals belonged on an island or across a river.

Pastoral subsistence economies can also be categorized in terms of mobility. The herd can be migratory, like the Lapps' reindeer; transhumant, like the Navajos' sheep; or wintered over, like the Yorkshire milk cows. A society dependent on herd animals will be more or less mobile depending on whether the animals are fed, left to forage, or hunted, as with the *cimarrón* cattle that proliferated on the Spanish-American savannas. Along with their herd animals, the Spanish introduced pastoralist values to the New World. "Ranching, the economic base of the Castilian reconquest, took precedence in social prestige and political power over farming," observes Farriss, "and the interests of stockmen prevailed over those of the conquered farmer on both sides of the Atlantic."[9] When horses began to multiply on the American grasslands, enabling native peoples from the plains to the pampas to move their encampments at will and raid at large, the European sense of superiority was shaken. A mounted warrior, refusing to come under obedience and take up the hoe, evoked the knight.

At the "Man the Hunter" Wenner-Gren symposium held in Chicago in 1966, ethnographic research on the Aborigines of Australia and the !Kung San of the Kalahari Desert showed that a preagricultural life was relatively easy. The implications were revolutionary. Anthropologists could no longer resort to theories of stadial cultural evolution going back to Aristotle. Hunting-gathering and pastoralism were not temporary states on the way to agriculture. Humans did not have an innate urge to cultivate grain and live in villages, and sedentism did not necessarily occur as soon as food production made it feasible. In places such as prehistoric Europe where hunter-gatherers and farmers shared the same environment, the former often ate better, had more leisure, and lived longer than the latter. In West Africa, identity was a function of subsistence: Kikuyu who hunted instead of farming were considered Ndorobo, while Ndorobo who adopted pastoralism became Maasai.[10] Paleopathologists found that in ancient America, as in the Middle East, a rise in agriculture and urban living meant a decline in health and longevity. In coastal Georgia, the advent of agriculture had been marked by declining nutrition and shorter stature, especially for women. In general, the more mobile a pre-Columbian population, the healthier its teeth and bones.[11]

The import of the new research on mission history was especially poignant. If agriculture did not improve the earthly existence of hunters and gatherers, if it actually had a health cost, then one of the principal justifications for reducing people to fixed settlements and relegating them to the lowest order of a hierarchical conquest society was forfeited. For many groups, the promise of a better life in the hereafter was insufficient to make the colonial compact anything more than conditional. On the Indian side of the Spanish-American frontier, societies contemplating Christianization silently weighed the security and goods they stood to gain by adopting fixed residence against the freedoms and foods they would lose by abandoning their seasonal rounds.

The sacraments through which the church conveyed grace were restricted in the Indies as elsewhere. Penance tended to occur once a year, during Lent. The Eucharist was rarely administered: laymen seldom received communion, and a neophyte's confessor could extend his postbaptismal period of probation indefinitely. The missionary orders resisted confirmation, which enabled the bishop of a diocese to examine the religious instruction of children and converts; Florida saw a bishop only twice in 170 years. Matrimony in formerly polygamous societies presented complicated cases of conscience that canonists were slow to resolve, such as how to distinguish natural marriage from concubinage or how to establish the rightful wife. Meanwhile, high sacerdotal fees discouraged some couples from marrying either in or at the church. Although every Christian within reach of a priest hoped for a "good death" with sins absolved, only leading citizens received the last rites, complete with extreme unction and the viaticum. Ordination, the threshold to the priesthood, was reserved for Spanish males, with peninsulars preferred to creoles and creoles to mestizos; Indians in the service of the church were restricted to auxiliary roles.[12]

For a proselytizing religion attempting to take root on distant frontiers, Roman Catholicism made few concessions to material circumstances. The "divine cult" called for irreducible paraphernalia and supplies. To say the simplest Mass in the poorest chapel, a priest had to assemble and preserve from sacrilege thirty-five separate items, one of them a stone altar. A properly furnished church possessed a permanent altar, a baptismal font, a set of liturgical vestments, a set of sacred vessels (or "ornaments"), religious statues and paintings, processional monstrances and crosses, torches and lanterns, parish registers, and bells of varying size, for a *doctrina* lived *"bajo campana."* The Spanish Crown's baptismal gift to a new congregation—a 1,000-peso start-up set of religious furnishings—effectively anchored the town, for the weight, volume, value, and holiness of the *sacra* made them difficult to transport. "Decent" worship further demanded consumables readily available in the Mediterranean world but unevenly distributed in the Indies: beeswax, incense, linen, olive oil, grape wine, and wheat flour. The wine and the wafer integral to the Mass were food injunctions, the inverse of food taboos. Through altar grants to priests of the Mass, the Crown made an effort to supply new churches with these necessities as well.[13]

The model for the reductions was monastic. A bell marked the hours for morning, noon, and evening prayers, to which the devout added special litanies, devotions, the Stations of the Cross, and the praying of the Rosary. The observing Christian presented himself at church on Sundays and the holy days set by the Council of Trent to hear Mass and receive instruction in elementary doctrine. During Lent, in preparation for his pre-Easter confession, he attended *doctrina* as often as a child, who went to class and recited the catechism at least three times a week and sometimes daily. Under this regimen of indoctrination, the normal rounds of hunters, gatherers, and slash-and-burn farmers became infractions of a religious rule.[14]

In his 1573 Ordinances of Pacification, Philip II institutionalized the conquest, giving notice that conquest by the sword must give way to conquest by the gospel. The royal standard passed to the missionary orders, enjoined to reduce the wild people peaceably, their expenses underwritten by royal alms. In the new order of things, the military's mandate was not to advance the frontier but to defend the advancing missionary. The 1574 Ordinance of Patronage, a move toward secularization, transformed members of the powerful and independent preaching orders into civil servants of the Crown, answering to a royally appointed bishop. Only in places too thinly settled to support an ecclesiastical hierarchy could the orders maintain a measure of autonomy. To these places they headed, increasing missionary manpower on the Spanish-American frontiers.[15]

Missions were more than sites of indoctrination; they were instruments of empire, deployed and subsidized for reasons of defense and strategy. In northwestern New Spain and New Mexico, they served as cities of refuge from Apache and Comanche raiders. On the long coasts of Chile, Florida, and California, they gave succor to seafarers and stood guard over the sea-lanes. The great arc of mission systems flung across the heart of South America upheld Spain's continental claims against Portugal's. But the program to Christianize and incorporate the people in Acosta's third category made slow progress. According to historian David J. Weber, up to the late eighteenth century, half of the vast expanse we think of as Spanish America was controlled by independent nations of Indians.[16]

Native peoples presented with a sparse frontier version of Christianity made a pragmatic calculation based on material considerations. An examination of those considerations, coupled with a knowledge of subsistence systems, allows the construction of a frontier Christianization model consisting of (1) a continuum of mobility on which to rank a given society from most to least mobile on the basis of its subsistence system at contact, (2) a spectrum of postcontact forces acting to change such a society's level of mobility at a particular place and time, and (3) a scale of Christianization ranging from indomitable to reduced—that is, from the restless life of *indios bárbaros* to the confined life of neophytes—on which to position the society after missionary contact. A formal invitation to enter Christendom placed a society on the scale of Christianization, but its position on the scale could vary. In this model, a society's level of mobility, rising or falling in response to the sum of forces acting upon it, becomes a measure of its resistance or receptivity to fixed residence, the tacit condition of conversion. Obviously, the more mobile a society, the greater the force required to bring it to the point of reduction and keep it there.

For most of Spanish America's scattered frontiers, historians have a working knowledge of the environment at the time of contact, the mobility levels of the indigenes, the postcontact forces with which they dealt, their experience with mission systems (pressuring them in the direction of sedentism), and whether or not their increased or reduced mobility outlasted the missions to become a new norm. This chapter focuses on nine representative regions: the Republic of the Guaranís, the Llanos de Mojos, the Maya lowlands, the Sierra Zapoteca, Florida, the Gran Chichimeca, the Chaco, Araucanía, and, for contrast, New France.[17]

The classic reductions, alternately extolled and deplored, are those of the Guaranís. Part of the extensive Tupí-Guaraní linguistic group, the Guaranís lived east of the Río de la Plata/Río Paraná in the forests and grasslands of present Paraguay and southern Brazil. They grew bitter manioc, maize, sweet potatoes, and squash in forest clearings in a classic case of slash-and-burn agriculture. When their garden plots, or *rozas*, became too distant, the villagers rebuilt their multifamily dwellings and explored the possibilities of a new place.[18] This habit of relocation, coupled with prophecies of "a land without evil" and a propensity for long-distance raiding, made the Guaranís open to mass migration. The early years of Spanish presence in Paraguay coincided with a major population movement across the Chaco. Thousands of Guaranís joined the Spanish expeditions to the Andes in the 1540s, and many stayed to join the heterogeneous Chiriguanás of the Charcas frontier, in what is now eastern Bolivia.[19]

The Guaranís of the Asunción region, known as Cariós, welcomed and offered wives to the Spanish, whom they saw as sources of iron tools and allies against their traditional enemies, the Payaguá on the Paraguay River and the Guaycurú of the Gran Chaco. Although it quickly became clear that the Spanish intended them for a labor force, the Guaranís were too decentralized to mount a unified resistance. Many fled into the forest.

In 1571 Philip II instructed the third *adelantado* of the Río de la Plata, Juan Ortiz de Zárate, to gather the natives into pueblos apart from the "vices and sins and bad customs" of creoles and mestizos and "by means of *religiosos* and other good persons to reduce them and convert them voluntarily to our holy Catholic faith and Christian religion."[20] The reductions would in turn support the colony. The first reductions, founded by Franciscans in Guairá (in the present Brazilian state of Paraná) in the 1580s and 1590s, doubled as *encomienda* pueblos. The Guaranís' consent to this compact can be explained by the appearance of paramilitary Paulistas (part-Portuguese, part-Indian expeditions from São Paulo), which began striking into the interior in search of slaves as early as 1585.

By 1609, when the groundwork was completed for the Jesuit Province of Paraguay, an administrative district covering eastern Bolivia, Argentina, southwestern Brazil, Uruguay, and Chile, the most remote forest dwellers were ready to seek asylum. By obtaining an exemption from the *mita*, or labor service, for natives "conquered by the gospel" and by locating their missions at a distance from colonial centers and controlling access to them, the Jesuits won the trust of the natives and the enmity of settlers, who accused them of monopolizing Indian labor.

The initial reductions in Guairá, Itatín, and Tapé turned out to be vulnerable to the Paulistas, who accelerated their raids, carrying off 60,000 Guaranís between 1628 and 1630 for the southern captaincies of São Paulo and São Vicente. Declaring that "indio bom é indio do padre" (a good Indian is a father's [priest's] Indian), the slavers concentrated on the reductions. In 1631, 12,000 mission Indians abandoned Guairá and headed south by canoe. On the way, half of them abandoned the enterprise and another

2,000 died, but the survivors of the exodus rebuilt their communities between the Paraná and Uruguay rivers in what is now the province of Misiones, Argentina. Ten years later, licensed by the Crown to carry firearms and commanded by chief Nicolás Ñeengirú, they defeated the Paulista forces in the battle of Mbororé. The Guaranís of the reductions in Itatín, similarly harassed, moved south of Asunción to the Tebicuary River in present Paraguay. Those of Tapé moved westward to the east bank, or Banda Oriental, of the upper Uruguay River in the present Brazilian state of Rio Grande do Sul. The three systems of reductions were then close enough together to be consolidated.

The resulting Jesuit Republic of the Guaranís served as a buffer state between the Portuguese and the Spanish for over a century. Its thirty reductions—fifteen in present-day Argentina, seven in Brazil, and eight in Paraguay—functioned as a federation of cities: producing *yerba mate* and textiles for export; practicing animal husbandry; creating their own art, music, and crafts; and achieving a high level of civilization in European terms, to the point of printing books in Tupí-Guaraní, the *lingua geral*. With a population that stabilized in 1732 at 144,000, the Republic had an army of 20,000, a third of which was cavalry. Its common herd of wild cattle increased to a million head, turning the Tapé Guaranís into horsemen and the aborigines of the vicinity into cattle hunters and supplying Colônia do Sacramento and Montevideo, rival settlements on the Platine littoral, with an export of hides.

The Charrúas and Minuanes of the littoral had a classic extensive mixed subsistence economy of hunting and gathering, with incipient agriculture. Because they were nomadic, which to a European meant without proprietary rights, and because they refused Christianization and incorporation into a European-style labor system, Portuguese and Spanish emigrants felt free to appropriate their hunting grounds. Moving northward into the Banda Oriental, the Charrúas and Minuanes came into conflict with the Tapé reductions. The result was an internal frontier between the aboriginal *indios bárbaros* and the agricultural-pastoral-artisanal mission Indians. The enmity that arose between the two groups would outlast the reductions and even the Portuguese-Spanish border wars.[21]

The older foes of the Republic were only biding their time. In the 1750 Treaty of Madrid, Portugal and Spain settled their differences in the south by agreeing to a territorial exchange: Portugal's Colônia for Spain's Banda Oriental. The 30,000 Tapé inhabitants were given four years to evacuate their seven reductions and relocate their herds. Disregarding their spiritual leaders, who were under orders to preach nonresistance, the "Sete Povos" took up arms and were defeated in the Guaraní War (1754–56). Although Charles III of Spain rescinded the treaty, the damage had been done. The Jesuits, long suspected of transmontane loyalties, fell victim to the rising tide of regalism, and between 1759 and 1768 the Society was expelled from the Portuguese, French, and Spanish empires in turn. In an unsympathetic political environment, the reductions declined and were gradually abandoned. Some of the Guaraní people, like their ancestors, sought refuge in the forests; some took their artisanal skills to the population centers of a burgeoning Platine economy; others headed toward the *cimarrón* herds of the savannas, where they helped to form the cattle culture of the gaucho.

Less well known than the Guaraní reductions but almost as successful were the Mojos (or Moxos) missions of the Upper Amazon, located in a tropical environment of forests and savannas on the Madeira River in what is now eastern Bolivia. Amazonian cultures could reach levels of population density as high as the Valley of Mexico's and probably underwent the same cycles of agricultural intensification and environmental overexploitation as the Lowland Maya, the Anasazi of the Southwest, and the Mound Builders of the Mississippi valley. Three centuries before the European arrival, the Arawakan chiefdoms of the Llanos de Mojos addressed the region's flood-drought problem with massive earthworks: mounds, causeways, reservoirs, and 50,000 acres of raised, ridged fields. At the time of contact, the savanna peoples' main cultivars were bitter and sweet manioc, peanuts, sweet potatoes, beans, squash, peppers, and maize, which they used to make an alcoholic beverage. They lived in central-based settlements strung along the riverside, with satellites on the open savanna. Fish supplied most of their protein, and they supplemented their diet by hunting and gathering.[22]

For thirty years after the conquest of Peru, the chimerical realm of the Gran Moxo was one of the goals of Andean-based parties of explorers. Actual contact with the chiefdoms came, however, from the east, as part of the rapid expansion that led Spaniards to found Asunción, a thousand miles up the Río de la Plata, in 1537 and Santa Cruz de la Sierra in 1561. By the end of the sixteenth century, slave-taking expeditions of Cruceños and Guaraní-speaking Chiriguanás were making regular forays into the savanna. Although Jesuits from Santa Cruz began work in the Llanos de Mojos in 1674, their superiors in the Province of Peru approved the venture only after a sufficient number of natives agreed to congregate in nuclear settlements under the indirect rule of the Jesuits, which they did in the hope of safety from their enemies and access to European goods. Because the Mojos and their neighbors were already semisedentary, mission life did not require them to change their basic mode of subsistence, merely to live in larger pueblos, raise cattle, and learn a common mission language, the Arawakan Mojo. By 1706 the pueblos of the Llanos de Mojos contained up to 30,500 Christians and were active in the Andean trade network.[23]

Although the Mojos reductions produced above the subsistence level, their income from exports was insufficient to meet their expenses. In a case of center supporting periphery, the Jesuit province covered the shortfall with a combination of investments in the secular economy, donations from benefactors, and Crown subsidies. The reason for the royal treasury's financial commitment was strategic. The Mojos mission system was one of those that stood as a barrier against the Portuguese advance, a front-line role that the Crown recognized in 1723 by granting the natives permission to use firearms. In the 1760s, Bourbon imperial policy reversed the center-periphery relation. The savanna became a theater of war, and the pueblos along the Madeira River stopped consuming royal revenues and began to produce them. In a move to concentrate authority, the Crown ordered the Jesuits out, but the mission culture that they and the Indians had created in the Bolivian Amazon endured.[24] If only by comparison to the abuses of the national period, the Mojos' experience with reduction must be judged successful. Like the irrigation-farming Yaquis of Sonora, they lamented the loss of the colonial pact and looked back on their life in the mission pueblos as a golden time.[25]

On the southern frontiers of New Spain, reduction met with mixed success. The Maya of the Yucatán and the lowlands of Chiapas and Guatemala were exceptions to the rule that civilization cannot exist apart from sedentary agriculture. The Spanish who arrived to begin the conquest of the Lowland Maya in 1527 found ceremonial centers centuries old and people with a sophisticated sense of time, who told their past in fifty-two-year cycles of ruin and renewal. While they waited for their greatness to return, the Maya traded cotton cloth, honey, wax, cacao, and salt and raised maize, beans, squash, and chiles in a pattern of shifting cultivation that made them especially difficult for authorities to count and control.[26]

Farriss identifies three types of population movement by Maya under colonial rule: flight across the frontier into an unpacified territory, or *despoblado;* drift to another community to escape their debts, labor obligations, and tribute; and dispersal to satellite settlements to fulfil the demands of shifting cultivation. First the men "made *milpa,*" clearing a space in the forest and planting maize, and then the family joined them. In the Yucatán as in Florida, the Franciscans were sure that only their watchfulness stood between their converts and utter depravity. "What was so disturbing to the Spanish ecclesiastical mind was precisely the freedom dispersed residence afforded, regardless of what the Indians in fact chose to do with it," Farriss observes. "The forest represented a threat to Christianity, a place where the Maya could revert to paganism and savagery."[27] In Chiapas, the Dominicans tried to eliminate what they regarded as a chaotic pattern of scattered settlement by forcing the population into closer, more "orderly" reductions, but their campaign was successful only in densely populated areas near Spanish towns, and even those places were subject to recurrent fugitivism.[28]

The Sierra Zapoteca of Oaxaca was a pocket frontier, isolated from the rest of New Spain by a terrain impenetrable to pack animals or horsemen. The Zapotec, Chinantec, and Mixe *serranos* in their rugged retreats, unconquered by Aztec warriors, resisted Spanish conquest until the 1550s and thereafter did their best to stay out of sight of the few Spanish and Tlaxcalan colonists sent to collect their tribute of cotton mantles and cochineal and the even fewer Dominican friars sent to Christianize them. Farming in the Sierra was subject to unpredictable rainfall and rapid land exhaustion, with low yields and the frequent clearing of new fields leading to a pattern of shifting settlement and abandoned villages. Pursuing the agenda of pacification, the Dominicans congregated the *serranos* into fewer, more accessible sites. To speed their indoctrination, the bishop of Oaxaca ordered the Indians to learn the language of Nahuatl, which was spreading throughout New Spain. The number of missionaries was so low, however, that many Indians saw their priest no more than six or eight times a year, which, considering the steep fees for his services, seemed enough. Communities observed saints' cults and holy days, but family devotions continued to center on ancestors and the spirits of trees, mountains, and rocks.[29]

The Indian societies of Florida presented Spaniards with a full range of the usual subsistence economies, and more. The Calusas, the people of a powerful chiefdom in south Florida, were sedentary but nonagricultural, basing their settlements squarely on marine resources. Secure in their naval power, and with access to European goods through salvage and Cuban fishermen, the Calusas were never Christianized. They expected missionaries to bring them fine gifts and then leave. On the Atlantic coast below

St. Augustine, the Ais and other groups of central-based wanderers were a security risk, trading with French, English, and Dutch vessels, but their marshy territory was incompatible with fixed settlement and thus with missions. The Guales and Oristas of present-day Georgia and South Carolina depended heavily on hunting, fishing, and gathering; they followed an annual round that took them from oak groves to estuaries, to scattered clearings for swidden agriculture, and back to the estuaries, where they maintained centers of redistribution. The eastern Timucuans inhabiting the barrier islands and coastal marshes east of the St. Johns River had a similar lifestyle.

After some first-generation resistance, the Guales and eastern Timucuans accepted the Spanish presence, iron tools, and missionaries. Their communal fields grew larger and their growing seasons longer, but their town sites continued to be transitory, leaving the landscape dotted with "old fields." In due course, the more agricultural western Timucuans, whose territory ran from the St. Johns west to the marshes of the gulf, were also Christianized, as were the Apalaches to their north, who had the richest soils and most intensive agriculture in all of Florida. The royal treasury in Mexico City underwrote the republic of Indians by adding a fund for chiefs to the presidio's annual subvention.

At their mid-seventeenth-century height the Florida mission provinces boasted 26,000 Christians in close to forty *doctrinas*, all prone to unseemly mobility. According to the Franciscans, the "bad and willful" Guales went "inland to pueblos of heathen, where they remain[ed] for one year and two without hearing Mass." The Timucuans, "content with little," often ran short of maize and went "into the woods to maintain themselves with plants and roots." Apalache matrons gathering hickory nuts to make lamp oil were said to be "wandering about in the woods," ready to commit "a thousand mortal sins." Florida's mission Indians clearly had not surrendered the right to move about.

Meanwhile, with the wandering Indians the missionaries were getting nowhere. The Yamassees, they protested, were "an indomitable, unreasonable nation" who would "by no means settle down, much less plant for their sustenance, or be found ever in a designated place." The Rinconada marshlands in back of Cape Canaveral were "full of idolaters and gentiles" who sustained themselves with fish and wild fruits. There had been some hope that gifts of iron hoes might "induce them to plantings and to live like rationals," but the Indians of the Rinconada had continued their wandering ways, "for no reason, . . . moved solely by their obstinacy and ignorance, like the sons of the woods that they are." Those of Mayaca, on the upper reaches of the St. Johns, would not "live like Christians"; the place was "irreduceable." Only after the English of Charles Town became buyers of Indians, and Creek slave catchers overran the peninsula, were the remnants of the wild nations driven to seek sanctuary under the guns of the fort in St. Augustine. The friars assigned to them, who did not know their languages, reported that the Costas were "an utterly useless nation," "vile by nature," who capriciously "leave their huts and go off to eat dates," while the Jororos "neither sow nor cultivate, but only wander about the whole year, men and women alike, searching the seashore for something to eat, killing alligators and other unclean animals." After living in proximity for 160 years, the Spanish and the wandering nations of Florida were still strangers.[30]

Spaniards, whose idea of conquest was to make themselves overlords of large numbers of productive people, ordinarily showed little interest in the lands or persons of wanderers. When valuable resources were identified beyond the borders of settlement, however, interest grew.

The Gran Chichimeca, a rugged and arid plateau between the eastern and western Sierra Madres, was home to four linguistic nations unconquered by the Aztecs: the Guachichiles, Zacatecos, Guamares, and Pames. All of the Chichimecos depended heavily on hunting and gathering, with dietary staples of mesquite bread, fermented agave juice, and cactus fruits, called *tunas*. Rainfall and warfare permitting, some groups grew maize and squash and resided in semipermanent villages, but the majority lived in caves and round huts on the shelves of canyons in terrain too rough for horsemen and so cactus-covered that it was called the Gran Tunal. When, shortly after the Mixtón War (1540–41), prospectors from Nueva Galicia discovered silver at Zacatecas and Guanajuato and planted mining settlements deep inside their territory, the Chichimecos began to raid the wagon trains for clothing, food, and horseflesh.[31]

In the Spanish worldview, only sedentary Indians could integrate themselves into the Spanish world as *indios de paz*. The Chichimecos, whose roaming left them without European-recognized rights to land, were *indios de guerra*. After years of conflict and bloodshed and several martyred Franciscans, the Spanish brought the Chichimeca War (1550–90) to a close with gifts and colonists. In a policy of "peace by purchase," a kind of reverse tribute, captains of peace gave the raiders wagonloads of the goods they had been taking by force. At government expense, four hundred Tlaxcalan families were transported to the frontier to found eight tribute-exempt pueblos, each of which was granted a year's supply of maize, ten yokes of oxen, a soldier, and a Franciscan. The viceroy of New Spain reported in 1590 that many nomads had already abandoned the sierras to learn the rudiments of agriculture. Once they became cultivators of the soil, said his successor, they and their children would forget the exercises of war.[32]

The descendants of the Chichimecos nonetheless persisted in the old ways. In 1774, the curate of a mission in Nuevo León complained that the Borrados had not made a harvest of maize or wheat for twenty-six years, although their ground was fertile and well watered. He himself had once given them oxen and seed corn, which they ate. "Their native inclination takes them to the countryside, where, not valuing the fruits that they might eat by their industry, they content themselves with anything wild and natural that comes along, such as tuna, mesquite, wild pig, deer, and mescal. And from this comes idleness, gaming, dancing, and a total disinclination to work the soil."[33]

The Guaycuruans of the Gran Chaco desert and its peripheries between the eastern slope of the Andes and the Paraná-Paraguay river system took pride in their nomadic culture and scorned the maize-growing Carió-Guaranís across the Paraguay, who were driven by their depredations to accept Spanish aid. Making war on the Guaycuruans was counterproductive. When Álvar Núñez Cabeza de Vaca, named governor of Asunción after his North American adventures, inquired what had been done to bring them under obedience, he was told that they could not be indoctrinated or "made industrious," for they never stayed more than three days in one place.[34] Moreover, thanks to the Spanish penchant for contraband, they had equipped themselves with iron tools and iron-tipped weapons.

Prominent among the Guaycuruan groups were the riverine Payaguás, who harassed shipping on the Paraguay River in their great war canoes, and the equestrian Abipones, Mocovís, Tobas, and Mbayás, who moved across the Paraguay into areas left empty by the destruction of Itatín, enserfed the Arawakan Guanás, one of the few agricultural groups in the Chaco, and raided the Guaranís to gain livestock and women. Reaching the height of their military strength in the early 1700s, these warrior groups pushed back the frontiers of the Spanish provinces of Tucumán, Paraguay, and Río de la Plata. In 1708 the governor of Tucumán informed the Crown that they had stolen many horses and become strong horsemen. Inasmuch as there was not the least hope of reducing them by gentle means and no peace with them was to be trusted, he intended to launch a "war of fire and blood" and "drive these barbarians out of the woodlands in which they shelter, where they live like wild beasts without polities or properties or anything like a human custom, thirsting like tigers for the blood of Christians."[35]

After the first of the governor's punitive expeditions, some of the more sedentary groups requested missions, and after 1740 most Guaycuruans spent some time in them. The push factors were epidemics and ecological pressures, including grazing damage, overhunting, and the decline of the *algarroba* (carob) groves. The pull factors were security, subsidies, easier access to iron lance points and sabers, and opportunities for short-term employment as ranch hands, hunters, and soldiers. The missions enjoyed mixed success. They failed to support themselves, for the natives resisted communal agriculture. The women planted and harvested, reverting to their old ways when *algarroba* and palm fruits were in season; the men spent much of their time drinking *chicha*, playing Spanish games of chance, and rustling cattle. According to historian James Schofield Saeger, "Guaycuruan men's desire for combat, which had provided security, sustenance, women, and prestige for centuries, could not be preached away." Nonetheless, those missions that continued to be funded after the expulsion of the Jesuits lasted until 1810, and in them many Guaycuruans found safety while they acquired the skills to fit into a changed world.[36]

The indigenous people of northern Chile had been part of the Inka empire for seventy or eighty years before the Spanish arrived. In that time they learned to tolerate foreign occupation, produce an agricultural surplus for the support of colonists and military garrisons, mine and refine precious metals for the payment of tribute, and raise pack animals. The Mapuche-speaking Araucanos of southern Chile did not pass through the Inka apprenticeship. They adapted readily to European technology, crops, and livestock, especially sheep and horses, but set limits on European demands and interference and in 1598 went on the offensive and expelled all the Spanish south of the Bío-Bío River. For the next two hundred years the Bío-Bío was the official boundary between Chile and Araucanía, flowing through a fortified border characterized by the violent exchange of women and children, weapons, and animals. The captaincy general of Chile was a *"tierra reputada por guerra viva,"* or combat post. The number of soldiers on the southern frontier rose to two thousand, and the captaincy's economy revolved around the military payroll and a legalized trade in captives and ransoms, but their annual *entradas* only expedited the transfer of Spanish goods into Indian hands.

Adapting to a raiding economy, the Araucanos moved their fields from the valleys into the sierras and broadened their subsistence base by hunting and gathering, like their Mapuche-speaking neighbors, the Pehuenches of the cordillera (suppliers of arrow poison) and the Huilliches of the southern coast below Valdivia (suppliers of ponchos). Low, well-watered mountain passes allowed the Pehuenches to move stolen cattle and other goods across the Andes. Bands of mounted Mapuches followed the same routes eastward to raid and trade with the Puelches of the pampas and the ostrich-hunting Tehuelches of northern Patagonia. The spreading horse culture, combined with expanding opportunities for exchange, led to the "araucanization of the desert." Throughout southern South America, native societies increased in military strength. Contraband on the southern route from Buenos Aires to Peru passed through their hands, and Spanish authorities had good reason to fear that they might make common cause with the Dutch, who in 1643 did briefly occupy Valdivia and open negotiations with the Araucanos.[37]

The Crown thus had strong strategic reasons for continuing to support the Jesuit missionaries who crossed the Bío-Bío to visit the lands of war. The natives, however, remained unreduced. In Paraguay and Bolivia, the Guaranís and Mojos turned to the reductions for sanctuary from raiders and slavers, but the Araucanos had no need of a refuge; in Chile, the Spanish were the ones under assault. Arauco could not have underwritten a Jesuit mission system had it desired one. Although there was a growing demand for the region's water-resistant woolen ponchos, no export emerged that was comparable to the *yerba mate,* cacao, or cotton mantles that sustained other mission systems and connected them to the nearest metropolis.

Unable to convert the *indios de guerra,* the Jesuits turned to sacramentalism, reviving the sixteenth-century flying mission in a new form. With their packs full of baptismal gifts, they rode into Araucanía every spring to baptize adults *in extremis* and the year's crop of infants, of whom a third would die before the age of reason. The sacramental crusade of the seventeenth-century flying mission served no secular purpose, for the Indians were left free of Spanish control, and the religious value of baptism without conversion was debatable. What it did accomplish was to fill the imagination of Catholic Europe with heroic missionaries sacrificing their lives to carry salvation to distant and dangerous vagabonds.

After the expulsion of the Jesuits, the Franciscans inherited the problem of the "baptized barbarians." Two centuries of evangelizing experience in the Americas had stripped the followers of Saint Francis of any illusions about peaceful conversion. They called on the Crown to reduce the Araucanos by force of arms to hear the word of God. The Indians' not residing in pueblos was the "chief obstacle" to their Christianization, asserted Father Ramón Redrado in 1775, for "scattered about in the mountains and plains, not listening to the voice of a missionary, they do not change in the least their barbarous customs."[38]

The flying missions into Araucanía raise disquieting questions about the parallel ventures in New France, which thanks to the Jesuit *Relations* have become the epitome of heroic evangelism. The missionaries who arrived at the settlements on the St. Lawrence River objected strongly to nomadism for the same reasons as priests elsewhere. Wandering in a wilderness was for beasts, not men; hearers on the move multiplied a preacher's logistical problems; and Christian precepts called for converts to be closely watched lest they lapse into the moral failings of natural man and their last state be worse than their first. In 1632, when the English marched out of the fort of Québec and the French returned to make a fresh start, the Jesuits took on the task of converting the Iroquoian Hurons and the Algonquian Montagnais. Both peoples lived in dispersed habitations and were relatively self-sufficient. They differed in their level of mobility.

Each fall the Montagnais, who lived in northern forests beyond the bounds of maize horticulture, split into small groups to hunt moose and caribou. Father Paul Le Jeune, who spent a winter with one such hunting band, returned convinced that the only way to convert the nomads was to get them to forsake their hunting and gathering ways and settle down. It "would be a great blessing for their bodies, for their souls," he wrote, "if those Tribes were stationary, and if they became docile to our direction." Material gifts and promises of protection from Iroquois raids attracted some Montagnais and other Algonquins to the village of Sillery near Québec, where the growing season was long enough for maize, but they did not take to fixed settlement, nor was that way of life compatible with the fur trade, their contribution to the colony's economy.[39]

The Hurons of the Great Lakes interior, who in the 1630s numbered around 30,000, were more promising candidates for Christianization, being farmers and town-dwellers. Three-quarters of their calories came from domesticated plants; they traded their surplus maize to the Algonquins of the Ottawa River valley; and they moved their towns no oftener than every six to twelve years. Some Huron Christians were actually starting to settle with the Jesuits in Guaraní-style reductions when the mission experiment was cut short. In the 1640s the Iroquois, armed with Dutch firearms, attacked Huronia, destroying the towns and scattering their inhabitants, then went on to raid Algonquin country. Some Algonquins came to the French for refuge, but they found the reductions too confining and the discipline of the seminary too severe for their children.

By 1649 the Jesuits in New France had given up on sedentism. No longer did they insist that the Indians come to them and settle in their vicinity. The later *Relations* emphasize their flying missions to the Hurons resettled in Iroquoia and to the mixed refugees of the Great Lakes region and the Illinois country. With little reason to hope that the natives to whom they ministered would ever turn their backs on savagery, the Jesuits fixed their minds on martyrdom.[40]

On the basis of this brief survey of native societies from the northern to the southern extreme of empire, some accepting and others avoiding reduction, one is drawn to agree with historian David Sweet that "Indians for the most part settled in missions only after having been badly battered by disease, famine, enslavement, the intensification of intertribal war brought about by contact with the Europeans, war with the conquerors themselves, or some combination of these pressures."[41] The Guaranís, slash-and-burn farmers at the time of contact, accepted reduction by Jesuits to escape the Guaycuruans and the Paulistas. The Mojos, who had combined riverbank farming with foraging, sought Jesuit protection from the Chiriguanás and the Cruceños. The Lowland Maya and the peoples of the Sierra Zapoteca, both of whom had practiced shifting cultivation at the time of contact, resisted Dominican efforts to congregate them. In the provinces of Florida, groups that had combined shifting cultivation with foraging continued to do so despite Franciscan disapproval. The peoples of the Gran Chichimeca were attracted to settlements by gifts and Franciscan mediation, but they were not converted from foragers into farmers. The Guaycuruans resided in missions seasonally but did not submit to a mission routine. The Araucanos held the Spanish at bay and developed an economy of raiding and contraband, with increased hunting and gathering. Like the natives of New France, they permitted Jesuits to visit and even baptize them but not to disturb their way of life.

Modern missiologists dismayed by the unapologetic arrogance of early modern missionaries would rather lay the blame for mission failures on the messengers than question the cultural fit of the message. Yet, just as all sheep are not of the fold, every society was not the stuff of conversion, and some missionaries came close to saying so. In 1570, Florida Jesuit Juan Rogel explained to his military patron why the Oristas were not accepting Christianity:

> The main obstacle to their conversion is their wandering scattered nine months a year. If we are to gather fruit, the Indians must join and live in settlements and cultivate the soil, raising sustenance for the whole year and once they are firmly fixed in one place preaching may begin. As this is not done we have had no results these four years, and would not for fifty.
>
> To unite them in this manner will be difficult and will take a long time to do it lawfully and not by compulsion or armed force. For they have been accustomed to living in this way for many thousands of years, and to want to take them from it would be like death to them. And even if they were willing, the land will not produce, being poor and miserable, and exhausting itself very quickly, and thus they themselves say that this is the reason they go about so scattered, moving from so many places.[42]

For some groups, baptism was a survival stratagem, and missions were refugee camps to be quitted when life returned to normal. Some who took to the woods to get away from Europeans were forced by external enemies, disease, or hunger to come to terms with them, if only temporarily. Others found that mission complexes could be put to use as inns, forts, granaries, trading posts, and livestock reserves. For those whose adaptation to horses yielded increased mobility and power, missions were places that begged to be raided.

What Bishop Antonio de Azcona Imberto said in the late seventeenth century about the Pampas Indians—"It has been observed in this kingdom that none of these wandering nations has ever been reduced to the faith"[43]—could have been said of mobile societies on the Spanish-American frontier generally. Those missionaries whose best efforts were failing to reduce the resistant peoples must have been troubled by the two reasons that suggested themselves. Either God had made some nations indomitable by nature, or the church itself, by forsaking universalism to focus on rites, rules, and reductions, had closed the door.

Notes

My sincere thanks to readers Jeremy Adams, James Brooks, Luca Codignola, Douglas Cope, Margarita Gascón, Jack P. Greene, Catherine Julien, Hal Langfur, James Muldoon, and David J. Weber.

1. José de Acosta, *De procuranda Indorum salute* [1588], ed. L. Pereña, 2 vols. (Madrid: Consejo Superior de Investigaciones Científicas, 1984–87), and *Natural and Moral History of the Indies*, ed. Jane E. Mangan, trans. Frances M. López-Morillas (Durham, N.C.: Duke University Press, 2002); Bartolomé de Las Casas, *Apologética historia sumaria* [ca. 1555], ed. Edmundo O'Gorman, 2 vols. (Mexico City: Universidad Nacional Autónoma, 1967). See also Anthony Pagden, *The Fall of Natural Man: The American Indian and the Origins of Comparative Ethnology* (Cambridge, U.K.: Cambridge University Press, 1982), 119–97, and D. A. Brading, *The First America: The Spanish Monarchy, Creole Patriots, and the Liberal State, 1492–1867* (Cambridge, U.K.: Cambridge University Press, 1991), 79–101, 184–95.

2. Amy Turner Bushnell, *Situado and Sabana: Spain's Support System for the Presidio and Mission Provinces of Florida*, Anthropological Papers of the American Museum of Natural History 74 (New York: American Museum of Natural History, 1994), 20–23; Antonine Tibesar, O.F.M., *Franciscan Beginnings in Colonial Peru* (Washington, D.C.: Academy of American Franciscan History, 1953), 36–50.

3. A. D. Wright, *The Counter-Reformation: Catholic Europe and the Non-Christian World* (New York: St. Martin's Press, 1982), 141, 277–79; Kenneth Mills, *Idolatry and Its Enemies: Colonial Andean Religion and Extirpation, 1640–1750* (Princeton: Princeton University Press, 1997), 204–5.

4. Peter A. Goddard, "Augustine and the Amerindian in Seventeenth-Century New France," *Church History* 67:4 (December 1998): 662–81; Stafford Poole, C.M., "The Declining Image of the Indian among Churchmen in Sixteenth-Century New Spain," in Susan E. Ramírez, ed., *Indian-Religious Relations in Colonial Spanish America* (Syracuse, N.Y.: Maxwell School of Citizenship and Public Affairs, Syracuse University, 1989), 11–19.

5. Nancy M. Farriss, *Maya Society under Colonial Rule: The Collective Enterprise of Survival* (Princeton: Princeton University Press, 1984), 92.

6. Robert Ricard, *The Spiritual Conquest of Mexico: An Essay on the Apostolate and the Evangelizing Methods of the Mendicant Orders in New Spain, 1523–1572*, trans. Lesley Byrd Simpson (Berkeley: University of California Press, 1966), 135–36; Tibesar, *Franciscan Beginnings in Colonial Peru*, 50; Bernardino Verástique, *Michoacán and Eden: Vasco de Quiroga and the Evangelization of Western Mexico* (Austin: University of Texas Press, 2000), xiii–xiv, 120–21.

7. For an example of Indians' being compared to gypsies, see the deposition of Fray Manuel Beteta, *doctrinero* of the pueblo of Nombre de Dios de Macaris, 8 July 1738, in "Auto on the State of the Doctrinas, St. Augustine, Florida, 9 June 1738 to 8 July 1738," Archivo General de Indias, *ramo* Gobierno: Santo Domingo [SD], *legajo* 865.

8. Amy Turner Bushnell, "The Sacramental Imperative: Catholic Ritual and Indian Sedentism in the Provinces of Florida," in *Columbian Consequences*, vol. 2, *Archaeology and History of the Spanish Borderlands East*, ed. David Hurst Thomas (Washington, D.C.: Smithsonian Institution Press, 1990), 475–90.

9. Farriss, *Maya Society under Colonial Rule*, 277.

10. Robert L. Bettinger, *Hunter-Gatherers: Archaeological and Evolutionary Theory* (New York: Plenum Press, 1991), 49; Susan Alling Gregg, *Foragers and Farmers: Population Interaction and Agricultural Expansion in Prehistoric Europe* (Chicago: University of Chicago Press, 1988), 37; V. Neckebrouck, *Paradoxes de l'inculturation: Les nouveaux habits des Yanomami* (Leuven: Uitgeverij Peeters, 1994), chap. 6, esp. 113.

11. Clark Spencer Larsen, *Skeletons in Our Closet: Revealing Our Past through Bioarchaeology* (Princeton: Princeton University Press, 2000); Richard H. Steckel and Jerome C. Rose, *The Backbone of History: Health and Nutrition in the Western Hemisphere* (Cambridge: Cambridge University Press, 2002).

12. On the availability of the sacraments, see Bushnell, *Situado and Sabana*, 97–99, and Ignacio Dalcin, *Em busca de uma "Terra sem Males." As reduções jesuíticas guaranis: Evangelização e catequese nos Sete Povos das Missões* (Porto Alegre: Edições EST, 1993), 89–95. For restrictions on ordination, see John F. Schwaller, "The Clergy," in *The Countryside in Colonial Latin America*, ed. Louisa Schell Hoberman and Susan Migden Socolow (Albuquerque: University of New Mexico Press, 1996), 123–46, esp. 128.

13. Bushnell, *Situado and Sabana*, 73–81.

14. Bushnell, *Situado and Sabana*, 90–97. Spanish parishioners in Florida observed thirty-eight holy days, and the Indians, thirteen. See Robert L. Kapitzke, *Religion, Power, and Politics in Colonial St. Augustine* (Gainesville: University Press of Florida, 2001), 13–14.

15. Amy Turner Bushnell, "Spain's Conquest by Contract: Pacification and the Mission System in Eastern North America," in Michael V. Kennedy and William G. Shade, eds., *The World Turned Upside Down: The State of Eighteenth-Century American Studies at the Beginning of the Twenty-First Century* (Bethlehem, Penn.: Lehigh University Press, 2001), 289–320, esp. 297–98.

16. David J. Weber, "Bourbons and *Bárbaros:* Center and Periphery in the Reshaping of Spanish Indian Policy," in Christine Daniels and Michael V. Kennedy, eds., *Negotiated Empires: Centers and Peripheries in the Americas, 1500–1820* (New York: Routledge, 2002), 79–103.

17. Omitted are the mission systems of Brazil and arid America, including those of northern New Spain and the Southwest on which Herbert E. Bolton based his model of the mission as a frontier institution. See "The Mission as a Frontier Institution in the Spanish-American Colonies," *American Historical Review* 23:1 (1917): 42–61.

18. On the Guaranís, see Juan Carlos Garavaglia, "The Crises and Transformations of Invaded Societies: The La Plata Basin (1535–1650)," and James Schofield

Saeger, "Warfare, Reorganization, and Readaptation at the Margins of Spanish Rule—The Chaco and Paraguay (1573–1882)," in *The Cambridge History of the Native Peoples of the Americas*, ed. Frank Salomon and Stuart B. Schwartz, vol. 3, *South America*, part 2, 1–58 and 257–86; Cayetano Bruno, *Las órdenes religiosas en la evangelización de las Indias* (Rosario, Argentina: Didascalia, 1992), 103–17; Thomas Whigham, "Paraguay's *Pueblos de Indios:* Echoes of a Missionary Past," in *The New Latin American Mission History*, ed. Erick Langer and Robert H. Jackson (Lincoln: University of Nebraska Press, 1995), 157–88; and Bartolomeu Melià, *El Guaraní conquistado y reducido: Ensayos de etnohistoria* (Asunción: Centro de Estudios Antropológicos de la Universidad Católica, 1988).

19. Hélene Clastres, *The Land-without-Evil: Tupí-Guaraní Prophetism* (Urbana: University of Illinois Press, 1995); Catherine Julien, "Warfare in Real Time and Space: Sixteenth-Century Expeditions from the Pantanal to the Andean Foothills," paper presented to the 50th International Congress of Americanists, Warsaw, Poland, July 10–14, 2000, and "Colonial Perspectives on the Chiriguaná," in *Resistencia y adaptación nativas en las tierras bajas Latinoamericanas*, ed. María Susana Cipolletti (Quito: Ediciones Abya-Yala, 1997), 18–76.

20. Bruno, *Las órdenes religiosas*, 103.

21. Juan Villegas, S.J., "La evangelización del indio de la Banda Oriental del Uruguay (siglos XVI–XVIII)," in Johannes Meier, ed., *Cristianismo y mundo colonial: Tres estudios acerca de la evangelización de Hispanoamérica* (Münster: Aschendorffsche Verlagsbuchhandlung, 1995), 69–111.

22. David Block, *Mission Culture on the Upper Amazon: Native Tradition, Jesuit Enterprise, and Secular Policy in Moxos, 1660–1880* (Lincoln: University of Nebraska Press, 1994); David Cleary, "Towards an Environmental History of the Amazon: From Prehistory to the Nineteenth Century," *Latin American Research Review* 36:2 (2001): 64–96; Anne Christine Taylor, "The Western Margins of Amazonia from the Early Sixteenth to the Early Nineteenth Century," in Salomon and Schwartz, *South America*, part 2, 188–256.

23. Bruno, *Las órdenes religiosas*, 129.

24. Block, *Mission Culture on the Upper Amazon*, 174–81; Bruno, *Las órdenes religiosas*, 129.

25. Cynthia Radding, "The Colonial Pact and Changing Ethnic Frontiers in Highland Sonora, 1740–1840," in *Contested Ground: Comparative Frontiers on the Northern and Southern Edges of the Spanish Empire*, ed. Donna J. Guy and Thomas E. Sheridan (Tucson: University of Arizona Press, 1998), 52–66.

26. Grant D. Jones, "The Lowland Mayas, from the Conquest to the Present," in *The Cambridge History of the Native Peoples of the Americas*, ed. Richard E. W. Adams and Murdo J. Macleod, vol. 2, *Mesoamerica*, part 2 (Cambridge, U.K.: Cambridge University Press, 2000), 346–91; Matthew Restall, *The Maya World: Yucatec Culture and Society, 1550–1850* (Stanford: Stanford University Press, 1997), 172–79.

27. Farriss, *Maya Society under Colonial Rule*, 199–214.

28. Amos Megged, *Exporting the Catholic Reformation: Local Religion in Early-Colonial Mexico* (Leiden: E. J. Brill, 1996), 56–57.
29. John K. Chance, *Conquest of the Sierra: Spaniards and Indians in Colonial Oaxaca* (Norman: University of Oklahoma Press, 1989).
30. Bushnell, "The Sacramental Imperative," 477–85, quotations from 480–85.
31. Philip Wayne Powell, *Soldiers, Indians, and Silver: The Northward Advance of New Spain, 1550–1600* (Berkeley: University of California Press, 1952), 3–45, 171; David Frye, "The Native Peoples of Northeastern Mexico," in Adams and Macleod, *Mesoamerica*, part 2, 89–135.
32. José Francisco Román Gutiérrez, *Sociedad y evangelización en Nueva Galicia durante el siglo XVI* (Zapopan: D.R. El Colegio de Jalisco, 1993), 25, 289–325, 387–93.
33. See "Queja de los indios de la misión de la Punta de Lampazos contra su alcalde mayor," in Eugenio del Hoyo, *Indios, frailes y encomenderos en el Nuevo Reino de León, siglos XVII y XVIII* (Gobierno de Nuevo León: Archivo General del Estado, 1985), 229–37, quotation from 235.
34. Melià, *El Guaraní conquistado y reducido*, 20.
35. Bruno, *Las órdenes religiosas,* 147–49, quotation from 148, translation mine.
36. James Schofield Saeger, *The Chaco Mission Frontier: The Guaycuruan Experience* (Tucson: University of Arizona Press, 2000), xiv–xv, 3–71, quotation from 35; Saeger, "Warfare, Reorganization, and Readaptation," 257–66.
37. Alvaro Jara, *Guerra y sociedad en Chile: La transformación de la guerra de Arauco y la esclavitud de los indios* (Santiago, Chile: Editorial Universitaria, 1971), 46–47; Kristine L. Jones, "Warfare, Reorganization, and Readaptation at the Margins of Spanish Rule: The Southern Margin (1573–1882)," in Salomon and Schwartz, *South America*, part 2, 138–87; Margarita Gascón, "La articulación de Buenos Aires a la frontera sur del Imperio español, 1640–1740," Universidad Nacional del Centro de la Provincia de Buenos Aires, *Anuario IEHS* 13 (1998): 193–213.
38. Margarita Gascón, letter to Amy Turner Bushnell, 3 September 2002; Jorge Pinto Rodríguez, "Frontera, misiones y misioneros en Chile: La Araucanía, 1600–1900," in *Misioneros en la Araucanía, 1600–1900: Un capítulo de historia fronteriza en Chile*, ed. Jorge Pinto Rodríguez et al.(Temuco, Chile: Imprenta Universidad de la Frontera, 1988), 17–119, quotation from 80, translation mine.
39. Carole Blackburn, *Harvest of Souls: The Jesuit Missions and Colonialism in North America, 1632–1650* (Montreal: McGill-Queen's University Press, 2000), 30–37, 50–52, 94–95, quotation from 94; Alain Beaulieu, *Convertir les fils de Caïn: Jésuites et Amérindiens nomades en Nouvelle-France, 1632–1642* (Québec: Nuit Blanche Éditeur, 1994), 140–42; Pierre Deffontaines, *Géographie et religions* (Paris: Gallimard, 1948), 134–35; Goddard, "Augustine and the Amerindian."
40. R. Douglas Hurt, *Indian Agriculture in America, Prehistory to the Present* (Lawrence: University Press of Kansas, 1987), 33–34; Beaulieu, *Convertir les fils de Caïn*, 140; Blackburn, *Harvest of Souls,* 36, 40; Louis J. Luzbetak, *The Church and*

Cultures: New Perspectives in Missiological Anthropology (1963; Maryknoll, N.Y.: Orbis Books, 1988), 96; Goddard, "Augustine and the Amerindian." Iroquoian reasons for war are discussed in José António Brandão, *"Your Fyre Shall Burn No More": Iroquois Policy toward New France and Its Native Allies to 1701* (Lincoln: University of Nebraska Press, 1997).

41. David Sweet, "The Ibero-American Frontier Mission in Native American History,"in Langer and Jackson, *The New Latin American Mission History*, 1–48, quotation from 32.

42. Juan Rogel, "Letter to Pedro Menéndez de Avilés, 12–9–1570, Havana," in Eugenio Ruidíaz y Caravia, *La Florida: Su conquista y colonización por Pedro Menéndez de Avilés*, 2 vols. (Madrid: Imprenta de los Hijos de J.A. García, 1893–1894), 2:301–8.

43. "Se tiene observado en este reino, que ninguna nación de estas que andan vagando se ha podido reducir a la fe jamás." Letters of Bishop Azcona to His Majesty, 8 August 1678, and 9 and 11 January 1683, quoted in Cayetano Bruno, *La evangelización de la Patagonia y de la Tierra del Fuego* (Rosario, Argentina: Ediciones Didascalia, 1992), 37.

8

Confessing the Indians

Guilt Discourse and Acculturation in Early Spanish America

Jaime Valenzuela Márquez
Translated by James Muldoon

The Significance and Functions of the Sacrament of Penance in the Counter-Reformation

Before I embark upon the topic that is the theme of this chapter, I must elaborate on the characteristics of the language and the practice of Catholic penitential practice that had developed in Europe before the conquest of Latin America. The Fourth Lateran Council (1215) provides a point of reference, for after the council this sacrament became an annual obligation for all the faithful, providing new responsibilities for the clergy:[1] in effect, the priest became responsible for gathering up declarations of sins and maintaining the seal of the confessional. This new approach gained renewed importance toward the end of the Middle Ages when the ancient communal penitential rite and general absolution—usually performed on Easter Sunday—was replaced by the practice of individual confession.[2]

The priest was expected to be ready, moreover, to ask the right questions, because from then on the confessor would hear the confession and ask questions of the penitent. From this modification of procedure arose a literature, the manuals of confession, designed to assist the clergy in this new responsibility. They provide true systematic summaries (*summae confessorum*) with lists of sins, questions, and rituals associated with the sacrament and were produced in a small volume that kept its cost down and facilitated its use in daily practice.[3]

The evolution of these manuals moreover followed the growing complexity of the individual "examination of conscience" that was linked together with the result generated for the new conception of sin imposed by the Lateran Council and with the appearance of a third place in the hereafter: Purgatory. As Jacques Le Goff has shown, Purgatory implied focusing interest on the individual death and on the judgment that followed.[4] It would be a period of temporary suffering, the length of which would depend primarily on the quantity and the quality of the faults committed during one's lifetime. The means of expiation needed to regain divine grace were a combination of persuasion exercised by the priest to encourage the necessary sentiment of guilt, as a step prior to preparing an examination of conscience that provided a detailed and complete confession of one's sins, and canceling the fulfillment of the symbolic punishment in light of those manuals.

In 1551, the Council of Trent strengthened the subject matter and the function of the dogmatic definition of the sacrament of penance.[5] Thus, rejecting the Protestant criticism, the church reaffirmed the sacramental nature and the divine character of its institution, the obligation of confessing all mortal sins, and the essential role that the priest was able to fulfill as the holder of the ritual key that could unlock the gates of Heaven to sinners, because he was able to absolve sins in the name of God. It strengthened and at the same time configured in minute detail the three acts that constitute confession: contrition, confession, and satisfaction.[6]

The first action indicates how the penitent should make an "open rejection" of the sins that he committed, accompanied by the intention to sin no more; that is contrition or repentance for having offended God.[7] Being "contrite," or psychologically dejected for the feeling of guilt, the penitent ought to submit himself to a serious examination of conscience, with the purpose of recalling mortal sins—confession of venial sins is optional—and the circumstances in which they were committed. The subsequent step is verbalization, or confession to the priest, listing in detail the sins that have been recalled. Then follows the absolution, which comes as a "judicial act," by means of which the priest pardons the sins and the postmortem punishment that they have merited, assigning to the penitent a symbolic temporal punishment for which satisfaction ought to be made. Completing this process, the "crime" against God is erased, because post-Trentine absolution has a performative function and not only a declarative one.[8] The penances for expiating sins, following ancient Christian tradition, consist of prayers, fasting, and the giving of alms.

This sacrament offers, therefore, a means for "negotiation" between the faithful and God, because the faithful can restore the privileged relationship that this last had created with them whenever it is considered necessary by means of the ritual stages foreseen for the occasion. The sacrament enables one not only to escape the eternal punishment of Hell, but also to reduce temporal punishment in a Purgatory that appears no less terrible.[9]

Nevertheless, the necessary requirement to ensure that this ritual "negotiation" has the hoped-for result consists of the fact that the individual holds himself effectively responsible for the sins he has committed and that he is truly disposed to correct them.[10] The penitent could eventually deceive the confessor, but he could not deceive the all-knowing God.[11] To accomplish this end it was absolutely necessary for the church to generate a persuasive and a dissuasive discourse, a discourse so powerful and convincing that it would keep the faithful in a permanent state of tension with regard to their next step to the hereafter.[12] Ivan Machado de Cháves, archdeacon of the cathedral of Trujillo, instructed confessors to pursue all possible means of persuading the penitent to have a real purpose of contrition and amendment; indeed, they should "suggest to him some of the reasons for the hideousness and the wickedness of sin, the brevity of human life and the certainty of death, and how life is all over in a moment, on which depends and has to begin an eternity of glory or of eternal punishment."[13] Not only must one avoid sin without having confessed, but the examination of conscience must be sincere and the telling of the sins complete and detailed because this is the only way for the sacrament to be valid and effective.[14]

The existential tension was nourished by the medieval Manicheanism that assigned absolute values in matters of justice, oscillating between the extremes of the fullness of grace and of punishment, with the tension finally occurring most often in ecclesiastical discourse. In effect, from theological texts to sermons, the church reflected a discourse that stigmatized earthly life as thoroughly sinful, characterized as being human with a weak will at the moment of being tempted by the Devil and "naturally" inclined to transgress divine laws.[15] The world was seen as the kingdom of wickedness, and this fact explained the frequent calamities that scourge humanity. Divine punishment was as frequent as the sinfulness of men, manifesting itself in epidemics, droughts, poor harvests, wars, famines, and so forth.

The logic that emanated from the conclusions of the Council of Trent and the discussions of later canonistic treatises aimed at generating a close connection between "contrition"—the rejection of sins for being faults committed against God, the desire not to return to sinfulness for the love of God—and "attrition"—the rejection of sins for fear of being condemned to Hell forever. Contrition emerged as the true fountain of repentance that leads, in contrast to the Protestant argument, to the remission of sins and to divine pardon.[16]

But the Counter-Reformation church was unable to avoid what Jean Delumeau defines as a "pastoral doctrine of dread" that maintained its sway as a tool of persuasion and of dissuasion until the eighteenth century. Moreover, in the case of Spanish America, the authors of the manuals of confession agreed that the native people, "because generally they are people of limited understanding, they do not reach the level necessary for contrition," and came to admit that they "are without sorrow and without repentance for their sins."[17] In the chapter devoted to instruction about the act of contrition to "rustics," Peña Montenegro proposed the image of the sinner's soul "as an enclosed place with armies of dogs, lions, bulls, serpents, and other wild animals that frightened it with their bellowings and destroyed it with their mouths and ripping it apart with their claws, and it as worms."[18] On his part, the catechism developed by Lorra Baquio asked, in Spanish and in Nahuatl, "Where will the wicked and the sinners go when they die?" and responded at once: "They will go to Hell, a place of eternal suffering, torment, and weeping because they did not heed the divine commandments, because they did not repent, because they did not correct themselves and because they did not earn pardon with tears for their sins, but died in them [in sin]."[19]

The "pastoral doctrine of dread" served, moreover, to nourish the legitimacy and the collective valuation of the sacrament of confession as the official ritual act—apart from the acts of voluntary expiatory mortification such as penitential processions and the wearing of hair shirts on the body—that allowed erasing "whatever sin however abominable and great that it is."[20] Moreover, all through the seventeenth century it was strengthened with the support of a Baroque aesthetic oriented to capturing psychologically and provoking specific sentiments in the spectators.[21] All these factors added up to the emphasis being placed on the anxiety-ridden moment of death, the revalorization of the omnipresent powers of evil in the world and the consequences for mankind that result, as manifested in the divine punishment from natural calamities.

In the case of the Spanish-American experience, rather than positive aspects and examples that could be imitated, there prevailed a minimalist morality that was predominantly negative with a discourse that identified the laws that could not be transgressed, the faults that ought to be avoided, the models that should not be imitated, and so forth.[22] A good example of this is the questions developed for interrogating the natives when they were confessing their sins.

Norms and Tools for the "New World"

Post-Trentine evangelization and confession in Latin America were generally adapted by means of the conciliar and synodal documents developed locally. In them was joined the European need to systematize the sacrament from the printed manuals that served as practical tools for the cleric who was evangelizing "on the spot" and that outlined the current doctrinal norms. The printing press arrived in Mexico about 1533 and at Lima about 1583. This last date coincides with the celebration of the Third Council of Lima, an event of great importance for the Christianization of South America, because it signified the adaptation and pastoral application of the results of Trent to local reality.

In effect, starting from these conclusions, three fundamental texts developed and extended their diffusion throughout the continent: one Christian doctrine, two catechisms (greater and lesser), and the first South American manual for confession, or *confesionario*. These three texts were printed in a trilingual version (Castilian, Aymara, and Quechua) in 1585, creating a complete manual for the use of local clergy.[23] In Mexico also, with the third council of that archdiocese (1585), there appeared the obligation to employ the bilingual manuals to teach and to hear the confessions of the Indians.[24]

A stereotypical transformation in the manuals of confession is obvious as much in their structure as in their doctrinal contents in spite of the development, notwithstanding that their elaboration, their specific content, and the human universes to which they were directed were diverse. Nevertheless, this transformation emphasized a structural incongruity in relation to the theological moment that was current in "Old World" Catholicism. In effect, confession of the interrogatory kind in force since 1215 had become obsolete after the Council of Trent stipulated that the penitent, after a "free" examination of conscience, ought to list his sins in order to enumerate them to the confessor. Nevertheless, this conciliar decision held no validity in America because the native people were not seen with the same level of maturity and "adult" responsibility that the new practice of confession assigned to the community of believing Europeans. The authors were certain that "invincible ignorance" made native people unable to declare their sins unless they were questioned in a detailed manner: "And truly some of these are so rustic that because of their limited understanding they neither learn nor have any concept of the obligation of confession."[25] Because of that, one author suggested that the reproofs that ought to accompany each commandment in the exhortations prior to confession ought to be "the easiest and intelligible ... for a people so incompetent, as these naturals are, and thus given to vice."[26]

The Spanish-American manuals, therefore, appear to be more like the medieval penitentials because they present the questions for the interrogation organized according to the order of the Ten Commandments, to which each is attached in very well developed texts, with other questions devoted to the capital sins, to the commandments of the church, to the five senses, to the cardinal and theological virtues, and so forth in the purest medieval theological tradition. Moreover, they reinforce the necessity of an exhaustive confession of one's sins, of the number of places in which the penitent committed them, and of their details and circumstances.

Following these same rules, the confessions of natives embodied pedagogically the moment of Catholic ritual in which the privacy of the faithful is evoked in its smallest and its largest details. The printed manuals thus present a list of generally very minute questions (with their corresponding translation into the local idiom or dialect) that enabled the priest to examine the private life of the penitent who stood before him. It is important to add that these manuals present themselves as a guide and support for the cross-examination, leaving to the discretion of the confessor the choice of questions best fitted to the status of the penitent, that is, the penitent's sex, age, social status, and so forth.

The interesting part for the historian who explores this topic is that in contrast to the stereotypical basis of the list of commandments and sins originally defined for the European world, the authors of the manuals for the Americas generally recognized the sociocultural reality for which they wrote, incorporating in their questionnaires a series of local practices and experiences that they saw in turn as the "sins of the New World."

The Language: From "Knowledge" to "Power"

Confronted with radically different cultures, the clergy learned quickly that if they wished to make the gospel message intelligible they would have to adapt it to the particular circumstances of Spanish-American reality. The manuals of confession were developed with this perspective in mind. The questions asked of the penitent should have a certain relevance to their circumstances given that the penitential questionnaire ought to support the teaching of Catholicism and the elimination of ancient ways of life.

The principal sacrament, baptism—because it is a solemn ritual in which abound symbolic acts and sacramental words accompanying the ritual—did not create greater linguistic problems for the missionaries. It is enough to recall the mass baptisms of native people who did not understand the language, the substance of the action, or the basic principles of the doctrine involved.[27] The fact resulting from the corresponding ritual steps marked out the immediate incorporation of the "ex-pagans" into the Christian world in a logic *ex opere operato* that allowed it to work despite the very different meanings that the various actors assigned to the event. Expediting the ritual was the first step, and teaching some of the doctrine as a condition of receiving the sacrament (above all on the part of the Franciscans, who indeed toward the middle of the sixteenth century stipulated the need to inculcate some basic teachings of the faith) did not develop much beyond rote memorization of a formal sort.

The essential support of the church for the "advanced" indoctrination of the native people was concentrated in the pastoral mission and in the systematic catechesis that developed on the part of the religious orders disseminated throughout the continent. In the Americas, the missionaries faced the problem of language and its effective codification: their great challenge was to transmit the substance of their message translated into vernacular languages.

In the context of the sacraments, penance posed a similar problem because of the need to direct the confession according to a detailed questionnaire. From this came the twofold effort that the authors of the manuals for the native people put forth. In the first place, it was necessary to adapt the more-or-less stereotypical texts that arrived from Europe to the local reality, integrating into the questionnaires the practices, behaviors, and values (those that were judged sinful) of the ethnic group to which the manuals would be sent. In the second place, there had to be an effort to translate the questionnaires into the languages or dialects of said groups because it was considered "necessary and imperative to know the true meaning and emphasis of the vocabulary and manner of speaking that they employ."[28] Given the complexity of these two tasks, it does not appear strange that the majority of the manuals of confession, as well as the catechisms and books of sermons printed for Spanish America, had been developed by priests with pastoral experience in the regions and among the peoples for whom they were destined.[29]

Thus the priest transformed himself into an ethnographer, responsible for systematizing the information gathered in contact "on the ground" and placing it at the disposal of the new agents of Christianization. This new role pointed to the necessity of probing deeply into the practices and the most intimate performances, and in all the cultural subtleties that could confuse the confessor.[30]

Therefore it was deemed necessary to have a practical guide to the people's daily habits, sexual practices, notions of morality, marriages in the forbidden degrees, and so forth. That is to say, to be able "to scrutinize diligently the sinner's conscience," it was essential to possess the most complete catalog possible of cultural codes through those that govern the people's behavior.[31] Juan Perez Bocanegra, for example, began his work with the declaration that it had taken more than twenty years to finish writing the book, and since then he had corrected it based on his long experience.[32]

It is from spoken knowledge, from the possession of a "body of learning," that the missionary church obtains the "power" to spread its strategy of cultural change and the implanting of its evangelical truth.[33] The power of the spoken word in post-Trentine Spanish America was based, as it happens, on the information gathered in the manuals ordered and systematized starting from the Ten Commandments and the different virtues and activities that a Christian ought to fulfill. That is to say, the "ethnographic" information had been digested ideologically by the author of the manual and made available in the text in the role of objects of ecclesiastical strategy. In the same way, beginning with the apparatus of Catholic doctrinal references, the manuals predetermined the practices and performances that ought to be stigmatized and about which the native people ought to generate a sense of guilt that would lead them to detest said practices and performances. The observation and "comprehension" of the Other thus acquired an instrumental purpose, and the cultural information was transformed into a tool for the use of the missionaries, leading, finally, to the destruction of the native culture.[34]

This same rubric lends insight into the preoccupation of the authors of the manuals with warning future users about the erroneous means by which the users had interiorized this sacrament among the native peoples, as discussed later in this chapter. The heterodox practices not only responded to the hybrid characteristic of syncretism produced in the process of religious transculturation, but also can be read as a countercultural strategy of these groups. From this also stemmed the interest of these authors to specify the counterstrategies employed to deceive the confessors, beginning with the most common and simple of those, which was the hiding of specific faults "that can be readily seen because he is constantly swallowing saliva and could not stop his knees from shaking, looks this way and that, and other signs."[35]

Another problem appeared at the moment of translating the questionnaires and declarations of faith described in the Spanish-American manuals into the vernacular languages and dialects. Here all the experience in the handling of idioms acquired by those religious figures active in missionary activity became important, because they were able to handle not only literal translation but also, particularly, the significant cultural specifics assigned by these people to their linguistic codes.

The great challenge for the Catholic missionary, therefore, was to link in the narrowest possible fashion the canonical-doctrinal significance of the concepts and substance of their religion to the native concepts and to their concrete use in local reality. But this goal collided with the problem of communication, which could be overcome only at the cost of sacrificing the developed Western meaning of the ideological corpus that they intended to instill in the numerous, diverse, and complex peoples who inhabited the "new world." To this problem should be added that very few priests were really prepared and well versed in these vernacular languages.[36]

Alonso de la Peña Montenegro emphatically pointed out that in the "new provinces of the infidels," where the priests were not deemed to handle well the local language,

> the preacher sins who wishes to preach and to propound the profound mysteries of our holy faith in language that he speaks poorly; the reason is clear, because someone who does not know the language very well places himself at risk and in manifest danger of teaching some errors or making offensive and absurd statements because he lacks the words, because of the limits of his vocabulary, and because he does not know the appropriate use of the words.[37]

The translators in this situation entered into an ambush that led to a mixed reconstruction of the signs and their significance.[38] In the first place, this occurred as a result of the fact that the native linguistic codes imposed an accommodation that often was substantial, because in general they did not possess the precise words and the translator had to appeal to conceptual approximations.[39] In the second place, and even more serious, many of the Christian and European concepts simply did not exist—nor did they have any place in the local vocabulary—so the authors and translators of these texts left the original words in Spanish or Latin. The manual of Perez Bocanegra, for example, had a treatise on the terminology regularly employed to translate into Quechua the word *baptism,* leading to the conclusion that the better solution was the hybrid word *baptizaiqui.*[40]

The redefinition of meaning that was articulated between the missionaries and the native people was bidirectional and aided in establishing the basis of the great process of cultural mixing and religious syncretism that developed throughout the continent and across the colonial centuries. Nevertheless, this redefinition should not be interpreted as attributable to the inevitable failure of the project of religious and cultural homogenization of the church in Spanish America.

Even though the aforementioned project did not fulfill the original objectives of the post-Trentine policy, the strategies outlined by the missionaries at a local level allowed an original process of cultural cooptation anchored in the need to know, manipulate, and accommodate the native languages. In other words, the fact of appealing to the words and meanings of the native languages to direct the Catholic teaching allowed the missionaries to "overload," in a way, that vocabulary—and the sociocultural practices and experience to which the words referred—with those meanings that were properly Catholic and European.[41]

Thus, in the acts of the first Spanish-American council, celebrated in Lima in 1552, the problem of the language of catechesis was discussed, recognizing the difficulty involved in making the native people aware of the meaning and of the obligations entailed in receiving the sacrament. Because of this challenge, the essential requirement of regular catechetical instruction and encouragement for the clergy to continue in the task of learning the local languages—and not teaching Spanish to the native people—were emphasized, thus recognizing that the problem was rooted in the lack of effective clerics. The council also recommended a better geographical distribution of the multilingual priests and an adequate sojourn in each location.[42]

The conclusions of the Second Council of Lima (1567) reinforced the program of the previous council: the linguistic problems had not been resolved, but recourse to interpreters remained forbidden. The council ordered the selection of those priests who already knew Quechua, that they might devote themselves to the administration of the sacrament; and for the first time on the continent, the council evoked the need to rely on a "practical manual" for the use of these confessors. The council further ordered that this manual should be composed for those who knew the native languages.[43] As mentioned above, the manuals were not developed until the Third Council, in the conclusions of which the ban on the use of interpreters was continued.[44]

Nevertheless, a century later, the manuals recognized the custom (by then made licit) of employing these cultural intermediaries and even showed the "obligation" of using them in the case where the priest observed insoluble obstacles to the effective administration of the sacrament.[45] The preoccupation became that of resolving the problems inherent in this cession of control, which involved leaving in the hands of a third party the knowledge of the secret of the confessional and the bidirectional interpretation of an essentially spoken ritual.

Heterodox Homologations: Native "Sins" and "Confessors"

From the beginning of the Christianization of the "new world," churchmen recognized the existence of indigenous experiences and practices that they were able to identify with those experiences and practices they were attempting to impose. This succeeded, for example, in the case of the notion of religious transgression that in both the Andean and the Mexican worlds the Catholic priests attempted to identify with the Western notion of sin, which provides a specific example of the problems of interpretation and translation that the priest encountered in Spanish America, as analyzed in previous paragraphs. In effect, both the content and the meaning of the notion as the appropriate linguistic sign that the authors took from the natives' languages to translate the term *sin* made reference to situations and contexts that were very different from the Christian notion of culpability.[46]

Internalized and associated with individual responsibility, the Christian notion of sin inscribes itself in a moral conception of life; contrition and absolution enable it to disappear. In the cosmology of the pre-Hispanic peoples, by contrast, the order of the universe depends principally on the gods and not on men, so the gods were the worse sinners. "Sin" existed therefore as a collective disorder and an injury that came from outside and was expressed in physical calamities such as sickness or natural disasters such as drought. From this relation between "sin" and calamity, the native peoples (at least in the case of Mexico) carried out a rite of expiatory purification aimed at restoring the lost order and that the "ethnographers" among the clergy identified with the sacrament of confession, although stigmatizing it as a "pagan" practice. The association seemed much clearer because the said ritual included rigorous fasting, penances, and bodily mortifications.

Hence the ecclesiastical chroniclers took pains to describe the characteristics and ritual formulations of these heretical practices, specifying the periods in which traditional fasting took place in native societies so that the parish priest and the missionaries would be able to detect its manifestation. In Peru, for example, the so-called destroyers of idolatry of the seventeenth century recorded the evidence of fasting associated with ceremonies of purification, which they labeled "confession."[47]

Robert Ricard, when describing the experience of confession in sixteenth-century Mexico, points out that the Franciscans responsible for the Christianization of the native population were careful to assign light penances "in order not to discourage the new converts, lest they shun the practice of confession or have occasion to hide their sins out of fear of what the punishment would be like." Nevertheless, some native peoples increased the penances, adding corporal punishments such as fasting and scourging. According to Ricard, they even thought themselves defrauded if the priest did not impose corporal penances. Many kept the practice of scourging themselves on Fridays in Lent as well as in times of drought or epidemics.[48]

The priests thus fell into an unresolvable dilemma, because these practices formed, at the same time, part of the native tradition and part of the privileged expiatory arsenal of the post-Trentine Catholic religious life. The permanent fear was that the Christianized natives would give themselves to such practices out of "pagan" zeal. From this apprehension arose the need to have recourse to a priest knowledgeable about the local cultures and to priest-*doctrineros,* sensitive to the subtleties of their parishioners and concerned about the instruction of their parishioners in correct doctrine and in the "correct" meanings of each ceremony.

The existence of notions of "sin" among the native people and the penitential practices associated with them, although they did not correspond to the world of Catholic representations, established a series of ambivalent positions and problems for the priest charged with distinguishing the false ones and eliminating them. This ambivalence became even more ambiguous to the extent that as time went by, the religious mixing gave way to hybrid practices even more dangerous for the church because they were able to be transformed in a cultural counterstrategy.

Thus it happened with the historical development of the pre-Spanish practice that the priests called "confession." In effect, at those times in which physical effects of a cosmological upheaval manifested themselves (diseases, droughts, etc.), the native people resorted to their traditional intermediaries before the deity so that they could proceed to the rites of purification and mortification that would allow the restoration of order. The manuals of confession frequently evoke the existence of these indigenous "confessors," pointing out that the priests would be dealing with a survival of pre-Spanish rituals. Nevertheless, these texts also denounce an eventual "supplantation," because on many occasions the native people confessed their sins to the previously mentioned representatives rather than to the Catholic priests.[49]

Explicit testimony about this comes to us from the process of the "extirpating of idolatries" carried out in the Andean zone of Cajatambo. Pierre Duviols has examined the declarations of Juan Guaraz, written down in 1656, in which Guaraz outlined the activities of Christobal Runtu and Pedro Allauca, two traditional "confessors." The witness described a particularly powerful ceremony in which were blended isolated words from the Christian vocabulary (such as *absolution*), Andean practices, and rules defined directly contrary to the Catholic commandments.[50]

Therefore a new phenomenon arose: a hybrid institution that retained pre-Spanish signs, rituals, and goals but had incorporated the symbolic spaces and concepts of the religion of the conquistadors. Hence, the evidence indicates that the native peoples resorted to their traditional "confessors," not only according to the pre-Spanish rationale for doing so, but also according to the church's understanding of the sacrament. In this way the parishioners confessed their individual sins with greater regularity to those "supplanters" than to the Catholic priest and even requested their consent to fulfill the obligation to confess annually to the church. Here came into play not only the correct doctrine but even the function and role of the priest.

The Role of the Priest

As pointed out previously, the Council of Trent, faced with the pressures of the Reformation, reinforced (among other things) the authority of the priest, who had the authority to hear confessions and the power to absolve the penitent in the name of God. Post-Trentine confession not only individualized the sins, emphasizing the need for awareness of them and the sense of responsibility that the sinner ought to experience, but also became aware of the relationship between the sinner and the priest that facilitates the various possible kinds of discipline for the conscience.[51]

The priest became a judge who ought to know all the aspects of sin and who would weigh and examine the gravity of the sins. In fact, the Trentine text points out that the faithful appear "as the guilty before the penitential tribunal." Another requirement is the obligation to confess all the occasions on which one has committed each sin, aiming at reinforcing the obligation of openness. As in the preliminary discussions—linked to the examination of conscience—as in the penitential interrogation, and especially for the sins "of the flesh," the priest was to act as a penitential inquisitor, suspicious of the native people who "are so slow-witted and usually arrive without having examined their consciences, so that as regards the number of their sins they say any number that comes to their minds."[52]

This conception of the role of the confessor served as the basis for all of the staged rituals and acts of expiation that clothed the administration of the sacrament both in Europe and in America, conforming to the aesthetic strategies developed by the Counter-Reformation.[53] In effect, with regard to the exhortations and sermons that precede confession itself, the texts were to set the tone and at times even their "setting." Three recurring themes were expected to be touched upon in these discourses: the symbolic space occupied by the priest, the theological nature of sin (that is, sin of action, thought, or omission), and the importance of the confidentiality of confession. These three themes gave rise to discourse of a profound emotional burden.[54]

In the first place, the priest was expected to explain to the native the unique character of the sacrament that the priest was conferring and the role that he would play as the agent of deity: being an ordinary man and therefore able to understand the weaknesses of the penitent, at the moment of the administration of the sacrament he would be transformed into a temporary incarnation of God, obtaining the right to record the penitents' secrets and the power to wash away their sins.[55] The Catholic priest presented himself in a classic role, easily associated by the native people with the leaders of their traditional religions. The priest thus became a privileged intermediary between the supernatural forces and mankind.

For this, the priest relied on an appropriate ritual dramatization, within which this preliminary moment allowed the arousal of the emotions necessary to lead the penitent with respect to the legitimacy of the said role, "softening him up" psychologically and, finally, inscribing him in the persuasive/dissuasive logic that nourished the strategy of Christianization. Thus, the priest acted in a Baroque fashion between the metaphors of fear and hope, between the diatribes threatening horrible punishments and the touching phrases tending to arouse true contrition:

> In order to persuade forcefully and to explain efficaciously to the Indians the mysteries and tenets of the Catholic faith and the commands of the law . . . , it is very useful . . . to illustrate these with examples and comparisons; and in the season of Lent which is when they make their confession, they must tell of some serious punishment that God reserves for those who fail to mention sins, weakening the integrity of the confession, because they are so earth bound that they are not so much moved by reason as by concrete examples.[56]

The missionaries stressed the difference between the exaggeration of the actions and the moderation of the words, for, as the appropriate doctrinal texts point out, the confessor ought to be agreeable and charitable in order to receive those who had fallen into sin.[57]

Exhortations and sermons also dealt with the nature of sin, utilizing a conceptual arsenal of metaphors and analogies that made the desired symbolic meaning comprehensible. The authors systematically resorted to concepts such as "poison," "stain," or "weed"; sin "stains and blackens and gives off a bad smell."[58] From this the texts explicated the effects of sin as "ulcers" in the soul of the sinner, which allowed including the useful metaphor of the spiritual priest-physician (similar to the judge) who "washes" and "cures" through the sacrament of penance that "is a general medicine for all the illnesses of the soul."[59] This theme is a recurring topic in the European as well as the Spanish-American manuals of confession.[60]

Ultimately, the sermons preached in the previous stage touch on the secrecy of confession. Confidentiality was a significant problem at the local level because the need to translate opened up close intimacy to a priest whom the penitent encountered on a daily basis. This evidently produced a great reticence, resulting from the sense of shame, fear, or antipathy that the parish priest was able to generate. This situation could annul the effectiveness of the sacrament because the penitent did not clear his conscience completely of all the sins that he had committed. For that reason, the Third Council of Lima foresaw the sending of special confessors to the Indian parishes.[61]

However, the role of the priest was forged not only in persuasive discourse, but also in the arrangements that regulated the administration of the sacrament. In effect, the confessor—besides being the "judge" and "spiritual physician" who invited the sinners to contrition, collected the evidence, evaluated the level of the sin, cured the soul, and gave the symbolic penance—also possessed repressive powers that he was able to exercise upon the parishioners who failed to fulfill their obligation to confess annually. Thus, after the First Council of Lima, there developed a classification of corporal punishments according to the kind of sin and the status of the sinner. These ranged from a few days in prison to public whipping and the shaving of the head.[62]

For its part, the First Council of Mexico (1555) had determined that priests responsible for the Indian communities ought to keep a register or list of their parishioners, reporting annually to the bishop the names of those who were resisting the priest's authority or those who neglected the sacrament, and to present this list for the special ecclesiastical visitors. This "statistical demography" of the population complied with the obligation to confess but was also inscribed in the necessity to control the well-known "Other" that the church promoted in its strategy of Christianization. The fact that a parishioner changed confessors constantly enabled him, eventually, to deceptively hide sins that only regular daily contact could observe. Thus the council added the ban on confessing outside of one's parish without the permission of the parish priest, a ban that weighed heavily on the leaders of the Indian communities.[63]

The Development of a Sense of Guilt as a Mechanism of Acculturation

The strategy of Christianizing the native peoples had to combine vigorous repression with an educational plan for "creating a sense of conscience" that mixed fear and hope, that channeled doctrinal content appropriate for individuals seen as infantile and only semirational by means of discursive allegories and emotive ritual forms. For this purpose, the church encouraged the creation of catechetical pamphlets (or *cartillas,* with the basic teachings and articles of faith and the commandments), prayer books (which usually contain the Our Father, Hail Mary, the Creed, and the Salve Regina), and practical manuals for use in the administration of the sacraments, all of which were "translated" into the vernacular languages and dialects.[64]

One of the means of persuasion/dissuasion that the church deployed in the "new world" was the generalization of the Catholic concept of sin and the implementation of the ritual apparatus that made absolution possible. Theologians, parish priests, and missionaries outdid themselves to produce catalogs of sins, patterned on the form of penitential questionnaires, in which they specified the indigenous practices, values, and ideas that ought to be stigmatized and then eliminated. Eradication of these elements would be accomplished through the generation of willpower of the interior of the consciousness of the individual. It is interesting to note, therefore, the pivotal role that willpower played in the shape of the strategy of the "spiritual conquest," which might best be defined as the permanent and systematic diffusion—through sermons, catechesis and questionnaires, and rituals linked to the liturgy of the sacraments—of the "individual" sense of sin.[65]

In the vision of the cosmos that overlay the world of the native people, that notion would have been seen not only as an attempted crime against the cosmic-social order of the community, but also as a transgression directly against the personal relation with the divinity. The sin committed by the individual deprives him of Christian grace and determines a punishment after death that moves, depending on his status, between the transitory darkness of Purgatory and the eternal torture of Hell. In this fashion, attrition for one's sins became the privileged psychological context by means of which the native people "incorporated" themselves into this sacrament.

It was that fear of divine punishment that enabled the church to begin the Christianization of the Indians by means of a process similar to the "emptying out" of the specifics of their cultural universes and an attempt at hegemony over their cognitive space. The "demonization" of certain practices, values, and behaviors—within which sexuality occupied a significant place, following the obsessiveness of the church with respect to that permanent source of temptation—became the base for displaying the strategy of persuasion/dissuasion that determined the essential relation between moral transformation and cultural transformation.[66] In other words, the effective Christianization of Latin America was expected to proceed through a process of inevitable acculturation. That process shaped itself within a strategy of global diffusion of Western European habits and values within which the priest of Indians (*cura de indios*) played a central role.[67]

The elimination of social practices and mental representations contrary to church teachings—and to Western European culture—was considered to be a logical consequence of the incorporation in the Indians' imagination of the conceptual arsenal, cosmic references, and ideological and symbolic codes of Christian origin. These elements defined and associated a "sense of guilt" (also of an individual character) with those acts, thoughts, or omissions and from this forged a profound general and permanent change that physical coercion alone could not ensure, a change that was perceived slowly but was unrenounceable: "Just as one can not climb to the high tower in a single bound, without stages, step by step, so also it is impossible to reach the fullness of the law in a single day, but removing bit by bit those things which over a long period of time shaped infidel societies."[68]

To ensure that outcome, indeed in the phase prior to the interrogation itself, the manual for confessors proposes a framework of analysis of reality, outlining a description of the world in which the Indian ought to make reference when he goes to confess his sins. In other words, the confessor defined "in negative" (if I may employ the vocabulary of photography) the standards of good conduct by presenting the sinful practices and values of the native people over the exogenous base of the Ten Commandments of the Christians.

The code of conduct of European civilization constituted, then, the moral and social model supporting the whole penitential questioning. To submit to confession, to accept that moment as codified, signified implicitly one's adherence in specific fashion to the rest of the system, integrating oneself into the society of the conquerors, regardless of how unorthodox the understanding of the original meaning of the sacrament.[69]

All the same, there can be no doubt that the methodological approach adopted in this chapter presents an obvious problem that relativizes the scope of this hypothesis. In effect, the sources with which I have worked focus on the questions of the confessors, not on the responses of the Indians—that is to say, the view of the cultural "interventionists" rather than the views of those who were imposed upon. And although the questionnaires reflect a local reality, this reality was presented after having been filtered through the codes, anxieties, and obsessions of their authors. The native universe thus appears in distorted fashion through the interpretive mirror of the post-Trentine clerical missionary.[70]

Nevertheless, for the purposes of the hypothesis, it is precisely this space of Western "cataloging" of the native practices deserving of censure or punishment that permits the study of one of the most important methods of Christianization of Spanish America. In other words, our modern attention does not point to the information given by the native person who was submitted to the questioning but to that information gathered, that is, elaborated and systematized by the manuals and "sent back" to the indigenous penitent clothed with the Catholic notion of sin and associated with a sense of individual responsibility for having committed sins.

This effort of moral discipline, which can be projected to a discipline of the social and political order, would have been reinforced by means of the immediate translation of the questionings into the local languages—for the practical use of the confessors. With this process of translation not only the acts and omissions but also the words that served to identify them would have become clothed within that tendency toward acculturation. The object being sought would obviously have been the changes of values and behavior of the individuals, that is to say, a cultural transformation, given the characteristics of the culpable practices.

Such acculturation, in this case, was not derived from repressive actions directed by the political or ecclesiastical authorities, because it was expected to happen as a result of the native's own will. It was he who, individually, would respond before the Christian God after death; therefore, it was he who, according to Catholic logic, ought to interiorize the notion of sin and ought to generate within himself the sense of sin before committing any of the indicated acts or omissions stigmatized by the church. Auricular confession of the stated sins before the priest, for his part, marked with an indispensable rite the expiation of those sins. This constituted an explicit mark of the materialization of the object of this strategy and a strengthening ritual that regularly reminded the native sinners of the list of cultural practices that they ought to eliminate from their daily lives and from their mental universe.

Notes

This article forms part of the research carried out in the winter of 2000 in the John Carter Brown Library (Providence, Rhode Island) as the María Elena Cassiet Research Fellow. I would like to acknowledge the helpful assistance of the staff of the library during my fellowship.

1. Jean Delumeau, *La confesión y el perdón. Las dificultades de la confesión, siglos XIII a XVIII* (Madrid: Alianza, 1992).

2. Cf. Nicole Lemaître, "Pratique et signification de la confession communautaire dans les paroisses au XVIe siècle," in Groupe de la Bussière, ed., *Pratiques de la confession. Des Pères du désert à Vatican II. Quinze études d'histoire* (Paris: Cerf, 1983).

3. Martine Azoulai, *Les péchés du Nouveau Monde. Les manuels pour la confession des Indiens, XVIe–XVIIe siècle* (Paris: Albin Michel, 1993), 20.

4. Jacques Le Goff, *La naissance du Purgatoire* (Paris: Gallimard, 1981).

5. Cf. John Bossy, "The Social History of Confession in the Age of the Reformation," *Transactions of the Royal Historical Society*, 5th Ser., no. 25 (London, 1975).

6. Louis-Marie Chauvet, "Pénitence," in Jean-Yves Lacoste, dir., *Dictionnaire critique de théologie* (Paris: PUF, 1998), 885.

7. Cf. Alonso de la Peña Montenegro, *Itinerario para parochos de indios, en que se tratan las materias mas particulares, tocantes a ellos, para su buena administración* (Madrid: Joseph Fernández de Buendia, 1688), 311–12, "Advertencias respecto a la contrición," John Carter Brown Library.

8. Chauvet, "Pénitence," 882–85. Cf., in Lacoste, *Dictionnaire critique*, the article "Peine" by Olivier O'Donovan.

9. Cf. Ludovico Bertonio, *Confessionario muy copioso en dos lenguas, Aymara, y Española, con una instruccion acerca de los siete Sacramentos de la Sancta Yglesia, y otras varias cosas, como puede verse por la Tabla del mesmo libro. Por el padre Ludovico Bertonio italiano de la Compañia de Iesus en la Provincia del Peru* (Impreso en la casa de la Compañia de Jesús, en la Provincia de Chucuito, por Francisco del Canto, 1612), 213–15.

10. Cf. another example collected by Bertonio, ibid., 222–25.

11. Cf. Juan Perez Bocanegra, *Ritual formulario, e institución de curas, para administrar a los naturales de este Reyno, los Santos Sacramentos del Baptismo, Confirmacion, Eucaristia, y Viatico, Penitencia, extremauncion, y Matrimonio, con advertencias muy necessarias* (Lima: por Geronymo de Contreras, 1631), 390.

12. Perez Bocanegra, *Ritual formulario*, 382.

13. Ivan Machado de Cháves, *Perfeto confessor i cura de almas* (Barcelona: por Pedro Lacavallería, 1641), 801. Another text, from the Franciscan Juan Baptista, emphasized the importance of the administration of the Eucharist as death approached: *Advertencias para los confessores de los naturales compuestas por el padre fray Ioan Baptista, de la orden del Seraphico padre Sanct Francisco, lector de theologia, y guardian del Convento de Sanctiago Tlatilulco: de la provincia del Sancto Evangelio* (México: Convento de Sanctiago Tlatilulco, por M. Ocharte, 1600), 75v.

14. Cf. Francisco de Lorra Baquio, *Manual mexicano de la administracion de los Santos sacramentos, conforme al Manual Toledano, compuesto en lengua mexicana*

por el Bachiller Francisco de Lorra Baquio, presbyter (México: por Diego Gutiérrez, 1634), 44.

15. Ibid., 18v.

16. Jean Delumeau, *Le péché et la peur. La culpabilisation en Occident (XIIIe–XVIIIe siècles)* (Paris: Fayard, 1983).

17. Baptista, *Advertencias para los confessores*, 2.

18. Peña Montenegro, *Itinerario para parochos*, 313.

19. Lorra Baquio, *Manual mexicano*, 30v–31.

20. Bertonio, *Confessionario*, 63; Delumeau, *La confesión*, 45–61.

21. Cf. José Antonio Maravall, *La cultura del Barroco. Análisis de una estructura histórica* (Barcelona: Ariel, 1980).

22. Azoulai, *Les péchés*, 21.

23. *Doctrina christiana y catecismo para instrucción de Indios*, facsimile ed. (Madrid: CSIC, 1985).

24. Luis Martínez Ferrer, *Directorio para confesores y penitentes. La Pastoral de la Penitencia en el Tercer Concilio Mexicano (1585)* (Pamplona: EUNATE, 1996).

25. Peña Montenegro, *Itinerario para parochos*, 434: "Si los indios y negros bozales que parecen ineptos para tener dolor y hacer examen de sus conciencias, tienen obligación a confesarse."

26. Perez Bocanegra, *Ritual formulario*, 386.

27. Cf. Rolf Foerster, "La conquista bautismal de los mapuches de la Araucanía," *Nütram* vol. 6, no. 3 (Santiago, 1990).

28. Alonso de Molina, *Confesionario mayor en la lengua mexicana y castellana [1569]* (México: UNAM, 1984), 2–2v.

29. Cf. Peña Montenegro, *Itinerario para parochos*, 122.

30. Cf. Perez Bocanegra, *Ritual formulario*, 105.

31. Baptista, *Advertencias para los confessores*, 13.

32. Ibid., 10.

33. Cf. Michel Foucault, *Vigilar y castigar. Nacimiento de la prisón* (México: Siglo XXI, 1976), 33–35; *L'archéologie du savoir* (Paris: Gallimard, 1969); *La verdad y las formas jurídicas* (Barcelona: Gedisa, 1993).

34. Cf. Tzvetan Todorov, *La conquête de l'Amérique. La question de l'autre* (Paris: Seuil, 1982), especially the chapter "Comprendre, prendre et détruire."

35. Perez Bocanegra, *Ritual formulario*, 111.

36. Ibid., 10.

37. Peña Montenegro, *Itinerario para parochos*, 122.

38. Cf. Paul Ricoeur, *Teoría de la interpretación. Discurso y excedente de sentido* (México: Siglo XXI, 1998); Michel Foucault, *Les mots et les choses* (Paris: Gallimard, 1969); Jorge Pinto, "La fuerza de la palabra. Evangelización y resistencia indígena (siglos XVI y XVII)," *Revista de Indias*, vol. 53, no. 199 (1993), 677–98; Berta Ares, "Relación del licenciado Michael de la Torre (Quito, 1574): Lengua, cultura y evangelización," *Cuadernos para la historia de la evangelización en Latinoamérica*, no. 3 (Cusco: Centro Bartolomé de Las Casas, 1988); Pedro Morandé, *Ritual y palabra*

(Lima: Centro Andino de Historia, 1980); Rodolfo Oroz, "La evangelización de Chile, sus problemas lingüísticos y la política idiomática de la Corona en el siglo XVI," *Boletín de la Academia Chilena de la Historia*, no. 66 (Santiago, 1962); Ricardo Salas, "Conquista, traducción y lenguaje misionero en el siglo XVI," *Mapocho*, no. 32 (Santiago, 1992); Patricio Cisternas, "Traducción, textos y alteridad durante la Conquista," *Boletín de historia y geografía*, no. 14 (Santiago, 1998); Francisco de Solano, comp., *Documentos sobre política lingüística en Hispanoamérica, 1492–1800* (Madrid: CSIC, 1991); Jaime Valenzuela Márquez, "El lenguaje y la colonización cultural de América en el siglo XVI," in Julio Valdeón Baruque, ed., *La cultura y el arte en la época de Isabel la Católica* (Valladolid: Instituto Universitario de Historia Simancas, 2003).

39. Cf., for example, Baptista, *Advertencias para los confessores*, 52–53v.

40. Perez Bocanegra, *Ritual formulario*, 46.

41. Cf. Georges Baudot, "Diablos, demonios y sortilegios en el proceso discursivo de la evangelización de México. Siglo XVI," in *México y los albores del discurso colonial* (México: Nueva Imagen, 1996); Serge Gruzinski, *La colonización de lo imaginario* (México: FCE, 1991).

42. Rubén Vargas Ugarte, *Concilios limenses (1551–1772)* (Lima: Tipografía Peruana, 1951).

43. Ibid.

44. Francesco Lisi, *El tercer concilio limense y la aculturación de los indigenas sudamericanos*, Salamanca (Universidad de Salamanca, 1990).

45. Peña Montenegro, *Itinerario para parochos*, 329–30.

46. Azoulai, *Les péchés*, 73–75; Lorra Baquio, *Manual mexicano*, 8.

47. Pierre Duviols, *Cultura andina y represión. Procesos y visitas de idolatrías y hechicerías. Cajatambo, siglo XVII* (Cusco: Centro Bartolomé de Las Casas, 1986), 90.

48. Robert Ricard, *La conquista espiritual de México. Ensayo sobre el apostolado y los métodos misioneros de las órdenes mendicantes en la Nueva España de 1523–1524 a 1572* (México: FCE, 1986), 215; Baptista, *Advertencias para los confessores*, 6; Peña Montenegro, *Itinerario para parochos*, vol. 2, tratado 5°, sesión III: "Sobre el tipo de penitencia que se ha de imponer a los indios."

49. Cf. Perez Bocanegra, *Ritual formulario*, 111, 133, 137, and 146.

50. Duviols, *Cultura andina*, 90–91.

51. Cf., for example, the "warnings" developed by Perez Bocanegra to serve as arguments against sacrilegious actions: *Ritual formulario*, 420; Molina, *Confesionario mayor*, 29–30.

52. Peña Montenegro, *Itinerario para parochos*, 306.

53. Azoulai, *Les péchés*, 23.

54. Ibid., 59. Cf. Juan Carlos Estenssoro, "Les pouvoirs de la parole. La prédication au Pérou: de l'évangelisation à l'utopie," *Annales HSS* (Paris: Nov.–Dec. 1996), 6.

55. Azoulai, *Les péchés*, 59.

56. Peña Montenegro, *Itinerario para parochos*, 77–78.

57. Cf. Machado de Cháves, *Perfeto confessor,* 793.
58. Lorra Baquio, *Manual mexicano,* 41v.
59. Machado de Cháves, *Perfeto confessor,* 822.
60. Cf. Perez Bocanegra, *Ritual formulario,* 90; Molina, *Confessionario mayor,* 4v; Peña Montenegro, *Itinerario para parochos,* 335: "El oficio de cura es de médico para curar las dolencias mortales del alma."
61. Lisi, *El tercer concilio limense,* passim.
62. Cf. Peña Montenegro, *Itinerario para parochos,* 62: "Si el cura para evitar pecados en su doctrina podrá castigar con azotes v otras penas a los indios."
63. Azoulai, *Les péchés,* 39.
64. Cf., for example, Luis Resines Llorente, *Catecismos americanos del siglo XVI,* 2 vols. (Salamanca: Junta de Castilla y León, 1992).
65. Cf. Bernard Dompnier, "Missions et confession au XVIIe siècle," in Groupe de la Bussière, *Pratiques de la confession;* Serge Gruzinski, "Aculturación e individualización: modalidades e impacto de la confesión entre los indios nahuas de México. Siglos XVI–XVIII," *Cuadernos para la historia de la evangelización en Latinoamérica* (Cusco: Centro Bartolomé de Las Casas, 1986), 1.
66. Cf. Pierre J. Payer, *Sex and the Penitentials: The Development of a Sexual Code, 550–1150* (Toronto: University of Toronto Press, 1984); Louise M. Burkhart, *The Slippery Earth: Nahua-Christian Moral Dialogue in Sixteenth-Century Mexico* (Tucson: University of Arizona Press, 1989); Regina Harrison, "The Theology of Concupiscence: Spanish-Quechua Confessional Manuals in the Andes," in Francisco Cevallos-Candau et al., eds., *Coded Encounters: Writing, Gender, and Ethnicity in Colonial Latin America* (Amherst: University of Massachusetts Press, 1994); Regina Harrison, "Confesando el pecado en los Andes: del siglo XVI hacia nuestros dias," *Revista de crítica literaria latinoamericana* 19 (1993), 37.
67. Cf. Peña Montenegro, *Itinerario para parochos,* vol. 1, tratado 4º, sesión X: "Si el cura de indios debe atender a enseñarles policía, y modo de vivir humano?"
68. Ibid., 116.
69. Azoulai, *Les péchés,* 66.
70. Cf. Mónica Barnes, "Catechisms and Confessionarios: Distorting Mirrors of Andean Societies," in Robert V. H. Dover et al., eds., *Andean Cosmologies through Time: Persistence and Emergence* (Bloomington: Indiana University Press, 1992).

9

Conversion in Portuguese America

Isabel dos Guimarães Sá

Introduction

The world of Christianity in colonial Brazil is difficult to render, especially if analyzed from the point of view of religious conversion. First, the variety of the subjects of conversion must be considered. Without taking miscegenation into account, three large broad groups needed integration in the Church: the Portuguese-born colonists and their descendants, the Amerindians, and the African imported populations.

The first Jesuits who arrived in the territory in 1549 were not reluctant to point at the religious faults and ignorance of the white Portuguese-born colonists who had settled there. It must be remembered that at the same time, and especially after the closing of the Council of Trent in 1563, internal missions were a priority of the militant church. If the European religious structures implemented over a millennium were insufficient in Europe, they were almost nonexistent for the Portuguese living in Brazil. As for the black population, the establishment of missions in Africa was virtually impossible because of the climate and the cultural resistance of African populations. Indoctrination was easier to do in Brazil, where the people imported from Africa could not escape the hegemony of the Portuguese, even if the priorities of conversion were undoubtedly concentrated on the Brazilian natives. Even if the results of the conversion of the latter were frustrating, as I show later in this chapter, most religious policies aimed at their conversion and made the other two groups largely secondary in the minds of the missionaries.

Evangelization legitimized the occupation of alien lands by the Portuguese and Spaniards: papal bulls gave them the right, and also the duty, to

Christianize all peoples they came in contact with in the colonized territories. No other European empires had the same obsession about converting other peoples to the Christian faith as did the Portuguese and Spanish.

Up to the creation of the Congregation for the Propagation of the Faith (Congregatio de Propaganda Fidei) in 1622, the Portuguese and Spanish Crowns enjoyed the monopoly of religious action in their colonies through the granting of a sequence of privileges issued by the papal court. The papal bulls sanctioned each country's rights over the newly discovered or conquered territories. These prerogatives (known as *padroado* in Portugal and *patronato* in Spain) were formed in the early years of their expansion.[1]

The privileges of the Portuguese *padroado* can be summarized as follows: the Crown decided on the building of cathedrals, churches, monasteries, and convents in the new territories. It also presented to the Holy See a small list of candidates to be nominated as archbishops or bishops for the overseas archdioceses and dioceses, as well as appointments to minor positions in the church hierarchy. The Crown also administered ecclesiastical revenues and rejected papal bulls that had not been previously submitted for its approval. All these prerogatives entitled the Crown to collect ecclesiastical taxes that would otherwise be paid to the Roman church.[2]

The context in which these privileges were given to the Iberian Crowns was easily integrated in the medieval Reconquest. In the formative years of the Portuguese *padroado*, expansion was seen as a crusade against the infidels. Its formation was as inseparable from the Portuguese conquests in Morocco as the conquest of Granada or the occupation of the Canary Islands was to the Spanish *patronato*.

The Portuguese *padroado* and the Spanish *patronato* restricted the Church of Rome's possibilities to develop religious action overseas, but a number of reasons explain why they were formed and why Rome took a number of years to try to correct this situation. In the first place, during the High Renaissance, popes had been absorbed in the amassing of new territories in the Italian peninsula. Second, they lacked organizational devices to implement the pope's authority in the new territories, especially as the Protestant Reformation exploded and the Catholic Church concentrated on recovering lost ground. Third, all the prerogatives that were conceded point to a lack of awareness on the part of the papacy of the importance that the new territories might develop in the future.

The Portuguese *padroado* suffered several setbacks in the East: the Jesuits were expelled from Ethiopia in 1634 and from Japan in 1639; the empire lost many of its fortresses in India and the island of Ceylon; and finally, the missionaries sent by the Propaganda Fide threatened its hegemony. Nevertheless, in Brazil the *padroado* managed to survive mostly unthreatened, in part because the Crown managed to acquire its entire territory after the expulsion of the French from Maranhão in 1615 and of the Dutch from Pernambuco in 1654. Brazil proved to be one of the more stable Jesuit provinces. The Society arrived in Portuguese America twenty years before settling in Spanish America and had a major role in the whole process of Christianization until the 1750s, despite some competition from other religious orders.

Perceptions of the Indians of Brazil: The Medieval Heritage

Attitudes toward the newly discovered peoples of America were influenced by the medieval cultural heritage. The Portuguese and the Spanish interpreted the life and mores of the Amerindians according to the tradition of demonology.

The medieval evolution of the Greek notion of barbarians had incorporated them with pagans, that is, non-Christians. Drawing mainly from Aristotle, the Thomistic tradition in the Middle Ages viewed non-Christians as living in a dark limbo, without light, faith, or salvation. They were imperfect human beings perpetually fighting one another in endless wars. This view crossed the Atlantic; to Europeans, Amerindians appeared as barbarians, engaged in perpetual fights and cannibal feasts.[3] When referring to Brazilian Indians, the Portuguese often used the expression "without law, without king, without God."

Colorfully painted naked bodies would be seen not only as evidence of the expulsion from Paradise, but also as impersonations of the Devil. Tribal dances became witches' Sabbaths; different sexual norms were evidence of degenerate devilish behavior; and cannibalism was seen as the ultimate proof of the Indians' evil nature. To the eyes of the Europeans, Brazil was the kingdom of Satan.

Founded by Saint Augustine, demonology had developed as a specific field of knowledge in the fifteenth century, with landmarks such as Johannes Nider's *Formicarius* (written between 1435 and 1437) and Jakob Sprenger and Heinrich Kramer's *Malleus Malleficarum* (1486). Carlo Ginzburg related demonology to the new social construction of witchcraft as practiced by groups of people and not by isolated individuals, as it emerged in the aftermath of the Black Death.[4] The Renaissance preserved the belief in the powers of the Devil as the inspiration of superstition, witchcraft, and idolatry: numerous works on the powers of the Devil were published in Europe.

In Portugal, no specific work devoted to demonology was published during the sixteenth century, and only two works of this kind (by Manuel do Vale de Moura and Manuel de Lacerda) were printed in the seventeenth century.[5] This small production contrasts with contemporary Spanish studies of demonology: between 1510 and 1618, six treaties were published in the sixteenth century and four in the seventeenth century. More than that, Spanish theologians related demonology to Amerindians. To José de Acosta, for example, the Devil had taken refuge in America after having been chased from the Old World with the arrival of Christ.[6]

Nevertheless, other Portuguese sources referred to this world of knowledge, including compilations of laws, jurisprudence, treaties on moral theology, manuals of confession, catechisms, parish priest manuals, sermons, and treaties of medicine. These works have revealed that Portuguese literate elites were familiar with the basic elements of the discipline of demonology, attributing phenomena such as witchcraft to the evil agency of the Devil. There was general agreement on the subject, with little dissent among the various authors.[7]

In Portuguese America, the Devil became the enemy of every missionary, as the source of idolatry: a permanent war was to take place between two opposite worlds, the Christian and the Barbarian. This dispute was present right from the beginnings of colonization. Although the bull *Sublimis Deus* issued by Pope Paul III on 2 June 1537 had established the human nature of Amerindians—proclaiming them capable of being indoctrinated—popular and elite views never stopped considering them as devilish beasts. These perceptions were in sharp contrast with the respect the Portuguese accorded Asian civilizations such as China and Japan.[8] The fact that the two were empires with visible social stratification, highly developed urban fortified systems, the presence of writing as well as a caste of literate elites, clothing and sophisticated rules of civility, and written laws created a pattern that implied the negative view of Amerindians. The latter were at the lower rank within a scale of values that accorded a higher level to most of the peoples with whom Europeans came in contact, including the Mexicans and the Incas.

The image of the Amerindians was built according to the colonial interests of the Portuguese, especially in what concerns the concept of a "just war" (*guerra justa*). In the terms of the law, the enslavement of the Indians was forbidden—the bull *Sublimis Deus* and royal decrees forbade it—but there were arguments that justified circumstances when the Portuguese might use the Indians as slaves. According to Beatriz Perrone-Moisés, the concept of a just war, developed in the context of the war against Islam during the Middle Ages, was adjusted in the sixteenth century to be applied to the Amerindians. Legitimate motives to fight against infidels included the refusal of conversion or hostility toward the propagation of the faith, the practice of hostile acts against the Portuguese and their allies, and the breaking of pacts. Portuguese legislation consistently confirmed that the hostility of the Amerindians toward the propagation of faith was a sufficient motive to declare war against the natives.[9]

Even if in theory the situations when war could be declared were restricted, in practice the colonists used this concept as a self-serving device to acquire the workforce they required. This was the case in the highlands of São Paulo, where the colonists and their allies (mainly *mamelucos*) made trips into the interior to fight the Indians, taking the captives to their estates as slaves. These expeditions made a major contribution to the integration of this area into the colonial economy.[10] They tended to be justified a posteriori with the hostility of the Indians, even though that hostility might have originated in previous aggression by the colonists.

The Agents of Christianization

It is hard to measure the efforts of Christianization without knowing who its agents were, how many there were, what goals they had in mind, and how they intended to achieve those goals. Neither is it easy to understand religious action without relating it to changing policies and relationships between the center and the periphery.[11] On the one hand, official policies governing evangelization were established by royal decree, as well as by the central administration of the religious orders. On the other hand, missionary action developed according to local dynamics, making it necessary to have in mind the evolution of the relationship between religious orders and the king, between them and their higher institutional authorities, and between colonists and missionaries.

Little is known about the first efforts at evangelization before the arrival of the Jesuits in 1549. Some Franciscans were aboard the fleet of Pedro Alvares Cabral, but there was little institutional interest in Brazil, either lay or ecclesiastical, during the first half of the sixteenth century. Nevertheless, the miscegenation of different ethnic groups started in this period. A new breed came into being: the *mamelucos,* sons and daughters of the first Europeans to settle in Brazil with the Indian women. The second generation of mixed bloods, daughters and sons of Indians and *mamelucos,* would be designated as *curibocas.*

With the importation of African slaves, the creation of new human types continued throughout the colonial history of Brazil. Four new ethnic categories were formed: *mulattos* (white father with black mother), *pardos* (white father with mulatto mother), *cafusos* (black father and Indian mother), and *cabras* (black father with mulatto mother). Brazilian-born Europeans were called *mazombos,* and second-generation black slaves were known as *crioulos.*[12] Also, different African ethnic groups with different religious backgrounds were brought into Brazil. Ethnic diversity in colonial Brazil was immense, and thus a history of its Christianization must take into account not only the Portuguese, the Amerindians, and the Africans, but also the intermixing of such broad large categories, with very diverse cultural and religious backgrounds.

The Jesuits

The Portuguese Empire was the first field of evangelization of the Jesuits (the order was scarcely two years old when Francis Xavier departed to India), beginning twenty years before their expansion in the Spanish or the French Empire. Historians have stressed the Jesuits' success in the Portuguese colonies, judging them the most successful of all the religious orders that were engaged in evangelization. We do not know, however, to what extent the extensive documentation of their missionary efforts by the Jesuits is responsible for leading scholars to overestimate their success while underestimating the efforts of those orders that did little to record their work for posterity. Moreover, in the whole Portuguese Empire, Brazil remains the area where the dominant role of the Jesuits remains unquestioned for the entire colonial period. They were the first religious order to arrive there and remained the most important until the 1750s, just before their expulsion from Portugal in 1759.

Significantly, the first six Jesuits arrived in Brazil in the same vessels that bore the new governor Tomé de Souza and a thousand men, with royal orders to build the city of the Saviour of Bahia, the capital of the colony. This group of Jesuits included the famous Manuel da Nóbrega, who would be its first mission superior, and provincial from 1553 to 1560. By 1570, another thirty-seven Jesuits had arrived from Portugal, joining forty-five men recruited locally.

Right from the first years in Brazil, the Jesuits helped the Portuguese Crown to gather new territories for the colony. This first contingent of Jesuits is supposed to have helped in the victory over the French in Fort Coligny and the subsequent founding of Rio de Janeiro. Also, they went farther south, to São Vicente, and then moved to the interior, to São Paulo de Piratininga, where they created a mission that would give birth to the city of São Paulo.[13]

By the end of the sixteenth century the province had opened three colleges: in Bahia, Rio de Janeiro, and Olinda. During the second half of the seventeenth century, after the expulsion of the Dutch from Pernambuco, a new expansion period followed, with an increase of the number of Jesuits and five new colleges (Santos, Espírito Santo, Recife, São Luís do Maranhão, and Belém do Pará).[14]

The first twenty years of the presence of the Jesuits in Brazil saw a major transformation in the methods of evangelization. Traveling missions were replaced by fixed settlements that included the residence, the college, and the *aldeia* (Indian village). The residence was a housing facility for the members of the order, while the college was used either in the teaching of the local elites or in the formation of recruits. Neither of these structures was concerned with evangelization of the Indians; the *aldeias* provided a fixed basis for conversion. Instead of traveling to indoctrinate, the Jesuits persuaded the Indians to settle in villages where a residing small group of Jesuits indoctrinated them. The increase in the number of these *aldeias* became possible with the amazing success of the Society, whose number of members did not cease to grow until the expulsion of the order (see table).

There were two separate provinces, one with Bahia as capital and the other in northeastern Brazil, Maranhão, formed after the expulsion of the French from the mouth of the Amazon. In the single province of Brazil, the Society's personnel would increase from 6 in 1549 to 169 in 1600. The next century would see a slow growth in its first half, only to increase again in the second half. By its last decade, there would be over three hundred Jesuits in the Brazil province and nearly five hundred in the years that preceded their expulsion. The province of Maranhão was to grow mainly during the eighteenth century, surpassing a hundred Jesuits in the 1730s (see table).

It would be a mistake, however, to assume that all of this staff was concerned with missionary action: many individuals were teachers in the Society's colleges or administrators in the bureaucratic machine and did

Number of Jesuits in Portuguese America (1549–1760)

Year	Brazil	Maranhão	Total
1549	6	—	6
1558	25		25
1568	61		61
1584	40		140
1600	169		169
1606	176		176
1610	165		165
1631	176		176
1641	159		159
1654[a]	162	26[b]	188
1664		11[b]	—
1679	188	34	222
1683	252	—	—
1690	—	54	—
1694	310	—	—
1716	324	—	—
1720	—	64	—
1722	367	69[b]	436
1730	—	102	—
1732	362	118	480
1735	417	117	534
1738	423		—
1741	431		—
1743	447		—
1748	471		—
1751		148	—
1753		136	—
1757	476	—	
1760		155	—

Source: Alden, *The Making of an Enterprise*, pp. 674–676.
a. The second wave of Jesuit missions in the State of Maranhão took off in 1652, after a first attempt in the 1640s.
b. The estimates for Maranhão are for the years 1655, 1663, and 1723.

not leave the urban centers. Charlotte de Castelnau-L'Estoile has shown that of 164 Jesuits listed in the 1598 catalogue, only 34 were concerned with the Christianization of the Indians. More than that, missionaries living in the *aldeias* were subaltern in relation to the urban ones, whose skills in theology or preaching ensured them the possibility of making the fourth vow (obedience to the pope), so that they might ascend to the higher posts in Jesuit hierarchy. The strictly missionary ones tended to be recruited in Brazil because of their linguistic proficiency. This analysis has also shown that the order lost much of its international character in Brazil: 86 percent of the missionaries were born either in Portugal or in the colony.[15]

The Changing Policies of Conversion

Debate about the strategies of conversion appeared during the first decade of the presence of the Jesuits in Brazil. Padre Manuel da Nóbrega favored military dominance over the Amerindians as a precondition of any efforts at conversion.[16] This policy, elaborated in 1556 and 1557, was radically opposed to the position of Bartolomé de Las Casas, who advocated peaceful means of religious proselytism. For Nóbrega, the policy seems to have been a response to the disappointments of his experience as a missionary, which had revealed the difficulties of making the natives truly understand the Christian faith. José de Anchieta, another Jesuit missionary, also supported the forced grouping of Amerindians in villages.

The first itinerant missions were replaced by fixed settlements with living-in missionaries, the *aldeias*.[17] This change required an alliance between the Order and the Crown, whose army was summoned to collaborate in the removal of the Indians from their original villages to the territories where the *aldeias* were to be found. Often, such villages were placed in strategic positions, as the Indians tended to be involved either in the construction of the colony's territory or in its defense. Most of the time, these villages were used as a frontier between areas dominated by the whites and enemy tribes, or even other Europeans settling in Brazil.

It has become a classical issue to compare the Jesuits' indifference toward African slavery with their protection of the Indians. Nevertheless, according to the logic of slavery until the eighteenth century, it was not forbidden to own slaves if they had been enslaved in a "just war" or as long as one was not responsible for their enslavement. Although Africans were, at least in theory, already slaves when the Portuguese took them, the justifications for fighting and enslaving Amerindians were not always recognized as legitimate.

This distinction was useful in economic terms, because the missionaries were as involved in the plantation economy as were the other colonists. They became owners of large estates, either raising cattle or, after the beginning of the seventeenth century, owning sugar plantations, where they used slaves as a workforce.

Nevertheless, "conversion" did not imply that the converts would be transformed into the equals of the Portuguese colonists. Indians were always the subjects of domination, never rising to posts in either the church or the civil hierarchy. As to the Africans, António Vieira (1608–1697), the most influential Jesuit who condemned the slavery of Amerindians, judged them as having at least gained eternal salvation. Blacks had been slaves in Africa, where they lived in hell; in Brazil their body would be still imprisoned while their soul was freed through baptism. The only recommendation of Vieira was that their owners treat them Christianly.[18]

The protection the Jesuits conceded to the Indians living in their villages was in itself a colonial project that clashed with the ambitions of the white colonists. The Jesuits wanted to restrict as much as possible the colonists' interference in the *aldeias,* especially the possibility of their claiming Indians to add to the workforce on their rural estates. Until the suppression of the Brazilian missions in 1760, the Jesuits were a colonial power and often fought against bishops or royal representatives.

An Enterprise or a Bureaucratic Organization?

Some recent work on the Jesuits has questioned the nature of this religious order. Dauril Alden, in a comprehensive book on the assistancy of Portugal, has viewed the Society as an enterprise because of its economic autonomy.[19] The idea that missions should be self-supporting led to their economic autonomy. By contrast, Charlotte de Castelnau L'Estoile has termed it a bureaucratic organization: an institution with a defined hierarchy, in which communication between the center (Rome) and the periphery produced a large amount of paperwork that was central to decision making among its members. This author drew attention to the specificity of the religious project of the Jesuits, whose main goal was conversion and not economic growth.[20]

It is difficult to choose between these two views, which do not seem incompatible (even if to refer to the Society as an enterprise in the contemporary sense seems anachronistic). On the one hand, it is difficult to deny the pragmatic sense of the Jesuits, even if controversial decisions such as becoming estate owners in Brazil finally won over their detractors. It is a fact that by the eighteenth century most Jesuit centers were provided with supporting sugar estates.[21] On the other hand, it seems that the control from the center was not always overwhelming and that many directives from above were adjusted to local circumstances, even at the cost of some disagreement between the province and Rome. Also, decision making from the center was not always predominant, and Jesuit provinces managed to present some controversial innovations as facts, even before Rome could put up obstacles to them. Such was the case with the creation of the *aldeias*, presented to Rome as *faits accomplis*, a result of the agency of the Jesuits in Brazil together with the governor Mem de Sá, who was then the representative of the political power in the colony.[22]

Other Religious Orders

Until 1581, the Jesuits appeared to be in charge of the evangelization of the Indians as natural allies to royal colonization. This decade, however, saw the rise of antagonism between the royal governor, Manuel Teles Barreto (1583–89), and the order.[23] This same decade is marked by the arrival of other religious orders such as the Benedictines, the Carmelites, and the Franciscans. It must be noted, however, that except for the Franciscans, these were not missionary orders. The Franciscans became the second religious order concerned with the conversion of the Indians and, like the Jesuits, attracted the enmity of colonists by preaching against Indian slavery.[24]

The Secular Ecclesiastical Frame: Bishoprics and Parishes

The increasing importance of Brazil led to the creation of the See of Bahia in 1551, two years after the first governor appointed by the king, Tomé de Sousa, started to build the city of Salvador. In 1676, Bahia was elevated to the metropolitan See of Brazil, in the same year that two new Brazilian dioceses were created: Rio de Janeiro and Olinda. A third new diocese would be created the following year in Maranhão. The diocese of Angola (created in 1596) was placed under the authority of Bahia in 1677, thus confirming the close ties between the two areas, which were linked by the slave trade. During the eighteenth century the dioceses of Pará (1719), Mariana, São Paulo, and Goiás (all founded in 1745) would follow.

The difference between the number of dioceses created in the Americas up to 1800 by each Iberian Empire is striking: seven in Brazil against forty-one in Spanish America. Even if one takes into account the larger areas controlled by Spain in the continent, it is a fact that the episcopal grid was tighter in the Spanish *patronato*. More than that, this grid was already in place by 1620, counting thirty-five dioceses by then, while Bahia was the only Brazilian diocese until 1676.[25]

Religious action on the part of the episcopal structures was far from being as influential as the one provided by the Jesuits and other religious orders. The dioceses did not develop missionary activities, religious training of future ecclesiastics being largely in the hands of the Jesuits well into the eighteenth century, and the confraternities of the Misericórdia fulfilled most charitable institutional duties. There were neither universities nor printing presses in Brazil, and this must have also limited the influence of the prelates. The only synod to take place in the entire colonial period was in Bahia, in 1707, which had as an outcome the publication (in Lisbon) of the only synodal constitutions edited in Brazil.[26] Bishops in Brazil limited themselves to diocesan visitations, rarely venturing out to the wilderness (except for the Amazonian expeditions of two bishops of Pará, D. Frei João de São José Queirós and D. Frei Caetano Brandão, in the 1760s and 1780s).

The Portuguese Crown was neither generous nor efficient in giving back to the ecclesiastical institutions the *dízimos* (church tax) it had collected on behalf of the Portuguese *padroado*. Certainly they had the obligation to fund religious action, but one can well understand why religious orders such as the Jesuits were always eager to have their autonomous sources of income, as referred to earlier in this chapter.

As a result, few parishes were created in Brazil. In the first century of the Portuguese colonization, the number of parishes did not exceed fifty; during the next century ninety were added; and in the first seventy-five years of the eighteenth century, after the gold rush in Minas Gerais, more than four hundred new ones were erected. There were single parishes almost as vast as metropolitan Portugal.[27] Many of these parishes were funded not by the *padroado* but by the community. The *paróquias coladas* (parishes created by the king, paid by the royal treasury) were rare, and bishops took the initiative of creating *paróquias encomendadas*. They would assign these parishes a priest, who would be remunerated by the parishioners themselves. Payments could include the payment of a tax known as *conhecença* (personal voluntary offerings on the occasion of the ministering of sacraments and also alms collecting during religious services).[28]

The weakness of the secular church structure explains in part why religious orders such as the Jesuits were so important in Brazil, although this can be viewed also as a cause-effect relationship. But this gap was also filled with private religious chapels, for example, the ones in rural estates such as the *engenhos* (sugar plantations) or cattle farms, which were financially more rewarding to priests than parishes. Also, collective structures such as confraternities and Third Orders helped to compensate for the failures of the parochial structure. These private religious structures created a domestic religion, often rural and distinct in character from that of the cities, where secular ecclesiastic official structures prevailed. Despite administrative difficulties in obtaining the permit to erect a private chapel, once the chapel was created the chaplains responded to their local masters, such as the boards of confraternities or the owners of the rural estates. Whenever both structures coexisted (parish and confraternity or private chapel) there were constant conflicts over the monopoly of the religious cult.

Private chapels and confraternities were fundamental in the development of Brazilian popular devotion. Everyday religion included also a segregation of spaces, as churches and chapels tended to avoid interracial mixing; whites preferred to have their own spaces either in churches or chapels. Some of the chapels of the sugar plantations would have a small room opposite the sacristy, where the members of the owning family, especially women, could attend mass without being seen. The number of domestic oratories was also high, and those allowed the diversification of private devotion to favorite saints, as well as personal (and less orthodox) cult forms.[29]

The Inquisition

Created by the pope in 1536 at the request of John III, the Portuguese Inquisition was never established in Brazil, in contrast with Spanish America, where there were inquisitions in Lima (after 1570), Mexico (1571), and Cartagena (1610). This does not mean that the inquisition did not make its presence felt in Brazil, however. The territory was under permanent surveillance. Several detection systems for deviant behavior were installed, and the accused would be sent to Lisbon, where they would be tried and sentenced. The first of such devices were inquisitorial visitations, in which inspection teams from the Lisbon Holy Office were sent to Brazil. The first covered the areas of Bahia and Pernambuco and took place between 1591 and 1595. There were similar visitations in this decade to the Azores, Madeira, and Angola. Other inquisitorial visitations in Brazil followed in the seventeenth century, although proceedings were published only for the one that occurred between 1618 and 1621.[30] After 1637 such visits were interrupted in Brazil as well as in Portugal because of their high cost in a context of a decade of political and economic crisis during the reign of Philip III, which was prolonged during the Restoration war (1640–

68).³¹ Also, a network of alternative control systems was put in place to inspect the colony's orthodoxy, which made such visitations by the metropolitan inquisition superfluous. The cooperation between the inquisition and the bishops was much improved, with the organization of diocesan visitations that paid due attention to deviant behavior, especially after the issuance of regulations by the Synodal Constitutions of 1707.³²

The emphasis of the inquisitorial accusations was not on matters of doctrinal orthodoxy but on sexual behavior. The colony had enjoyed a reputation for loose mores since the first Jesuits reported on the habits of the white colonists. In matters of religious practices, authors have reported on their heterodoxy, that is, the gray frontier between licit and illicit piety, as well as the Brazilian clergy's indifference to superstitious practices, marked by the juxtaposition of different cultural universes.³³ The inquisitorial accusations were not directed at the African populations, New Christians, or native populations. "Sexual offenses" (such as sodomy, fornication, and bigamy) perpetrated by Old Christians were the main crimes prosecuted.³⁴

Confraternities and Religious Life

Confraternities represented the adherence of the local populations to Catholicism. They were an expression of the religiosity of the laity, linking formal ecclesiastical structures to communities of believers. They encouraged the practice of everyday religious life and made sure that the events in the ritual calendar were duly celebrated. Confraternities proved to be the most efficient religious institutions at the local level: they organized processions; arranged for the building of churches and maintenance of religious equipment; ensured the payment of priests for the regular cure of souls; and provided the locals with a sense of social importance through membership. They were the only religious structures available in the mining area of Minas Gerais, where religious orders were forbidden by the king. The urge to tax every pound of gold extracted in the area on behalf of the Crown had led the monarchy to deny authorization for the building of convents and monasteries there. Two motives accounted for this decision: first, religious orders would have been financially dependent upon the Crown, as was every religious structure of the *padroado;* second, convents and monasteries would inevitably attract pious donations and bequests from the populations.

In northeastern Brazil, the chapels of the *"engenhos"* fulfilled similar functions, providing spiritual services both to slave masters and to their workers. Private arrangements and associations created under the initiative of the local populations (even if under the auspices of the local religious orders) were at times more important locally than parishes. Confraternities allowed the populations to compensate for the weak religious structures set up by the *padroado régio*.

Strictly hierarchical and discriminating in their requirements for membership, there were confraternities to match virtually any social situation, and the number of confraternities to which each person was able to belong was a sign of distinction. From the Misericórdias to the Third Orders, limited strictly to local white elites, one could find confraternities for almost every social or ethnic group in Brazil. More than ensuring the celebration of weekly masses or the receiving of sacraments, they made religious cult a part of daily life in the colony.

The world of confraternities was strictly hierarchical. At the top were the confraternities of the Misericórdia and the Third Orders of the Carmelites and Franciscans, which forbade admission to nonwhites and where membership was a privilege of the rich and wealthy: merchants and businessmen, estate owners, royal officials. Beneath them, but also meant for white men, were the confraternities of the Santíssimo Sacramento, Nossa Senhora da Conceição, and São Miguel e Almas. Significant differences existed among these three groups of religious associations.

The Misericórdias were lay confraternities for white men, under royal protection, enjoying preeminence either in local power or in the practice of institutional charity, often administering major hospitals and *recolhimentos*[35] (conservatories for women in which they were secluded but did not take vows, and could leave the premises). Their patrimony was based upon the accumulation of pious legacies and circulated on the money market to finance sugar crops or other financial needs, mostly of the elites who integrated them.

The Third Orders recruited their members in the same social strata, often overlapping with the Misericórdias but with significant differences: Misericórdias were *numerus clausus* confraternities, whereas Third Orders did not limit the number of members. The latter also admitted women, a situation that contrasted with most existing confraternities. Members of the Third Orders were particularly concerned with daily devotion, and brothers took vows after a period of novitiate. In fact, they attempted to imitate the life of the religious order to which they were attached, functioning as lay branches to the religious orders that patronized and tutored them. In Bahia, they made available the more prestigious burial grounds to the wealthy.

Confraternities such as Santíssimo Sacramento, Nossa Senhora da Conceição, and São Miguel e Almas were typically post-Tridentine, often were attached to a parish, and were concerned with the organization of daily religious life, as well as liturgical feasts. In spite of being meant for white men, they were not as elite as the Third Orders or the Misericórdias.

In Brazil, confraternities were particularly important to the African populations, both slaves and freedmen. They provided a means by which some autonomy for the black and mulatto populations and control by the white colonists could be negotiated. In fact, whites were ever present as part of black confraternities, sometimes as members of the directing boards and other times as patrons. Such confraternities could group individuals of African origin according to their color (black and mulatto tended to go to separate confraternities).[36] African slaves gathered in the confraternities of Our Lady of the Rosary, Santa Ifigénia, and São Benedito; *crioulos*, mulattos, and freedmen joined the irmandades das Mercês; *pardos* joined the brotherhoods of São Gonçalo Garcia. Nevertheless, this typology is only indicative, because even if their regulations (*compromissos*) prescribed admission to certain groups, membership practices were more permissive; a confraternity for black Africans might, for example, include *crioulos*, mulattos, and freedmen.

The grouping of Africans could go as far as constituting different confraternities according to African ethnic origin. This was the case in Rio de Janeiro and Bahia, even if in other areas such as Minas Gerais several different ethnicities were admitted in the same confraternity. In this region, the confraternities of the Rosary included mixed-origin slaves, with a variety of both Sudanese and Bantu ethnicities.[37]

Women and Religion

Religion in the empire was a male business, as was nearly every aspect of colonial life. The few women of Portuguese origin who existed in the different parts of the empire were urged to enter the marriage market. Lack of Portuguese brides was genuine, but perhaps not the longing of Portuguese males for white women, for these men found plenty of women locally. Also, for inheritance reasons, most parents wished to place their daughters in convents and did so by sending them to Portugal.

Convents for women in the Portuguese colonies were few and founded late, because the policy of the Crown was to delay their establishment as much as possible. There were only three foundations in the seventeenth century: Santa Monica in Goa in 1606, the barefoot Carmelites of Macao in 1633, and the Poor Clares of the Desterro in Bahia in 1677. It is significant that in the Spanish Empire, by the 1620s, there were already thirty-six convents for women, fifteen of those located in Mexico City. The difference in the number of female convents in the two empires can be explained in the patterns of colonial emigration. The Spaniards tended to emigrate with their wives and were encouraged to do so by the Crown, whereas Portuguese men left Portugal alone, either as single men or leaving their wives and children behind. Nevertheless, the foundation of convents was much desired by the colonial Portuguese elites, who constantly applied to Lisbon for authorization to erect them.

The policy of the Crown, however, was to reduce the number of convents as much as possible and delay as long as possible their foundation. This policy resulted in the sending of daughters of colonists to the metropolitan convents, a practice that the Crown tried to forbid in 1732.[38] The will to found convents can be explained either in the inheritance strategies that favored the exclusion of some women from the marriage market or in the undeniable attraction that the status of nun and the ideals of sainthood exerted upon women.

The alternative to placing women in cloisters was the *recolhimento*, which allowed the cloistering of women according to monastic rules without the requirement of taking vows. The *recolhimentos* were convenient because they permitted women (if sometimes only in theory) to reenter the marriage market and because the Crown was not so restrictive about their foundation. In practice, most *recolhimentos* in Brazil became surrogate convents, and life inside their walls was not much different from classic female withdrawal from the world.[39]

Despite the opposition of the Crown, the number of convents and *recolhimentos* increased during the eighteenth century. In the preceding century, there had been only the previously mentioned Clarists of the Desterro in Bahia and two *recolhimentos*, one in São Paulo and the other in Olinda. However, another five convents were created in Brazil in the second third of the eighteenth century: two in Bahia (Lapa and Mercês), two in Rio de Janeiro (Ajuda and Santa Teresa), and one in São Paulo. As to the number of foundations of *recolhimentos*, they mounted to eight: four in Bahia, two in Minas Gerais, two in Pernambuco, and another in Maranhão.[40]

A low participation of women of Portuguese origin in the public activities of confraternities can be expected, although few studies on the subject have been published. Women were not welcome outside the domestic sphere, except for attending the mass at church, and even so, women of high status would travel to churches in coaches and litters that concealed them from public exposure. As for devotional activities organized by confraternities, one can suspect white women of being honorary sisters (mostly through widowhood) of elite confraternities such as the Misericórdias rather than active participants. Nevertheless, in Brazil, white women could enter the Third Orders as members (and not just as representatives of a deceased husband or father) and participate actively in their devotional life. However, even though these women could attain some leadership positions over other female members, male tertiaries monopolized the higher posts in the directing hierarchy.

The religious sphere of women was thus preferably either domestic or reclusive (and tightly controlled by men, such as the episcopal hierarchy or the confessors). Some devout women who did not enter a *recolhimento* or a convent developed forms of religious living inside their homes. Even if women chose not to go to that extreme, the existence of private chapels and oratories provided women with secluded religious structures that entertained their devotion, a devotion that could not have been as orthodox as the Church of Rome would have wished for. The case of Rosa Maria Egipcíaca da Vera Cruz is illustrative: an African woman, an ex-prostitute, claimed that the Jesus child came every day to her house and combed her hair, and she reciprocated by breastfeeding him.[41]

Conclusions

No one gives up entirely a previous identity, religious or social, just by the fact of being indoctrinated. Missionaries were aware that the process of conversion would take several generations, and they were often discouraged by meager short-term results. Conversion was accompanied by the acquisition of Christian modes of living, which implied covering genitals with clothes, adopting monogamous heterosexuality, or giving up cannibal feasts. Numerous obstacles made Christianization a difficult goal. There was passive and active resistance by Indians who would not give up their frames of thought or simply replace them with new ones. The tendency was to juxtapose different systems of belief and forms of behavior that were often contradictory. Despite the Jesuit tradition of producing a literature of propaganda concerning the success of missions, recently explored sources have revealed the utmost discouragement of most mission superiors, who named Brazil the "barren vineyard" and accused the Indians of believing without faith and thus of being virtually incapable of assimilating the Christian message.[42]

Even the children, whom the Jesuits considered the best converts, remained in contact with their communities and did not give up their culture entirely. Also, one of the fears of the Jesuit administrators was the acculturation of isolated missionaries to the Indian culture, a sea of difficulties that implied a hard-to-solve contradiction: missions might be sterile and the conversion work difficult to perform and dangerous to the salvation of the missionaries, but it legitimized the presence of the order in Brazil. Missionizing represented the purpose of the Society itself, whose conversion project was at the basis of its very existence and spread across the continents.

One episode illustrating the intricate weaving of different religious cultures that emerged as the result of missionary action is the *santidade* of Jaguaripe, studied by Ronaldo Vainfas in *A Heresia dos Índios*. Mamelucos, fugitive slave Amerindians and Africans, and even Portuguese colonists participated in a hybrid religious cult in Jaguaripe, a frontier territory in Bahia. The cult (1580–85) included a mixture of elements of Jesuit doctrine, as apprehended by Indians and *mamelucos*, with Amerindian traditional religious ceremonies; it incorporated millenarian expectations, as the followers were promised a land without evil and the enslavement of the whites. Strategic moves from an ambitious landowner, Fernão Cabral de Taíde, aided by the *mamelucos*, attracted this community of fugitives to his *engenho*. Reactions of other landowners, whose Amerindians and African slaves had fled to the *santidade*, were followed by the intervention of the governor, Teles Barreto, who put an end to the rebellion at the command of a military expedition in 1585. Vainfas rightly assumed this episode to be proof of the active resistance by the colonized to the presence of the white colonists, including the Jesuits. It is also significant that several white persons, starting with Fernão Cabral and his wife, paid respect to the cults performed in the *santidade* of Jaguaripe, demonstrating the gap between popular and elite religion.[43]

The subjects of conversion cannot be seen as passive objects. For example, there is the case of the Indian tribes who chose an alliance with the colonizers to fight their common enemies. Less evident is the situation in which Amerindians negotiated between what the missionaries were trying to teach them and the issues they chose to believe, or the interpretations they gave to the new Catholic rituals they performed. For obvious reasons, and as a measure of their subaltern position, their motivations and strategies have left few traces. I know of no account of an Indian (albeit Christianized) having left a record of his or her encounters with the Portuguese missionaries.

Religious practices proved to be less sensitive to the frontiers between licit and illicit practices than they were in Europe, the latter having been practically ignored by the clergy.[44] Private chapels, especially in the sugar plantations, were the rule, and the role of parish priests was often precarious, especially in areas that were later integrated into the colonial economy. As a result, the populations enjoyed less surveillance from the ecclesiastical authorities, and their devotional practices included a great degree of unorthodox behavior.

As to the Indians, it is to be expected that the full success of their conversion depended on their full integration into the colonial society. But Indians in Brazil were as devastated by epidemic mortality as were native populations elsewhere in America. In the long run, the missions contributed to the destruction of the overwhelming majority of tribes, either physically or culturally.

Notes

1. In 1433 the Portuguese king, D. Duarte, was already granting spiritual jurisdiction over the Madeira Islands to the Order of Christ, and in 1455 the bull *Romanus Pontifex* recognized the Crown's rights to rule spiritual matters in the newly discovered territories. The Spaniards started their efforts in papal court to obtain the same prerogatives in the 1480s, in the context of the fight against Spanish Muslims and the colonization of the Canary Islands. Only in 1508 did Jules II grant the bull *Universalis Ecclesiae*, which enabled the Spanish Crown to rule spiritual matters in the Americas.

2. Cf. C. R. Boxer, *The Church Militant and Iberian Expansion* (Baltimore, 1978), chap. 3.

3. Ronald Raminelli, *Imagens da colonização: A representação do Índio de Caminha a Vieira* (Rio de Janeiro, 1996), 53–55.

4. Carlo Ginzburg, *História Nocturna: Uma decifração do Sabat* (Lisbon, 1995), 77.

5. Manuel do Vale de Moura, *De incantationibus seu ensalmis* (Évora, 1620); Manuel de Lacerda, *Memorial e antídoto contra os pós venenosos que o Demónio inventou e per seus confederados espalhou, em odio da christandade* (Lisbon, 1631).

Cf. José Pedro Paiva, *Bruxaria e superstição num país sem "caça às bruxas,"* *1600–1774* (Coimbra, 1997), 15–80.

6. Cf. Laura de Mello e Souza, *Inferno Atlântico: Demonologia e colonização, séculos XVI–XVIII* (São Paulo, 1993), 13–46. See also José de Acosta, *Historia Natural y Moral de las Indias* ed. Jane E. Mangan, trans. Frances M. Lopez-Morillas (Durham, N.C., 2002).

7. José Pedro Paiva, *Bruxaria,* 15–80.

8. Raminelli, *Imagens da colonização,* 148–52.

9. Cf. Beatriz Perrone-Moisés, "Aldeados, aliados, inimigos e escravos: Lugares dos índios na legislação portuguesa para o Brasil," *Congresso Luso-Brasileiro "Portugal-Brasil: Memórias e Imaginários." Actas* (Lisbon, 2000), vol. 1, 147–64.

10. John Monteiro, *Negros da Terra: Índios e bandeirantes nas origens de São Paulo* (São Paulo, 1994), 209.

11. Charlotte de Castelnau-L'Estoile, *Les Ouvriers d'une vigne stérile: Les Jésuites et la conversion des Indiens au Brésil, 1580–1620* (Paris, 2000).

12. Jorge Couto, *A construção do Brasil* (Lisbon, 1995), 312–13.

13. On the first 21 years of the Jesuits in Brazil, cf. Jean-Claude Laborie, ed., *La mission jésuite du Brésil: Lettres et autres documents (1549–1570)* (Paris, 1998), 7–62.

14. Dauril Alden, *The Making of an Enterprise: The Society of Jesus in Portugal, Its Empire, and Beyond, 1540–1750* (Stanford, 1996), 71–75, 218–26.

15. Castelnau-L'Estoile, *Les Ouvriers d'une vigne stérile,* cf. 197–98, 199–256, and 183.

16. See *Cartas do Brasil e mais escritos do P. Manuel da Nóbrega Opera Omniaf,* introduction by Serafim Leite (Coimbra, 1955).

17. Castelnau-L'Estoile, *Les Ouvriers d'une vigne stérile,* 108.

18. José Oscar Beozzo, "500 Anos de Evangelização," *Extensão* 2, no. 3 (1992): 33–45.

19. Alden, *The Making,* ix.

20. Castelnau-L'Estoile, *Les Ouvriers d'une vigne stérile,* 19, 235.

21. Alden, *The Making,* map 3.

22. Castelnau-L'Estoile, *Les Ouvriers d'une vigne stérile,* 107.

23. Castelnau-L'Estoile, *Les Ouvriers d'une vigne stérile,* 257.

24. Caio Boshi, "As Missões no Brasil," in F. Bethencourt and K. Chaudhuri, eds., *História da Expansão Portuguesa* (Lisbon, 1998), vol. 2, 396–402.

25. José Pedro Paiva, "Pastoral e evangelização," in João Francisco Marques and António Camões Gouveia, eds., *História Religiosa de Portugal* (Lisbon, 2000), vol. 2, 283.

26. *Constituiçoens primeiras do Arcebispado da Bahia feitas e ordenadas pelo illustrissimo e reverendissimo senhor D. Sebastião Monteiro da Vide, Arcebispo* (Lisbon, 1765).

27. Guilherme Pereira das Neves, *Dicionário da História da Colonização Portuguesa no Brasil* (Lisbon, 1994), 22–23.

28. Eduardo Hoornaert, ed., *História da Igreja no Brasil*, 4th ed. (São Paulo, 1992), vol. 2, pt. 1, 284–85; Cristina de Cássia Pereira Moraes, "Faço o que Vossa Mercê manda, mas olha o que eu faço. . . . Um estudo sobre a religiosidade na constituição da sociedade em Goiás—1736–1770," *Congresso Luso-Brasileiro "Portugal-Brasil: Memórias e Imaginários." Actas* (Lisbon, 2000), vol. 1, 174.

29. Luis Mott, "Cotidiano e Vivência Religiosa: Entre a Capela e o Calundu," in Laura de Mello e Souza, ed., *História da Vida Privada no Brasil* (São Paulo, 1997), vol. 1, 161–220.

30. Ronaldo Vainfas mentions three other inquisitorial visitations, although they do not seem to involve the appointment of Portuguese inquisitors travelling to Brazil, having been performed by local ecclesiastics. Two of them took place in 1627 (one to Pernambuco and the other to the south), and the third one in 1646. Vainfas, *Trópico dos Pecados: Moral, sexualidade e Inquisição no Brasil*, 2d ed. (Rio de Janeiro, 1997), 225.

31. See Francisco Bethencourt, "A Inquisição," in João Francisco Marques and António Camões Gouveia, eds., *História Religiosa de Portugal* (Lisbon, 2000), vol. 2, 95–131.

32. Caio César Boschi, "As visitas diocesanas e a Inquisição na Colônia," *Revista Brasileira de História* 7 (São Paulo, 1987): 151–84.

33. Mott, "Cotidiano," 196–202.

34. Vainfas, *Trópico*, 240, 344.

35. On the Brazilian Misericórdias, cf. C. R. Boxer, *Portuguese Society in the Tropics: The Municipal Councils of Goa, Macao, Bahia, and Luanda, 1510–1800* (Madison, Wisc., 1965); A.J.R. Russell-Wood, *Fidalgos and Philanthropists: The Santa Casa da Misericórdia of Bahia, 1550–1755* (London, 1968); and Isabel dos Guimarães Sá, *Quando o rico se faz pobre: Misericórdias, caridade e poder no Império Português, 1500–1800* (Lisbon, 1997).

36. Patricia A. Mulvey, "Black Brothers and Sisters: Membership in Black Lay Brotherhoods of Colonial Brazil," *Luso-Brazilian Review* 17 (Madison, Wisc., 1980): 253–79; A.J.R. Russell-Wood, "Black and Mulatto Brotherhoods in Colonial Brazil: A Study in Collective Behavior," *Hispanic American History Review* 54 (Durham, N.C., 1974): 567–602.

37. Célia A. R. Maia Borges, "As irmandades do Rosário: Culturas em negociação," *Congresso Luso-Brasileiro "Portugal-Brasil: Memórias e Imaginários." Actas* (Lisbon, 2000), vol. 1, 317–18.

38. Leila Algranti, *Honradas e devotas: Mulheres na Colônia. Condição feminina nos conventos e recolhimentos do sudeste do Brasil, 1750–1822* (Rio de Janeiro, 1993), 67–81.

39. Algranti, *Honradas e devotas*, 322.

40. Caio Boschi, "Ordens Religiosas, clero secular e missionação no Brasil," in F. Bethencourt and K. Chaudhuri, *História da Expansão Portuguesa* (Lisbon, 1998), vol. 3, 304.

41. Mott, "Cotidiano," 179–83.

42. On the difficulties of conversion, cf. Castelnau-L'Estoile, *Les Ouvriers d'une vigne stérile,* especially 9–20, 497–500.

43. Ronaldo Vainfas, *A heresia dos Indios: Catolicismo e rebeldia no Brasil colonial* (São Paulo, 1995).

44. Mott, "Cotidiano," 196.

10

Making Papists of Puritans

Accounting for New English Conversions in New France

Evan Haefeli

Despite Whiggish notions of the superiority of Protestantism, English "Puritans" could be converted to Roman Catholicism, as occurred with several hundred in colonial America. The Puritans were prisoners of war on the frontiers of European expansion, captured by French and Native raiding parties launched from Canada. The number of converts was relatively small (roughly 2,309), but the ideological significance of their conversion was great, marking an undeniable French Catholic victory in the spiritual battle for supremacy in North America. The loss was a bitter one for New England. Ever since then, the stories of these apostates have fascinated ministers, antiquarians, and scholars of all sorts. That so little is known about them has only sharpened the interest.[1]

How did the French convince New England Puritans to convert to Catholicism? Scholars have relied heavily on speculation and circumstantial evidence to understand why these individuals adopted the faith their culture so fiercely rejected. James Axtell has made the most systematic effort to explain the phenomenon, suggesting four reasons why captive New England Puritans might have embraced French Catholicism (and nationality—for him the conversion was a cultural as well as a religious phenomenon). First is the captives' "simple gratitude for being delivered out of the hands of the Indians and relief at having survived the painful journey from the English colonies." Second is "the prisoners' natural reluctance to undertake the arduous trip home, particularly if they knew that their immediate family had been killed or carried to Canada." A third reason was the possibility of employment, especially for men who could work as shoemakers, weavers, and mill builders and operators in a New France that needed their talent and labor. Yet, as Axtell notes, few men availed themselves of the special incentives the French used to try to retain these men. Axtell's fourth and final suggestion is that the New Englanders converted out of "love—for French spouses, converted kinsmen and friends, or the Mother Church."[2]

Axtell's speculations probably apply best to a group of men he was not studying. There was in New France a hitherto overlooked group of Englishmen who were quite prone to conversion and assimilation into French Catholic society. They were not Puritans or even New Englanders. They were English and had emigrated directly from Europe. Often young and poor, they had been captured while serving as soldiers or sailors on or around Newfoundland. For a number of them, life in Canada was clearly preferable to the hard service they had known before, but not enough is known about them yet to speak with certainty about the nature or number of their conversions.[3]

As Axtell points out, most of the known New England converts were not men but women and children. The Puritans most likely to convert were "girls between the age of seven and fifteen" at the time of their capture. This gives a peculiarly gendered twist to the idea that love and gratitude played a role in conversion. That love was more likely to strike a Puritan woman than a man undoubtedly had something to do with the scarcity of women in New France in the seventeenth and early eighteenth centuries. As the work of William Foster shows, female captives could find opportunities and avenues of empowerment in New France, while male captives generally encountered dispossession and humiliation. But that so many of the converts were children—girls—indicates that there was something about the process of proselytizing in New France that worked well with the young and female but not as well with the adult and male.[4]

In part because of the nature of the records, hypotheses on why New England captives converted tend to stress social causes. As Axtell points out, if one accepts contemporary English reasoning, "the converts were either compelled against their wills, or were too young to know any better." It cannot be denied that a degree of coercion was used to obtain these conversions. As the comparatively well documented case of the Deerfield captives shows, the isolation of children from each other and their parents, the use or threat of beatings, and threats of being returned to the Native warriors who had captured them in the first place combined with favorable treatment for those who did convert, to limit the extent to which conversion was a religious choice. Furthermore, women who converted tended to be widows or young women who had to convert in order to marry—a vital source of protection and legitimacy in a society with at least some men willing to abuse their vulnerable status. Sometimes these female converts married other English captives, not Frenchmen, and returned to New England once the war was over. Nevertheless, the need for self-preservation in a foreign society clearly helped these sexually mature women fall in love with Canadian men and the Catholic Church.[5]

Social factors can help explain why conversion would make sense to certain people. But observers must still account for what was fundamentally a religious process involving the replacement of one set of doctrines by another. Turning Puritans into Catholics bore little resemblance to missionary efforts among Native Americans. There, as scholarship has shown, French missionaries often worked to create a fit between Catholicism and Native traditions, producing a new, Native American variant of Catholicism. Converting New Englanders was quite a different matter. Puritans, even the children, were full of anti-Catholic attitudes, and they were intimately familiar with scripture. Their knowledge of Christianity made them appealing objects of conversion, but their Puritanism posed a challenge.

Understanding the religious dimensions of the conversion process is difficult because it was the most personal and least documented aspect of the converts' experience. The few sources describing this ideologically charged event have to be treated with great care. The most detailed accounts of French proselytizing activities come from Puritan men. These sources are hostile at best. These writers, the learned minister John Williams, author of *The Redeemed Captive Returning to Zion*, for example, composed their narratives in large part to show how they used their biblical knowledge to confound the arguments of the papists.

A striking number of the men's accounts come from the War of the Spanish Succession. Though many captives taken during the War of the League of Augsburg converted and remained in Canada, most of them were poorer frontier folk who were not encouraged to record their experiences either in New France or in New England. The War of the Spanish Succession, by contrast, produced a burst of captivity narratives, both published and unpublished, because many of the captives managed to return to New England shortly after being taken. Prisoner exchanges played an important role in the course of the war, as well as in the politics of both New France and Massachusetts. Undoubtedly an awareness of the political and religious significance of their experience encouraged many of the returning captives to compose an account of their captivity, even if said account was not formally published. John Williams' narrative was the most famous and influential because it not only was published, but it contained a relentless refutation of Catholicism and a denunciation of Catholic proselytizing of captives in New France that rendered it a potent weapon in the ideological war against the religion of the French.[6]

Statements from converts provide little insight into the process of conversion. They are generally brief responses to relatives' urgings to return to New England. Many claimed they could not, for fear of endangering their souls. Esther Wheelwright, a captive Puritan girl who became a nun, saw Providence working for her (and against Puritanism) when it brought her to New France. Writing to her mother in 1747, some forty years after her capture, Esther told of how

> I want nothing necessary as to Temporals, and as to Spirituals such continual favours do I receive from heaven that are beyond expression. Oh, what joy, what pleasure, what consolation would it give me, my dear Mother if you had the happiness of knowing this holy religion which a kind providence hath made me embrace since I left you. An established religion which our Forefathers professed for a long time with much need and fervour until the ... Schisme.

These attitudes reflect at least some of the arguments used to convert the former Puritans. As one priest told the captive soldier Joseph Bartlett, "Who knows (said he) but that God hath sent you to know the true way of worship." Nonetheless the statements attest to little more than the truth and depth of the conversion. To understand how it was achieved one must look elsewhere.[7]

Two little-known sources offer the best testament to date of the way religion was used to convert Puritans in general, and the powerful effect it had on children in particular. The first is from an account composed by a Deerfield boy named Joseph Kellogg. The other comes from the Mohawk family of the Deerfield girl Eunice Williams, who was taken in the same 1704 raid. Both converted while living in Native American households near Montreal. Eunice never returned to settle in New England. Kellogg returned to New England at the end of the war, reconverted to Protestantism, and pursued a successful career as a frontier commander and translator.

As these accounts indicate, their conversions involved theological persuasion and religious arguments and strategies that would have been familiar to anyone in Europe, albeit with a particularly American twist. Though both report the conversions at some distance—Joseph sometime after he had returned to New England and its faith, Eunice only indirectly through her descendants—they offer an otherwise unavailable window on the conversion process. That one account involves a boy and the other a girl also gives us some material with which to speculate on possible gender differences in proselytizing techniques, though definitive conclusions are impossible.[8]

These conversions were products of a very particular time and place: the Montreal region during the War of the Spanish Succession. This particular context is vital to understanding French proselytizing efforts. Later wars saw no such wave of conversion and adoption of New England captives. In part this was because more adult men, and fewer women and children, were captured. But more important, the French evangelical zeal to convert captives faded.

When Eunice and Joseph arrived in Canada in 1704, the island of Montreal was a peculiar place. It had originally been granted as a seigneury to a group of evangelical laymen in the 1640s. Joined together in the Société de Notre Dame de Montréal, they hoped to set up a model Counter-Reformation society and convert Native Americans through the example of their pious lives. But Montreal Island was located at the pivotal point connecting the French settlements along the Saint Lawrence to the lands of the Iroquois and the English, their frequent enemies, as well as to the fur trade of the Great Lakes. It did not take long for war, trade, and diplomacy to overtake the settlement. Ville-Marie became the fortified trading town and administrative center of Montreal. The Society of Notre Dame folded. But the seigneury was taken over by another outgrowth of the Counter-Reformation, the Sulpician order. Sulpicians were wealthy, elite Frenchmen determined to promote strict Catholicism. Though not as evangelically active as the Jesuits, the Sulpicians did run several missions in and around Montreal, where English captives soon fell within their orbit.[9]

The Sulpicians advocated cultural and religious assimilation more vigorously than Jesuits and applied it to Native Americans and New Englanders alike. Speaking of the Sulpicians' missionary work with Native peoples, one of their leading priests declared, "We believe that they profit by living among us, and not in their own land; that they must be taught our language, that their women must wear skirts and their men hats and pants; that they must adopt French housing; learn animal husbandry, and how to sow wheat and root vegetables; and that they must be able to read and hear mass and be taught the holy rites." That was in 1684. As the cycle of imperial wars with England began in 1689, the Sulpicians applied the same imperative to assimilate to Puritan captives. According to Joseph Kellogg, the Sulpicians also "persuaded the indian to marry the english propounded such & such to them, and though the indians at first unwilling they persuaded them to it, to secure them there." Indeed, he noted that "several of them that are yet with the Indians are such as by the instigations of the Priests & Jesuits have on their knees promised God and the Virgin mary to live and die with the Indians, and are by them threatened with Eternal damnation if they break their vow."[10]

In 1704, the Catholic activists of New France had reason to feel that they were finally gaining the upper hand over Protestant heresy. The 1685 Edict of Nantes had put a violent end to public Protestantism within France. Many thousands of French Protestants had been forced to convert or flee as a wave of militant Catholic evangelicalism swept across France. Catholics in New France evidently saw their war against New England as part of a larger effort to roll back Protestantism on both sides of the Atlantic. They told Joseph Kellogg that "it was but a little while & all of the English were good Catholicks, and not the name of a protestant among them."[11]

Much of the zeal for converting Puritans was concentrated in a group of priests (both Jesuit and Sulpician), noble military officers, and wealthy merchants living in and around Montreal. At the center of this community was the household of Jacques Le Ber. One of the wealthiest men in the colony, Le Ber had earned enough as a fur-trade merchant to purchase a title of nobility. He participated actively in an extraordinary devotional movement dedicated to continuing Montreal's original pious mission. His daughter, Jeanne Le Ber, became the colony's first and most famous religious recluse. His son Pierre was a pious religious painter devoted to the decoration of Montreal's religious buildings. The Le Bers supported the women's lay religious order of the Congregation de Notre Dame, which ran a hospital and school under the direction of the future saint Marguerite Bourgeoys.[12]

Connecting these groups with the English captives was the Sulpician father Henri-Antoine Meriel de Meulan, who was distinguished by his fluency in English. Meriel was instrumental in at least twenty, but probably far more, Puritan conversions. No other priest in New France came close to his diligence. Toward the end of the War of Spanish Succession,

Meriel returned to France, where he died. His death put an end to the great era of captive Puritan conversions in New France.[13]

Joseph Kellogg describes the report of his conversion as "some few short hints of the many artifices used to persuade the English children to stay" in New France. Coercion came at the top of his list. He was first isolated and alienated from any embodiment of English Protestant culture: "By the priests' means all the grown persons were put away." He (like the other children) was then informed "that unless I really hated my father and mother I could not be saved." Meanwhile, "the Indians prohibited the children speaking together in the English tongue, if we did speak it must be in the Macqua [Iroquois] language." He was then "forced by my master to go to church. He forced me to cross myself when I was unwilling, he threatened to beat me, & would by force take my hand, & make it for me, would deny me victuals unless I would conform to them." The stick did not come without a carrot, for the priests showered Joseph with kindness and attention if he accommodated to their demands. He remembered how the "priest always humoured me, giving me any thing if I complied with them."[14]

All of these coercive techniques are attested for in the accounts of other returned captives. When the captive John Williams arrived at an Abenaki village in Canada, he saw there "several poor children who had been taken from the Eastward the summer before, a sight very affecting, they being in habit much like Indians and in manner very much symbolizing with them." His captive son Stephen arrived at the same village several months later. Stephen noticed that some of the English children "would scofe at me when before the indians whorse than the indian children, but when alone they would talk familiarly with me in English about their own country, etc., whereas when before the indians they would pretend they could not speak english." In his opinion it was "no wonder that children that are small will not speak to their friends when they come to see them, but they will scofe and deride them, because the indians have taught them so, will be angry if they do otherwise."[15]

Joseph Kellogg's narrative dwells on the psychological and theological aspects of the conversion campaign. According to him, his proselytizers employed a relentless education in the lies of Protestantism and the wonders of the Catholic religion to push him from one faith to the other. They "used all their art to make us in love with their religion," he recalled, and "were often crying against our religion." They said that "the rise of our religion was King Henries the eights wickedness, that he killed two wives, & married his own daughter, that he had six wives one after another: for which wickedness he was excommunicated by the Pope." Only after this did Henry "by means of Luther's and Calvin's apostasie make himself Lord and master of religion." As for Martin Luther and John Calvin, both "were very wicked" and driven by base motives to break with the Mother Church. The priests claimed that "Luther himself said he had eaten a bushel of salt with the Divel, that Calvin was enraged because when a cannin expecting a bisoprick he failed in it, and in discontent he ran away, and took a nun with him with whom he lived in whoredom, and that for these wickednesses he was whiped and branded at Geneva." The great founders of Protestantism were thus presented as a series of vicious sinners who deviated from the true church for their own selfish and wicked ends.[16]

The French priests even tried bare intellectual intimidation. They used the English children's reliance on the Bible to disprove the reliability of Protestantism, claiming the Protestant "bibles were defective and did not contain all." They pointed out that the English had taken out the Apocrypha from their scriptures. They asserted that "there was but one true religion in the world, & that among the English there were a great many religions." One Jesuit went so far as to explain to Joseph "that I ought to believe him because he was more learned & had more knowledge than I had, and that he had quitted all to come & instruct the poor people in the right way."[17]

Unlike adult Puritans, English children could not quote the Bible chapter and verse against their captors; nor were they equipped to attack the Catholics for false practices. Joseph Bartlett, for example, threw Father Meriel's claim that "we hold nothing but what we can prove by your own bible" in his face by asking "what proof ... have you of such a place as Purgatory, or a middle place for departing souls?" When Meriel replied "in Luke xvi. 22—And he died, and was carried by angels into Abraham's bosom," Bartlett retorted, "Abraham had gone to heaven." The captive soldier then argued that Purgatory was impossible, for "it was appointed unto men once to die, and after death is the judgment, Hebrews ix. 27; and in Ecc. xi. 3." Joseph Kellogg's minister, John Williams, could claim that "it is absurd to believe that a priest uttering a few words over a wafer not above an inch square can make it a god or the body of Christ entire as it was offered on the cross," but young Joseph did not have the education or scriptural knowledge to counter his proselytizers as John did.[18]

The French touted the power of the very idolatry that New England's ministers denounced, from sacraments to miracles and relics. One priest claimed that "he could by the host or sacrament cast out divels at any time." Protestantism, by contrast, was proved all the more wrong for its failure to produce miracles, as Joseph related: "They told me a pretence of Calvin's working a miracle that he killed instead of raising of the dead." Joseph's Jesuit mentor explained that "miracles were on[e] great mark of the true church, and though there were none in our country, yet I should see one there." He then took Joseph to watch a religious procession bless some fields plagued with worms that "were eating their grain." The boy watched as "they went in procession saying of their prayers, & sprinkling holy water." Then he saw how "within a little time all the worms were gone away."[19]

Joseph's masters endeavored to demonstrate that "their religion was confirmed by miracles" by confronting him with a series of miracle stories involving American and European saints. Key in his conversion (and evidently that of Eunice) was the story of the devout Mohawk woman Kateri Tekakwitha. Though she was not yet a saint during Joseph's captivity, the Jesuits intended to see her canonized, and a number of French colonists respected her spiritual power even in 1704, only a few years after her death. One Sulpician told Joseph that "he had heard of great miracles wrought by Saint Katherine—here note that this Saint Katherine, was a Macqua [Mohawk] squaw, that was dead & sainted—but he did not believe them and was strook deaf." Only after the priest had gone "to her tomb & confessed his sin & asked her pardon and prayed that he might be restored" was he immediately cured. Joseph was then told of a nun at Montreal who "was very sick and had a grievous pain in her side." She sent for "a tooth of Saint Katherine, and a dish which she used to use, which she put in her mouth & drank in the dish," after which the nun "was cured." Joseph was also told of another "saint, that had been dead above a hundred years, and that his body was yet whole, only one arm that the Pope had cut off for a relick." Miraculously, "when they were going to cut it off many years after his death, he pulled in his arm to oppose or hinder it," until they "told him, that what they were doing was by order of his Superior, and that he was to obey, and thereupon he yielded, and when it was cut off, it bled as much as though he had been alive."[20]

Miracle stories served polemical ends. To quiet the Protestant critique of transubstantiation, Joseph was told a story about Saint Francis Xavier "for the proof . . . that Christ's body could be in heaven, and in the Host." Once, while on a sea journey, some men had left Saint Francis Xavier's ship in a small boat when suddenly a great storm struck and drove them away from the ship. Saint Francis spent the storm "praying to god sometimes kneeling, sometimes walking." When the captain told him he "was concerned about the men in the boat," the saint "assured the men in the ship, that the men in the boat would come again in a little time." And so they did. When asked how they had weathered the storm, the boatmen responded that they had "had an excellent steerman, & that was Saint Xavier, that all the while was a pilot to them so that this same saints body was at the same time in the ship & boat at a distance." As for Purgatory, Joseph wrote, one man

> assured me that after his mother had been dead many years she appeared to him one night & told him that she was in great distress in purgatory, but must not fail of getting so many masses & prayers said for her and she should be delivered, and that after so many masses & prayers said for her she appeared to him again in the same place, and with a shining countenance, telling him she was now happy in paradise, and told him what was become of many that had been dead some years before.[21]

In the end, the power of Catholic relics and a well-ingrained sense of obligation procured Joseph's conversion. Joseph fell sick with smallpox after his first year of captivity. At the height of his illness, when the thirteen-year-old boy's sores were "white and just ready to run," he wrote, "a Jesuit came to me, and told me my case was very hazardous, and that he had used all ordinary means but without success." Then the Jesuit held out the hope of extraordinary help. By chance, "when he was looking over his medicines some of the relick" of Saint Katherine "came into his hand, but though he knew the great virtue in them, he dare not give them to me, because I was not a Roman Catholic in heart, and told me I was near dying, and that if I would now promise, that I would confess, & be Roman Catholick, if upon taking some of these relicks I should have help, he would give them to me." The desperately ill boy accepted the divine deal. The Jesuit gave him "something under the name of the relicks of the rotten wood of the coffin, after which I slept better, & grew better." Once Joseph "was recovered," the Jesuit reminded him "of the promise that I had once made, & how angry God would be with me if I did not make good my promise." And so Joseph "went to Montreal and in the Jesuits church with a lighted wax candle" in his hand he "read over their creed," and on his knees he promised "God and the Church to live and die in their religion and land." And so he was "wrought upon by their insinuations to be a Roman Catholic."[22]

The closest approximation to a narrative of a Puritan girl's conversion is the oral tradition passed down in the Mohawk family of Eunice Williams. Though the sources vary in quality, it seems safe to conclude that Eunice had less choice than Joseph in the matter of conversion. Joseph recalled that the "Indians indulge english boys abundantly, let them have the liberty they will, while they outwardly conform to them, and so an easy way of life and libertinism is more prevailing with them than any affection they have to religion." Girls did not have the same freedom of movement and action, even in a Mohawk village. Joseph's narrative implies that male conversions were superficial and (perhaps) that female conversions were more profound. Perhaps this implication should not be taken at face value, as Joseph was obviously trying to convince others that his conversion was less than perfect and that the converts remaining in New France would easily return to Protestantism. Nonetheless, it does point to a perceived gender difference that cannot be ignored.[23]

Part of the difference between Joseph's and Eunice's experiences lay in their host communities. Joseph lived in a small, multiethnic village on Montreal Island. Eunice lived in the large Mohawk town of Kahnawake, across the Saint Lawrence River from Montreal. Jesuits had established a mission there shortly after the Mohawk community emerged in the 1670s. Nearly as populous as French Montreal, Kahnawake was nominally Catholic and allied to the French, but culturally and politically it was quite autonomous. Its warriors joined Frenchmen on raids against New England and took many captives for reasons having to do with their own so-called mourning-war culture.

Originating untold centuries before the arrival of Europeans, mourning-war customs dictated that captives from enemy communities had to be taken to replace relatives who died a sudden, unexpected, or untimely death. The Mohawks were matrilineal. Thus it was women who called on young men to bring them captives to assuage their grief, and women (the matrons of the affected matriline) who determined what became of the captive. Men were often tortured to death in revenge. Women and children were often adopted directly into Mohawk families or held as slaves.

The Jesuit mission ensured that Catholicism would be a part of the process, but it merely added to an age-old custom of adoption and cultural conversion. The powerful community of Kahnawake converted and adopted more Puritans than all the other Native villages in Canada combined. Jesuits certainly had a role in the process, but, as with all affairs at Kahnawake, it was probably more an auxiliary than a guiding one. Natives like those at Kahnawake were effectively, Axtell writes, "the best cultural missionaries and educators on the continent."[24]

The story of Eunice's conversion abounds in mourning-war imagery. Eunice, the story goes, was taken to replace a child lost to a Mohawk woman only a few years before, a classic example of mourning warfare at work. Once she arrived in Kahnawake, "the relations of her adopted mother took much notice of her, and the children were instructed to treat her as one of the family." Kateri Tekakwitha "was held up to [Eunice's] view" as a model of devout behavior. According to the family tradition, this affected Eunice greatly. She converted and soon acquired a reputation for "great piety and strictness." Catholicism apparently complemented but did not supplant traditional Mohawk techniques for the assimilation of captives. With such an enthusiastic welcome, it is not surprising that after several years captive children such as Eunice might prefer to stay at Kahnawake with a family they knew than return to a virtually forgotten life back in New England.[25]

Mohawk family tradition remembers Eunice's conversion as a rather straightforward spiritual and cultural awakening. Contemporary evidence indicates that her experience must have been a bit scary. At one point during her first year of captivity her father, the minister John Williams, managed to visit her for an hour. He later wrote of how the seven-year-old girl "was very desirous to be redeemed out of the hands of the Macquas and bemoaned her state among them." With relief he noted that "she could read very well and had not forgotten her catechism." But she was clearly ill at ease. This minister's daughter knew her Protestantism well enough to be suspicious of the Catholic Mass. She told her father that the Mohawks "profaned God's Sabbaths and said she thought that a few days before they had been mocking the devil, and that one of the Jesuits stood and looked on them." John Williams, determined to keep his daughter Protestant, told her to "pray to God for His grace every day. She said she did as she was able and God helped her. But," she added, "They force me to say some prayers in Latin, but I don't understand one word of them; I hope it won't do me any harm." All her father could do was tell her "she must be careful she did not forget her catechism and the Scriptures she had learned by heart." After he left she passed on his words to the other captives "and said she was much afraid she should forget her catechism, having none to instruct her." John only saw her once more for a few minutes in Montreal: "I improved to give her the best advice I could." But it was not enough. Within a few years she had "forgotten to speak English," was converted, and was married to a Mohawk.[26]

The conversion accounts of Joseph Kellogg and Eunice Williams provide a vital entry point into the role of religion in the conversion of Puritan captives in New France. By relating the experiences of children they address the experience of the majority of New England captive converts, who were both young and female. They also provide some basis for understanding possible gender differences in the captives' relationship to Catholicism. Though the Mohawk holy woman Kateri Tekakwitha clinched the conversions of both, their relationship to her varied. Kateri helped save Joseph's life, whereas she was an object of emulation for young Eunice. The Catholicism that confronted Joseph was polemical, aggressive, and manipulative, as evangelical priests preyed on his hapless individuality. Eunice's conversion was a family effort, led by her adopted Mohawk kin. Priests stood at the fringe of her conversion, which also seems to have been much more gradual—cumulative, almost—rather than the sudden, near-death decision of poor Joseph.

Helpless, isolated, and constantly exposed to the wonders of Catholicism, both Puritan children entered the Roman faith with the help of a Native American "saint." A great deal of social pressure surrounded the indoctrination of both captives. However, the cause and inspiration—saints, relics, and miracles—evident in both stories make it clear that, despite the claims of English polemicists and Axtell's speculations, religion was at the heart of their conversion experience.

Child captives (the majority of those converted) were concerned about their souls, not the hazards of frontier travel or job incentives. They gave in to wonder as much as coercion. Conversion gave them religious power in a world where they had little else. Their relative powerlessness probably rendered their conversion more complete than that of Native American proselytes.

French and Mohawk Catholics made no attempt to apologize for their faith or to modify it to Protestant sensibilities. Indeed, in the case of Joseph and his compatriots on Montreal Island, attacking Protestantism went hand-in-hand with promoting Catholicism. The children's Christianity may have aided the process. They knew enough to understand what the priests were talking about but not enough to refute the priests' claims as their elders could. Caught between highly trained and active priests and Kateri Tekakwitha, deprived of the moral and intellectual support of their elders, the Protestantism of New England child captives did not stand much of a chance.

Notes

I would like to thank William H. Foster III, Kevin Sweeney, James Muldoon, and an anonymous reviewer for their constructive comments on an earlier draft of this chapter.

1. For an overview of this phenomenon, see James Axtell's chapter on "The English Apostates" in his *Invasion Within: The Contest of Cultures in Colonial North America* (New York: Oxford University Press, 1985), 287–301. I am using the term *Puritan,* as most American scholars tend to do, as ethnic shorthand for the Reformed Protestants who inhabited New England.

2. Axtell, *Invasion Within,* 291–93.

3. Evan Haefeli and Kevin Sweeney, *Captors and Captives: The 1704 French and Indian Raid on Deerfield* (Amherst: University of Massachusetts Press, 2004), 244–45; Marcel Fournier, *Les Européens au Canada: Des origins à 1765* (Montreal: Les Éditions du Fleuve, 1989), passim.

4. Axtell, *Invasion Within,* 291–93; William Henry Foster III, "Women at the Centers, Men at the Margins: The Wilderness Mission of the Secular Sisters of Early Montreal Reconsidered," in *Women and Religion in Old and New Worlds,* ed. Susan E. Dinan and Debra Myers (New York: Routledge, 2001), 93–112; William Henry Foster III, *The Captors' Narrative: Catholic Women and Their Puritan Men on the Early American Frontier* (Ithaca, N.Y.: Cornell University Press, 2003).

5. Axtell, *Invasion Within,* 295. On the Deerfield captives, see Haefeli and Sweeney, *Captors and Captives,* 147–63, 238–49.

6. On the war and prisoner exchanges, see Haefeli and Sweeney, *Captors and Captives,* 164–207. Important narratives from the War of the Spanish Succession are John Williams, "The Redeemed Captive Returning to Zion," in *Puritans among the Indians: Accounts of Captivity and Redemption, 1676–1724,* ed. Alden T. Vaughn and Edward W. Clark (Cambridge: Harvard University Press, 1981), 167–226; Stephen Williams, *What Befell Stephen Williams in His Captivity,* ed. George Sheldon (Deerfield, Mass.: Pocumtuck Valley Memorial Association, 1889); Cotton Mather, *Good Fetch'd Out of Evil* (Boston: B. Green, 1706); and Joseph Bartlett, "Narrative," in Joshua Coffin, *A Sketch of the History of Newbury, Newburyport, and West Newbury from 1636 to 1845* (Boston: Samuel G. Drake, 1845), 331–34.

7. For two female captives who claimed they "would come hum if it was not for the sake of ther soules," see Esther Williams to Stephen? Williams, Feb. 28, 1709/10?, folder "Papers Relating to the 1704 Attack on Deerfield," case 8, box 28, The Reverend John Williams and Family, Gratz Collection, Historical Society of Pennsylvania; Esther to Mary Wheelwright, 26 September 1747, in Emma Lewis Cole-

man, *New England Captives Carried to Canada,* 2 vols. (1925; Bowie, Md.: Heritage Books, 1989), vol. 1, 429–30; Bartlett, "Narrative," 333.

8. For Joseph Kellogg's life, see Coleman, *New England Captives,* vol. 2, 99–100. For the closest thing possible to a biography of Eunice, see John Demos, *The Unredeemed Captive: A Family Story from Early America* (New York: Alfred A. Knopf, 1994). Demos is aware of the Kellogg source, although he does not examine it at length.

9. See Haefeli and Sweeney, *Captors and Captives,* chaps. 2, 8, 12.

10. Sulpician cited in Louise Duchêne, *Habitants and Merchants in Seventeenth Century Montreal,* trans. Liana Vardi (Montreal and Kingston: McGill-Queen's University Press, 1992), 9; Joseph Kellogg, "When I Was Carryed to Canada . . . ," verso, folder "Papers Relating to the 1704 Attack on Deerfield," case 8, box 28, The Reverend John Williams and Family, Gratz Collection, Historical Society of Pennsylvania.

11. Kellogg, "When I Was Carryed to Canada," verso.

12. For Jacques, Jeanne, and Pierre Le Ber, see *Dictionary of Canadian Biography,* 14 vols. (Toronto: University of Toronto Press, 1967–1998), vol. 2, 374–78.

13. For Meriel's life, see *Dictionary of Canadian Biography,* vol. 2, 467–68. For Meriel's proselytizing activities (which often include the Le Bers and their associates), see Coleman, *New England Captives,* vol. 1, 160, 206, 238, 247, 320–21, 329, 356–58, 401, and vol. 2, 6–7, 49, 68.

14. Kellogg, "When I Was Carryed to Canada," recto and verso.

15. J. Williams, "Redeemed Captive," 183; S. Williams, *What Befell Stephen Williams in His Captivity,* 9–10.

16. Kellogg, "When I Was Carryed to Canada," recto.

17. Ibid., verso.

18. Bartlett, "Narrative," 333–34; J. Williams, "Redeemed Captive," 216.

19. Kellogg, "When I Was Carryed to Canada," recto and verso. For a similar procession in Acadia, which failed to impress its Puritan observers, see John Gyles, "Memoirs of Odd Adventures, Strange Deliverances, etc.," in *Puritans among the Indians: Accounts of Captivity and Redemption, 1676–1724,* ed. Alden T. Vaughn and Edward W. Clark (Cambridge: Harvard University Press, 1981), 127–28.

20. Kellogg, "When I Was Carryed to Canada," recto. On Kateri Tekakwitha, see *Dictionary of Canadian Biography,* vol. 1, 635–36; and Daniel K. Richter, *Facing East from Indian Country: A Native History of Early America* (Cambridge: Harvard University Press, 2001), 79–90.

21. Kellogg, "When I Was Carryed to Canada," recto and verso.

22. Ibid., recto and verso.

23. Ibid., verso.

24. See Haefeli and Sweeney, *Captors and Captives,* chaps. 3, 8, and 11; Axtell, *Invasions Within,* 302. Beginning with Alden Vaughn and Daniel K. Richter, "Crossing the Cultural Divide: Indians and New Englanders, 1605–1763," American Anti-

quarian Society *Proceedings* 90 (1980): 23–99, Axtell's exuberant portrayal of Native success in converting colonists to their ways—as first published in his famous essay, "The White Indians of Colonial America," *William and Mary Quarterly*, 3d Ser., 32 (1975): 55–88—has been steadily modified but not wholly undone.

25. Charles B. de Saileville, "A History of the Life and Captivity of Eunice Williams, Alias, Madam De Roguers, Who Was Styled 'The Fair Captive,'" [1842], 18–19, 28, 26, 56–57, 65, 97–98, Neville Public Museum, microfilm edition, reel 7, on deposit in the State Historical Society of Wisconsin Area Research Center in Green Bay. For Mohawk Christianity at Kahnawake, see Demos, *Unredeemed Captive*, 151–54.

26. J. Williams, "Redeemed Captive," 189. For Eunice's life, see Demos, *Unredeemed Captive*.

11

Gold for Glasse

The Trope of Trade in English Missionary Writings

Laura M. Stevens

The history of British mission in America is one in which words outweighed deeds and cultural production exceeded conversion. The early modern English, and later the British, talked a great deal about their desire to Christianize the indigenous peoples of America.[1] These intentions did translate into projects, including the Praying Indian towns organized by John Eliot, the Church of England's mission to the Mohawks, and Eleazar Wheelock's foundation of "Moor's Indian Charity School" as well as Dartmouth College.[2] On the whole, however, these attempts were few and feeble, especially in comparison with the efforts of the Spanish and the French. When missionary projects did not fail through the resistance of the Indians or the indifference of the British, war and disease rendered the work tragically redundant, destroying those native peoples who had accepted their invaders' religion.

Despite this failure to engender widespread conversion among American Indians, the British devoted much paper and ink to expressing their evangelical aspirations and seeking funds for missionary work. They produced sermons, journals, letters, and even a few poems. These texts are too numerous to list here, but major collections of missionary writings include the New England Company's seventeenth-century "Indian tracts," which describe the efforts of Eliot, the Mayhew family, and other Puritans to convert the indigenous peoples of New England; the sermons and reports published from 1702 onward by the Church of England's Society for the Propagation of the Gospel in Foreign Parts (SPG), a group devoted to providing Anglican clergy for colonists but also to converting Indians and African slaves; the publications of the Society in Scotland for the Propagation of Christian Knowledge (SSPCK); and the narratives of the Indian Charity School written in the 1760s and 1770s by Wheelock.[3]

Ironically, these texts can be seen as the primary accomplishment of British mission in the American colonies, as their influence often exceeded the effectiveness of the projects they were written to promote. This influence was subtle but palpable, shaping British images of America, modern strategies of fund-raising, and imperial notions of the relation between benevolence and power. This shared cultural influence is all the more striking because it, along with a set of recurring rhetorical strategies, connects a group of texts divided by their emergence from different denominations and competing projects across a span of more than one hundred years.

Missionary writings helped an audience in England and Scotland envision, and feel involved in, the distant unfolding of imperial endeavor. They assisted in the task of making America intelligible to a metropolitan British audience, especially one steeped in a biblically influenced understanding of the world. They also participated in the complex emotional process of prompting the British to develop a national identity.[4] Such an identity included an understanding of imperial dominance as a globally desired extension of British benevolence, the reception of which could be reciprocated, if only poorly, by the wealth of empire. It also included an understanding of Britishness based not on place or power but rather on collectively expressed feeling for the plight of Britain's others.

My project here is to trace part of the role missionary texts played in the development of British imperial rhetoric, by showing how these writings borrowed, and then reread through the lens of scripture, a prominent image of early modern travel writings. This was the image of American gold traded for the glass and other trinkets offered to Indians by European travelers. First symbolizing the exploitation of colonized peoples, and then more generally the bilking of the powerless, this image came to signify the opposite of its original connotation because of its application to Christian conversion. It was this rhetorical shift that made possible the catastrophic event wryly summarized by Vine Deloria: "It has been said of missionaries that when they arrived they had only the Book and we had the land; now we have the Book and they have the land."[5]

Missionary writings, which drew upon a rich repository of scriptural references to trade, transformed the trope of gold exchanged for glass into a sign—first of Britain's obligations to its colonies and then of the intangible but eternal rewards that conquest would bring to the conquered. Focusing on Paul's comment in Romans 15:27 that "if the Gentiles have been made partakers of [the Jews'] spiritual things, their duty is also to minister unto them in carnal things," these texts presented colonialism as an act of spiritual charity.[6] They reconfigured colonial commerce as a cycle of reciprocal circum-Atlantic exchange involving an endlessly replenished currency: the prayers and pity of the British. Most importantly, missionary texts configured Christianity as an exportable commodity, the spiritual "gold" that Britain should exchange for the material "glass" of America. The piteous spectacle of Indians being cheated by Europeans, refracted through Paul's description of a charitable collection for the impoverished Christians of Jerusalem, reconfigured the idea of intercontinental commerce. Seeking to convert the "poor Indians" of America, these texts ended up overturning an image that had been used to indict the exploitation of those Indians. On a rhetorical level, selling the idea of saving souls helped make possible the idea of selling England's glass for America's gold.

"They Bartered Like Idiots": Early Modern Images of Indian Trade

It is well known that the missionary and imperial aspirations of early modern Europe were intertwined. Whether European desires to save the souls of America's indigenous peoples were sincere or not, the public expression of those desires rationalized efforts to conquer those peoples and own the resources of their land.

Columbus's first descriptions of the islands upon which he had stumbled make this point clear. Emphasizing that the Taino Indians there "do not carry arms and do not know of them," he suggested simultaneously that they would be easy to conquer and convert. "They ought to make good slaves," he wrote, "for they are of quick intelligence since I notice that they are quick to repeat what is said to them, and I believe that they could very easily become Christians, for it seemed to me that they had no religion of their own."[7] Besides their mimicry, paltry weaponry, and apparent lack of religion, one of the strongest signs of their pliability was their inability to negotiate a profitable trade. As Columbus noted in the same letter, the poignancy of the Indians' overly generous bartering proved the ease with which Europe could rob or redeem these people:

> They ... give objects of great value for trifles, and content themselves with very little or nothing in return. ... It even happened that a sailor received for a leather strap as much gold as was worth three golden nobles, and for things of more trifling value offered by our men, ...

> the Indians would give whatever the seller required. . . . Thus they bartered, like idiots, cotton and gold for fragments of bows, glasses, bottles, and jars.[8]

In describing this exchange Columbus failed to recognize the expectations of reciprocity and the nuances of status-determination that surrounded indigenous American systems of gift giving.[9] He also neglected the possibility that the Taino found gold to be as inconsequential as the sailors considered their own "trifles" or that they attached a metaphorical and ceremonial importance to the glass.[10] With stunning confidence in his interpretive ability, he was quick to see this exchange as evidence of economic innocence.

Showing that with this passage "Columbus reads the Indian system of valuation (whatever it was) as an empty prefiguration of his own," Joshua Bellin has observed, "a glass bead is worthless and a pearl precious only in systems of exchange value."[11] Echoing Stephen Greenblatt's comment that this letter epitomizes the European fantasy of "the grossly unequal gift exchange: I give you a glass bead and you give me a pearl worth half your tribe," Bellin has pointed out that Columbus described the Indians as "naive consumers beyond Europe's wildest dreams."[12] The profits of a few sailors suggested the effortless gain of future treasures.

Moral self-congratulation accompanied the assessment of potential wealth in this letter. Columbus juxtaposed his sailors' eagerness to exploit the Indians with his own insistence that they be treated favorably:

> I forbad [these trades] as being unjust, and myself gave them many beautiful and acceptable articles which I had brought with me, taking nothing from them in return; I did this in order that I might more easily conciliate them, that they might be led to become Christians, and be inclined to entertain a regard for the King and Queen, our Princes and all Spaniards, and that I might induce them to take an interest in seeking out, and collecting, and delivering to us such things as they possessed in abundance, but which we greatly needed.[13]

With this anecdote Columbus set in place a vision of intercontinental contact that would unite diverse expressions of European desire.[14] Wonder at the Indians' financial naiveté, concern to save them from injustice and divine wrath, fervent hopes to win their "regard" and receive their wealth—all these reactions became central to the discourse of colonialism.

Underlining the contrast between unjust sailors and the just admiral who commands them is a distinction between shortsightedness and foresight that is more intellectual than moral. Columbus's initial insistence on fair trade will, he hopes, encourage the Indians' excessive reciprocity. It is an investment, promising a payoff in gold and labor. Christian conversion plays a dual role in this vision of exchange: fair trade will help lead the Indians to Christianity, and Christianity will keep the trade fair. For what except the gospel can match the wealth that the Indians "abundantly possess" but Spain "greatly need[s]"? Christianity is the only commodity that can balance the intercontinental books for Columbus, offering compensation for conquest.

At the core of Columbus's formulation is this vision of "gold for glasse," of treasure bartered for its shiny imitation. This trope became central to descriptions of global exploration. It also acquired a broad metaphorical register in the early modern period, suggesting many forms of poor judgment. After killing his wife Desdemona out of ill-founded suspicions over her fidelity, for example, Shakespeare's Othello referred to himself as

> one whose hand,
> Like the base Indian, threw a pearl away
> Richer than all his tribe. (5.2.344–46)

Shakespeare's choice of metaphor, if indeed he did refer to an American Indian here, emphasizes Othello's gullibility in the face of Iago's manipulation.[15] Stressing his tendency to trust appearance, these lines also link prodigality to naiveté. Othello does not really trade; rather, he throws his treasure away. Instead of focusing on a desire for what glitters, this reference emphasizes a prerequisite eagerness to discard that which is more valuable than it seems. Indians toss away pearls because they do not understand their value. Othello, likewise, has tossed away the love of his wife because he was made to distrust its authenticity. The absence of any trade, even for glass, heightens his suicidal sense of loss.

More than a century later Eliza Haywood echoed Shakespeare's romantic inflection of this trope in *The City Jilt* (1726), a narrative of love betrayed by greed. Near the end of this story the callous Melladore, who seduced and then abandoned the heroine Glicera so that he could marry a wealthier woman, finds that Glicera has obtained ownership of the deed to his now bankrupt estate. Throwing himself on her mercy, Melladore writes to her: "Like the foolish *Indians*, I have barter'd *Gold* for *Glass*, exchang'd the *best* for one of the *vilest* that ever disgraced the name of Woman."[16] Although Melladore describes himself as bartering rather than discarding a treasure, the emphasis on poor discernment echoes Othello. Like Othello he has judged badly in matters of love, failing to see the value of true gold.

Besides asserting the cost of ignorance, the trope of trade also could suggest the exploitation of innocence. This meaning applied especially when intangible resources were balanced against material ones. John Milton used this image at the beginning of the Civil War in *The Reason of Church Government Urg'd against Prelaty* (1642). In an autobiographical interlude he pondered the moral burdens that accompany the acquisition of spiritual knowledge, justifying his criticism of England's bishops as a duty placed on him by the privilege of his education. Those who have received gifts of knowledge should distribute them cheaply, he argued, not hoard them while they sell false treasures at high prices. This autobiographical defense enhanced his attack on the Church of England, because he then contrasted his own generosity with episcopal greed. Expanding on the "burden" of the educated, Milton wrote,

> And that which aggravates the burden more is that (having received amongst his allotted parcels certain precious truths of such an orient lustre as no diamond can equal, which nevertheless he has in charge to put off at any cheap rate, yea for nothing to them that will) the great merchants of this world, fearing that this course would soon discover and disgrace the false glitter of their deceitful wares wherewith they abuse the people, *like poor Indians with beads and glasses,* practise by all means how they may suppress the venting of such rarities, and such a cheapness as would undo them, and turn their trash upon their hands.[17]

Overlapping images of global commerce become a vehicle of Puritan attack. While cheating "poor Indians" by selling them glittering trash, England's bishops have hoarded the treasures entrusted to them by God, those spiritual truths of "orient lustre" that they were supposed to give away. Europe's exploitation of other lands becomes a symbol of England's exploitation by its church.

As he applied the trope to the domestic realm, Milton added a spiritual dimension. The suggestion of simony, the selling of religious benefits for material gain, created an intersection between axes of spiritual and material worth. Through this accusation Milton made explicit Columbus's implied vision of an intercontinental reciprocity involving a payment of Christianity for gold, compensating for the false currency of glass.

Other seventeenth-century writers used the trope of gold for glass in similar ways. Robert Boyle, best known for his scientific work, invoked this image in his moral writings. "The Aretology," one of his (until recently) unpublished essays, notes: "Vertu by an aduantagious Exchange for vs [us], serves her followers as the [silly] Indians do our Mariners, giuing them for Beads and Whistles and Gugaws, precious wares and substantiall meat."[18] Rather than taking the perspective of the cheated Indians, Boyle focused on the "aduantagious Exchange" the virtuous enjoy for their avoidance of vice, just as the European sailors gain from trade with Indians.

The essay "Of Felicity" (1646) by the Interregnum writer John Hall also uses the trope of gold for glass to mourn the abandonment of spiritual happiness for material gain: "We have [felicity] brought home to our own doores; . . . [T]hose happy soules that *claspe* hold of it. . . . They can set a true *estimation* of those *sublunarie* things, that others are contented so to overbuy, more Sottish [than] the Barbarous Indians to exchange Gold for Glasse."[19] As with *Othello* and *The City Jilt*, Hall's reference to Indians signifies a poor bargain prompted by the duplicity of appearance. Like Boyle and Milton, Hall harnessed a moral prescription to the image of the duped Indian, warning his readers not to make an equally poor bargain.

Clearly a variety of seventeenth-century writings replicated Columbus's depiction of naive Indians exchanging their treasures for the trash of those who would become their conquerors. In their appropriation of this trope they took for granted the distinction between real and apparent worth suggested by exchange. That is, the allusion to Indians and trade conveyed the supremacy not only of reality over appearance, but also of the intangible—whether romantic or moral—over the quantifiable. These texts also took for granted the idea that exchange was to the detriment of Indians.

Ironically, this last interpretation does not apply to the texts that claimed to be most interested in the welfare of Indians: missionary writings. Although these texts also adopted the trope of gold for glass, they realigned the meanings Columbus had assigned to it by diminishing the real worth of gold in the face of spiritual goods. This change is understandable when considered in the context of scripture and its complex treatment—both metaphorical and literal—of wealth. It also makes sense when one considers the delicate task these writers faced: raising funds to convert Indians by soliciting many of the very people gaining wealth from the exploitation of Indians. This adjustment made it possible for missionary writers to invoke a sense of moral obligation while presenting a model of fair exchange that would not alienate an English or British audience.

Understandable though their motives were, the writers of these texts played an important if unintended role in developing a rhetorical justification for colonialism. What Columbus took as an example of exploitation that he had rectified to make possible the Indians' acceptance of Christianity, British missionaries later presented as an emblem of salvation.

"To Barter Gold for Brass, and Pearl for Trifles": Missionaries and the Trope of Trade

When British missionaries and their supporters raised funds to convert Indians, they often did so by invoking their readers' sense of Christian duty even as they evoked their acquisitive desire. Sometimes they attempted this twofold task directly, arguing that contributions to mission would enhance Britain's wealth. Martin Benson, bishop of Gloucester, insisted in his sermon before the SPG, "For were we but wise enough to consider only the Advantage of our Trade in *America* ... we should take care to propagate the Christian Revelation which ... enjoins all those Virtues that make Commerce gainful, and prohibits all those Vices that bring Poverty in their Rear."[20] Nathaniel Eells, a minister involved with Wheelock's school, went so far as to pair a capitalist with a Christian mission. "[T]he vast Consumption of british Manufactures among [them]," he claimed, "would teach the Nation how to make a *Gain* by promoting *Godliness*."[21] Although they would lose short-term wealth, contributors to missions would enhance colonial assets in the long run, turning savages into consumers as well as Christians.

Most missionary texts did not make such a direct link between charity and trade. Rather, they spoke through a metaphorical language that imitated the Gospels' treatment of riches. In the Gospel of Matthew, for example, Jesus emphasized the importance of giving up wealth: "It is easier for a camel to go through the eye of a needle, than for a rich man to enter into the kingdom of God" (Matt. 19:24). He also relied on the language of wealth, however, to emphasize the value of this kingdom: "[T]he kingdom of heaven is like unto a merchant man, seeking goodly pearls: Who, when he had found one pearl of great price, went and sold all that he had, and bought it"(Matt. 13:44-46). Such images allowed Jesus to use material acquisition as a metaphor for spiritual gain, even as he demeaned riches in the face of spiritual reward. These images also can be seen to equate material with spiritual value. The kingdom of God may be greater than all one's wealth, but there is a suggestion of equivalence in the parables, brought about by references to purchase. Although the kingdom of God is more valuable than all earthly treasure, it is like something that can be bought. Thus the Gospels' adoption of a metaphorical economy, whether or not it was intended by its writers to do so, can lend itself to an economic vision of religion.

In his epistle to the Romans, Paul also juxtaposed material with spiritual wealth. At the end of his letter to the church in Rome, he wrote,

> But now I go unto Jerusalem to minister unto the saints. For it hath pleased them of Macedonia and Achaia to make a certain contribution for the poor saints which are at Jerusalem. It hath pleased them verily; and their debtors they are. For if the Gentiles have been made partakers of their spiritual things, their duty is also to minister unto them in carnal things. (Rom. 15:25–27).

Paul's formulation suggests not only the virtue of charity, but also the imperative of spiritual and material exchange. Describing the gentiles' charity as a debt for the Jewish church's communication of the good news had the effect of placing a fulcrum between the balanced values of material and spiritual wealth. Generosity is there, but it is prompted by obligation. As Paul would have it, the conversion of the gentiles has merited compensation to the Christian Jews.

Drawing on these scriptural references, many writers of missionary texts evoked images of wealth to make two claims. First, they asserted that the conversion of heathens was as valuable as it was costly, meriting donations and superseding in importance any wealth the British would gain from America. Second, they suggested that Christianity was a compensation Indians deserved for the riches they had lost. Taken together, these claims could be, and eventually were, made to suggest a fair payment of Christian conversion for colonial wealth. A survey of missionaries' references to exchange suggests a gradual shift from stressing the debt owed to America's natives for their loss of material gold, to emphasizing the spiritual gold that Britain brought to America.

J. D., or John Dury, stressed the expense and importance of conversion in one of the earliest missionary texts, *The Glorious Progress of the Gospel amongst the Indians in New England*. He exhorted his readers, "*Come forth ye Masters of money*, part with your Gold to promote the Gospel; let the gift of God in temporal things make way, for the Indian receipt of spirituals."[22] This text appeared just before Parliament passed an "Act for the promoting and propagating the Gospel of Jesus Christ in New England," which called for a nationwide collection to support the conversion of Indians and incorporated the New England Company to distribute those funds.[23] Emboldened perhaps by Parliament's endorsement, the text made direct appeals for contributions. Dury emphasized the importance of the mission even as he stressed its cost. Rather than suggesting a transatlantic reciprocity, he pinned his appeal upon Christian obligation: "If you give any thing yearly," he concluded, "Remember Christ will be your Pensioner." The main compensation suggested for these contributions was spiritual. For parting with their gold the English would underwrite the Indians' reception of spiritual wealth and receive God's blessing.

Whereas Dury stressed a duty to be generous, Joseph Caryl, an Independent preacher of London, framed his fund-raising plea six years later with references to prosperity. In his preface to Eliot's *Late and Further Manifestation of the Progress of the Gospel* (1655), he proclaimed,

> O let old England rejoyce in this, that our brethren who with extream difficulties and expences have Planted themselves in the Indian Wildernesses, have also laboured night and day with prayers and teares and Exhortations to Plant the Indians as a spirituall Garden, into which Christ might come and eat his pleasant fruits. Let the gaining of any of their souls to Christ . . . be more pretious in our eyes [than] the greatest gaine or return of Gold and Silver. This gaine of soules is a Merchandize worth the glorying in upon all the Exchanges, or rather in all the Churches throughout the world. This Merchandize is Holinesse to the Lord: And of this the ensuing Discourse presents you with a Bill of many particulars, from your spiritual Factory in New England.[24]

Like Dury, Caryl sought money for missions in New England. Unlike Dury, he did not stress a Christian obligation to be charitable. Rather, he suggested that Indian converts were the profits England would reap from its colonizing labor. Instead of stressing the expense of mission, he conveyed its value through images of abundance. His words replicated England's colonial aspirations in miniature, linking the pursuit of material prosperity to spiritual growth. Mission takes place first through tropes of plantation, so that America is transformed into an orchard. Wild inhabitants of an uncultivated land, Indians become the fruits of a "spirituall Garden." The text then replaces gardens with gold, placing plantation within commerce. As Christ eats the garden's "pleasant fruits," images of these spiritual products are returned across the Atlantic, circulated among readers, and accepted as imported goods. The tone of the last sentence resembles a report to stockholders, promising a "Bill of many particulars," as if it were a list of assets and expenses. Mission in America is thus made to suggest the accrual of English wealth.

Between these two texts, both published under the auspices of the New England Company, one can see a shift in the presentation of spiritual versus material value. Where Dury promised his readers only the gratefulness of God, Caryl relied upon images of wealth to convey the spiritual benefits of charity. Where Dury coaxed his readers to give, Caryl sold the idea of giving. Dury saw a straightforward purchase of spiritual benefits for the Indians with English gold. Material wealth, as it moves westward across the Atlantic, converts into spiritual. Although images of trade are central to Caryl's description, those images make the Indians items of, rather than participants in, exchange. Clearly, though, their conversion is construed as a benefit to themselves as much as to the English. Missionary work is made a source of mutual profit.

Both Caryl's and Dury's prefaces were written in the early, optimistic stages of Christian missions in North America. By the end of the seventeenth century, especially after King Philip's War had destroyed most of New England's "Praying Indians" and alienated many indigenous survivors, missionaries began to acquire a tone of pessimism and urgency.[25] Although they adapted images of exchange to their projects, they did so less to emphasize the value of Indian conversion than in recognition of the great debt England owed America's natives for what they had suffered. This shift may have reflected a growing familiarity with the language of debt, especially after the founding of the Bank of England in 1690.[26] It also, however, was a response to glaring evidence of colonial exploitation, Indian demise, and evangelical failure.

In 1693 Patrick Gordon, a Scottish Episcopalian minister, appended a proposal for spreading the gospel in pagan countries to his *Geography Anatomized*, a cultural survey of the globe. In relation to North America Gordon wrote of the great embarrassment to England,

> That those very *Indians* who inhabit near on the English Pale . . . should still continue in most wretched ignorance. . . . O Christians.

Shall we covet and thirst after their *Talents* of Gold? and yet keep hid in a Napkin that *Talent* entrusted to us. Shall we greedily bereave them of their *Precious Pearls?* And not declare unto them the knowledge of the Pearl of Price. No! No! Let us not act as others have done in making *Gold* our *God,* and *Gain* the sole design of our Trading.[27]

Focused on what he saw as the theft of America by the English, Gordon did not even mention trade. Citing parables about the kingdom of God, he stressed the kingdom's value and reminded his readers of their duty not to hoard its blessings. He sharpened this reminder by pairing the allusion to the spiritual gold of God's kingdom with a reference to the Indians' material gold. Rather than selling the idea of supporting missions by alluding to the riches of America, he suggested that those who have acquired wealth from the Americas owe some return.

Gordon drafted part of this proposal in a letter to the SPG, and it was transcribed into the society's journal in 1701.[28] The next year the SPG sent Gordon to Jamaica, Long Island, as one of its first missionaries.[29] Although Gordon's death shortly after his arrival prevented any sustained contribution to the SPG's efforts, his publication may have influenced the society's preachers. In 1704 Gilbert Burnet, the well-known Latitudinarian and chronicler of the Civil War, appealed to merchants, noting: "You great Dealers in Trade, who have had so plentiful a Harvest in Temporal things, from the Productions of those Countries, and from the Industry of our Colonies settled among them, are, in a more especial manner, bound to minister to them in Spiritual things."[30] As he alluded to Paul's formulation, Burnet told his audience that they owed America a debt that could be repaid through charitable contributions. He thus suggested that financing missionary work translated to a spiritual expiation for material gain.

Other SPG preachers, such as George Stanhope, dean of Canterbury, emphasized the idea of spiritual debt by comparing merchants to sailors acquiring Indian gold with European glass. Presenting this image with reference to Paul's vision of spiritual-material exchange in 1714, however, he reversed the usual description of transatlantic trade. Emphasizing the "obligation" of all Christians to spread the word of God, he wrote,

> But this Obligation seems to be drawn yet closer, upon All, whose Fortunes are owing to any Commerce with those Ignorants and Unbelievers. For, may I not be allowed to turn to *St. Paul's* Argument, and affirm upon this Occasion, that to Them, whose Strength and Toil is consumed in the Service of your Carnal Things, Some Debt is

contracted, Some Title thereby convey'd, to the Spiritual Advantages, they might receive from you? This were to act like generous Traders indeed; To barter Gold for Brass, and Pearl for Trifles; in returning the noblest and most useful Treasure, for Riches, which they knew not either the Use, or the Value of.[31]

Whereas gentile Christians of the early church had offered material help to Jewish ones in return for sharing the spiritual wealth of Christ, Stanhope suggested that the British owed a spiritual debt to those who had given them material wealth. The change was subtle but significant. The order and the origin of the spiritual-material exchange were overturned. This reversal allowed Stanhope to validate the very trade that the image of gold for glass condemned. The Indians gave away their gold because they did not understand the use of it. By taking their gold and repaying them with spiritual wealth, the British were described as donating spiritual pearls for material trinkets.

Rather than badgering his audience into charity out of guilt, Stanhope tried to prompt their generosity by offering a pleasing image of mutually profitable trade. A few years later Edward Chandler, bishop of Coventry and Litchfield, expanded upon this strategy by presenting a moral vision based upon reciprocity:

> Natural Justice guides Men to be kind to that People, and Benefactors to those Places, by whom, and where they live, thrive, and prosper. . . . The moral sense whereof is this, that we return good, wherever we receive good: Return it not in Beads and Baubles, but in a Species, which may indeed cost us little, but to them, that are without Christ, and without God in the World, is of inestimable Value.[32]

Although he cited "natural Justice," Chandler echoed Paul when he stressed the importance of repaying goodness. He sought to gather money for missionary work by depicting colonialism as an exchange of gifts. Describing America as England's "benefactor," Chandler called his audience to express their thanks to America by offering a gift of "inestimable Value," the knowledge of Christ.

The idea of mission allowed Chandler to reverse the usual vision of gold traded for glass: Britain now gives true gold instead of the "beads and baubles" other colonists have offered for the wealth of America. At first cheated of their treasure, the Indians now are being given something more lasting and useful. Their gain has not required Britain's loss but in fact has enabled the country's continued enrichment.

Conclusion: "We Are More Poor, They More Rich by This"

The idea of spiritual wealth flowing to America in exchange for temporal riches became a cliché in missionary writings, especially Anglican ones, through the middle of the eighteenth century. In 1709 William Dawes, bishop of Chester, said in a sermon before the SPG that "we cannot make them a more rich amends, for all these Advantages, for all these their carnal Things, than be letting them *reap our spiritual ones.*"[33] Several decades later Benson proclaimed, "*We abundantly reap temporal things* thence, and it is just therefore that we should *sow spiritual things* there."[34] Perhaps John Waugh, dean of Gloucester, made the point most persuasively in his sermon of 1722 when he wrote,

> Nor can we otherwise do Justice, or express our Gratitude to those poor Infidels, from whose Countries we have drawn such immense Wealth ... than by repaying them *spiritual* for temporal Riches. This, as it is an easie Expence to the Contributors, for so great Gains, so will it be a Means of procuring to those that receive the Advantage of it, a Treasure of inestimable Value, *The Knowledge of the only true God, and Jesus Christ whom he hath sent.* A Treasure, which St. Paul set so great a Value upon, that he looked upon the most pretious things as nothing worth, as Dung and *Dross.*[35]

By drawing on Paul's epistle, Waugh was able to suggest the worthlessness of worldly goods even as he stressed the bargain his readers would enjoy by funding missions. The British suffer only an "easie Expence," in exchange for which they receive both material wealth and the awareness of Indian conversion. The "Infidels" of foreign lands lose wealth they hardly knew existed, and in return they receive the invaluable word of God. Everyone gains, and nobody loses, in this vision of intercontinental exchange.

The trope of trade allowed the British in their most optimistic moments to imagine an inexhaustible circulation of wealth around the Atlantic basin, enriching every participant and saving every soul. As Philip Bisse, bishop of Hereford, said, "All Zeal naturally spreadeth, without spending its Force; and rather increaseth its Fervour, the farther it goes."[36] Long before Adam Smith wrote the *Wealth of Nations,* missionary texts taught their readers to transcend the zero-sum game of a mercantilist vision, seeing piles of wealth made endlessly expandable through global circulation. While raising money for the salvation of the Indians, then, missionary writers transformed a symbol of the Indians' exploitation into one of their spiritual compensation.

Later missionaries focused far less on tropes of exchange. In his fundraising narratives of the Indian Charity School, written in the 1760s and 1770s, Eleazar Wheelock rarely described his work as part of a fair trade with, or a debt owed to, Indians. When he discussed his school in financial terms, he was more likely to stress the comparative bargain that Indian conversion presented in comparison with the price of waging war. Near the conclusion of the Seven Years' War he speculated that "if one half which has been, for so many Years past expended in building Forts . . . had been prudently laid out in supporting faithful Missionaries . . . the instructed and civilized Party would have been a fair better Defence than all our expensive Fortresses, and prevented the laying waste so many Towns and Villages."[37] After he announced his intention to focus on the education of Anglo-American missionaries rather than Indians, his focus shifted altogether.[38]

Factors including the French and Indian War, a growing sense of British entitlement, and a weakening of transatlantic ties between Britain and the colonies probably influenced this rhetorical shift. Another important factor no doubt was the growing poverty of those Indians who remained in areas by then filled with European colonists. William Warburton, bishop of Gloucester, juxtaposed spiritual with material wealth in his SPG sermon of 1766, but with an important change. He wrote that "the Aborigines of the Country, Savages without Law or Religion, are the principal Objects of our Charity. Their *temporal,* as well as *spiritual,* condition calls loudly for our assistance."[39] Unlike his predecessors, Warburton did not refer to an exchange, reciprocal or not, but rather stressed the Indians' temporal *and* spiritual needs. A sense of specific obligation disappeared under the general rubric of charity.

In 1633, George Herbert's "Church Militant" included a prophecy of true religion moving westward from its seat in England to a new home in America. Prompting this transfer was an eastward flow of wealth from America to Europe, which it was corrupting. Of America Herbert wrote,

> My God, thou dost prepare for them a way,
> By carrying first their gold from them away,
> For gold and grace did never yet agree;
> Religion always sides with poverty.
> We think we rob them, but we think amiss:
> We are more poor—they are more rich by this.[40]

Celebrating the arrival of Protestants in the New World, Herbert portrayed the church on the brink of transition, about to abandon a corrupt Europe for an innocent America from which the Spanish had already taken much wealth.[41] He transformed the impoverishment of America into enrichment, toying with the term as he linked colonialism to divine will. By having the Spanish take their gold, God prepares the Indians for Christianity. The English also help the natives by making them financially poor, while transforming that poverty into spiritual wealth. Writing when the only English attempt to convert America's natives had been the abortive establishment of Henrico College near Jamestown,[42] Herbert reversed Paul's description by seeing conversion as compensation for theft. That his vision influenced at least some missionaries is suggested by the fact that these lines appeared forty years later in Daniel Gookin's *Historical Collections of the Indians in New England*. Gookin, who was the superintendent of Indian affairs in Massachusetts during King Philip's War (and a supporter of Eliot), quoted this poem as he described the piety of the "Praying Indians," mourned their treatment during the war, and called for more missionary efforts.[43]

A letter from the missionary Gideon Hawley to the Massachusetts Historical Society, describing his almost forty years of missionary work with the Mashpee Indians on Cape Cod, presents us with a wry fulfillment of Herbert's prophecy. Writing in 1794, Hawley described his first meeting with the Mashpee in the late 1750s:

> The natives here appeared in a very abject state.... They were dressed in English mode; but in old tattered garments and appeared below a half naked Indian in possession of his Liberty.... Their children were sold or bound as security for the payment of their fathers' debts.... These Indians and their children were transferred from one to another master like slaves. Nevertheless to console them they had the Christian religion.[44]

Like Herbert, Hawley paired material poverty with spiritual wealth. He described the latter as compensation for the former, consoling the Mashpee for the loss of their wealth and freedom. Although Hawley depicted himself as trying to ameliorate the Indians' material conditions, his description of their status presents an uncanny repetition of Herbert's vision. The impoverishment of America's natives for the benefit of its colonizers is overshadowed by their spiritual enrichment.

Stephen Greenblatt has observed that "the whole achievement of the discourse of Christian imperialism is to represent desires as convertible and in a constant process of exchange . . . . The rhetorical task of Christian imperialism then is to bring together commodity conversion and spiritual conversion."[45] This chapter has explored one aspect of this intersection between spiritual and financial conversion, as displayed in British missionary writings from the seventeenth and eighteenth centuries. From the time of Columbus's first encounter with the natives of what would soon be called America, one of the most important images of that encounter was that of gold traded for glass.

It is one of the cruel ironies of imperial history that, even as they condemned the exploitation of America and sought to save the souls of its natives, British missionaries set in place a religious rhetoric that bridged the benevolent and the acquisitive desires of Europe in relation to America. Describing colonial commerce through biblical descriptions of charity and the kingdom of God, they made it possible for the British to see Christian conversion as fair compensation for the sufferings of America's natives. Condemning material wealth even as they sought financial support for their projects, emphasizing the cost of promoting Christianity and the debt of Britain to America, missionaries presented spiritual conversion—with the accoutrements of European acculturation—as the most valuable export Britain had to offer America. Their writings made it possible for the British, and later the citizens of the United States, to believe that spreading the gospel among the Indians would amount to offering them true gold for their own spiritual glass.

Notes

Portions of this chapter are derived from chapter 1 of Laura M. Stevens, *The Poor Indians: British Missionaries, Native Americans, and Colonial Sensibility* (Philadelphia: University of Pennsylvania Press, 2004).

1. I use the terms "English" and "Scottish" when referring to texts published before the Act of Union between England and Scotland in 1707, as well as to the English-speaking people who wrote or read them. I use "British" to describe texts, authors, and readers situated after 1707 unless they emerge specifically from an English or a Scottish context. I also resort to the more inclusive term "British" when describing a group of texts or a trend that encompasses the date of union.

2. On the work of Puritans in New England, see Henry William Busk, *A Sketch of the Origin and the Recent History of the New England Company* (London, 1884); William Kellaway, *The New England Company, 1649–1776, Missionary Society to the American Indians* (London: Longman, Green, 1961); Neal Salisbury, "Red Puri-

tans: The 'Praying Indians' of Massachusetts Bay and John Eliot," *William and Mary Quarterly*, 3d Ser., 31 (1974): 27–54; Francis Jennings, *The Invasion of America: Indians, Colonialism, and the Cant of Conquest* (Chapel Hill: University of North Carolina Press, 1975); James P. Ronda, "'We Are Well as We Are': An Indian Critique of Seventeenth-Century Missions," *William and Mary Quarterly*, 3d Ser., 34 (1977): 66–82; William Simmons, "Conversion from Indian to Puritan," *New England Quarterly* 7 (1979): 197–218; Robert James Naeher, "Dialogue in the Wilderness: John Eliot and the Indian Exploration of Puritanism as a Source of Meaning, Comfort, and Ethnic Survival," *New England Quarterly* 62 (1989): 346–68; Harold W. Van Lonkhuyzen, "A Reappraisal of the Praying Indians: Acculturation, Conversion, and Identity at Natick, Massachusetts, 1646–1730," *New England Quarterly* 64 (1990): 396–428; Daniel Mandell, "'To Live More Like My Christian English Neighbors': Natick Indians in the Eighteenth Century," *William and Mary Quarterly*, 3d Ser., 48 (1991): 552–79; Hilary E. Wyss, "'Things that Do Accompany Salvation': Colonialism, Conversion, and Cultural Exchange in Experience Mayhew's *Indian Converts*," *Early American Literature* 33 (1998): 39–61; Richard Cogley, *John Eliot's Mission to the Indians before King Philip's War* (Cambridge: Harvard University Press, 1999). On the Church of England's Society for the Propagation of the Gospel in Foreign Parts, see David Humphries, *An Historical Account of the Incorporated Society for the Propagation of the Gospel in Foreign Parts* (London, 1730); Earnest Hawkins, *Historical Notices of the Church of England in the North American Colonies* (London, 1845); C. F. Pascoe, *Two Hundred Years of the S.P.G.: An Historical Account of the Society for the Propagation of the Gospel in Foreign Parts, 1701–1900* (London, 1901); E. C. Midwinter, "The S.P.G. in America," in *S.P.G. Archives Lectures* (Westminster: S.P.G., 1936–37), 3–12; G. E. Edwards, "Life in Old Documents," in *S.P.G. Archives Lectures* (Westminster: S.P.G., 1936–37), 13–22; Frank J. Klingberg, *Anglican Humanitarianism in Colonial New York* (Philadelphia: Church Historical Society, 1940); Hans Cnattingius, *Bishops and Societies: A Study of Anglican Colonial and Missionary Expansion, 1698–1850* (London: S.P.C.K., 1952), 7–37; H. P. Thompson, *Into All Lands: The History of the Society for the Propagation of the Gospel in Foreign Parts 1701–1950* (London: Billing and Sons, 1951); Margaret Dewey, *The Messengers: A Concise History of the United Society for the Propagation of the Gospel* (London: Mowbrays, 1975); Daniel K. Richter, "'Some of Them . . . Would Always Have a Minister with Them': Mohawk Protestantism, 1683–1719," *American Indian Quarterly* (fall 1992): 471–84; Daniel O'Connor et al., *Three Centuries of Mission: The United Society for the Propagation of the Gospel, 1701–2000* (London: Continuum, 2000). On Wheelock's and his student Samson Occom's work, see James Dow McCallum, ed., *The Letters of Eleazar Wheelock's Indians* (Hanover, N.H.: Dartmouth College Publications, 1932); Leon Burr Richardson, ed., *An Indian Preacher in England* (Hanover, N.H.: Dartmouth College Publications, 1933); Harold Blodgett, *Samson Occom* (Hanover, N.H.: Dartmouth College Publications, 1935); James Axtell, "Dr. Wheelock's Little

Red School," chap. 4 of Axtell, *The European and the Indian: Essays in the Ethnohistory of Colonial North America* (New York: Oxford University Press, 1981). For general sources on British missionary projects in colonial America, see George Warren Hinman (New York: Fleming H. Revell, 1933); Henry Warner Bowden, *American Indians and Christian Missions: Studies in Cultural Conflict* (Chicago: University of Chicago Press, 1981); James Axtell, *After Columbus: Essays in the Ethnohistory of Colonial North America* (New York: Oxford University Press, 1988); Margaret Connell Szasz, *Indian Education in the American Colonies, 1607–1783* (Albuquerque: University of New Mexico Press, 1988); Hilary E. Wyss, *Writing Indians: Literacy, Christianity, and Native Community in Early America* (Amherst: University of Massachusetts Press, 2000).

3. See, e.g., Thomas Shepard, *New England's First Fruits* (London, 1643). In assuming Shepard's authorship I follow Cogley, *John Eliot's Mission*, 278, citing Thomas Werge, *Thomas Shepard* (Boston, Twayne Publishers, 1987). See also Richard Willis, *A Sermon Preach'd before the Society for the Propagation of the Gospel in Foreign Parts, at Their First Yearly Meeting on Friday February 20th. 1701/2. At St. Mary-le-Bow* (London, 1702); and Eleazar Wheelock, *A Plain and Faithful Narrative of the Original Design, Rise, Progress, and Present State of the Indian Charity-School at Lebanon, in Connecticut* (Boston, 1763). On these texts see George Parker Winship, *The Eliot Indian Tracts* (Cambridge: Harvard University Press, 1925); Samuel Clyde McCulloch, "The Foundation and Early Works of the Society for the Propagation of the Gospel in Foreign Parts," *Huntington Library Quarterly* 8 (1945). On the SSPCK, see Henry Hunter, *A Brief History of the Society in Scotland, for Propagating Christian Knowledge in the Highlands and Islands; and of the Correspondent Board in London* (London, 1795); and Frederick V. Mills Sr., "The Society in Scotland for the Propagation of Christian Knowledge in British North America, 1730–1775," *Church History* 63 (1994): 15–30.

4. I am influenced here by Benedict Anderson's theories about the role that printed texts played in the development of nationalist identity. Benedict Anderson, *Imagined Communities: Reflections on the Origin and Spread of Nationalism*, rev. ed. (New York: Verso, 1991).

5. Vine Deloria Jr., *Custer Died for Your Sins: An Indian Manifesto* (London: Collier-Macmillan, 1969), 101.

6. All biblical quotations in this paper come from the Authorized King James Version.

7. Christopher Columbus, *Letter to the King and Queen of Castile (First Voyage)* [1493], in *The English Literatures of America, 1500–1800*, ed. Myra Jehlen and Michael Warner (New York: Routledge, 1997), 13.

8. Columbus, *Letter to the King and Queen*, 13–14.

9. Daniel K. Richter, *Facing East from Indian Country: A Native History of Early America* (Cambridge: Harvard University Press, 2001), 6–7; Michael P. Morris, *The Bringing of Wonder: Trade and the Indians of the Southeast, 1700–1783* (Westport,

Conn.: Greenwood Press, 1999), 1–3; Daniel K. Richter, *The Ordeal of the Longhouse: The Peoples of the Iroquois League in the Era of European Colonization* (Chapel Hill: University of North Carolina Press, 1992), 22–23.

10. Christopher L. Miller and George R. Hamell, "A New Perspective on Indian-White Contact: Cultural Symbols and Colonial Trade," *Journal of American Studies* 23 (1986): 311–28.

11. Joshua Bellin, *The Demon of the Continent: Indians and the Shaping of American Literature* (Philadelphia: University of Pennsylvania Press, 2001), 42–43.

12. Stephen Greenblatt, *Marvelous Possessions: The Wonder of the New World* (Chicago: University of Chicago Press, 1991), 110, quoted in Bellin, *Demon of the Continent*, 42.

13. Columbus, *Letter to the King and Queen*, 13–14.

14. Although this vision of unequal exchange usually applied to the Americas, it sometimes appeared in reference to Asians or Africans. Joanna Lipking mentions "the promise that opens a 1665 collection called *The Golden Coast* that 'a man may gain an estate by a handful of beads, and his pocket full of gold for an old hat.'" Joanna Lipking, "The New World of Slavery—An Introduction," in *Oroonoko*, by Aphra Behn, ed. Joanna Lipking (New York: Norton, 1997), 76.

15. There continues to be uncertainty about the reference to the "Indian" in this line, as the folio edition of Shakespeare's plays refers to "the base Iudean," while the quarto edition substitutes "the base Indian." E.A.J. Honigmann concluded, "The best analysis, is, I think, Richard Levin's 'The Indian/Iudean crux in *Othello*' (SQ 33 [1982], 60–67), which ends with a telling point. It is appropriate for Othello to compare himself with the Indian, whose action results from ignorance, and 'very inappropriate for him to compare himself to Judas, whose action was regarded as a conscious choice of evil.'" E.A.J. Honigmann, "Longer Notes," in William Shakespeare, *The Arden Shakespeare "Othello,"* ed. E.A.J. Honigmann (Surrey, U.K.: Thomas Nelson and Sons, 1997), 342–43.

16. Eliza Haywood, *The City Jilt*, in *Three Novellas by Eliza Haywood*, ed. Earla A. Wilputte (1726; East Lansing: Michigan State University Press, 1995), 105; emphasis in original.

17. John Milton, *Complete Poems and Major Prose*, ed. Merritt Y. Hughes (Indianapolis: Odyssey Press, 1957), 665; emphasis mine.

18. Robert Boyle, "The Aretology" (1645), in *The Early Essays and Ethics of Robert Boyle*, ed. John T. Harwood (Carbondale: Southern Illinois University Press, 1991), 73–74. See also a similar reference to Indians in another essay in the same work, "The Doctrine of Thinking," 196.

19. John Hall, "Of Felicity," in *Horae Vacivae, Or, Essays. Some Occasional Considerations* (London, 1646), 25–27; emphasis in original.

20. Martin Benson, *A Sermon Preached before the Incorporated Society for the Propagation of the Gospel in Foreign Parts; at Their Anniversary Meeting in the Parish-Church of St. Mary-le-Bow, on Friday, February 15, 1739–40* (London, 1740), 10.

21. Nathaniel Eells to Nathaniel Whitaker, Stonington, January 12, 1767, in Richardson, *An Indian Preacher in England*, 198; emphasis in original.

22. J.D., afterword to *The Glorious Progress of the Gospel, Amongst the Indians in New England*, ed. Edward Winslow (London, 1649). Richard Cogley identifies J.D. as "John Dury, the Scottish-born ecumenist then residing in England" in *John Eliot's Mission*, 67.

23. An Act for the promoting and propagating the Gospel of Jesus Christ in New England, in *Acts and Ordinances of the Interregnum, 1642–1660* [July 27, 1649], vol. 2, 197. See also Kellaway, *The New England Company*, 15.

24. Joseph Caryl, preface to *A Late and Further Manifestation of the Progress of the Gospel Amongst the Indians in New-England*, by John Eliot (London, 1655).

25. On the fate of the Praying Indians in King Philip's War, see Jill Lepore, *The Name of War: King Philip's War and the Origins of American Identity* (New York: Vintage, 1998), chaps. 1, 5; Jenny Hale Pulsipher, "Massacre at Hurtleberry Hill: Christian Indians and English Authority in Metacom's War," *William and Mary Quarterly*, 3d Ser., 53 (1996): 459–86.

26. There is a large body of scholarship on the philosophical implications of the development of modern finance and public debt, beginning with the work of J.G.A. Pocock, *Virtue, Commerce, and History: Essays on Political Thought and History, Chiefly in the Eighteenth Century* (New York: Cambridge University Press, 1985).

27. Patrick Gordon, *Geography Anatomized: Or, A Compleat Geographical Grammer.... with a Reasonable Proposal for the Propagation of the Blessed Gospel in All Pagan Countries* (London, 1693), 208; emphasis in original.

28. "Proposals for Propagating the Gospel in all Pagan Countreys," By Mr. Patrick Gourdon [sic]. Item 7, Appendix A, *USPG Journal*. See Reference to "Proposals," January 16, 1701, vol. 1, Journal A, USPG Papers, Rhodes House Library, Oxford, U.K.

29. O'Connor et al., *Three Centuries of Mission*, 5–6.

30. Gilbert Burnet, *Of the Propagation of the Gospel in Foreign Parts. A Sermon Preach'd at St. Mary-le-Bow, Feb. 18. 1703/4. Before the Society Incorporated for That Purpose. Exhorting All Persons in Their Stations, to Assist So Glorious a Design* (London, 1704), 22.

31. George Stanhope, *The Early Conversion of Islanders, a Wise Expedient for Propagating Christianity. A Sermon Preached before the Incorporated Society for the Propagation of the Gospel in Foreign Parts; at Their Anniversary Meeting* (London, 1714), 23; emphasis in original.

32. Edward Chandler, *A Sermon Preached before the Incorporated Society for the Propagation of the Gospel in Foreign Parts; at Their Anniversary Meeting* (London, 1719), 25.

33. William Dawes, *A Sermon Preach'd before the Society for the Propagation of the Gospel in Foreign Parts, at the Parish-Church of St. Mary-le-Bow, on Friday February 18. 1708/9* (London, 1709), 22; emphasis in original.

34. Benson, *A Sermon Preached*, 12; emphasis in original.

35. John Waugh, *A Sermon Preached before the Incorporated Society for the Propagation of the Gospel in Foreign Parts; at Their Anniversary Meeting* (London, 1723), 30–31 emphasis in original.

36. Philip Bisse, *A Sermon Preach'd before the Incorporated Society for the Propagation of the Gospel in Foreign Parts; at Their Anniversary Meeting in the Parish Church of St. Mary-le-Bow, on Friday the 21st of February, 1717* (London, 1718), 4.

37. Wheelock, *A Plain and Faithful Narrative*, 11.

38. Wheelock made this announcement in *A Continuation of the Narrative of the Indian Charity-School, in Lebanon, in Connecticut, from the Year 1768, to the Incorporation of It with Dartmouth-College, and Removal and Settlement of It in Hanover, in the Province of New-Hampshire, 1771* (Hartford, Conn., 1771).

39. William Warburton, *A Sermon Preached before the Incorporated Society for the Propagation of the Gospel in Foreign Parts; at Their Anniversary Meeting* (London, 1766), 16; emphasis in original.

40. George Herbert, "The Church Militant," in *The Works of George Herbert*, ed. F. E. Hutchinson (Oxford, U.K.: Clarendon Press, 1941), 190–98, ll. 247–54.

41. David S. Shields, "Then Shall Religion to America Flee," in *Like Season'd Timber: New Essays on George Herbert*, ed. Edmund Miller and Robert DiYanni (New York: Peter Lang, 1987), 282.

42. On Henrico College see Alden T. Vaughan, *Roots of American Racism: Essays on the Colonial Experience* (New York: Oxford University Press, 1995), 115; Peter Walne, "The Collections for Henrico College, 1616–1618," *The Virginia Magazine of History and Biography* 80 (1972): 259–66; Robert Hunt Land, "Henrico and Its College," *William and Mary Quarterly*, 2d Ser., 18 (1938): 453–98.

43. Daniel Gookin, *Historical Collections of the Indians in New England* [1674] (Boston, 1792), 20.

44. Gideon Hawley to Dr. Thacher, January 1794, Letters of Gideon Hawley, Gideon Hawley Papers, Massachusetts Historical Society, Boston.

45. Greenblatt, *Marvelous Possessions*, 71.

Contributors

Amy Turner Bushnell is retired from the College of Charleston and is now a research associate at the John Carter Brown Library, Providence. She is the author of several books, among them *Establishing Exceptionalism: Historiography and the Colonial Americas* (1995).

Peter A. Goddard is associate professor of history at the University of Guelph. He has published articles and book chapters on aspects of seventeenth-century Jesuit culture and missionary activity, including studies of Jesuit diabolism and the influence of Saint Augustine in Jesuit missions to New France.

Isabel dos Guimarães Sá is an assistant professor at the Universidade do Minho, Braga. She is the author of *Quando o rico se faz pobre: Misericórdias, caridade e poder no império português, 1500–1800* (1997) and *As Misericórdias Portuguesas de D. Manuel I a Pombal* (2001).

Evan Haefeli is assistant professor of history at Tufts University. He is the coauthor, with Kevin Sweeney, of *Captors and Captives: The 1704 French and Indian Raid on Deerfield* (2003).

Dennis Channing Landis is the curator of European books at the John Carter Brown Library. He was the editor of the six-volume bibliographical series *European Americana: A Chronological Guide ... 1493–1750* (1980–97) and the author of *Literature of the Encounter* (1991).

Barbara De Marco is managing editor of the journal *Romance Philology* and principal editor at the Research Center for Romance Studies at the University of California, Berkeley. She is coeditor, with Jerry R. Craddock, of *Documenting the Colonial Experience, with Special Reference to Span-*

ish in the American Southwest (1999–2000), a two-volume special issue of *Romance Philology.*

Mark Meuwese is completing his Ph.D. in history at the University of Notre Dame. He has been a fellow at the John Carter Brown Library.

James Muldoon is professor of history emeritus at Rutgers University and a research scholar at the John Carter Brown Library. His publications include *Varieties of Religious Conversion in the Middle Ages* (1997) and *Empire and Order: The Concept of Empire 800–1800* (1999).

Annie Parker is a graduate student in the history department at the University of Iowa.

Daniel T. Reff is associate professor in the Division of Comparative Studies in the Humanities at Ohio State University. His published work includes *Disease, Depopulation, and Culture Change in Northwestern New Spain 1518–1764* (1991).

Laura M. Stevens is assistant professor of English language and literature at the University of Tulsa. She is the author of *The Poor Indians: British Missionaries, Native Americans, and Colonial Sensibility* (2004).

Jaime Valenzuela Márquez is professor of history at the Pontificia Universidad Católica de Chile. He is the author of *Bandidaje rural en Chile central: Curico, 1850–1900* (1991); *Las liturgias del poder: Celebraciones públicas y estrategias persuasivas en Chile colonial (1609–1709)* (2001); and *Fiesta y legitimación política: Del Chile borbónico al republicano* (forthcoming).

Index

Abenaki people (Canada), captives among, 221
Abipone people (Paraguay), 158
Absolution, as judicial act, 170
Abyssinian Church, 104
Acadia, religious processions of, 229n19
Acaxee people (Mexico), religious beliefs of, 25, 26, 28
Acculturation: to Christianity, 3, 186; of Jesuits, 210; of neophytes, 178, 211; role of guilt in, 184–87
Acosta, José de, 103, 105, 107; on Chinese, 142; on Amerindians, 143; *De procuranda Indorum salute*, 112, 142; *Historia natural y moral de las Indias*, 142; influence of, 113; on native languages, 112; on propagation of Gospel, 106; on Satan, 195
"Act for the promoting and propagating the Gospel of Jesus Christ in New England," 240
Act of Union (1707), 247n1
Adam, in Puritan theory, 80–81
Agreda, María de, 44
Agriculture, Amerindian: extensive, 146; Guaraní, 162; intensive, 146, 153; and longevity, 147–48; Mayan, 153; slash-and-burn, 146, 150; Yaqui, 154
Ahome people (Mexico), religious beliefs of, 25
Ais (Amerindians), 156
Albany (New York), Mohawk neophytes at, 132
Aldeias (mission villages), 198, 202; colonists' interference in, 201; missionaries in, 199; Tupís in, 126, 133
Alden, Dauril, 201
Algarroba (carob) trees, 159

Algonquian dialect, 84; Eliot's study of, 78
Algonquians: alliance with Iroquoians, 61; communities of, 71; conversion narratives of, 90; exposure to Christianity, 124; war with Iroquoians, 162. *See also* Praying Indians
Allauca, Pedro, 181
Almaráz, Felix D., 53n14
Alvares Cabral, Pedro, 196
Amazon River, French expulsion from, 198
Amerindians: Acosta on, 143; administration of Eucharist to, 148; agriculture of, 146, 147–48, 150, 153, 154, 162; antimaterialism of, 60; bartering ability of, 233–34; celebration of Holy days, 36, 46, 49n1, 149, 165n14; Chilean, 145, 159; conception of sin, 179–81; confession for, 172, 173–74; *congregación* of, 144–45; consumption of manufactured goods, 238; cosmic-social order of, 185; cost of Christianization for, 148; distinctions among, 103; economic naiveté of, 234, 235; enslavement of, 196–97, 201; of Florida, 155–57, 162; gift-giving systems of, 234; as gypsies, 146, 164n7; *hechiceros*, 26, 27, 47; interpretation of Protestantism, 140n37; Jesuit view of, 70; mobility levels of, 150; natural virtue of, 64–65; of Nueva Galicia, 48; papal bulls on, 195; of Paraguay, 158, 160; Patagonian, 160; penance for, 180; prayer books for, 185; Protestant understanding of, 104–5, 115n5; Recollects' view of, 62–65, 68–69; religious beliefs of, 18, 25–29; response to European expansion, 119; rituals of, 43, 180; shrines of, 26–29; as ten lost tribes, 7, 50n2, 88; willpower of, 185. *See also* Neophytes

256 Index

Amerindians, Brazilian: conversion of, 192–211; effect of medieval attitudes on, 194; enslavement of, 196–97; just war against, 195–96; military dominance over, 200; Portuguese perceptions of, 194–96. *See also* Guaraní people; Tupí people

Amerindians, Mexican, 24–31; *caciques* of, 25; priesthood of, 26; *principales*, 24, 26–27; religious beliefs of, 25–28; resistance by, 155; women, 27

Amerindians, New England, 246; civil life of, 87; conversion narratives of, 86, 90, 91–93, 97n49; cultural conquest of, 79; Eliot's evangelization of, 78–94; English obligation to, 241–44, 245; as example to English, 88; reciprocity with English, 243; relations with Puritans, 79–80, 84–86; response to Eliot, 80. *See also* Praying Indians

Amerindians, New Mexico, 36–49; *hechiceros*, 47; in Pueblo Revolt, 5, 38, 45–48, 55n21

Anabaptists, 89

Anasazi people (Southwest), 153

Anderson, Arthur, 49

Anderson, Benedict, 249n4

Angola (Brazil): diocese of, 202; inquisitorial visitation at, 204

Antichrist, pope as, 102

Antinomian Controversy (1636–38), 80; assurance following, 85; hypocrisy in, 81, 82–84, 90, 91, 92–93, 96n23; Richard Mather in, 97n64; sanctification in, 82; Shepard's response to, 82–84

Antonine Plague, 21

Anuas, Jesuit, 18, 26

Apostolic Age, end of, 100, 103, 109, 111

Araucanía, 159; Jesuits in, 160; reductions in, 150

Araucano people (Chile), 159; Franciscan missions to, 161; raiding economy of, 160; resistance by, 162

Argentina, reductions in, 152

Arianism, 19

Aristotle, 2; concept of society, 12, 14; on nature of man, 142

Armenian Church, 104

Armstrong, Guyda, 15n9

Arnauld, Antoine, 105

Arróniz, Othón, 50n3

Artifacts, Catholic: proliferation of, 42–44, 49

Asia, Jesuits in, 12

Asunción (Paraguay), 153; Guaranís of, 151

Augustine of Canterbury, 4

Augustine of Hippo: *Confessions*, 2, 15n8

Autos sacramentales, 50n3

Avontroot, Jan, 116n35

Axtell, James, 215, 216, 227

Ayeta, Fray Francisco de: *memorial* of, 38, 45–48

Ayvinos people, 26

Azcona Imberto, Antonio de, 163

Azores, inquisitorial visitation at, 204

Azpilcueta, Father Martin, 26, 27

Aztecs, 157

Bahia (Brazil): confraternities of, 207; convents in, 208; inquisitorial visitation at, 204; Poor Clares of the Desterro, 208; Synod of (1707), 203, 205

Balduin, Friedrich, 103

Bank of England, 241

Baptism: Calvinist ideology of, 129; in Catholic missionization, 105; mass, 175; pre-conquest rites of, 105; Quechua conception of, 178; as survival stratagem, 163

Baptismal gifts, royal, 149

Barbarians, medieval concept of, 194

Barclay, Thomas, 133

Bartlett, Joseph, 218, 222

Batuco people, 26, 27

Baudot, Georges, 51n6

Bedembach, Felix, 103

Belém do Pará (Jesuit college), 198

Bellarmine, Cardinal Robert, 101–2, 107, 108; Lutheran response to, 102, 105–6

Bellin, Joshua, 234

Belon, Pierre, 104

Benavente de Motolinía, Toribio, 145

Benavides, Fray Alonso de: *memorial* of, 38, 44–45

Benedictines, in Brazil, 202

Benson, Martin, 238, 244

Index

Benzoni, 105
Bible, individual interpretation of, 106
Bío-Bío River (Chile), 159, 160
Birabin, J. N., 21
Bishops, medieval: orthographic practices of, 17
Bisse, Philip, 244
Boak, A. E., 21
Board games, as teaching techniques, 70
Bolivia, Jesuits in, 160
Borrado people (Spanish America), 158
Boyle, Robert: "The Aretology," 237–38
Brandão, D. Frei Caetano, 203
Brazil: African slaves in, 192, 207; Benedictines in, 202; confraternities in, 203, 204, 205–7, 209, 213n35; convents in, 208; conversion efforts in, 10–12, 192–211; domestic religion of, 204; Dutch expulsion from, 124, 132, 135, 194; Dutch invasion of, 128; Dutch-Indian relations in, 119; Dutch West India Company in, 118; ecclesiastical structure of, 202–4; epidemics in, 125, 211; gold rush in, 203; inquisitorial visitations in, 204–5, 213n30; Jesuits in, 10–11, 126, 192–211, 212n13; lay preachers in, 122; mission systems of, 165n17, 201, 210; neophytes in, 205–7; *paróquias encomendadas* of, 203; Portuguese colonists of, 122, 192, 196, 201, 210; religious life in, 205–7; religious plurality in, 137n13; rural estates of, 203; schools in, 121, 137n10; Sephardic Jews in, 122; sugar plantations, 204, 205–6, 211; Synodal Constitutions (1707), 203, 205. *See also* Amerindians, Brazilian
Brébeuf, Jean de, 70
Breckling, Friedrich, 110; as chiliast, 111; *Synagoga Satanae*, 111
Brightman, Thomas, 102
Brutscher, Johann, 102
Bulls, papal: on Amerindians, 195; on New World, 192–93, 211n1
Burgundians, conversion of, 19
Burnet, Gilbert, 242
Bushnell, Amy Turner, 7–8

Cabeza de Vaca, Álvar Núñez, 38, 158

Cabral de Taíde, Fernão, 210
Cafusos (African-Amerindians), 197
Cajatambo (Andes), 181
Cajetanus, Cardinal: on just war, 106
California, missions of, 149
Calixt, Georg: *Discurs von der wahren Christlichen Religion*, 104
Calov, Abraham: *Systema locorum theologicorum*, 106
Calusa people (Florida), resistance by, 155–56
Calvin, John, 107; in conversion narratives, 222
Calvinism: ideology of baptism, 129; Mohawk conversion to, 127–30, 133
Calvinists: English, 101; militant, 137n5
—Dutch, 118–35; anti-Catholicism of, 123–24, 134; in Brazil, 123; educational programs of, 121, 137n10; expulsion from Brazil, 124, 132, 135, 194; millennialism of, 120; in New Netherland, 123, 139n25; pastors of, 122, 123; prestige among Mohawks, 131; view of Jesuits, 123, 124, 134. *See also* Missionaries, Dutch Calvinist
Camerarius, Philipp, 106, 115n20
Campo, Andrés de, 40
Canary Islands: colonization of, 211n1; European settlement of, 4–5; Spanish occupation of, 193
Cannibalism, 194
Captivity narratives, Puritan, 217–25
Capuchins, 58
Cardenas, Father Lorenzo de, 26, 27
Cariós (Guaraní people), 158; of Asunción region, 151
Carmelites: in Brazil, 202; confraternities of, 206; of Macao, 208
Carob, 159
Caron, Raymund, 111
Cartagena (Colombia), inquisition in, 204
Caryl, Joseph, 240–41
Castelnau-L'Estoile, Charlotte, 199, 201
Catechesis: language of, 178; of neophytes, 175, 178
Catechism: Mohawk teachers of, 132; pamphlets, 185

258   Index

Catholicism: baroque, 72; Brazilian, 202–4; corruption in, 101; feasts of, 30; Gallican, 69; Old World, 173; paraphernalia for, 43–44, 53n15, 148–49; primitive, 14; Puritans' conversion to, 11, 215–28; ritual supplies for, 42–44, 53n15; universality of, 104; use of images, 23; as "white magic," 70, 77n53
Catiti (Amerindian), 55n22
Cattle farms, Brazilian, 203
Cayuga Indians, 126
Celts, shrines of, 20
Ceremonies, religious: of conquistadors, 42, 53n14; following Pueblo Revolt, 45–48; hybrid, 41; syncretism in, 41
Ceylon, Portuguese loss of, 194
Chaco (Spanish America), reductions in, 150
Chamier, Daniel, 108
Chandler, Edward, 241–44
Charles V (king of Spain), 1, 144
Charrúa people (South America), 152
Chávez, Fray Angélico: *Coronado's Friars*, 41, 52nn8,10, 53nn12–13
Chemnitz, Martin: *Loci Theologici*, 102–3
Cherokees, literacy of, 140n34
Chiapas (Mexico), reductions in, 155
Chicha (drink), 159
Chichimeco people, 143, 145; culture of, 158
Chichimeco War (1550–90), 157
Children, Puritan: conversion to Catholicism, 218–19, 221–28
Chile: Amerindians of, 145, 159, 160, 161, 162; missions in, 149
Chiliasm, German, 111
China: Acosta on, 142; civilization of, 195; Jesuits in, 12
Chinantec people (Mexico), resistance by, 155
Chinard, Gilbert, 64
Chiriguaná people, 143, 151, 162; slavers among, 153
Christ: Mediation of, 105; parable of wealth, 238
Christianity: accommodation to local cultures, 12, 31; acculturation to, 3, 185; and civilization, 2–3, 143, 209; as colonial commodity, 233; following demographic collapse, 21; Huron understanding of, 67–68; as imperialism, 247; missionary obligation in, vii; primitive, 14; in Roman empire, 18–19; syncretism in, 6, 41, 50n3, 74, 177, 178, 181, 210–11; as trade for gold, 237–43; transference of emotion to, 22; universal, 8
Christianization: agents of, 196–97; as civilization, 2–3, 143, 209; of civilized peoples, 142; and colonial development, 63; cost for Amerindians, 148; early medieval, 2–3; mobility within, 146, 161; nature as barrier to, 69; of nonsedentary peoples, 145–46; of pagan sites, 4, 18; of Peru, 144; resistance to, 2, 14; reversal of, 146; of South America, 173. *See also* Conversion; Evangelization; Missionization
Christmas, Amerindian celebration of, 36, 49n1
Church, medieval: as city-state, 3
Church architecture, Franciscan, 43, 49, 54n16
Cíbola, Seven Cities of, 38–39, 40, 52n9; Franciscans' search for, 41
Cicero, Marcus Tullius, 65; on nature of man, 142
City-states, ancient, 2–3
Civility: association with religion, 86, 97n53; of Hurons, 64–65
Clovis (Frankish king), conversion of, 2, 15n5
Cogley, Richard W., 84, 87, 94n4, 251n22
Cohen, Charles, 79, 96n35, 97n49; *God's Cares*, 81
Colleges, Jesuit: in Brazil, 198
Colonialism, 63; and divine will, 246; as spiritual charity, 233
Columbus, Christopher: on Amerindian trade, 233–35, 237, 238; on slavery, 233
Comenius, Johann Amos, 113; *Methodus linguarum novissima*, 112
Confession, 9, 171, 172; according to Ten Commandments, 174, 176; confidentiality in, 183–84; Council of Lima on, 184; cultural intermediaries in, 179; individual, 169–70; of neophytes, 173–74;

Index   259

post-Trentine, 9, 173, 182; pre-Trentine, 173; role in conversion, 9; role of priest in, 182–84; syncretism in, 177, 181; in traditional religions, 181
Confession manuals, 169–70; ethnographic information in, 176–77; language of, 175; Mexican, 173; New World imprints, 173; penance in, 183; Spanish American, 172–79, 183, 186; translation of, 177–78; worldview of, 186
Confraternities, Brazilian, 203, 204, 205–7; recruitment into, 206; women in, 209
Congregación, 144–45. *See also* Reductions (settlement)
Congregation de Notre Dame (Montreal), 220
Congregation for the Propagation of the Faith, 104, 193; creation of, 13
Conhecença (tax, Brazil), 203
Conscience: development of, 184; examination of, 182
Conversion: affective experience in, 91; aggressive approach to, 22; of agricultural societies, 8, 9, 144; civil, 63; commodity, 247; as compensation for theft, 246; decontextualization in, 70–71; definitions of, 137n4; early Christian, 2, 19; hierarchical society in, 8; as indeterminate process, 58; within kinship networks, 68; linguistic problems in, 9–10, 14, 174–79; of marginalized persons, 139n26; millennialism in, 62, 210; motives for, 210–11; of nomadic peoples, 7–8; personal, 15n8; quantifiable, 58; reward and punishment in, 67–68; social dimension of, 63. *See also* Christianization; Evangelization; Missionization
Conversion, Catholic: in Brazil, 10–12, 192–211; following depopulation, 107, 125–26; fear in, 59, 68, 71, 172; gift giving in, 161; modern, 69–72; in New France, 5, 57–64; versus Protestant, 2; from Puritanism, 11, 215–28; Puritans' motives for, 216–17; Recollects' beliefs concerning, 67; role of confession in, 9; as sacramental imperative, 146; Spanish approach to, 4–5; techniques in, vii, 4–5, 7, 37–38, 40, 45, 57–58, 59, 68, 71, 72; as theater, 5, 36, 37, 50n3
Conversion, medieval, 1, 14, 62–69; versus modern, 57–74; Protestant view of, vii
Conversion, Protestant: versus Catholic, 2; of Catholics, 102; coercive, 86; expense of, 239–40; to Puritanism, 78–94; Puritans' accounts of, 78–79, 83–84, 88; Puritans' beliefs regarding, 80–82, 88, 93–94, 95n10, 96n39; role of gift giving in, 130–31, 140n33; role of literacy in, 131; role of trade in, 130, 234, 238–43; in seventeenth-century thought, 101
Conversion narratives, Amerindian, 86, 90, 91–93, 97n49
Conversion narratives, Puritan, 217–27; coercion in, 221–22; divine providence in, 218; gender in, 225; Luther in, 222; miracle stories in, 223–24; psychological aspects of, 221; Purgatory in, 222, 224; transubstantiation in, 223
Coronado, Francisco Vásquez de, 39; Franciscans accompanying, 38, 40, 41, 52n10, 53n12
Cortés, Hernán, 1, 107
Costa people (Florida), 157
Cotton, John, 82, 95n16, 101
Council of Mexico (First, 1555), 184
Council of Trent (1551), 144; confession following, 9, 173, 182; effect on South America, 173; missions following, 192; on penance, 170, 171; on priesthood, 170
Councils of Lima: First (1552), 178, 184; Second (1567), 178–79; Third (1583), 173, 184
Counter-Reformation: aesthetic strategies of, 182; Augustinian thought in, 144; effect on New World, 1; and missionization, 13; in Montreal society, 219, 220; penance in, 169–73
Covenant Chain alliance, 128, 139n28
Crioulos (Brazilian slaves), 197; confraternities of, 207
Cruceño people (Spanish America), 162
Cruz, Fray Juan de la, 41
Cults: of saints, 22, 23–24, 31; of Virgin Mary, 55n21

Cultural fusion, 37, 50n3
Culture, Amerindian: Chichimeco, 158; fasting in, 180; Guaycurú, 158; priests' knowledge of, 180; Protestant understanding of, 104–5, 115n5; rejection of, 12; Western cataloging of, 187
Culture, missionary: Franciscan, 59–61; Jesuit, 61–62
Cumaná (Venezuela), *congregación* in, 145
Curibocas (Amerindian-Portuguese), 197

Dannhauer, Johann Conrad, 103, 108, 109
Dartmouth College, 231
Davenant, John, 108
Davidson, H. R. Ellis, 20
Dawes, William, 244
Debt: public, 251n26; spiritual, 241–44
Dedekennus, Georg, 103
Dellius, Godfried, 118, 129, 139n29; gift giving by, 130–31, 140n33
Deloria, Vine, 232
Delumeau, Jean, 172
De Marco, Barbara, 4–5, 7
Demonology, 194–95
Demos, John, 229n8
Dépaïsment (conversion technique), 71
Depopulation, 138n21; conversion following, 107, 125–26; of Iroquoians, 139n21; in Spanish New World, 106; of Tupí peoples, 125, 138n21. *See also* Epidemics
Déracination (conversion technique), 71
Disease. *See* Epidemics
Dízimos (church tax), 203
Dominicans: on accommodation, 12, 13; disagreements with Jesuits, 12; reductions by, 155, 162
Dorantes, Esteban de, 39
Duarte (king of Portugal), 211n1
Dunte, Ludwig, 103
Dury, John, 109, 251n22; *The Glorious Progress of the Gospel*, 239–40, 241
Dutch: expulsion from Brazil, 124, 132, 135, 194; trade with Mohawks, 119, 126–27, 132. *See also* Calvinists, Dutch; Missionaries, Dutch Calvinist

Dutch Reformed Church: Calvinists in, 120; and Dutch West India Company, 137n7, 138n15; literacy program of, 131; missionary policies of, 11, 118–35; mission schools of, 132; in New York, 118, 125, 129, 135, 138n19; Recife Council, 133; support for Tupí, 128, 130
Dutch West India Company (WIC): alliance with Tupí, 128, 130, 132; in Brazil, 118; chartering of, 120; compensation from, 121–22, 137n11; and Dutch Reformed Church, 137n7, 138n15; missionary program of, 120; in New Netherland, 118;
Duviols, Pierre, 181

Eastern Orthodox Church, 104
East Indians, Acosta on, 142
Eckhard, Heinrich: *Pandectis controversiarum*, 102
Eckhard, Melchior Sylvester, 103
Economy: intensive agricultural, 146, 153; pastoral subsistence, 147; subsistence, 146, 150
Edict of Nantes (1685), 220
Eells, Nathaniel, 238
Ehinger, Elias: *Velitatio epistolaris*, 102
Eichsfeld, Christian, 103
El Dorado, 1
Eliot, John, 15, 101; beliefs concerning Amerindians, 7; biography of, 94n1; conversion methods of, 80, 85; evangelization of, 78–94; *Late and Further Manifestation of the Progress of the Gospel*, 240; Massachuset Bible, 99; Cotton Mather's memoir of, 79; preaching by, 80, 85, 86; study of Algonquian dialect, 78, 84; writings of, 80, 84. *See also* Praying Indians; Praying Towns
Eliot Tracts, 79, 80, 94n3, 231; corruption in, 87–88; depravity of Amerindians in, 85, 94; English audience of, 87; rhetorical themes of, 84–85, 87, 92
Engenhos (sugar plantations), chapels of, 204, 205–6, 211
England: conquest of New Netherland, 119, 124, 128; North America colonies of, 124;

imperial rhetoric of, 232; obligation to Amerindians, 241–44, 245; reciprocity with Amerindians, 243; theft of America, 242. *See also* Missionaries, English

Epidemics: among Mohawk, 125, 127, 139n21; in Brazil, 125, 211; clerics' prevention of, 35n55; in Mexico, 29, 30–31; protection by Christianity, 133; role in missionization, 159; in Roman Empire, 21, 22; smallpox, 125; in Spanish New World, 29, 106, 143. *See also* Depopulation

Escalante, Fray Silvestre Vélez, 55n22

Espejo, Antonio de, 42

Espírito Santo (Jesuit college), 198

Essequibo (Guiana), 110

Ethiopia, Jesuit expulsion from, 193

Eusebius, 103

Evangelization: of African slaves, 122; in Dutch North America, 136n3; legitimization of, 192–93; of nomadic peoples, 145; Portuguese crown on, 196; post-Trentine, 173; written word in, 119. *See also* Christianization; Conversion; Missionization

Faith, anxiety concerning, 81, 82–84, 90, 91, 92–93, 96n35

Farriss, Nancy, 144, 154, 155

Fasting, in Amerindian culture, 180

Fear, in conversion techniques, 59, 68, 71, 172

Ferdinand and Isabel (king and queen of Spain), pluralism under, 143

Fletcher, Richard, 16n19

Flint, Valerie I. J., 22

Florida: Amerindian societies of, 155–57, 162; missions of, 149; reductions in, 150

Food taboos, 149

Foraging, 162

Foster, William, 216

France: and Amazon. *See* Amazon River, French expulsion from

Franciscans: on accommodation, 12, 13; apostolic poverty of, 59–60, 74; culture of, 59–61; disagreements with Jesuits, 12; early modern, 75n6; missionary methods of, 7; preaching of, 60–61; understanding of psychology, 50n2. *See also* Recollects

Franciscans, French: apocalyptic tradition of, 5; conversion beliefs of, 58, 72; in New France, 5, 58, 72; preaching by, 58

Franciscans, Portuguese: in Brazil, 196, 202; confraternities of, 206

Franciscans, Spanish, 4; accompanying Coronado, 38, 40, 41, 53n12; in *conquista*, 61; daily life of, 54n17; in Florida, 156; in Guairá, 151; martyrdom of, 5, 40, 45, 157; *memoriales* of, 37; in Mexico, 144; millenarianism of, 57, 144; missionary methods of, 37–38, 40, 45, 57–58; in New Mexico, 38–48, 52n7; pastoralism of, 57; in Peru, 144; *primeros doce*, 36, 37; in Pueblo Revolt, 38; in South America, 160–61; use of theater, 5, 36, 50n3; in Yucatán, 155

Francis Xavier, Saint, 223–24

Francke, August Hermann, 112–13

Franks, conversion of, 19

Freedmen, confraternities for, 207

Freeman, Bernardus, 122, 132

Fundamentalism, conversion in, 16n6

Fur trade, 219

Gante, Pedro de, 37–38, 49n1; correspondence of, 51n6

Gaul: population decline in, 21, 32n10; Roman influence in, 19–20

Genève, Charles de, 62

Geography, ancients' knowledge of, 106, 107

Gerber, Christian: *Unerkannte Sünden der Welt*, 112

Gerhard, Johann: *Loci theologici*, 104–6; refutation of Welz, 110–11

Germans: conversion of, 19; theologians, 6–7, 13, 100. *See also* Lutherans

Gift giving: Amerindian system of, 234; in conversion, 130–31, 140n33, 161

Ginzburg, Carlo, 194

Glass, exchange for gold, 232–33, 235–36, 243, 247

Goiás (Brazil), diocese of, 202

262   Index

Gold, exchanged for glass, 232–33, 235–36, 243, 247
The Golden Coast (1665), 250n14
Gómez Canedo, Lino, 51n5
Gookin, Daniel: *Historical Collections of the Indians in New England*, 246
Gordon, Patrick: *Geography Anatomized*, 241–42
Gospels: pre-conquest knowledge of, 105; treatment of riches, 238–39; universal preaching of, 6–7, 13, 100, 101, 102–3, 106–8
Goths, conversion of, 19
Gottfried, Johann Ludwig, 107
Grace: for non-Europeans, 114; in Puritan theology, 82, 83, 85; sin as sign of, 92
Grafton, Anthony, 15
Granada, Luis de, 105
Granada, Spanish conquest of, 193
Gran Chaco region (Spanish America), 158; Guaycurú of, 151
Gran Chichimeca (Sierra Madres), 157; reductions in, 150, 162
Gran Moxo (imaginary realm), 153
Gran Tunal (Sierra Madre), 157
Gray, Edward G., 94n4
Greater Antilles, islanders of, 143
Great Migration, 82
Greek Orthodox Church, 104
Greenblatt, Stephen, 234, 246–47
Greenland, Protestant missions to, 114
Gregory I (pope), 4, 6
Gregory XV (pope), 104
Gregory of Nyssa, 21–22
Grössel, Wolfgang, 109, 112, 113, 115n11
Grotius, Hugo, 115n5
Groulx, Lionel, 74n5
Guachichile people (Mexico), 157
Guairá (Brazil): Franciscans in, 151; reductions in, 151–52
Guale people (Florida), 156
Guamare people (Mexico), 157
Guanajuato (Mexico), silver at, 157
Guaná people (Arawakans), 158
Guaraní people, 165n18; agriculture of, 162; serfdom of, 158; reduction of, 150–51, 152, 162

Guaraz, Juan, 181
Guasave people (Mexico): Holy Week celebrations of, 29; religious beliefs of, 25
Guaycurú people, 151; culture of, 158; missionization of, 159, 162
Guilt: as acculturation mechanism, 184–87; discourse of, 169–87; in penance, 170
Guimarães Sá, Isabel dos, 10

Haefeli, Evan, 11
Hall, David, 82
Hall, John: "Of Felicity," 237
Hamlet, William, 84
Hawley, Gideon, 246
Haywood, Eliza: *The City Jilt*, 235–36, 237
Henrico College (Virginia), 246, 252n42
Henry VIII (king of England), 222
Herbert, George: "Church Militant," 245–46; *The Temple*, 99
Herding, 147
Heurn, Justus van: *De legatione Evangelica ad Indos*, 108
Heyling, Peter, 108
Historia de los mexicanos por sus pinturas, 51n6
Holy days, Amerindian observance of, 36, 46, 49n1, 149, 165n14
Honigmann, E.A.J., 250n15
Hoornbeek, Joannes, 112; *De conversione Indorum & Gentilium*, 108, 109
Horcasitas, Fernando, 49n1
Horn, Georg, 115n5; *De origine Americanarum*, 108
Horse pastoralism, 145
Hospitalières, 71
Huelsemann, 108
Huilliche people (Spanish America), 160
Huitziton (Mexican chieftan), 50n2
Human development, theories of, 8
Human nature: Puritan ideas concerning, 80–81; sinful, 171
Human rights abuse, in New World, 101, 106
Human tradition, papal dogma on, 105
Hunnius, Ägidius: *Tractatus de s.s. majestate*, 103
Hunter-gatherers, 146

Hurons: baptism of, 67; *civilité* of, 64–65; competition with Mohawks, 127; Jesuits' conversion of, 57–74, 161–62; mission of Saint Joseph to, 59; Recollects' conversion of, 58, 60–61, 67, 69, 73–74; reductions of, 161–62; religious beliefs of, 66–67; as rustics, 69; society of, 64–65; understanding of Christianity, 67–68; war with Iroquois, 162; women, 65
Hutchinson, Anne, 82
Hutter, Leonhart, 103
Huya Aniya, Yaqui belief in, 25, 34n41
Hypocrisy, concerning sin, 81, 82–84, 90, 91, 92–93, 96n23

Iberia, Roman influence in, 19, 20
Identity, national, 232, 249n4
Ignatius, Saint, 70
Immaculate Conception, Feast at Isleta, 46
Incas, conquest of, 143
India: Portuguese loss of, 194; Protestant missions to, 114; relationship to Indies, 106
Indian Charity School (Lebanon, Conn.), 232, 245, 252n38
Indians, Praying. *See* Praying Indians
Indies, relationship to India, 106
Inquisition, 104; Portuguese, 204–5, 213n30; Spanish American, 204
Ireland, conversion of, 8
Irmandades das Mercês (confraternity), 207
Iron Age, religion of, 20
Iroquoian language, 221
Iroquoians: alliance with Algonquians, 61; depopulation of, 139n21; Dutch interpreters among, 132; exposure to Christianity, 124; Jesuits among, 161; war of 1640s, 74, 162
Iroquois League, 126, 127, 139n24
Islam: missions to, 104; Spanish, 143
Isleta Pueblo (New Mexico), recapture of, 46
Itatín (Spanish America): destruction of, 158; reductions in, 151, 152

J. D. *See* Dury, John
Jaguaripe, *santidade* of, 210
Jamaica (Long Island), missions at, 242

Jansenists, 69
Japan: Acosta on, 142; civilization of, 195; Jesuit expulsion from, 193
Jennings, Francis, 86
Jeremiads, Puritan, 87
Jerome, Saint, 57, 103
Jesuits: on accommodation, 12, 13; belief in transformation, 57–58, 61, 62; as bureaucracy, 201–2; in China, 12; culture of, 61–62; disagreements with older orders, 12; Dutch Calvinist view of, 123, 124, 134; humanism of, 69; linguistic studies of, 73; missionary methods of, 4–5, 7, 70, 198; orthographic practices of, 17; papacy on, 12; pragmatism of, 201; propaganda of, 209–10; rationality of, 70, 72, 73, 76n48; *ratio studiorum*, 69; teaching practices of, 70, 198; transformation of pagan space, 17–18; view of Amerindians, 70; view of neophytes, 71; view of slavery, 200
Jesuits, French, 5–6, 124; among Iroquoians, 161; among Mohawks, 119, 127; in Canada, 5; conversion of Hurons, 57–74, 161–62; conversion techniques of, 71, 72; efficacy of, 69; martyrdom of, 162; New France mission of, 69, 161, 162; *Relations* of, 161; relations with Recollects, 73, 74n5, 77n55; use of *dépaïsment*, 71; use of ritual, 72; use of shamanism, 72
Jesuits, Portuguese, 10; acculturation of, 210; aid to Crown, 198; in *aldeias*, 199; in Brazil, 10–11, 126, 192–211, 212n13; Brazilian colleges of, 198; conflict with colonists, 126, 139n23; conversion policies of, 200–201; expulsion from Ethiopia, 193; linguistic proficiency of, 200; missionary methods of, 198; missions to Tupí, 119, 131, 138n16, 140n35; in plantation economy, 200
Jesuits, Spanish: *cabecera* churches of, 29; conversion techniques of, 4–5, 57–58; expulsion from South America, 160; in Llanos de Mojo, 153–54; in Mexico, 17, 24–31; Paraguay reductions of, 9, 160; sacramentalism of, 160; spatiotemporal paradigm of, 31; *visita* chapels of, 29

Jews: in Brazil, 122; missions to, 104; Spanish, 143
Jororo people (Florida), 157
Juan (Tewa Amerindian), 56n23
Juchipila (Zacatecas), 48
Jules II (pope): *Universalis Ecclesiae*, 211n1
Jumano people (New Mexico), 44
Jurieu, Pierre, 114
Justice, natural, 243
Justinian, dialogues of, 105

Kachina dance, 47
Kahnawake (Mohawk town), adopted Puritans in, 225–26
Katherine, Saint, 223, 224
Kellaway, William, 94n4
Kellogg, Joseph, 218, 219, 229n8; coercion of, 221, 222; conversion narrative of, 221–25, 227; smallpox of, 224; on Sulpicians, 220
Kikuyu (West African people), 147
King Philip's War (1675–76), 78, 93, 241, 246
Kivas, destruction of, 48
Kramer, Heinrich: *Malleus Malleficarum*, 194

Lacerda, Manuel de, 195
Laet, Johan de, 115n5
Lagunero people, 28
Lalemant, Jerôme, 67
Landa, Diego de, 61
Landis, Dennis, 6, 13
Las Casas, Bartolomé de, 105, 106, 142, 200; *congregación* by, 145; influence of, 113
Last rites, restrictions on, 148
Lateran Council (Fourth, 1215), 9, 169; on sin, 170
Le Ber family, 220, 229n12
Le Caron, Father Joseph, 58
Le Clercq, Chrestien, 65, 73; *First Establishment of the Faith in New France*, 59
Le Goff, Jacques, 21, 170
Leibniz, Gottfried, 113
Le Jeune, Paul, 70, 161
Lent, Amerindian celebration of, 180
León-Portilla, Miguel, 49n1
Lery, 105
Leyden, missionary training in, 109
Lima (Peru): councils of, 173, 178–79, 184; inquisition in, 204
Lipking, Joanna, 250n14
Llanos de Mojos (Spanish America), reductions in, 150, 153–54
López, Diego, 44
Lorra Baquio, Francisco de, 172
Lugh (sun god), 20
Luther, Martin, 6, 103; on Apostle Paul, 100; in conversion narratives, 222
Lutherans, 7, 13; conversion of Catholics, 102; missionization by, 99–117; in New York, 122; response to Bellarmine, 102, 105–6

Maasai (West African people), 147
Macao, Carmelites of, 208
Machado de Cháves, Ivan, 171
Madeira: inquisitorial visitation at, 204; spiritual jurisdiction over, 211n1
Mamelucos (Amerindian-Portuguese), 196, 197; cults of, 210
Mandelslo, Johann Albrecht von, 107; *Morgenländische Reisebeschreibung*, 116n27
"Man the Hunter" Wenner-Gren symposium (Chicago, 1966), 147
Mapuche people, 160
Maranhão (Brazil): convents in, 208; diocese of, 202; French expulsion from, 194; Jesuits in, 198
Martin of Tours, Saint, 19, 22, 28
Martyrdom, 26; of Franciscans, 5, 40, 45, 157; of Jesuits, 162; narratives of, 53n12
Mashpee Indians, 246
Mass, Catholic: as performance, 37; supplies for, 43–44, 53n15, 149
Massachusetts, Protestant missionaries in, 7. *See also* Praying Indians
Material goods, exchange for spiritual goods, 239–45
Mather, Cotton, 79
Mather, Richard, 88, 92; in Antinomian Controversy, 97n64

Maurits, Johan, 118
Mayaca (Florida), Amerindians of, 157
Mayans: agriculture of, 153; civilization of, 154; Franciscans among, 155; reduction of, 150, 154–55; repression of, 61; resistance by, 162
Mayhew, Thomas, 79, 101
Mayhew family, 231
Mayo people (Mexico), religious beliefs of, 25
Mazombos (Brazilian creoles), 197
Mbayá people (Paraguay), 158
Mbororé, battle of, 152
Meisner, Balthasar, 104
Mem de Sá (governor of Brazil), 202
Mendieta, Gerónimo de, 57; *Historia eclesiástica*, 38, 65
Meriel de Meulan, Henri-Antoine, 220–21, 229n13
Meuwese, Mark, 7, 11
Mexico: epidemics in, 29, 30–31; Franciscans in, 144; inquisition in, 204; Jesuits in, 17, 24–31; place names in, 30; precolonial rituals of, 49n1; printing in, 173; religious transformation of, 49; shrines of, 26–29. *See also* Amerindians, Mexican
Mexico City, convents of, 208
Michoacán (Mexico), *congregación* in, 145
Micmac people, 65
Middle Ages: Christianization in, 18; conversion in, vii, 1, 16n17
Millenarianism: Calvinist, 120; in conversion practices, 62, 210; of Franciscans, 57, 144; in missionization, 110; of Recollects, 72; Welz's, 116n35
Miller, Perry, 96n41
Milton, John: *The Reason of Church Government Urg'd against Prelaty*, 236–37
Minas Gerais (Brazil): confraternities of, 207; convents in, 208; gold rush in, 203; religious structures of, 205
Minuane people (South America), 152
Misericórdias (confraternities, Brazil), 203, 206, 207, 213n35; women in, 209
Misiones (Argentina), reductions in, 152
Missionaries: ethnographic knowledge of, 176; institutional culture of, 59; intellectual framework of, 15; saints, 22; secular role of, 59; systems of reference, 59; transformation of pagan space, 4, 18
Missionaries, Catholic: disagreements among, 12; linguistic techniques of, 10; martyrdom of, 26; and nonsedentary societies, 8; oversight of, 13; preaching by, 12; Sulpician, 219–20, 223; techniques of, 3, 12; training of, 104. *See also* Dominicans; Franciscans; Jesuits
Missionaries, Dutch Calvinist, 7, 110, 118–35; among Mohawks, 118–19, 121, 123, 127–30, 132–35; among Tupí, 11, 117n35, 118–19, 121–123, 127–35, 129, 137n14, 140n30; baptism of Tupís, 140n30; catechizing by, 134; educational policies of, 121, 134, 137n9; ideology of, 122; opponents of, 116n34; pastors among, 122, 123; salaries of, 121–22; techniques of, 12; training for, 109. *See also* Calvinists, Dutch
Missionaries, English, 108, 109; Anglican, 13; education of, 245; fund-raising by, 240; in Massachusetts, 7; pessimism of, 241; trade tropes of, 238–43. *See also* Puritans
Missionaries, medieval, vii, 2–3; and New World missionaries, 3–4; Protestant view of, 6
Missionaries, Protestant: conversion techniques of, 3, 6, 12; in Greenland, 114; in India, 114; linguistic problems of, 11; Lutheran, 99–117; preaching by, 12; Swedish, 99; training of, 109; in West Indies, 114
Missionaries, Spanish: approach to conversion, 4–5; catechesis by, 175, 178; cultural information for, 176–77; cultural intervention by, 186; medieval roots of, 3–4; persuasive strategies of, 185. *See also* Franciscans, Spanish; Jesuits, Spanish
Missionary literature, English, 99; cultural influence of, 232; trade with Amerindians in, 231–47

Missionization: cost of, 112, 240, 242, 247; and Counter-Reformation, 13; effect on health, 148; effect on mobility, 150; following demographic collapse, 21; in German theology, 6–7, 13, 114; millenarianism in, 110; plantation tropes of, 240–41; Protestant view of, vii, 6, 101; and Reformation, 13; resistance to, 155–59, 162–63; role of epidemics in, 159; syncretism in, 178; and theology, 6–7, 12–13, 100. *See also* Reductions (settlement)

Missionization, Lutheran, 99–117; cost of, 112; support for, 111–12

Missions, Catholic: of Florida, 156–57; following Council of Trent, 192; as frontier institutions, 165n17; as instruments of empire, 149–50; internal, 192; in New France, 5, 57–64; in Ordinances of Pacification, 149; Protestant criticism of, 105, 121; raids on, 163; secularization of, 149

Missions, New England: Eliot's, 78–94; ethnohistorical studies of, 79, 93; fundraising for, 240

Missions, New Mexico, 39; furnishings of, 43; royal support for, 42–44; sacred space of, 54n16

Missions, South American, 150; Brazilian, 165n17, 201, 210; center and periphery in, 154; exports of, 160; *reducción* into, 150–63; subsidies for, 154

Mita (labor service), 151

Mixe people (Mexico), resistance by, 155

Mixton War (1541), 48

Mobility: anthropological classifications of, 146–47; within Christianization, 146, 161; effect of missionization on, 150. *See also* Nomads; Reductions (settlement)

Mocoví people (Paraguay), 158

Moebius, Georg, 107–8, 116n27

Mohawk language: missionary pamphlets in, 121; written, 122, 131

Mohawks: adoption into, 225–27; alliance with Dutch, 132; alliance with English, 128; baptism of, 130; catechist teachers among, 132; Catholic, 127, 129, 133, 134, 138n17; competition with Hurons, 127; conversion to Calvinism, 127–30, 133; Dutch mission to, 118–19, 121, 123, 127–30, 132–35; epidemics among, 125, 127, 139n21; Jesuits among, 119, 127; literacy of, 119, 121, 131–32, 134, 140n36; marriages with Dutch, 132; matrilineality of, 225; mission schools for, 132; political alliances of, 129–31, 133–34; pro-French, 129; protection of Christianity for, 132–33; Protestant rituals of, 135; trade alliances of, 130–31, 134; trade with Dutch, 119, 126–27, 132; traditional religion of, 119, 125, 126, 133, 134; women, 132

Mojo people (Upper Amazon), reduction of, 153–54, 162

Monarchy, Portuguese: on evangelization, 196; Jesuit aid to, 198; policy on convents, 208; prerogatives in New World, 193; taxation by, 203

Monasticism, 19; and reduction, 149

Monogamy, for neophytes, 3, 148

Montagnais (Iroquoians), 161

Montreal Island: Counter-Reformation society in, 219, 220; multiethnic inhabitants of, 225

Mornaeus, Philippus: *De veritate religionis Christianae*, 107

Morocco, Portuguese conquests in, 193

Morrison, Karl F., 58

Mortification, in Amerindian religion, 181

Mound Builders, agriculture of, 153

Mourning wars, 225, 226

Mulattos, Brazilian, 197; confraternities for, 207

Müller, Johannes: *Gründliche Antwort und Widerlegung*, 102

Muslims: expulsion from Spain, 143; missions to, 104

Naeher, Robert, 96n41

Nahuatl language, 155; catechism in, 172

Nahuatl people, theater of, 50n3

Nantes. *See* Edict of Nantes

Naranjo, Pedro, 47–48

Nature: as barrier to Christianization, 69; God's will in, 96n41

Ndorobo (West African people), 147

Ñeengirú, Nicolás, 152
Neophytes: acculturation of, 178, 211; Brazilian, 205–7; catechesis of, 175, 178; children, 210; civilization of, 3, 9; coercion of, 186, 201; confession of, 173–74; daily life of, 54n17; enmity with unconverted, 152; indoctrination of, 149; Jesuit view of, 71; languages of, 10, 109, 112; mobility restrictions on, 150; Mohawk, 132; monogamy for, 3, 148; probation for, 148; recidivism of, 6, 14, 58; syncretism of, 210–11. *See also* Amerindians; Reductions
New England Company, 231, 240, 241. *See also* Amerindians, New England
New France: conversion in, 5, 57–64; English in, 216; Franciscans in, 5, 58, 72; Jesuits in, 69, 161, 162; Recollects in, 58, 59, 60; reductions in, 150; social divisions in, 71
New Mexico: Acts of Obedience and Vassalage in, 53n14; Amerindians of, 36–49; Franciscan architecture of, 43, 49, 54n16; Franciscans in, 38–48, 52n7; missions of, 39, 42–44; Oñate expedition to, 42; Pueblo Revolt, 5, 38, 43, 45–48; reconquest of, 45; source documents for, 55n18
New Netherland: Calvinist ministers of, 123, 139n25; Dutch West India Company in, 118; English conquest of, 119, 124, 128; literacy in, 121
New World: ancients' knowledge of, 108; apocalyptic view of, 1; Catholic sources on, 100; effect of Counter-Reformation on, 1; European contact as, 131, 140n34; European intellectuals on, 113; German Protestants on, 6–7, 13, 100; gospel in, 100; Herbert on, 245–46; intellectual framework for, 14–15; papal bulls on, 192–93, 211n1; Satan in, 27–28, 31, 50n2, 111, 194–95; wars of religion in, 11
New World, Portuguese: conversion in, 192–211; royal prerogatives in, 193
New World, Spanish: colonization rights in, 99; conquest of, 17, 143–44; epidemics in, 29, 106, 143; guilt discourse in, 169–87; human rights abuse in, 101, 106; mercantilism in, 17; Protestant view of, 113–14; reductions in, 150–51; sins of, 174
New York: Calvinists in, 11, 121, 137n10; Dutch Reformed Church in, 118, 125, 129, 135, 138n19; Lutherans of, 122; mass baptisms in, 129
Nicolai, Philipp, 104; *Historia regni Christi*, 103; *Tractatus de regno Christi*, 106
Nider, Johannes: *Formicarius*, 194
Nizá, Fray Marcos de: *Relación*, 38–39, 52n8
Nóbrega, Manuel da, 197, 200
Nomads: Christianization of, 7–8, 145–46, 161. *See also* Mobility; Reductions (settlement)
Nossa Senhora da Conceição (confraternity), 206, 207
Nueva Galicia, Amerindians of, 48

Olinda, Hilletie van, 132
Olinda (Brazil), diocese of, 202
Olmos, Andrés de, 51n6; *Tratado de las antigüedades mexicanas*, 38
Oñate, Juan de, 42, 53n14
Oneida Indians, 126
Onondaga Indians, 126
Order of Christ, 211n1
Ordinances of Pacification (1573), 149
Ordinances of Patronage (1574), 149
Ordination, restrictions on, 148, 165n12
Orista people (Florida), 156; resistance by, 163
Ortelius, Abraham, 107
Ortiz de Zárate, Juan, 151
Osiander, Johann Adam, 108
Otermín, Antonio de, 45–47
Other World, communication with, 20
Our Lady of the Rosary (confraternity), 207

Padilla, Fray Juan de, 40–41, 53n12
Padroado (papal prerogative, Brazil): religious structures of, 205; setbacks to, 193–94; taxation in, 203
Paganism, as religion of place, 20
Pagans, European: conversion of, 19–21; Iron Age, 20; rejection of Christianity, 111–12; Roman tolerance of, 20
Pame people (Mexico), 157

Pampas Indians, resistance by, 163
Papacy: as antichrist, 102; bulls on Amerindians, 195; bulls on New World, 192–93, 211n1; on Jesuits, 12; primacy of, 105
Pará (Brazil), diocese of, 202
Paraguay: Amerindians of, 158, 160; Jesuits in, 9, 160; reductions in, 9, 151, 160
Paraíba (Brazil), Dutch in, 128
Pareus: *Ad Romanos S. Pauli apostoli epistolam Commentarius*, 108
Paris, Yves de, 60
Parker, Annie, 6, 7, 9
Paróquias coladas (parishes), 203
Pastorale de la peur, 59, 172; Recollects' use of, 68, 71
Pastoralism: Franciscan, 57; horse, 145
Patagonia, Amerindians of, 160
Patrick, Saint, 8
Patronato (papal sanction, Spain), 193; diocese of, 202
Paul (apostle), 244; Luther on, 100; on preaching of gospel, 105; on spiritual obligation, 232–33, 239, 242–43
Paul II (pope): *Sublimis Deus*, 195, 196
Paulistas (paramilitary, Brazil), 151, 152, 162
Payaguás people (Paraguay), 158
Peasants, European: conversion of, 2, 4, 14, 16n19, 144; kinship networks of, 68
Pehuenche people (Spanish America), 160
Pelagianism, 19
Peña Montenegro, Alonso de, 172, 177
Penance: for Amerindians, 180; in confession manuals, 183; in Counter-Reformation, 169–73; guilt in, 170; language problems in, 175; medieval, 174; negotiation in, 171; rituals of, 169; theological discourse on, 171–72
Penitential questionnaires, 175, 185; social models in, 186–87; translation of, 177, 187
Perez Bocanegra, Juan, 176, 178
Pérez de Ribas, Andrés, 18, 31; *Historia de los Triumphos de Nuestra Santa Fee*, 53n12; on Mexican religion, 26, 27–28, 29
Peripeteia (reversal of fortune), 69
Peripety paradigm, 58
Pernambuco (Brazil): convents in, 208; Dutch expulsion from, 194; inquisitorial visitation at, 204, 213n30

Perrone-Moisés, Beatriz, 195–96
Peru: conquest of, 143; Franciscans in, 144
Petatlán Pueblo (New Mexico), 39
Peter Martyr, 105; influence of, 113; on propagation of gospel, 106
Phelan, John Leddy, 5–6, 57
Philip II (king of Spain), missionary ordinances of, 149, 151
Pierron, Jean, 70
Pietism, 112–13
Población (settlement), 145
Pocock, J. G. A.: *Virtue, Commerce, and History*, 241, 251n26
"Point to Point" (board game), 70
Polybius, 106
Poor Clares of the Desterro (Bahia), 208
Popé (Amerindian), 47, 55n22
Porta, Konrad, 103
Portugal: in Brazil, 128, 139n27; Brazilian colonists of, 122, 192, 196, 201, 210; conquests in Morocco, 193; incorporation into Spain, 123; loss of India, 194; war with Potiguars, 128, 139n27. *See also* Monarchy, Portuguese
Potiguars (Tupí people), war with Portuguese, 128, 139n27
Praying Indians: adaptation of Puritanism, 93; church membership for, 92; confessions of, 91; conversion narratives of, 91–93, 97n49; exclusion from covenant, 91; gathering churches among, 89; orthodoxy of, 89–90, 97n41; questions to Eliot, 86; religious progress of, 87, 88–89; as sons of Adam, 86, 90, 91; teaching of, 85; visit to Providence, 89. *See also* Algonquians; Amerindians, New England; Praying Towns
Praying Towns, 78, 86, 231; effect of King Philip's War on, 78, 93, 241, 246; population of, 78; property rights in, 87; as proto-reservations, 86; purpose of, 8–9. *See also* Reductions
Preaching: castigatory, 63; by Catholic missionaries, 12; Eliot's, 80; of fear, 73; Franciscan, 58, 60–61; Recollect, 60–61, 73; by SPG, 242
Priests: as agents of deity, 182–83; Celtic, 20; Council of Trent on, 170; as ethnogra-

phers, 176, 180; as penitential inquisitors, 182; resistance to authority of, 184; ritual dramatization by, 183; role in confession, 182–84
Priscillianism, 19
Processions, sacred: Acadian, 229n19; in Brazil, 205; Mexican, 30–31, 37; in New Mexico, 44; Spanish, 24
Protestantism: Amerindian interpretation of, 140n37; universal character of, 120
Protestants: view of missionization, vii, 6, 101. *See also* Calvinists; Lutherans; Puritans
Protestants, French: conversion to Catholicism, 220
Protestants, German: view of missions, 6–7, 13, 114
Providence, divine: in conversion narratives, 218; Puritan belief in, 78–79
Providence (Rhode Island), Praying Indians at, 89
Pueblo Revolt (New Mexico, 1680), 5, 38, 55n21; leaders of, 47, 55n22; mission furnishings in, 43; public ceremonies following, 45–48; Taos in, 45; unbaptism in, 47, 48
Pufendorf, Samuel: *Politische Betrachtung der geistlichen Monarchie des Stuhls zu Rom*, 114
Purgatory, 105, 170, 171, 185; in conversion narratives, 222, 224
Purification, in Amerindian religion, 181
Puritanism: conversion beliefs in, 80–82, 88, 93–94, 95n10, 96n39; conversion to Catholicism from, 11, 215–28
Puritans: accounts of conversions, 78–79, 83–84; on Amerindian trade, 236; captivity narratives, 217–25; capture by French, 215; conversion to Catholicism, 11, 215–28; ecclesiology of, 89; French proselytizing of, 217–19, 221–28; jeremiads of, 87; missionary expertise of, 113; relations with Amerindians, 79–80, 84–86; systems of understanding, 78–79; view of grace, 82, 83, 85; view of human nature, 80–81; view of salvation, 80–83, 90; written covenants of, 87. *See also* Missionaries, English

Quakers, in New York, 122
Quechua language, 178, 179
Quenstedt, Johann Andreas, 108
Quetzalcoatl (deity), 26
Quiroga, Vasco de, 145
Quistorp, Johann: *Annotationes in omnes libros Biblicos*, 106

Ranching, 147
Recidivism: Jesuit view of, 71; of neophytes, 6, 14, 58
Recife (Jesuit college), 198
Recife Council (Dutch Reformed Church, 1644), 133
Recolhimentos (women's conservatories), 206, 208, 209
Recollects: beliefs on conversion, 67; civilizing mission of, 61; conversion of Hurons, 58, 60–61, 67, 69, 73–74; millennialism of, 72; missionary activism of, 60; in New France, 58, 59, 60; *pastorale de la peur*, 68, 71; preaching of, 60–61, 73; relations with Jesuits, 73, 74n6, 77n55; shamanistic practices of, 67, 73; use of rational explanation, 66; view of Amerindians, 62–65, 68–69. *See also* Franciscans
Reconversion: of Praying Indians, 92; repentance in, 96n26
Redrado, Father Ramón, 161
Reductions (settlement), 11, 145; in Araucanía, 150; in Argentina, 152; in the Chaco, 150; in Chiapas, 155; by Dominicans, 155, 162; in Florida, 150; in Gran Chichimeca, 150, 162; in Guairá, 151–52; of Guaraní, 150–51, 152, 162; of Huron, 161–62; in Itatín, 151, 152; by Jesuits, 9, 160; in Llanos de Mojos, 150, 153–54; of Mayans, 150, 154–55; of Mojo people, 153–54, 162; monasticism and, 149; in New France, 150; in Paraguay, 9, 151, 160; in Sierra Zapoteca, 150, 155; in Spanish America, 150–63; in Tapé, 151, 152–53. *See also* Missionization; Mobility; Praying Towns
Reff, Daniel, 3, 4, 7
Reformation, Protestant, 6; missionary practice and, 13
Relaciones Topográficas, 23

Religion, Amerindian: confession in, 181; Huron, 66–67; intermediaries in, 181; Mexican, 25–29; Mohawk, 119, 125, 126, 133, 134; Tupí, 119, 125, 126, 133, 134, 138n20
Religious images, desecration of, 47, 48
Religious sites, pagan: Christianization of, 4, 18
Renaissance, demonology in, 194–95
Republic of the Guaranís (Spanish America), 152; reductions in, 150
Restoration war (1640–68), 204–5
Ricard, Robert, 37, 43, 180
Rio de Janeiro (Brazil): confraternities of, 207; convents in, 208; diocese of, 202; founding of, 198
Río de la Plata (Spanish America), 158
Rio Grande (Brazil), Dutch in, 128
Rio Grande do Sul (Brazil), 152
Rodríguez, Fray Agustín, 42
Rogel, Juan, 163
Roman empire: commerce in, 19–20; epidemics in, 21, 22; population decline in, 21; spread of Christianity through, 18–19; toleration in, 20
Romanus Pontifex (papal bull), 211n1
Ross, Alexander, 108
Runtu, Christobal, 181
Russell, J. C., 21

Sacraments, restrictions for Amerindians, 148. *See also* Baptism; Penance
Saeger, James Schofield, 159
Sagamos (witch doctors), 70
Sagard-Théodat, Gabriel, 73; *Dictionary of the Huron Language*, 73; *Grand Voyage*, 63; *Histoire du Canada*, 58, 63–67
Sahagún, Bernardino de, 51n6; *Historia general de las cosas de la Nueva España*, 38; *Psalmodia Christiana*, 36–37, 49
Saint Lawrence Seaway, French settlements along, 219
Saints: feasts of, 24; intercession by, 23, 24; invocation of, 105; missionary, 22; relics of, 22, 23, 29, 31. *See also under first names of saints*
Salas, Juan de, 44

Salvador de Bahia (Brazil), Dutch capture of, 120
Salvation: preparationist view of, 83; Puritan view of, 80–83, 90
Sánchez Chamuscado, Francisco, 42
Sanctification, in Antinomian Controversy, 82
Sandia Pueblo (New Mexico), 48, 55n21; recapture of, 47
Santa Cruz de la Sierra, founding of, 153
Santa Fe (New Mexico), *cabildo* of, 55n21
Santa Ifigénia (confraternity), 207
Santa Monica (convent, Goa), 208
Santarén, Hernando de, 26
Santíssimo Sacramento (confraternity), 206, 207
Santos (Jesuit college), 198
São Benedito (confraternity), 207
São Gonçalo Garcia (confraternity), 207
São José Queirós, D. Frei João de, 203
São Luís do Maranhão (Jesuit college), 198
São Miguel e Almas (confraternity), 206, 207
São Paulo (Brazil): colonists of, 196; convents of, 208; diocese of of, 202; founding of, 198
Saravia, Adrian, 111, 112
Satan: Huron belief in, 66; in New World, 27–28, 31, 50n2, 111, 194–95; Puritan discourse of, 86; as source of idolatry, 195
Savoyards, missionization of, 62
Schelguigius, Samuel: *Dissertatio historico-theologica de statu ecclesiae evangelicae*, 108
Schenectady (New York), Mohawk neophytes at, 132
Scourging, in Amerindian culture, 180
Sedentism, Amerindian, 146–47, 150; Mayan, 154
Self, formation of, 58, 61
Seneca Indians, 126
Sete Povos (Tapé group), 152
Settlements, Amerindian: in Christianization, 144–45, 146; renaming of, 17–18. *See also* Reductions
Settlers, Christian: Brazilian, 122, 192, 196, 201, 210; moral standards of, 10, 16n18

Seven Years' War, 245
Sexuality, Amerindian: demonization of, 185; Portuguese perception of, 194
Shakespeare, William: *Othello*, 235, 236, 237, 250n15
Shamanism: curing in, 125; Jesuits' use of, 72; Recollects' use of, 67, 73
Shamans, Amerindian: effect of epidemics on, 29; *hechiceros*, 26, 27; of New Mexico, 47
Shepard, Thomas: on Antinomian controversy, 82–84; Cambridge confessions of, 90–92, 98n76; on Praying Towns, 87; sermons of, 80; *The Sincere Convert*, 111
Shrines: Amerindian, 26–29, 30; celtic, 20; Spanish, 23–24, 30
Sierra Zapoteca (Oaxaca), reductions in, 150, 155
Sillery (Algonquin community), 71, 161
Silver, Mexican, 157
Sin: Amerindian conception of, 179–81; in Antinomian controversy, 81; and calamity, 180, 181; catalogs of, 185; Christian conception of, 179; contrition for, 172; divine pardon for, 172; in Eliot Tracts, 87; expiation for, 170, 180, 187; Fourth Lateran Council on, 170; hypocrisy concerning, 81, 82–84, 90, 91, 92–93, 96n23; interiorization of concept, 187; metaphors for, 183; minimalist model of, 172–73; mourning of, 84, 96n37; "New World," 174; perdurable nature of, 60, 62; punishment for, 81, 172, 185; responsibility for, 171, 187; sermons on, 183; as sign of grace, 92; temptation to, 185; theological nature of, 182; verbalization of, 170. *See also* Confession
Sin, original, 80, 90–91; Amerindian beliefs and, 132
Sinaloa (Mexico), Amerindians of, 24
Slavers, Creek, 157
Slavers, Brazilian, 151; among Chiriguanás, 153
Slavery: Columbus on, 233; Jesuit view of, 200
Slaves, African: in Brazil, 192, 207; confraternities for, 207; evangelization of, 123
Slaves, Amerindian, 196–97, 201

Smallpox, 125, 224
Smith, Adam: *Wealth of Nations*, 244
Société de Notre Dame de Montréal, 219
Society, Aristotle's concept of, 12, 14
Society for the Propagation of the Gospel in Foreign Parts (SPG), 231, 238, 244; preachers of, 242
Society for the Propagation of the Gospel in New England, 109
Society in Scotland for the Propagation of Christian Knowledge (SSPCK), 231–32
Soler, Vincent: *Cort ende sonderlingh Verhael van eenen brief van Monsieur Soler*, 117n35
Sousa, Tomé de, 197, 202
South America: Christianization of, 173; missions of, 150; post-Trentine, 173
Space, sacred: Mexican, 27–28, 31; of mission churches, 54n16; pagan, 20; in paganism, 120; Spanish, 23–24; transformation of, 4, 18, 22, 28–29, 31
Spain: conquest of Granada, 193; expulsion of Muslims, 143; geography of, 30; incorporation of Portugal, 123; New and Old Christians in, 144; parish churches of, 29; religions of, 143; shrines of, 23–24, 30; supernatural beliefs in, 23–24, 30; war with United Provinces, 120
Spener, Philipp, 112
Spenser, Edmund, 8
Spicer, Edward, 34n41
Spirituality, and material wealth, 239–45
Sprenger, Jakob: *Malleus Malleficarum*, 194
Stanhope, George, 242
Stevens, Laura, 13
Strabo, 106
Sulpicians, 219–20; in Puritan conversion narratives, 223
Sulpicius Severus: life of St. Martin, 22, 28
Summae confessorum. *See* Confession manuals
Supernatural: demonology, 194–95; Spanish belief in, 23–24
Surinam, 110
Sweden: colonists in North America, 124
Sweet, David, 162

Index 271

Syncretism, religious, 6, 50n3, 74; in ceremonies, 41; in confession, 177, 181; in missionization, 178; of neophytes, 210–11

Taino people, Columbus on, 233
Taos (New Mexico), 125; in Pueblo Revolt, 45; reconquest of, 5
Tapé (Spanish America): reductions in, 151, 152–53; Sete Povos of, 152
Tecpatzin (Mexican chieftain), 50n2
Teellinck, Willem, 120
Tehuelche people, 160
Tekakwitha, Kateri, 223, 226
Teles Barreto, Manuel, 202, 210
Tello, Fray Antonio, 38, 50n2; *Crónica miscelánea*, 40–41; sources of, 52n11
Ten Commandments, confession according to, 174, 176
Tentzel, Willem: *Monatliche Unterredungen*, 109, 116n34
Tepechitlán (Zacatecas), 48
Tepehuan people (Mexico), idols of, 26
Theater: conversion as, 5, 36, 37, 50n3; Nahuatl, 50n3; and religious ceremonies, 51n5
Theology: covenant, 80–81; preparationist, 80, 83, 95n21
Theology, German: missions in, 6–7, 13, 100
Third Orders (confraternities, Brazil), 206, 207; women in, 209
Thirty Years' War, 99, 100, 106
Thomas, Saint (Apostle), 7, 16n14; in Brazil, 108
Tiguex (New Spain), 40
Timucua people (Florida), 156
Tlaloc (deity), 27
Tlaltenango (Zacatecas), 48
Tlaxcalan (Spanish America), 157–58
Tobas people (Paraguay), 158
Toledo, Francisco de, 145
Torquemada, Juan de: *Monarquía Indiana*, 38
Totherswamp (Praying Indian), 91
Trade, Amerindian: Columbus on, 233–35, 237, 238; Dutch-Mohawk, 119, 126–27, 132; early modern images of, 233–38; in English missionary literature, 231–47; Puritans on, 236; role in conversion, 234, 238–43
Trade, scriptural references to, 232
Transubstantiation, in conversion narratives, 223
Treaty of Madrid (1750), 152
Tree worship, 27
Tribal societies: conversion of, 8; under Roman Empire, 19
Trinity, in Catholic missionization, 105
Tsiaonentes, Marie, 133
Tucumán (Spanish America), 158–59
Tupí-Guaraní language, 150; catechisms in, 121, 122; printing in, 152; written, 131
Tupí people (Brazil): in *aldeias*, 126, 133; alliance with WIC, 128, 130, 132; baptism of, 140n30; body ornaments of, 133, 141n38; Catholic, 123–24, 133, 134; conversion to Calvinism, 127–30, 133; depopulation of, 125, 138n21; Dutch missions to, 117n35, 118–19, 121–123, 127–35, 129, 137n14, 140n30; Dutch sources on, 135n1; Jesuit mission to, 119, 131, 138n16, 140n35; literacy of, 119, 121, 131, 134, 140n35; political alliances of, 129–31, 133–34; Potiguars, 128, 139n27; protection of Christianity for, 132–33; Protestant rituals of, 124; teachers among, 131, 132; trade alliances of, 130, 134, 140n31; traditional religion of, 119, 125, 126, 133, 134, 138n20; visit to United Provinces, 128; 139n27
Turks, missions to, 104
Tzapotlán (New Spain), 40

Ubeda, Fray Luis de, 41
United Provinces: Portiguars' visit to, 128, 139n27; Protestant morals in, 120; war with Spain, 120
Unschuldige Nachrichten (journal), 111
Urban VIII (pope), 104
Ursinus, Johann Heinrich, 107; *Historisch- und theologischer Bericht*, 111; *Richtiges Zeigerhändlein*, 111; *Widerholte Erinnerung*, 110, 111

Vainfas, Ronaldo, 213n30; *A Heresia dos Índios*, 210
Vale de Moura, Manuel do, 195
Valenzuela Márquez, Jaime, 9
Vargas, Diego de, 45
Vaughan, Alden T., 94n4
Vega, Garcilasso de la, 113
Veiel, Elias, 112
Vera Cruz, Rosa Maria Egipcíaca, 209
Vera Paz (Guatemala), *congregación* in, 145
Verhulst, Willem, 120
Vieira, António, 201
Ville-Marie (Montreal), 219–20
Virgin Mary: cults to, 55n21; desecration of image, 47; Mexican shrines of, 29, 30; as mother goddess, 4; veneration in Spain, 23–24
Vitoria, Francisco de, 105, 113
Voegler, Valentin Heinrich: *De religione Judaica et Judaeurum conversione dissertatio*, 107–8

Waban (Praying Indian), 92
Wale, Anton van, 109
Wandering. *See* Mobility; Nomads
War, just, 106, 195–96
Warburton, William, 245
War of the Spanish Succession: conversion narratives from, 217; prisoner exchanges during, 228n6
Wars of religion: German, 7; in New World, 11
Warwick, Jacques, 64
Waugh, John, 244
Wealth: Jesus's parable of, 238; material versus spiritual, 239–45
Weber, David J., 150
Weigel, Valentin, 107
Welz, Justinianus von, 112, 113, 117n36; *Eine Christliche und treuhertzige Vermahnung*, 109–10; *Ein kurtzer Bericht*, 109; millennialism of, 110, 116n35; refutations of, 110–11; supporters of, 112

Wendelin, Marcus Friedrich, 108; *Exercitationes theologicae*, 107
West Indies, Protestant missions to, 114
Wheelock, Eleazar, 231, 232, 238, 245; *A Continuation of the Narrative of the Indian Charity-School*, 252n38
Wheelright, Esther, 218
Williams, Eunice, 218, 219, 229n8, 230n26; contact with father, 226–27; conversion narrative of, 225, 226–27
Williams, John, 221, 222; captive daughter of, 226–27; *The Redeemed Captive Returning to Zion*, 217
Williams, Roger: Narraganset vocabularies, 99
Williams, Stephen, 221
Willpower, Amerindian development of, 185
Winthrop, John, 82
Women, Amerindian: Huron, 65; Mexican, 27; Mohawk, 132; Zuaque, 30
Women, Portuguese: in confraternities, 209; religious life of, 207–9
Women, Puritan: conversion to Catholicism, 216–17, 225, 226–27, 228n7
Woods, Ian, 15n9

Xixime people (Mexico), 26
Xumana people (Mexico), baptism of, 44

Yamassee people (Florida), 156–57
Yaqui people (Mexico), 27–28, 31; agriculture of, 154; belief in Huya Aniya, 25, 34n41; sorceresses of, 27
Yucatán, Franciscans in, 155

Zacatecas (Mexico), silver at, 157
Zacateco people, 157
Zamora, Margarita, 31
Zapotec people (Mexico), resistance by, 155
Zentgraf, Johann Joachim: *De obligatione Evangelicorum*, 111
Zuaque people (Mexico), 30
Zuni people, 26; conversion of, 37

BV
2755
.S65
2004